Public School Finance
ECONOMICS AND POLITICS

Jesse Burkhead, Professor of Economics at Syracuse University, is author of *Government Budgeting* and coauthor of *Decisions in Syracuse* and *River Basin Administration and the Delaware*. He has served as an economist with the U.S. Bureau of the Budget and as a consultant to educational organizations, and supervised a three-year Project for Research in Educational Finance.

Public School Finance
ECONOMICS AND POLITICS

JESSE BURKHEAD

With chapters by
Bertram M. Gross and
Charles S. Benson

SYRACUSE UNIVERSITY PRESS 1964

Library of Congress Catalog Card 64:14856

This study was made possible in part by funds granted by Carnegie Corporation of New York. The statements made and views expressed are solely the responsibility of the author.

Manufactured in the United States of America
by The Heffernan Press Inc., Worcester, Mass.
and bound by Vail-Ballou Press, Binghamton, N.Y.

Contents

Tables

Figures

Preface

In this country the responsibility for the support of public education is intergovernmental in character. School districts and other local government agencies, the states, and the national government all share in the determination of support levels. These decisions are economic, reflecting choices among alternative government programs and choices between public and private use of resources. The decisions that are made about public education are broadly political; they are made by administrators and elected officials as representatives of the electorate. The decisions are shaped by societal attitudes and values and by the interaction between community leadership and value structures. The nature of these decisions is the subject matter of this volume.

American society has always professed to place a high value on education, and on public education in particular. The implementation of this value judgment, however, requires that continued efforts be put under way to channel adequate resources to the support of the public schools. To be sure, there have been important increases in the quantity of resources used in elementary and secondary education in the years since World War II. Thousands of classrooms have been built; hundreds of thousands of new teachers have been trained. Very large increases in enrollment have been absorbed, for the most part with considerable success; teachers' salaries have been improved. However, there is ample evidence that these gains have not been sufficient for the task at hand.

In the fall of 1963 New York City teachers threatened a strike because city and state officials were unwilling or unable to organize additional fiscal support for the City's school system. Until a few weeks before the opening of classes the teachers of the State of Utah refused to sign their contracts because of similar unwillingness on the part of state officials. After four years with no public schools, seventeen hundred Negro children in Prince Edward County, Virginia, were finally enrolled in privately supported institutions. In large cities the continued inadequate education of many young people adds to the number of unemployables. If public education is to be strengthened to overcome these deficiencies, it will be necessary to devote a larger fraction of the nation's resources to the support of elementary and secondary education, and to organize these resources effectively.

It is the thesis of this volume that the necessary resources are available. There is no danger that in the short run standards of living or the performance of the American economy will be impaired by modest additional taxes for increased support of education. Furthermore, in the long run standards of living and the performance of the economy will very likely be enhanced by the diversion of such resources.

There are some grounds for guarded optimism on the financial outlook for public elementary and secondary education. It is possible that as a nation we are at the beginning of a period in which education will be even more highly valued than is now the case. The philosophy and practice of "continuing education" may catch hold, and "cradle to grave" education of all kinds and varieties, formal and informal, liberal, cultural and technical, may come to be a part of a new way of life. It is also possible that we are at the beginning of a technological revolution in educational methods with communication techniques that will infuse the educational establishment with new zeal, new enthusiasm, and new efficiency. New programs and new technologies, if they eventuate, will be important not alone for what they accomplish in themselves, but for their impact on community attitudes toward education.

There is great strength in the decentralized system of public education that we have in this country and in the accompanying patterns of intergovernmental fiscal support. This intergovernmental system provides a maximum of flexibility in adaptation to national, state and local educational needs and resources. But as in all matters economic, there is a cost. The price we pay for decentralization consists of the waste of resources in some districts and the inadequate availability of resources in other districts.

At several places in this volume, and in a number of different contexts, it is suggested that the strength of the decentralized system can be preserved, and that existing deficiencies can be remedied by new organizational structures for participative planning for educational policy and for educational finance. Unless such structures are developed the resources that are available to be mobilized will not be secured or used to their maximum effectiveness.

This volume is based on the findings of the Project for Research in Educational Finance, a three-year study of the socioeconomic and political factors that influence the support of public elementary and secondary education.

Eleven of the chapters in this volume are summaries of the monographs published by the Syracuse University Press as *The Economics and Politics of Public Education Series.* The responsibility for the summaries is my own, however, and not the authors'. I have attempted to emphasize generalized findings, to deemphasize research technique, and to stress the issues of public policy. There is one omission in terms of coverage. The present volume does not contain a summary of William Wasserman's study, *Education Price and Quantity Indexes,* which was deemed to be sufficiently technical to fall outside this more general orientation. It is hoped that what is reported here will encourage readers to examine the more detailed research findings, methodology, and references contained in the monographs. Two chapters were specifically commissioned for this volume: Chapter II, "The Administration of Public Schools," by Bertram M. Gross, and Chapter IX, "State Aid Patterns," by Charles S. Benson. Chapter I is intended to provide a general economic framework for public school finance, Chapter XV to provide some organizational prescriptions.

My personal and professional debt to large numbers of persons who have contributed to this project over the past three years is a substantial one. These include, first and foremost, the authors of the monographs, who did the work of research and writing. In addition, staff members of the U.S. Office of Education, the New York State Department of Education, the National Education Association, faculty of schools of education, and social scientists interested in public education have extended indispensable help to the project. These specific contributions have been acknowledged in the individual monographs.

My own immediate staff—Mrs. Edna Hockensmith, secretary to the project, and Robert Fairbanks, research assistant, have been of greatest help. My colleagues in the Department of Economics, particularly Jerry Miner and Seymour Sacks, have been available for continuous consultation. Both the project and this volume have specifically benefited from the advice and counsel of Professors Richard C. Lonsdale and Robert C. Stewart of the Syracuse University School of Education, who have served as general project consultants and who have helped project authors to avoid at least some of the pitfalls that befall "outsiders" who write about an area foreign to their immediate professional experience. John C. Honey, then of the Carnegie Corporation staff, provided most valuable advice on the organization of the project at its inception. Margaret Mahoney, of the Carnegie Corporation staff, has been continuously helpful to the project.

This book is divided into three sections. The first four chapters deal with matters of general concern to public education—economics and administration, and the utilization of resources within education. The next five chapters are directed to the economics and politics of state and local finance; the following five chapters review issues related to general federal aid to education and examine experience with some existing federal aid programs. The concluding chapter offers some suggestions for new organizational arrangements.

JESSE BURKHEAD

Syracuse, New York
Fall 1963

I. The Economics of School Finance

In 1962-63 outlays for public elementary and secondary education in the United States amounted to about $16 billion. States and local governments spent more on public schools than on any other program. For all levels of government, public elementary and secondary education ranked second in importance only to national defense and constituted 10 per cent of all governmental expenditures. Thus, in terms of sheer magnitude, decisions about the allocation of resources to this part of the public sector are important.

It would be comforting if there were firm economic guidelines that could be followed by political decision-makers in judgments about resource allocation for public education. Unfortunately, this is not the case. Economic criteria are necessarily imprecise where outputs cannot be measured. There is, however, a growing body of knowledge about the economic value of education; there is an analytical framework for describing the considerations that ought to determine public finance decisions in this area; there is a set of institutional parameters that appears to be significant in shaping decision processes. It is the purpose of this chapter to outline these three.

The Economic Value of Education

In the last few years economists have discovered the significance of education as a determinant of economic growth.[1] A partially new terminology has come into existence. "Investment in education" is employed as a substitute for "expenditures on education." Such terms as "the economics of human resources," "investment in human beings" and "human capital formation" have entered the literature. Economists have also begun to examine other aspects of human resources, such as health,[2] and outlays for nonphysical capital such as research and other knowledge production.[3] These developments may well mark a major shift in emphasis in economic analysis and research—away from the study of physical capital and toward the study of nonphysical capital, or investment in the human agent.

This new emphasis is a logical outgrowth of the nature of contemporary economic problems. The scientific revolution of our time, it

The author is indebted to Joseph A. Kershaw for comments on an earlier draft of this chapter.

is commonly observed, requires new quantities and qualities of skilled manpower. The demands for highly developed technical skills seem continuously to outrun supplies. Research in industry, in government, and in the universities is highly valued and research workers have a prestigious position in society. Improvements in technology, affecting all phases of contemporary living, from national defense to suburban swimming pools, appear to depend on research, and research in turn on technical skills and education.

The worldwide concern for economic growth has also been a major influence in the redirection of thinking toward the role of human resources. In the underdeveloped nations growth problems are at the center of public policy. Resources are scarce and decisions must be made as to whether economic growth can be better encouraged by outlay for elementary education or for public health, by the construction of a new steel mill or by teacher training programs. Economists are pressed to provide answers, crude and tentative as they may be.

For the advanced industrial economies it is thought that problems of assuring an equilibrium of income, employment and prices—the avoidance of severe depression or inflation—are relatively easy to deal with. To assure a continuous increase in per capita income, however, is much more difficult. As economists have examined the determinants of the growth in income, for example in the U.S. economy, it has been discovered that the qualitative improvement of human resources is an important explanatory variable.

There are other factors at work to encourage this type of research. The international competition among economic systems gives rise to strong national efforts to increase total output. Educational systems are evaluated in terms of their ability to contribute to this end. Educators do battle with their critics in terms of the quantity and quality of education that is thought to be internationally competitive. Questions are raised as to whether nations are spending too much or too little for various kinds and varieties of education. Educational policy, and the economic and other values of education, are matters of great public concern.

The economists' recent attention to human resources has already produced stimulating and provocative findings. However, this area is a most difficult one for economic analysis. In any program affecting the quality of human resources the costs and benefits are elusive. Most such programs, including education, do not have end products that can be defined, let alone measured. Hence the efficiency of alternative arrangements cannot easily be evaluated. Moreover, in education the student's time is an input for the system and thus, conceptually, is a cost of production. But the student himself, and his knowledge and ability, is also the system's output. Such interdependencies are not easy to untangle.

Nevertheless, this research will increase our understanding of the economics of human resources and of the probable consequences of specific expenditures. There is always some usefulness in systematic thinking, even when numbers cannot be attached to all of the influences that are at work.

No effort will be made here to survey the whole of the recent literature on the economics of human resources or even on the economics of investment in education. Excellent surveys are available elsewhere.[4] What will be attempted is a brief statement and evaluation of selected recent findings concerning the value of education as an investment, some comments on the value of education as consumption, and a description of cost-benefit analysis. This will serve as a general preliminary to a specific examination of the fiscal framework for public education.

Education as Investment

As economists turned their attention in the decade of the 1950's to a study of long-run patterns of economic growth in the U.S. economy, one important finding emerged: increases in output could not be explained solely on the basis of increases in physical capital accumulation and increases in the number of workers.[5] A "third factor" has been at work, defined to include "changes of all kinds in the capital stock embodied in men, physical and 'mental,' and also changes in the efficiency of physical capital and economic organization and structure."[6] Attention thus came to be directed toward the measurement of the components of this "third factor." This has encouraged inquiry into the economics of research and invention, the economics of health, and, of course, education.

Much of the research on the relationship between education and output has been done by Theodore W. Schultz of the University of Chicago and a group associated with him. Schultz, for example, has estimated the annual volume of gross investment in formal schooling at all levels in the United States from 1900 to 1956.[7] He finds that total investment in education, defined to include both direct costs and foregone earnings, has been rising rapidly in relation to nonhuman investment since the turn of the century—from 9 per cent to 34 per cent of gross physical investment. Further, these increases apparently go far to account for the "third factor"; investment in education contributes to productivity increases. The ratio of total capital—both physical and human—to output has been reasonably constant over this half century.[8]

Using quite different techniques Denison has estimated the contribution of education to economic growth for the years 1909-57.[9] He assumes that three-fifths of the earnings differentials that are associated with educational attainment in comparable age groups are in fact directly attributable to education. The remainder must be attributed to such factors as motivation and ability. With this assumption Denison estimates that education contributed about 23 per cent of the growth in total real national income and about 42 per cent of the growth of real national income per person employed for the years 1929-57. Increases in education contributed only about half this much to economic growth in the period 1909-29 and between 1960 and 1980 will contribute somewhat less than in the 1929-57 period.

A related line of inquiry has explored the costs and returns on education at various levels. Here an effort has been made to measure the profitability of investment in education by comparing its costs with the returns that may be attributable directly to the increased education. In this context returns are measured as the differential earnings of those who have been educated, as compared with those who have not been educated. College training lends itself much better to this kind of measurement than does elementary and secondary education. For the former Becker has estimated that in 1940 private returns on college education for urban white males, after taxes, was 12.5 per cent. In 1950 the comparable figure was 10 per cent.[10] When total costs, including those not paid by the students, are used as the basis for measurement, net returns are lowered to about 9 per cent in both 1940 and 1950.

Schultz, in another set of estimates, concluded that in 1958 the rate of return on high school education was 11.8 per cent, and on college education 10.9 per cent.[11] These are higher than average rates of return on business investment. The conclusion has been reached, by both Schultz and Becker, that further investment in education would bring a social gain in that returns would exceed those obtainable, on the average, from investment in physical capital in the market economy. However, the differential rates of return are not very great as between investment in education and in physical capital.

The foregoing brief and selective summary does not do justice to the procedures that underlie the estimates. Those who have been engaged in the analysis of the economic value of education have been generally careful to make their assumptions explicit and properly to qualify their conclusions. There are, nevertheless, some serious conceptual problems here with the measurement of the quantity of investment in education, with the methods of attributing effects on economic growth to changes in such stock, and with the measurement of returns on education in terms of earnings differentials. The difficulties that have been encountered with the concept of foregone earnings are illustrative.

It is part of economists' stock in trade to instruct noneconomists that resources are scarce and that the use of resources for one purpose precludes their use for another. If resource inputs are devoted to the provision of, say, secondary education, they will not be available for some other purpose. If that "other purpose" is the provision of health services, then the (opportunity) cost of an increment of educational service may appropriately be measured in terms of the foregone opportunities to enjoy an increment of health services.

As applied to the evaluation of investment in education the concept of opportunity cost requires that, in measuring investment, not only shall the direct inputs of educational cost be taken into account, but also the loss of earnings occasioned by keeping students out of the labor market. In this approach for elementary education the loss in earnings would be trivial; for secondary education it would be much more important; for higher education very substantial. One set of estimates puts the foregone earnings of high school students at an amount more than equal to the institutional costs of elementary and secondary education in 1957-58, and the foregone earnings of college and university students at more than twice as much as institutional costs.[12] The inclusion of foregone earnings in estimates of investment in education thus adds very greatly to the totals of investment cost and reduces the resulting calculations of the rate of return.

The inclusion of foregone earnings in educational costs is quite appropriate for an individual who wishes to calculate his own net return from an investment in education but it is much more questionable in application to estimates of the full cost to society of investment in education for a nation.[13] It is possible to imagine that several thousands of students now in college could find alternative employment, although job opportunities have recently been limited for this age group. But it is difficult to imagine that several million high school and college students could find employment without a reordering of the work force, and indeed of the whole economy, to lower skill levels. Marginal comparisons and opportunity cost concepts have no meaning applied to greatly different kinds of economic organizations.

There are comparable kinds of conceptual difficulties in the estimates of returns on investment in education by way of differential earnings. The task here is to measure those earnings differentials that are attributable solely to the educational component and to eliminate those differentials attributable to sex, ethnic background, ability, and other factors. This problem has been recognized by Becker, who has most ingeniously attempted to control for the "other factors," but in fact, the identification of all factors that contribute to earnings differentials is not possible. Students who attend college are different from those who do not. On the average those who attend college are presumably more highly motivated, come from families with higher incomes, and have been exposed to more educational influence in the home. A college degree opens up job opportunities that are not available to those of equal ability but without degrees, and family influence will assist the graduate to find more lucrative job opportunities. Earnings differentials are thus the resultant of a complex of interdependent forces. In this kind of multiple matrix it is very difficult to measure the specific contribution of formal education.[14]

At this stage of the research on the economics of education, it is not possible to evaluate the significance of the inclusion of foregone earnings or the failure to isolate all of the factors that contribute to earnings differentials. Some estimate of foregone earnings would seem to be appropriate for inclusion, but how should this estimate be arrived at? Similarly, until alternative procedures are available for estimating the factors affecting earnings differentials, it is difficult to judge the significance of the determinants now omitted from the analysis. It may well be that separation of the social from the private benefits of education is simply not possible and that, no matter how ingenious the estimates, this crucial measurement will remain permanently elusive.

Education as Consumption

No matter how tentative the findings, economic analysis is better equipped to examine education as an investment than to examine education as a consumer good. In fact, there is little that economists can contribute to an evaluation of why goods and services are wanted; demands that are made effective in the market can be measured, but it is not regarded as the province of economics to explore the psychological or social derivations of such demands.

Nevertheless, in any attempt to appraise the value of education, the significance of education as a consumer good cannot be avoided. Education may be demanded by individuals, or by a society, as an investment in higher income in the future, or as an investment in economic growth. But it is also demanded as a thing in itself, to be consumed and enjoyed simply as "cultural attainment." Neither can the investment and consumption aspects be separated. Students are not trained independently in the acquisition of skills and in their ability to enjoy the world around them. The vocational and cultural aspects of education cannot be separated at any level, in kindergarten or in graduate school.

It might be anticipated that there would be substitution between the investment and the consumption aspects of education at different stages of economic development. Vocational education would have more value in a developing society, but as per capita incomes increase and the society becomes more affluent, the value of education as a consumer good, however that may be defined, would rise.

Interestingly enough, expenditures on public elementary and secondary education do not appear to have followed this pattern with any considerable regularity in the United States. Hirsch has found that over the period 1900-58 the income elasticity of such expenditures was 1.09.[15] An increase of 1 per cent in personal income was associated with an increase of per pupil expenditures in average daily attendance of only slightly more than 1 per cent. Elementary and secondary public education thus have a lower elasticity of expenditure with respect to personal income than consumer durables such as automobiles.

However, this perspective is altered if higher education is treated as consumer expenditure with its investment aspects ignored. The inclusion of expenditures for public and private higher education would appear to raise the coefficient of elasticity to a value of about 2.0.[16] The perspective might be altered further if estimates were available over long periods of time for all outlays for education, including education in the home, in the church, on the job, and at commercial vocational schools. Machlup's pioneering estimates for the two years 1955-56 and 1957-58 suggest that this would be the case.[17]

Expenditures on elementary and secondary public education, viewed as a consumer outlay in relation to personal income, thus do not appear to increase more rapidly than income, but expenditures for education as a whole do increase more rapidly than income. In short, as a consumer good education may be valued as highly as other "luxury" goods.

Expenditures on education may be justified as a consumer good or as an investment good. Evidence to date suggests that, viewed solely as an investment good, past outlays represent an economic use of resources. If to this investment value is added an increment derived solely from the satisfaction of consumer preferences, there is every reason to conclude that expenditures on education have brought handsome returns.

Costs and Benefits

One promising approach to the analysis of the economic value of education lies in the application of cost-benefit techniques. Cost-benefit has long been used by federal agencies in the analysis and justification of water resource development projects. It has also come to be increasingly employed for the examination of the feasibility of metropolitan development projects, such as urban renewal and highway construction.

As employed in the water resource field, this technique requires that monetary values be attached to all project benefits "to whomsoever they may accrue," and that these benefits be discounted to a base year to permit comparison with project costs, likewise expressed in terms of a base year. If benefits exceed costs, the project is economically justifiable. In counting benefits, values are attached to both the direct benefits that come from the output of products such as water and power, and also to indirect benefits, such as land value enhancement, that may result from the project. Every effort is made to attach dollar values to project programs such as recreation, whose benefits may be somewhat intangible.

Although cost-benefit analysis has been employed by the federal government for some 25 years in the evaluation of water resource programs, there continue to be difficulties in its use, both conceptually in terms of what should and should not be counted, and in securing adequate data. Equally or perhaps even more formidable problems would be encountered in applications of cost-benefit analysis to education. Nevertheless, the effort would appear to be worthwhile since the results should be useful for educational program decisions.

Weisbrod has outlined a general approach to this analysis for the entire range of education—elementary, secondary, and higher.[18] Costs would include both institutional outlays and the social costs of income foregone while students are in school. Benefits would be those that accrue to individuals and those that accrue to society. Under the first heading Weisbrod would estimate the financial return to individuals that is derived from the investment in education. In addition, he would estimate the value of the "financial option" to individuals, defined as benefit that accrues from the opportunity for still further education. A third individual benefit would be included—the nonmonetary "opportunity options" that individuals may enjoy as a result of their education: broadened employment choices and insurance against technological change.

The benefits of education that are external to the student would be divided into three groups: residence-related beneficiaries—those whose welfare is improved, for example, because children are kept off the streets; employment-related beneficiaries—the employer interest in well-trained workers; and society in general—a kind of catch-all category to pick up such values as general literacy and pursuit of the societal goal of equality of opportunity.

This broad, aggregative approach to the measurement of the costs and benefits of education does not, of course, avoid all the conceptual and measurement problems that are inherent in the approach to education as an investment. However, cost-benefit analysis can be applied to much smaller educational policy problems. Vocational education in an urban school system, for example, would appear to lend itself to this technique. It should be possible to compile some generally adequate estimates of costs and gains for incremental changes in outlays for vocational education and thus to arrive at a crude kind of quantitative basis for making judgments about expansion and contraction.

As it has been employed by federal water resource development agencies, cost-benefit analysis has been most useful where comparisons are made among projects that are roughly similar in character. Alternative port development projects along the same river, for example, are susceptible to reasonably accurate comparisons. But far more serious difficulties are encountered when efforts are made to compare large multipurpose projects located in different regions. In application to educational policy the same limitations would very likely obtain. It should be possible to estimate, with reasonable accuracy, costs and benefits from the construction of language laboratories in high schools. It would be much more difficult to estimate with confidence the benefits and costs of language laboratories as compared with the benefits and costs of vocational education.

The economic analysis of investment in education and analysis of the costs and benefits of education is in its infancy. Much additional research is now in progress and it can be expected that much more will be undertaken, not only in the economics of education but in other aspects of human resources. Thus far the operational content of the research is meager. Neither the conceptual apparatus nor the empirical work has reached the point of providing answers to those who must make decisions about whether this or that educational program should be expanded or contracted—whether more or fewer resources should be channeled to the support of specific programs. As Vaizey has put it:

> The most comprehensive study of the subject reveals no simple way of judging what should be spent on education in comparison with other items of government expenditure. It is silly, indeed, to expect a simple answer. Education is an extremely complex part of the complicated social mechanism; and the education system as we know it is the result of the interaction of various combinations of forces; and the structure of politics (especially democratic politics) is there to take decisions in these matters, decisions which will be affected in only some degree by economic considerations.
>
> Nevertheless, economic considerations do exist; and it is important to try to be rational about them.[19]

Optimum Public Spending and Taxation for Education[20]

The purpose of a theory of the public finances of education is in many ways similar to the purpose that lies behind the measurements of the economic value of education. Public finance theory should provide a framework for orderly examination of the factors that determine the optimum level and the composition of government revenue and expenditure. Ideally, the theory should be operational, that is, the determinants should be susceptible to measurement. Very often, however, the measurement possibilities are limited.

In the context of a consumer-directed market economy, a complete theory of expenditures for public education should seek to explain the following: (1) The theory should provide a framework for determining whether educational services should be produced publicly or privately. (2) It should suggest, on the basis of a concern for proper allocation of resources, redistribution of income, and economic stabilization, the appropriate amount of expenditure for education. (3) The theory should point to the appropriate pattern of taxes for raising these revenues. (4) The theory should indicate the level of government that is to be responsible for the support of various components of public education. Only the second and fourth of these considerations will be examined here.[21]

Resource Allocation: Equating Benefits and Costs

A strict application of the principles of economic efficiency would provide educational spending up to the point where the benefits of additional spending were just equal to the burdens of the necessary taxation plus such amounts of foregone earnings as should be taken into account. The equating of benefits and tax costs would be achieved for each individual and business which used educational services. In this view the benefits of education are reflected in the willingness of households and business firms to pay for various levels of elementary and secondary education provided in a community. Burdens are measured by the value to households of the increased consumption and saving they could have obtained from the funds taxed away for educational expenditures.

Household demands for education are based on the value of educational services to the pupil or his family. These demands reflect desires of parents for education so that their children's lifetime earnings will be higher, or because parents believe education will heighten the children's enjoyment of life. Household demand for education also encompasses the value of education to persons unrelated to pupils who find satisfaction in the education of others because of the cultural, political, and interpersonal characteristics of an educated society. Derived demand for education by producers, similar to their demand for productive inputs, is an additional component of the total demand for education. Increased outlay for education in a community provides a more productive work force, and so long as the value of the increased output due to greater educational skills of the workers exceeds the cost of additional educational services and higher wages paid, the producers stand to gain from increased outlay. A summation of producers' and consumers' derived demand comprises the total demand for educational spending. Theoretically, where total demand is equal to the unit cost of goods and services an economically efficient level of output is achieved.

Foregone earnings may also be included as a part of the cost of education, although this treatment is open to some question, as noted above. If these are counted, the cost of education will be greater than the taxes to provide the necessary funds. Thus, for a given level of benefits, the optimum level of expenditures would be lower than if earnings foregone were ignored.

Resource Allocation: Effects on Production

Another problem in the determination of the total demand for education, in an approach using a market basis, arises because educational attainments often yield scientific, administrative, and other cost-reducing discoveries. The original discoverers or their employers may, for a short time, obtain an economic gain from the sale of their uniquely productive innovation, but the social gains of widespread use will not appear as part of any private demand for education because it cannot be privately captured. As a result, the economically correct level of derived demand for education by producers should include the indirect cost-reducing effects of increased levels of education which increase the productivity of other producers.

The effects of one producer's behavior on the costs of production of other producers, called "external effects" or "external economies," occur over time as well as at a given moment. Increased educational outlays which raise productivity make higher rates of economic growth possible. Growth may be more rapid because an increased product can provide more capital goods (i.e., buildings, machines) while consumption remains unchanged or rises by less than the increase in productivity. However, most of the gains from more rapid economic growth will be enjoyed by future generations whose preferences exert no influence on the current use of economic resources. Market-determined outlays for education, therefore, will not adequately reflect the value to future generations of the contribution to economic growth from contemporary levels of spending for elementary and secondary education. Here the private market approach to education fails to register the social demand of future generations.

The complex nature of the total demand for education is a result of the many economic effects of education that cannot be captured through a market transaction because they accrue to others besides the student. A market solution to the output of goods or services is an ideal one only when private or personal benefits and costs are the sole significant elements. Private demand for education does not reflect satisfactions gained by individuals other than students and cost reductions for firms other than those whose employees receive education. Since the market fails to register these consequences the amount of education supplied is inadequate. Theoretically, the economist can say that the total demand, including private and nonprivate elements, should determine educational outlays. The virtual impossibility of determining the magnitude of these public elements renders the concept of an educational optimum nonoperational.

The level of educational spending consistent with private and nonprivate consumer and producer demand, even if attained, still would not necessarily be an optimum from an economic standpoint. The relationships between levels of public education and income distribution and economic stability are also involved in the determination of educational spending.

Income Redistribution

Education outlays in excess of the amounts demanded by individuals and business firms may be undertaken as an income redistribution technique. Families with low incomes and a lack of knowledge of the potential returns to education are not likely to demand heavy educational outlays, but the community may decide that increased educational services should be consumed by children in such families. As a way of redistributing income and controlling the use of the extra income, additional education is provided without assessing extra tax liabilities on low-income families.

The issue here is whether the recipient should decide on the disposition of redistributed income. When the shortcomings of consumer sovereignty in determining a family's outlay for education are taken into account, there is no clear economic answer to this problem. Supporters of the market economy emphasize that transfer payments have the advantages of providing social and cultural values of freedom of choice, but few would dissent from the proposition that a necessary step in breaking the chain of successive generations of poverty and lack of motivation is satisfactory elementary and secondary education for children. Especially where the future of children is at stake, a doctrinaire adherence to the principles of consumer sovereignty by policymakers may doom still another generation to a marginal life economically, socially, and culturally.

Economic Stabilization

Educational spending to promote economic stability is not consistent with contemporary theories of controlling business cycles, although increased educational outlays have been proposed as antirecessionary measures. Plans for new school buildings, for example, could be kept in readiness and implemented when there were indications of unemployment.

A broader view is that educational outlays are justified by their economic, social, political, and other benefits and, therefore, adequate levels of public education should be provided regardless of the desirability of government expenditures for stabilization purposes. Stabilization policy should aim at providing full employment, stable prices, and adequate rates of economic growth, and in so doing must take into account the level of demand for goods and services produced by governments. The determination of the quantity of public services to be provided should, in turn, be based on an appraisal of needs and desires for such services assuming that stabilization policies achieve full employment. If stabilization aims are confused with supplying the proper amounts of public goods and services, resources will not be used where they yield the greatest benefits.

Educational Spending by Different Levels of Government

The concept of an ideal division of responsibility among the various government levels for financing and providing public elementary and secondary education has been much discussed. From an economic point of view, one aspect of the issue is to allocate responsibility so that final and derived demands for education are reflected in the total amount of educational spending, while, at the same time, tax burdens are assessed in relation to benefits received. Insofar as income in the form of education is preferred to transfer payments as a redistribution technique, further educational outlays must be provided without assessing taxes in accordance with benefits. In addition, government responsibilities should be distributed so as to minimize the costs of educational services as well as the costs of tax collection. In the context of the present federal system in the United States, such objectives imply the involvement of all levels of government in financing public education.

Local Government. At the local level governments are most capable of adapting the quantity of spending and the character of the public school system to the demands of those using the schools and to the business firms and individuals who will be most immediately affected by the nature of elementary and secondary schools. The dominance of local governments in operating public schools in the United States today is largely the consequence of these circumstances. However, only a portion of total educational spending should be locally determined and financed. Benefits accruing to persons and business firms outside the boundaries of the local government must also be reflected in educational revenues and expenditures for local pupils. Also, local taxes are unlikely to be redistributive even within the local community; redistribution across regions requires state and federal participation. Further, even though expenditures are under local control, local revenue systems may be incapable of effective tax administration and state and federal taxation may be a superior way of raising revenues from residents for education. The widespread benefits of education and problems of local tax administration require the participation of state and federal governments in educational finance.

State Government. Apart from the role of the state in consequence of the extensive benefits of education and difficulties faced by local tax administration, considerably more extensive state participation would be justified if state operation of local public schools resulted in substantially reduced costs. The success of school district consolidation programs in recent years has greatly reduced the number of inefficiently small school systems and while considerably more consolidation is needed in a few states, there appears to be no necessity for actual state operation to achieve economically sized school systems. State operation might, however, provide strong incentive for educational research and experimentation which individual local school systems now find hardly worthwhile. States can also act as purchasing agents and guarantors of credit for local schools. However, if states are not to abandon concern for differences in local community attitudes toward education, they must allow local variations in educational spending and services. It appears, then, that states can best reduce educational costs by promoting consolidations, by engaging in and supporting basic research on educational methods, and by using the financial strength of the state to obtain the most favorable terms for local school purchases and bond issues.

Federal Government. In the determination of educational outlays the central government alone can make effective the consideration of nonmarket benefits which cross state boundaries by granting to local school governments funds derived from the entire nation. Also, only the central government, through a system of taxation and grants, can redistribute income regionally and thereby modify the economic base out of which local school spending is derived.

A further economic task for the central government is use of the federal tax system to obtain revenues to be repaid to the localities. An advantage of such a procedure is that the federal government can effectively employ more equitable taxes, such as the personal income tax, and greater reliance on federal taxation would lessen pressures on competitive tax concessions by state and local governments to induce industrial location. Also, instead of requiring the maintenance of the myriad of small tax collection agencies that result when every local and state governmental unit collects taxes, the federal government is able to administer tax collections with a single central staff employing modern data processing and auditing techniques.

Intergovernmental Responsibilities. The ultimate general pattern of governmental responsibility that follows from these economic concerns is that local governments operate the schools and have the power, within standards set by the state, to hire staff, determine curriculum and length of school day and term, and perform other vital educational functions. In addition, these local units contribute toward local educational outlays an amount determined by the local communities' demand for education. The funds for these outlays should come from local residents and business firms according to acceptable standards of equitable burden, although they may be raised by the state or even the federal tax system and returned to the point of collection. To this amount is added the demand for education emanating from benefits of education obtained by persons residing outside the locality. The funds for these outlays come from sources outside the local government. Finally, state and federal grants to local schools to redistribute income in the form of educational services provide additional sources of funds for educational spending by local systems.

The Institutional Setting

The foregoing normative model of public school finance in an intergovernmental system provides a general framework for appraising existing patterns of taxes and expenditures for public education. The model is not, however, capable of being used operationally for policy decisions about optimum levels of spending for public education, nor for decisions about the appropriate level at which taxes are to be imposed. The benefits of education to households and to business firms cannot be measured with accuracy. Differences among local, state, and national benefits cannot be determined with precision. In short, the demands for education can only be approximated.

These approximations must find expression through the political process. Political decisions about resource allocation are not made solely in a context of economic efficiency considerations. They are also a product of the traditions of our system of fiscal federalism, which has assigned differing responsibilities to national, state, and local governments; these levels of government have developed differing institutional arrangements for discharging these responsibilities.

Responsibilities Among Levels of Government

These intergovernmental patterns can be appropriately examined in terms of Richard A. Musgrave's three-branch approach to the public sector.[22] In Musgrave's framework the public budget may be divided conceptually into three components. The first is allocations, wherein decisions are made about the provision of government goods and services for such purposes as national defense, education, streets and roads, police and fire protection. The second branch embraces decisions about economic stabilization, where government taxes and spends to control fluctuations in total economic activity. The third branch consists of decisions about the distribution of income among individuals and among major economic sectors and regions.

The allocations branch, with the exception of the provision of national defense and the conduct of foreign affairs, is intergovernmental—that is, almost all public programs, including public education, are supported by national, state, and local governments. This is due not to the attribution of benefits to these levels, but to the fact that the supporters of specific programs have access to the political structure at many points. Resources for public education, for example, that may not be available at the local level may be sought at the state level, and inadequate access to state and local resources will encourage efforts to enlist additional support from the national government. Neither does this proceed through any simple process of exhausting first one source and then another. The supporters of specific programs may proceed simultaneously at all these levels to seek additional financing. This pattern of intergovernmental decision-making affecting the resources available for public programs may appropriately be regarded as a source of tremendous strength and flexibility. Shifts in these arrangements have provided a means for the accommodation of program requirements to what would otherwise be seriously inhibiting institutional restrictions on public policy.

Economic stabilization, however, is not intergovernmental. Since the 1930's and increasingly since the Employment Act of 1946, the federal government has assumed almost sole responsibility for measures that are designed to maintain a high level of income and employment. These responsibilities may not be assumed vigorously; the measures adopted may be inadequate to the task; but the responsibility is clear.

No such stabilization responsibility exists for states and local governments. Public works programs in a state or even occasionally in cities may be undertaken in part with a view to their employment effects, and there may be occasional state-level programs designed to deal with structural and regional unemployment problems. But, in general, state and local governments are in the position of adapting and accommodating their policies to a national stabilization program.

The distribution of income is also a national responsibility, expressed in terms of attention to the impact of expenditures and revenues on income groups, among regions within its economy, and among industrial and occupational groupings. On the expenditure side of the national budget the concern for low income groups is expressed in various outlays such as for welfare and distressed areas. On the revenue side the budget reflects a whole series of decisions made consciously and unconsciously to influence the distribution of income among the rich and the poor. Controversy over tax policy, frequently couched in terms of the progressivity or regressivity of burdens, is a manifestation of national responsibility for the distribution of income.

State and local governments are much less concerned with distributional considerations in the formulation of budget policy. Although state and local government expenditures probably have some mildly redistributional effect from the rich to the poor, state and local government revenue structures tend to be regressive, offsetting, in part, the progressivity of the federal revenue system. Distributional considerations are by no means irrelevant in state and local government finance; but very often they are obscured by controversy over which group of the poor shall bear additional taxes.

Operating Characteristics

To these important differences in responsibility for the branches of the public sector must be added significant institutional differences that influence the operating character of the public finances at different levels of government. The first of these centers on the differential access to taxable capacity.

The sum total of the wealth and income of the fifty states is, of course, equal to the total wealth and income of the nation. Therefore, state and local taxable capacity is equivalent to the taxable capacity of the national economy. Nevertheless, the national government has tax advantages not possessed by state-local governments. Some of this advantage may be attributed to a higher level of administrative ability in the national government, and some to the greater ease in taxing transactions that cross state lines. But most of the advantage is a product of the historical accident or design that has given the federal government major control over the personal and corporate income tax.

A second set of institutional differences between national government finances and state-local finances turn on considerations that affect debt financing. Although there is much popular concern about federal deficits and the national debt, in fact, rather substantial deficits are incurred in peacetime years without perceptible impact on national solvency however defined. The national Treasury has no need to worry about the mere provision of funds. The Federal Reserve System can be asked, or coerced if necessary, into serving as an agency to purchase whatever Treasury securities are necessary to provide whatever funds are required.

State and local governments are in a very different position vis-à-vis their deficits and debts. Not only are there frequent state constitutional restrictions limiting indebtedness but, in addition, these governments do not have access to the central banking facilities of the Federal Reserve. Hence state and local governments must be concerned about their "credit" in the conventional sense in which this term is used in the private sector. As a result, state-local expenditures are much more limited by available revenue than is the case with the national government.

State and local governments are "open" economies. Securities issued by these units are very likely to be held by "foreigners"—institutions and persons living outside the jurisdiction. The payment of debt charges is thus a transfer of local income to "outsiders." Also, a state or local government may lose population and economic activity and find itself with a capital plant that must be amortized by those who remain. All such factors limit the use of borrowed funds.

A third set of differences relates to the structure of local government—a structure virtually unchanged since the beginnings of the nation. Apart from school districts, whose boundaries have altered continuously with the process of redistricting, and some annexation by cities, the basic spatial pattern of counties and municipalities has seldom been realigned. In consequence, the existing boundaries of political jurisdictions, as has been commonly observed, are less and less harmonious with economic regions. The population of the central cities spills over to form new suburbs, and metropolitan areas come to be economic regions in polycentric or multinucleated patterns. But there is no metropolitan regional government with jurisdictional competence to deal with areawide problems. Economic activity crosses and recrosses local government boundaries. The taxable capacity represented by the flow of local economic activity eludes the grasp of the governmental units involved.

The multiplicity or fragmentation of local government leads to a number of serious and unfortunate fiscal consequences. The absence of areawide taxing jurisdiction forces counties, municipalities, and school districts to undertake all manner of patchwork arrangements to bolster their inadequate finances. Operating under continuous fiscal pressure, local governments adopt narrowly based sales taxes and flat-rate income taxes, and seek from state legislatures permission to levy special excises on specific types of transactions. Special district governments are organized to provide water, sewerage, fire protection, lighting, public health, and streets and roads. Bond financing is undertaken and service charges are imposed to support the bond issue. The fragmentation of local revenue structures that established the original straitjacket and forced the creation of the special districts thus ends up with an even larger number of governmental units.

It seems likely that no other advanced industrial nation has differences in governmental service levels as great as those in the United States. With such a multiplicity of local governmental units, the costs and benefits of government services are distributed in a haphazard fashion. A public welfare program paid for largely by a central city may benefit the needy who have moved from rural areas. Public schools paid for in one community may provide vocational training that benefits employers in another community.

These disparities in the distribution of the costs and benefits of local government services lead to a peculiar kind of competition within a metropolitan area. Each jurisdiction attempts to compete for public benefits and at the same time attempts to minimize tax costs. Business firms and householders seek to locate within the local jurisdiction that provides a maximum of public benefits from governmental services with a minimum of tax costs. This brings pressure on local units to shift public service costs to other jurisdictions. The possibilities for cooperation among governmental units within a metropolitan area are thus jeopardized as each unit seeks its maximum fiscal advantage.

Within a typical metropolitan area much of the fiscal antagonism centers on conflicts between the central city and the outlying suburban and exurban areas. Although precise calculations are impossible to obtain, there is a general consensus among most students of local government that central cities operate at a continued disadvantage. The central city is the major source of employment and of income produced within the metropolitan region, but the outmovement of residences, commercial activity, and, increasingly, of industry, diminishes the proportion of the property tax base that can be reached by the central city government. At the same time, central city costs do not decline proportionately to the shift in economic activity. To keep the city viable as a place of employment, large outlays are necessary for police and fire protection and for the construction of arterial highways and downtown parking facilities. City residents will typically pay a disproportionate share of such outlays either directly or indirectly as construction of new public facilities removes property from tax rolls.

At the same time, the changing ethnic and income composition of the central city produces two additional and unfortunate consequences for governmental programs and finances. As low-income ethnic minorities come to make up a larger proportion of the central city population, social and economic cleavages between the central city and the suburbs become sharper, and possibilities are diminished for cooperative areawide solutions for common problems. Second, the changing socioeconomic character of the central city increases the need for public programs to improve housing, combat delinquency, provide recreation facilities, and, in general, to undertake needed social and economic urban renewal. Needs are increased relative to resources. Low income families concentrate in the city and this alone makes for fiscal imbalance.

Finally, state and local finances operate in an institutional setting characterized by rather different citizen attitudes toward taxpaying and spending than is the case with the national government. It is difficult to measure these attitudes with any degree of precision but their presence is undoubted.

State and local governments seem to occupy an unhappy position as residual legatee of the fiscal pressures of a high-tax society and have inherited the consequences of the long-standing antigovernment tradition of American society. In this tradition public goods and services are thought to be inherently inferior to private goods and services. The public sector "lives off" the private sector. The citizen works one day in five to support the bureaucracy. Private activity is productive; public activity is unproductive. The possibility that a high-tax, high-expenditure community could provide a larger measure of public and private welfare and hence of total welfare is not seriously entertained in this view. A calm appraisal of the relative costs and benefits of public and of private expenditures is indeed difficult; there is no straightforward technique for measuring and comparing outcomes. But the possibility for rational decisions about resource allocation, particularly at state and local levels, is often precluded by the widespread refusal to recognize that public sector activities can be productive of increases in private welfare.

Economic Models and Political Choice

As economists continue to improve their measurements of the value of education as an investment and develop further the possibilities of cost-benefit analysis, there will be increased possibilities for rational choice in decisions about resource allocation in the public sector. Estimates of benefits of other governmental programs will facilitate comparisons among governmental programs, and between the public and the private sectors. But for the immediate future decisions concerning the finances of public education must be, of necessity, political decisions in the broadest sense of that term.

As matters now stand, the political process alone is capable of reaching decisions about social values and the way in which the taxes necessary to realize such social values should be apportioned. Only the political process can express the value judgments inherent in decisions about the distribution of income and the volume of resources that should be devoted to education in the interests of an improved distribution of income. There are no market measurements capable of providing other than the most tentative of guides for the allocation of taxes to support education.

An ideal political process should be quite as capable of serving as a mechanism for resource allocation as an ideal market system. In fact, the political process, if it functions well, can satisfactorily record and reconcile the public want-satisfactions of diverse interests and groups and is superior to a market in reflecting the intensity of wants. In the real world, of course, political processes can be as imperfect as market processes and it would be most unwise to attempt sweeping generalizations about the effectiveness of either in reaching an optimum allocation of resources for public and private use.

In most important ways the finances of public education are similar to all other public finance problems. Educational finance shares the same tax base—federal, state, and local—with other public functions. Taxes to support education have the same kinds of economic impacts as taxes to support other governmental functions. Citizen attitudes toward government, favorable or unfavorable, will come to influence taxes and expenditures for education in much the same fashion that such attitudes influence taxes and expenditures for national defense, for welfare, for health and hospitals.

In short, school finance is a creature of the same institutional structure and value system that shapes attitudes and decisions about all public and private economic and political activity.

II. Administration of the Public Schools

As as result of the necessary efforts of school administrators to mobilize funds for public education, the impression has become widespread that more money will solve most educational problems.

Certainly, a lot more money for public education would remove many harmful constraints. It would facilitate the payment of more appropriate teachers' salaries, the construction of more adequate space, the use of better equipment, the development of better teaching materials, and a significant expansion in basic and applied research in the learning process and teaching methods. But more money would merely make it easier for school administrators to obtain the larger volume of resources that seems required. It could not by itself assure the effective use of these resources to meet America's needs for more and better educational services.

Moreover, the competition for public funds is so great that additional increments in expenditures per student will probably be both small and gradual. The size and rate of these increments, in fact, will unquestionably be affected by the extent to which school administrators demonstrate through actual performance and clearly formulated proposals their capacity to use additional funds effectively.

It is therefore pertinent to examine the nature of school administration. This is in line with the increasing attention given throughout the world to the administration of all organizations with important functions in society. Before discussing school administration, however, some prefatory remarks are desirable on the concept of administration and the growth of administrative thought. The characteristics of public school administration which are common to the administration of all other organizations will then be discussed. This will lead to an analysis of some special characteristics of public school administration. The concluding section of this chapter will discuss the need for three general improvements in school administration: a new role concept for school administrators, the encouragement of teacher self-development, and a new approach to national, state and local educational planning.[1]

This chapter was written by Bertram M. Gross, professor of political science, Syracuse University.[2]

What Is Administration?

[illegible] nany other widely used words, "administration" and "ad-[illegible] or" are highly ambiguous. Different people—and indeed, sometimes the same people—often use the same words to refer to entirely different ideas or activities. This confusion is compounded by indiscriminate use of such terms as "scientific administration (or management)" and "administrative (or management) science." In the general discussion that follows an effort will be made to define these rather slippery words, particularly in application to public education.

The Guidance of Organizations

As here used, "administration" refers to the process of guiding or leading organizations, or members, units or aggregations thereof, toward the achievement of certain purposes. More colloquially, this is equivalent to running an organization or getting things done with or through the other members of an organization.

The administrative process takes many forms. The most obvious is the direction or supervision of subordinates. Equally important, administrators mobilize the human, material and financial resources that are required for an organization to operate. To do this and to get results, they influence superiors and colleagues as well as subordinates. Moreover, a large amount of administrative activity is externally oriented. It is aimed at overcoming the resistance of, or obtaining support from, outside individuals and groups.

This is a broad concept of administration, this definition embracing the total operations of units, organizations and systems. This includes the official governing bodies of school systems and the top executives of every system and individual school. It includes the head of every unit, section or department, no matter how small or humble. It includes all the many "assistants-to" and deputies who actually assist their chiefs in the guidance of schools and systems. It includes all staff advisers and special committees that participate in the process.

This is a far cry from administration as mere paperwork or the clerical handling of routine procedures. It has nothing in common with the conception of administration as consisting of lifeless organizational forms or visionary plans. It relates, rather, to the full-bodied reality of people in action.

This is also a far cry from the idea of administration as an unproductive burden on the shoulders of those who do the really productive work. The activity here referred to by the term is an indispensable prerequisite to the productive operation of any organization. When properly performed, it can make all other activities in an organization more productive. In any one situation, of course, there may be too many administrators as a whole and too few of them capable of high-quality work. Yet in other situations there may not be enough administrators to facilitate the use of new and more complex techniques or to formulate and attain new and higher goals. As will be indicated later, this is probably true of many public school systems. To be more effective in meeting the needs for public education it may well be necessary to initiate more ambitious undertakings whose complexity will require a considerable increase in both the quantity and quality of administrative activity.

The Study of Administration

The art of administration is one of the oldest in the world. It was first developed by tribal chieftains, kings and their advisers, heads of armies, and the builders of religious institutions. It has been developed still further by the administrators of the great economic, governmental, religious, and educational organizations that are the basis of modern civilization.

But the scientific study of administration started only in the 20th century. Although it has progressed rapidly in recent years, it is still in its infancy. It is not yet based upon enough direct observation of actual behavior. It does not yet provide a clearly defined set of terms and concepts. It has not yet made sufficient use of recent advances in psychology, anthropology, sociology, political science, and economics. It has not yet caught up with the wisdom of practical administrators.

During the first half of the 20th century the most important advances in the study of administration centered around one or another special aspect of the subject. Production engineers have developed specific techniques for improving work methods in both office and factory. Personnel specialists have devised valuable techniques for use in recruiting, promotion, wages and salaries, disciplinary action, and collective bargaining. Psychologists and "human relations" specialists have developed methods of measuring and improving workers' morale. Economists, accountants, and budget experts have fashioned an impressive set of tools on the financial side of an organization's operations. New techniques are constantly being developed in these areas and in internal information systems, public relations, and the procurement and maintenance of materials and equipment. However, in many of these areas there has been a tendency for specialists to neglect the work of others and equate their own work with administration as a whole. The more enthusiastic specialists, particularly those whose techniques are highly quantitative in nature, have sometimes labelled their own handicraft "scientific management" or "administrative science."

There is also specialization in terms of different types of organizations. Special colleges, faculties, and departments have dealt separately with the administration of business organizations, of civilian government organizations, and of military organizations. Attention has also been concentrated on the administration of schools, hospitals, and libraries. But most of these special fields of administration are characterized by ambitious instructional programs unsupported by a sufficient foundation of research and theory. They also exhibit a tendency to exaggerate the differences between one type of organization and another and neglect the advantages that might be reaped through the cooperative exploration of common problems.

The great advance in administrative thought in the second half of the 20th century is in the development of a general approach to the administration of organizations. This is an approach which uses the observation of behavior to formulate imaginative generalizations concerning the entire process by which administrators guide organizations toward the achievement of objectives. It is an approach which can be used in integrating the specialized techniques of administration and indicating their relevance to particular situations. It is an approach which draws upon relevant theory and research from all the intellectual disciplines, without regard for traditional disciplinary boundaries. The study of school administration has already been greatly enriched by more intimate contact with this new and more general stream of thought.

The Common Characteristics of All Administration

In a certain sense all human beings have something in common. In part, the common element stems from the biological basis of human life. In part, it stems from the social setting in which they live and the common elements in human experience.

One of the things people have in common is the way they behave in organized groups. This, in turn, determines those elements which are common to the administration of all organizations.

People-In-Organizations

An organization consists of people working together to achieve certain purposes. To put it more abstractly, an organization is the interrelation among these people. Those who comprise an organization will invariably use certain nonhuman resources such as buildings, equipment, materials and machinery. But these material things are not the organization. They are merely passive elements that are used by the organization's members.

One of the most conspicuous aspects of an organization is the formal division of labor among its members. In larger organizations this becomes exceedingly complex. Still more complex, however, and much less conspicuous is the network of informal relations that develops within every organization. An inevitable response to the formal division of labor, these informal relations may work both to supplement and to frustrate the formally established patterns.

The people involved in an organization's activities are motivated by certain needs and interests. These needs are multiple. They are complex. They vary from time to time. They are often conflicting—both within a single person and among different persons.

A common element in all human motivation is made up of survival needs. These include such simple things as food, drink, sleep, shelter and also protection against aggression or threats to security. Another common element is found in the belonging needs. These include the needs for companionship, affection, and love, and for being a part of something larger than one's self. On the other side of the coin from belonging needs are the needs for differentiation. These needs are met by status, respect, and power.

Finally, there are the needs for self-development—also referred to as self-fulfillment or self-actualization. These needs are met by learning, by esthetic and intellectual pursuits, and by creative efforts of any type. They may flourish in an atmosphere of freedom and independence—particularly when the survival, belonging, and differentiation needs are being met.

The various goods and services produced by organizations—economic as well as cultural and governmental—are mainly designed to meet combinations of these human needs. In an exchange economy money is a basic prerequisite for meeting certain of these needs. It is used to command goods and services that are sold. Money thus provides an important—albeit not the only—basis for security, status, and power.

Organizations-In-Environments

No human organization is a closed system. It is rendered open by four channels that relate the organization to its environment: entries and exits, which transform outsiders into members and members into insiders; multiple membership, which results in members' loyalties to outside groups; resource exchange, which involves the absorption of inputs in the production process and the delivery of output produced; and mutual or reciprocal influence on the part of both members and outsiders.

The relation of mutual or reciprocal influence is an extremely complex one. Every organization is in an environment composed of large numbers of individuals and groups playing a large variety of roles. An extremely important role is that of client (or consumer) for the organization's output. Other important roles are those of suppliers, advisers, controllers, and opponents. Any of these roles may be played by any type of organization, and many organizations play many of these roles at the same time. The intangible role of public opinion must also be recognized.

Any organization, accordingly, is surrounded by a complex array of people, units, organizations, and opinions that interrelate with it. An oversimplified picture of this "encirclement" is provided by Figure 1.

FIGURE 1
THE IMMEDIATE ENVIRONMENT OF ORGANIZATIONS

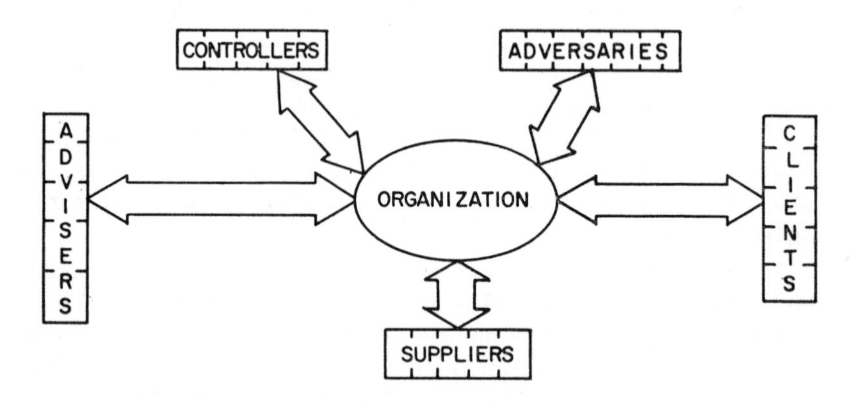

There is considerable variation in the visibility of the specific individuals and groups in these categories. Some of them, indeed, are well known to everyone in the organization; others are known to few organization members other than those who conduct dealings with them. Some operate in an open and above-board manner; others are behind-the-scenes operators.

Apart from its immediate environment, every organization is also part of a broader social system, as suggested by the outer boundaries on the chart. This social system includes the cultural values, political structure and resource base of the country or region.

Complex Purpose Patterns

Every organization is characterized by some pattern of accepted purposes. These purposes are multiple, changing and differently perceived by different people. They are rooted in the divergent needs of different members and interested outsiders. A major task of the administrator is to bring these divergent purposes together into some acceptable pattern.

In brief, administrators try to guide organizations toward (1) satisfying certain human needs, (2) providing certain outputs for use by their clients, (3) mobilizing certain resources, (4) making efficient use of scarce inputs, (5) maintaining the organization's viability, (6) observing certain codes of behavior, and (7) doing all these things as rationally as possible.

A brief explanation is in order on each of these purpose categories.

Satisfaction of Needs. The highest purpose of any organization is to satisfy needs. Those whose needs must be taken into account are the members of the organization. Unless participation in the organization meets some of their needs, members will leave the organization or withhold their full energies from the organization's activities.

But no organization can survive without satisfying some needs of nonmembers also. The most direct group of nonmembers are its clients. For example, the direct clients of schools are the students, who are the recipients of educational services.

The direct clients, however, are not the only ones whose needs are satisfied by an organization's operations. A business corporation tries to provide good business for its suppliers, dividends for its stockholders and reliable debt service for its bankers. An ordinary government agency may be responsive to a great variety of interests beyond those of its immediate clients, including those of other government agencies. Above all, any government agency—and every public school system—is expected to serve the public interest.

In the case of public schools the network of indirect interests is extremely large. In the immediate sense benefits are also received by the students' families and their future employers. In a broader and more far-reaching sense, however, substantial benefits are enjoyed by the entire nation—from the schools' contribution to the cultural, intellectual, and moral level of its students. This is particularly true for any nation where the great majority of the citizenry attend the public schools in their early years.

Output. An organization aims to satisfy the needs of its clients by producing certain services or goods. Its "product mix" sets forth the various types of output—together with quality specifications and quantity goals for each type. The product mix of a school is composed mainly of educational services, the nature of which is indicated by its curriculum.

A large part of every organization's activity, however, goes into the production of intermediate outputs. These are used by other units in the organization (as in the case of building maintenance, record keeping, or a committee report proposing a new curriculum) or are merely parts of the final output (as with a single class session).

Mobilization of Resources. Resources are those services or goods which are needed in the production of output. Resource mobilization is the process of obtaining and maintaining a supply of such inputs from the external environment or from within the organization or system. The major resources are personal services, equipment, and materials. Money is an indispensable element in obtaining the needed amount and quality of these inputs. Hence the initial phase of resource mobilization usually centers on the raising of funds. In the case of public schools, which do not charge for their services, these funds are raised from local taxes, public bond issues, or financial aid from state and federal agencies.

Money is not a direct resource, however. It may serve, for example, to attract persons capable of providing good teaching services. But the availability of more money may not automatically bring a sufficient supply of good teachers into existence for schools as a whole.

Efficiency in Use of Scarce Inputs. Whenever there is a perceived scarcity of desired inputs, organizations and administrators aim at economizing on input in relation to output. Efficiency purposes consist of input-output relationships. Thus an organization may aim at getting more output with the same amount of input or the same amount of output with less input.

In a narrow sense, efficiency may be thought of in terms of any single type of input—for example, building space. If a school suffers from a scarcity of classrooms, it is therefore interested in the most efficient possible use of all available space. It may achieve this purpose by improvements in the design and distribution of the available space and by raising the student-space ratio. But overcrowding may also result in a decline in the quality or quantity of educational services, with a resulting decline, not an increase, in efficiency.

In a broader sense, efficiency must be thought of in terms of the use of all inputs—buildings, personal services, and supplies. These can be expressed most simply in terms of total monetary expenditures, which provide the only way of adding all the miscellaneous input elements. Thus the efficiency of a school or school system is a relationship between its total expenditures and its total output of educational services. The difficulty of identifying this relationship will be dealt with below.

Viability. In a minimal sense, viability means survival. If the organization does not survive, it cannot get anything done. Survival is the indispensable prerequisite for achieving any other purpose or purposes.

The alternative to survival is not so clear. At times it may mean utter disintegration. It may also mean division into surviving parts, integration into a larger whole, reorganization, or merely a few new administrators and a new name. What from one viewpoint may look like death may turn out to be rejuvenation or reincarnation.

In a larger sense, as distinguished from one or another form of survival, viability means growth. If an organization does not grow, it cannot get ahead of competitors or opponents; it cannot hope to do a "bigger and better job." Hence for most organizations, in fact, the daily "struggle for survival" is seen as the struggle to expand the capacity to produce, resist stress, or adapt to new conditions.

In the case of a local or state school system, accordingly, it is not sufficient to aim at the best possible educational services in the immediate future. It is also essential to aim at the growth of the system's capacity to meet future needs. The growth of a system, however, has many implications for its components. It inevitably requires the merger, reorganization, elimination, or change of individual schools, departments, programs, or procedures. Growth also requires considerable change in the personal capacities of its teachers, administrators, and suppliers of supporting services.

Observance of Codes. Every organization aims at doing things "the right way." To some extent, the nature of "the right way" is set forth in external codes—laws and regulations, moral and ethical prohibitions and prescriptions, and professional principles. Many of these are written. Some of the most powerful are unwritten.

"The right way" is also determined by the code of the organization. This will in part reflect the external codes, particularly when these are supervised by enforcement agencies. In greater part, however, the code of the organization expresses certain types of behavior that have been deemed necessary to serve the interests of members and that have been hallowed by custom and habit.

In the case of public schools the most obvious codes are embodied in state law, local ordinances, and regulations of various state and local agencies. Moral codes are also of great importance. Public servants in general—and teachers in particular—are often expected to set a "better example" than other citizens.

With the maturation of teaching as a profession, professional codes of ethics are also important. These have been promulgated by the National Education Association and by teachers' associations in various states. For the more vigorous schools and school systems, however, these merely provide a framework, or starting point. The more successful administrators aim at establishing a special code of service for their schools or school system, a code embodied more in the "spirit of the place" than in any written document.

Rationality. All members of an organization often aim at doing things rationally. This means the selection of the means best adapted to attain a set of purposes—from satisfactions and output down to rationality itself. To state the matter in another way, it means devising behavior sequences that appear to be causally related.

Rationality may be divided into two components. One is technical rationality, which calls for the application of the latest and best results of scientific and technical research and theory. The other is administrative rationality, which requires the selection of the best possible methods of guiding organizations. This form of rationality, unfortunately, is still based too much on intuition and too little on research and theory.

As with any purpose category, however, there may frequently be a major gap between desire and attainment. Intended rationality may be little more than a fancy rationalization of the irrational. The administrator's rationality may, in the judgment of his peers or of those who come later in the great advantage of hindsight, be little more than a muddle.

In the case of the public schools, technical rationality has been impeded by a shocking lag in research, both basic and applied, in education and learning. This lag is particularly serious, albeit not often recognized, in a field as basic as the psychology of learning, where most researchers have preferred to concentrate on animals and infants. One of America's outstanding psychologists has identified the problem as follows:

> This same half-century saw American psychology move away from its earlier concern with the nature of learning as it occurs in school. The psychology of learning tended to become involved with the precise details of learning in highly simplified short-term situations and thereby lost most of its contact with the long-term educational effects of learning. For their part, educational psychologists turned their attention with great effect to the study of aptitude and achievement and to social and motivational aspects of education, but did not concern themselves directly with the intellectual structure of class activities.[3]

In the applied field the situation is also highly unsatisfactory. Although some university schools of education have tried to lead the way, the overwhelming majority of local and state school systems have devoted an almost unbelievably small amount of resources to research and experimentation. This contrasts rather sharply with the resources that have been invested on the technical aspects of such other public undertakings such as road construction, water supply, and sewage disposal—to say nothing of the vast research undertakings in industry.

A new impetus to applied research in educational methods has been recently provided by the National Defense Education Act and the accompanying activities of the United States Office of Education. Under NDEA, with additional support from various foundations, ever-greater attention is being given to the development of improved curricula (particularly in the physical sciences, mathematics and languages), experimentation with new methods of classroom organization and new methods of instruction, including visual aids and teaching machines.

In all these areas technical progress has been accompanied by a certain amount of gadgetry for its own sake. It becomes fashionable to use certain methods even where their relevance to particular teaching-learning situations may be highly questionable. The inventors, innovators, and reformers themselves often contribute to this by exaggerated claims for their devices and methods. Yet this is probably an inevitable accompaniment of technical progress—and not nearly as dangerous as technical stagnation.

Power, Cooperation, and Conflict Processes

Any useful understanding of administrative rationality must start with the realization that administration is an endless process. It consists not of separate activities but of interlocking activities. It is hard to find the beginning and still harder to find the end. Every achievement creates new difficulties, every solution new problems.

This process is one of constant change. Neither the people involved in an organization's activities nor their purposes ever remain immobile. Organizations come into being, grow, contract, or even die. Their members enter and leave. Of those who remain, some grow wiser and all get older. Even if the process of change is not evident from outside or is not formally legitimatized, it takes place beneath the surface.

Yet one should not lose sight of the more static aspects of administration. They must be included as part of the picture—just as the banks are a part of a river. The form and the structure are merely the more stable parts of the ongoing process.

There have been many efforts to slice up the administrative process into specific processes. One of the first slicings—done by Henri Fayol back in 1916—divided it into planning, organization, command, control, and coordination. Luther Gulick reformulated this into POSDCORB—Planning, Organization, Staffing, Direction, Coordination, Reporting and Budgeting. Others have singled out the techniques of budgeting, accounting, systems analysis, personnel management, records management, and public relations. Still others prefer such "higher level" concepts as planning, decision-making, communicating, activating, assembling resources, evaluating performance, and improving performance.

There is no end to the possibilities of subdividing administration into more specific processes. New insights will always reveal new and significant aspects of a complex subject. New techniques will always be developed, while the older techniques constantly are being refurbished. At a deeper level of analysis, however, it is possible to describe the administrative process in terms of two clear-cut propositions.

The first of these is that *administration is a process of acquiring and using power.* Power is here used in the sense of influence or the ability to get things done.

The essence of any organization is that it pools individuals' energies and abilities into the power of the group to do things that could not be done at all, or as well, by the individuals acting separately. In this sense any organization—whether an army, a government department, a business or a woman's club—is a system of power.

In guiding an organization, or any unit or combination thereof, any administrator is handling power—somewhat like the man behind the steering mechanism of an automobile or airplane. But to guide the power system, he must develop his own capacities to influence people.

In part, the administrator's own power stems from the formal authority attached to the position which he holds. People expect him to sit in the driver's seat and—up to a certain point—will be inclined to go in the direction he chooses.

But the greatest mistake in administration is to equate formal authority with administrative power as a whole. Authority is never a sufficient source of power or a guarantee of sufficient power. Administrators must actively set out to acquire power. They must develop, through action, their abilities to influence people and groups. This involves much more than the crude use of commands, punishments, and rewards. It also involves the use of persuasion, advice, suggestion, consultation, and reciprocal influence.

When personal influence is highly developed, it may well exceed authority. Some persons exercise power with little or no authority. Many administrators exercise power far beyond the legitimate borders of their authority.

In either case, power has no automatic relationship to responsibility. As often pointed out, administrators may get drunk with power and exercise their influence with little sense of responsibility to their organization or to society as a whole. Yet a school administrator without power cannot act responsibly to further the objectives of public education. Power may ennoble and elevate as well as corrupt. It is a sword that can cut in any direction.

The second proposition is that *administrators participate in relationships of both cooperation and conflict among the members of an organization and between the organization and its environment.*

The first half of this double-barreled proposition emphasizes the process of social cooperation. Without a minimal degree of cooperation no organization can develop the power to get things done and is therefore doomed to fall apart. This cooperation may be based on a passionate dedication to common objectives. Or it may stem from a mere *quid pro quo* understanding in which each member succeeds in attaining purely personal objectives. The organization, in turn, must enjoy some degree of cooperative relations with its environment. This is often described by using the term "cooperative system" to refer to the larger and looser entity comprised of an organization and the outsiders with whom it relates in a regular fashion.

The remainder of this proposition states that conflict is the other side of the coin from cooperation. Within any organization, internal conflicts are inevitable. Different people mean divergent interests and divergent perceptions of the purposes of the organization or the best ways to obtain them. The division of labor within an organization automatically creates conflicting interests between the divided units. There is always some kind of competition within an organization as to how the separate units can best be coordinated—and as to who should be authorized to coordinate.

Conflicts with the environment are also inevitable. Whenever an organization tries to achieve certain objectives, there are obstacles in the path. At the very least these will take the form of inertia or passive resistance. Often they take the sharper form of competition for scarce resources or of direct opposition.

The negative potential of such conflicts is obvious. Conflicts that go too far will make it impossible for an organization to satisfy the needs of members, clients, and others in the community. This will frustrate and may imperil the existence of the organization.

What is less obvious, however, is that within limits conflict has a positive potential. Internal conflict can overcome dull routine and can help produce new ideas and new leaders. External conflicts can keep an organization on its toes.

The good administrator—whether operating on intuition alone or on the basis of clearly formulated concepts—sees both sides of the coin. He knows that he is engaged in a perpetual process of both cooperation and conflict. He knows that a large part of his job is to bring people to work and think—and feel—together. He also knows that he and his cohorts must be prepared to fight.

The Special Characteristics of School Administration

To a considerable extent, administering a school, a part of a school, or a school system is like administering any organization. But this does not mean that general knowledge of administration reveals everything that is important about school administration. It does not mean that a successful businessman, army officer, or police chief would be—merely by virtue of his administrative performance elsewhere—capable of being a successful school principal or superintendent. There are special characteristics of school administration which make it very different from the administration of other organizations.

In fact, the administration of any individual school, unit, or system is in some ways unique. The differences among public schools are at times probably almost as profound as the differences between schools and other organizations. These differences stem from such factors as goals, personality, methods, curriculum, level, student body, the specific relation of the school to the local structure of government, the local line-up of political forces, public support, and cultural environment. Such unique characteristics can be learned only by experience in, and with, a specific school situation.

Although it is possible to isolate and analyze the individual factors that combine in various ways to produce the unique "flavor" of administering an individual school organization, these characteristics will be laid to one side in order to examine characteristics which seem common to school organizations as a whole. Although the major frame of reference here is public school administration in the United States, much of the discussion will be relevant to public school administration in other countries, even in those that are less developed economically.

A Special Form of Public Politics

In a certain sense every organization has a "private politics" of its own, consisting of its internal rivalries for position and power. In this sense school organizations are probably little different from any other organization.

Every governmental organization is also involved in a public form of politics. Its operations are a matter of widespread public concern. Its deeds and misdeeds are publicly investigated and discussed. Its administrators are held publicly responsible for their actions. Above all, it must actively compete with other public agencies for the financial support without which it cannot properly operate. Even though appointments and promotions may be free from influence by party politicians, the organization operates in a highly political environment.

The politics of schools and school systems, in turn, is a special form of politics. The education of the young is a subject of intense interest to most families. It is tied up deeply with traditions, prejudices, and religious beliefs. The political significance of these matters is dramatically illustrated by the continuing controversies concerning racial integration in the schools, religious instruction, and public aid to religious schools. Its less dramatic but day-to-day aspects are illustrated by the unending public controversies on school bond issues, school taxes, the distribution of state educational funds, and the question of federal aid to education.

Thus, whether or not the top administrators of local and state school systems like to use the term, they are involved—in the broader sense of the term—in politics. They "build fences" to strengthen their support. They try to divide the opposition. They try to win over neutrals. Yet no matter what they do, some school administrators feel so heavily buffeted from all sides that they do little more than respond to stimuli. They "play it safe." Only the more able administrators—those who have developed the skills and wisdom of "statesmen"—are capable of taking the initiative and becoming creative influences upon their environment.

A new element is also entering school politics: a national, as distinguished from a purely state or local, aspect. This occurs as the quantity and quality of public education becomes increasingly a national issue. The National Defense Education Act was enacted under the Republican administration of President Eisenhower. The national aspects of public education have figured strongly in the politics of the Democratic administration of President Kennedy. In future decades there will be more rather than less attention to public education by the federal government. It is highly unlikely that this will result in the diminution of educational politics in either the states or the localities. It will merely add another dimension to the public politics of public education.

Unusually Close Contacts with Clients

Schools have much closer contacts with their immediate clients, the students, than do most organizations. This gives rise to certain special characteristics of school organizations and their administration.

There is no intermediary between students and school. The students come directly to the school to get its services. Apart from vacation periods the total time they spend on the school premises is usually the largest single slice of waking-hour time devoted to any single activity. The total time spent in one school or another usually covers the students' entire period of puberty and a significant part of earlier growth and later adolescence. The total amount and variety of interactions between students and teachers may far exceed the interaction between students and parents.

In hotels, hospitals, and jails, of course, the clients actually live on the premises for a certain period of time. But with the exception of the chronically hospitalized and the "long-timer," this is a relatively short period in comparison with the ordinary time span of public education. And in none of these cases are the clients themselves expected to exert themselves in the way that is expected from students in school. In none of them must the organization go so far as teachers do in evaluating the active performance of the clients. In none of them are the clients themselves organized in groups as formal and cohesive as the classes in a school. In none of them do the clients go so far in identifying themselves with the organization or even regarding themselves as members of it. All these are special characteristics of the relations between a school and its students. Hence an important task of school administrators is the provision, utilization, maintenance, and improvement of the space and facilities needed by students—in short, continuous attention to client needs.

Still more important, however, is attention to the fact of continuous contact with young people, whose implications are many and varied.

For one thing, this contact can be very exciting. The process of human growth in childhood, puberty, and adolescence is a wonderful thing, wonderful to watch, and wonderful to take part in as a member of an educational organization. The stream of students is endless—and endless also the different personalities and their patterns of growth and learning. The future belongs to them (in fact, not merely in commencement addresses) and to the extent that the school can affect their growth it can help shape the future.

On the other hand, there are characteristics—it may even be said, occupational hazards—associated with this contact. Because of their superior knowledge and their positions of higher authority, both teachers and school administrators can easily develop an overauthoritarian approach to students. Instead of serving its legitimate role in helping achieve the school's objective, this authority may serve the more narrow personal purpose of self-aggrandizement, as the teacher dominates the pupils or the administrator does the same over both teachers and student body. This occupational hazard is rendered more dangerous whenever intimate contact with young people and immature minds monopolizes a person's life and displaces any significant contact with older people, mature minds, and tougher substantive problems.

Another aspect of school-student intimacy is that public schools do not engage in any significant competition in order to attract students. Since students are assigned to their individual schools largely on a geographical basis, selection is usually automatically determined rather than being based on parental or student choice. The students will come to a school because they are sent there. The spur of competition may not be as sharp as in the case of private schools and institutions of higher learning.

Intangible and Complex Output

A common problem is faced by the administrators of all organizations that provide freely available public services. They cannot use monetary units to add up the total quantity of their output, nor can they have a common measure applicable to both output and input. This makes the estimation of efficiency extremely hazardous.

Where the public services are more tangible—as with street cleaning, fire fighting, water supply, and traffic control—the problem can be more readily handled. It is easier to identify just what is being done or should be done. It is easier to reach informed judgments as to quantity and quality.

Educational services are among the most intangible of all services.

It is possible to estimate the time spent in performing them but very difficult to estimate the quantity or quality of the actual output. Educational services are also more complex than most other intangible services. This complexity derives from the cooperative nature of the learning process. On the one side are the educational services provided by teachers. These may include such activities as (1) transmitting information and explanations, (2) motivating students to learn, (3) posing problems, (4) providing demonstrations, (5) proposing student action, and (6) evaluating student performance. On the other side are the contributions of the students: (1) their personal capacities, (2) their own motivations and processes of development and maturation, and (3) the amount of energy and imagination they devote to the learning process. The importance of these contributions by the students is recognized, of course, by the very existence of systems for giving grades to students. Yet the progress or lack of progress made by students cannot readily be attributed solely to either the students' contributions or the teachers' services. Whatever is learned in schools is learned as a result of both.

To make an accurate appraisal of the teachers' services, it would be necessary to focus on the marginal increment in student learning over a given period of time. Thus the progress of a student receiving one set of teaching services would be compared with that of a substantially similar group receiving another set of teaching services under substantially similar conditions. The difference between their rates and paths of progress would then be presumed to result from the differences in teaching services. The actual marginal increment in learning would also be compared with an ideal increment, that is, optimum learning goals established on the basis of experience concerning how much progress students can make under ideal conditions and an ideal set of teaching services.

In the production of education there are no simple units of measurement. On the one hand, the learning process itself is multidimensional; it involves values and abilities as well as knowledge and, as in so many other aspects of human behavior, those aspects susceptible to precise measurement often turn out to be the least significant. On the other hand, the specific contribution of teaching devices to this complex process is even harder to pin down. Many courses merely serve as indirect catalysts, providing an atmosphere or framework conducive to student learning and development. Many students learn despite their teachers or as a result of sharp conflict with them. It is thus exceedingly difficult for schools to identify their products clearly in a truly meaningful fashion, appraise their quality and calculate their quantity. Probably more than any other organization, they "shoot in the dark."

Under these circumstances it is often necessary to use "service surrogates" of quality and quantity. These surrogates are aspects of the teaching-learning process that can be evaluated or counted. They serve as substitutes for, or representatives of, teaching services for the purpose of quality and quantity calculations.

Quality Surrogates

The quality of any service may be defined as the extent to which it lives up to certain specifications. In turn, specifications are always multidimensional. The most important quality specifications are those relating to the satisfaction of the needs or interests of those for whom the services are provided. Other specifications relate to the characteristics of the services themselves, the methods used in providing them, and the input factors which enter into their provision.

Client satisfactions. Since human satisfactions—like needs and interests themselves—are locked within the minds and hearts of individuals, certain surrogates must be used to appraise their extent. In services or goods that are sold on the market, the degree of satisfaction may be inferred from consumer willingness to pay a given price. This measure is not available in the case of public education. Similarly, it is not possible to use the pattern of consumer choice, since pupils are generally assigned to schools on a relatively fixed geographical basis. This leaves two major surrogates: presumed results and expressed opinions.

Aspects of student performance can be measured in (a) a specific course or program, (b) a subsequent course or program, and (c) subsequent activity after completion of an educational program. Presumed results in terms of the effects on productivity, citizenship, and culture are rarely susceptible to quantification.

The quality of teaching services may also be judged in terms of the opinions of (a) students themselves, an extremely powerful influence on the judgments of others, (b) other teachers, and educational organizations, (c) parents of students, and (d) subsequent employers of students.

Product characteristics. Here attention may be focused upon the curriculum. The quality of teaching services may be inferred from the degree of conformance with or deviation from one's ideas concerning an ideal service mix. This pattern may vary in terms of the subject matter of courses. It may vary in terms of the specific handling of any subject—whether in terms of level of difficulty, the needs of different groups of students or different approaches to it.

Methods used. Another indirect indicator is found in the use of approved or promising teaching methods. This includes various methods of motivating students, posing problems, transmitting information and explanations, initiating student action and evaluating student performance. It also includes the use of books, audio-visual aids, teaching machines and all other relevant devices or equipment.

Input factors. In education the major input is teaching manpower. The quality of teaching may therefore be inferred from various indicators that are presumed to bear upon the quality of the teachers. These may include (a) formal degrees received, (b) subsequent studies undertaken, and (c) length and type of teaching experience. The inference may also be made that a larger total expenditure per student indicates a higher quality of teaching services received by students. The same inference is made with respect to specific categories of expenditures—particularly teachers' salaries and construction of facilities.

Quantity Surrogates

The quantity of intangible services is even harder to pin down than their quality. It would be impossible to count the pieces of knowledge, skills, and interests acquired by students. Here, as with other intangible services, there is no choice but to use instead the number of clients, the duration of services rendered, and the quantity of inputs.

The number of clients. The total quantity of services provided by a school system, school, or teacher is often expressed in the number of students served. This number may then be broken down into various groupings of students, with appropriate attention to the number of drop-outs from the beginning to the end of a school program. Special attention is usually given to the number of graduates.

The duration of services. In a certain sense the quantity of teaching services may be calculated by counting courses, course duration or course credits. The teaching load of individual teachers is customarily measured by course hours (modified perhaps by a calculation of the number or duration of preparations). Such quantification can be made more meaningful by multiplying course duration by the number of students. Thus the total services of a school may be expressed in terms of student-hours or student-years.

Input factors. Inputs—in the form of total costs—also appear on the quantity side. Thus an increase in total costs provides a way of summarizing increases in the number of students, courses, course durations and student-durations.

In the case of each of these surrogates there is often reason to infer something significant from them concerning quality or quantity. But none of these surrogates must ever be confused with teaching services themselves. The actual amount of help given to student learning processes may go down as the number of students goes up. Some people with advanced degrees or numerous publications make wretched teachers. An impressive new teaching device may in actuality detract from the learning process. And, as already suggested, student performance is the product of student input as well as teachers' contributions. The use of these surrogates may thus give a misleading picture. Even when all used together, they can give only a partial picture. Administrators must use them, but must do so with great care and never take them too seriously.

Improvements in School Administration

In the case of any activity as varied as administration, it is extremely easy for any observer to find a dozen points where improvements may be needed. In fact, any administrator whose performance is good enough to be worth improving can himself readily indicate dozens of things that he and his organization should do better.

School administration is no exception. It would be possible to compile a long list of reforms, starting with such venerable ones as reorganization and consolidation and going through every aspect of school budgeting and personnel practices. But this is a task better left to school administrators themselves. When nonschool administrators approach this area, it is more useful to deal with the broadest and most fundamental aspects of administration.

Three of these aspects will here be discussed: the role of the school administrators, the encouragement of teacher self-development, and the approach to educational planning. If progress can be made on these strategic matters, there will be a firm basis for the school administrators themselves to move toward other needed improvements.

A New Role for School Administrators

As noted above, the first half of the 20th century has witnessed important transformations in the concept of administration. These decades saw a decline in the image of administrators as authoritarian despots. They saw a rise in applications of the scientific method, human relations, and democratic leadership, with increasing attention to the concept of professional administration.

The ideal of professional administration is indeed a high one. It implies a serious effort to develop an organized body of administrative knowledge and skill, to provide for both the pre-career and mid-career training of administrators, and to develop a code of administrative ethics. It also implies a recognition of the fact that no administrator can ever afford to lose himself in administration. Just as a teacher always teaches some subject matter, an administrator must administer something. He must be intimately acquainted with the changing purpose pattern of his organization and the processes, power, cooperation, and conflict within it and in relation to the surrounding environment.

The ideal of professional school administration is still higher. This ideal implies a combination of at least two professional approaches. The school administrator must not only have a professional approach to administration, he must also have a professional approach to—and preferably a professional background in—teaching. He must commit himself to making his own contribution—no matter how small—to the maturation of both.

A new role for public school administrators is slowly emerging. The professional school administrator increasingly addresses himself to the formulation and achievement of certain purpose patterns through the cooperative action of people inside and outside the organization. He is interested in student and public needs for educational services and the personal needs of teachers and other employees. He tries to obtain the best possible "product mix" of teaching services and related activities. He is involved not only in mobilizing whatever resources are needed but also in making the most effective and efficient use of them. He appreciates the importance of current investment in the future strength and capacity of the school or school system. He is interested in developing high internal codes of behavior. He actively seeks both technical and administrative rationality.

Although this role is little more than that intuitively developed by the best school administrators for many decades, its explicit formulation and application will emerge slowly. It will call for the retooling of some present administrators and the replacement of others. In the long run it will call for a new generation of public school administrators, a generation dedicated to serving the learning needs of students through the mobilization of creative energies inside and outside the schools. This will call for an active administrator role in promoting the growth and self-development of teachers and all other staff members in the schools. Above all, it will mean that administrators themselves will set the tone for this widespread learning process by continuously trying to learn from the advancing tide of theory and research and from the experience of themselves, of other schools, and of other organizations. This, in turn, means a still greater role than before for the various organizations that have been doing pioneer work in the development of a professional approach to school administration.

Encouragement of Teacher Self-Development

For many years there has been attention to the question, "How can we get better teachers in the public schools?" More recently, public school administrators have given increasing attention to the equally important question, "How can we improve the capacities of present teachers and keep them from leaving the field?"

One of the answers has been to increase teachers' salaries. In fact, campaigns to raise teachers' salaries have become important issues in thousands of communities. Some real progress has been made. Yet across-the-board salary increases affect only the relative attractiveness of teaching as compared with other ways of earning a living. It does not by itself provide incentives for better teaching performance. Accordingly, there have been many efforts to introduce into schools merit rating devices previously developed in other types of organizations. In business and government such devices have proved feasible only when used in connection with routine types of work; and even in such cases they tend to exacerbate interpersonal relations. Their suitability to educational organizations is highly questionable.

Some public school administrators have begun to think of "rank systems" analogous to those in colleges and universities. Under such a system a limited number of high-ranking positions—with the title "Master Teacher" or perhaps "Professor"—would be established. To achieve such a rank much more would be expected than mere seniority, courses, and degrees. The basic criterion would be creative work in teaching, as judged by peers and responsible superiors together rather than by officials alone. Such a system would establish a line of career advancement for teachers rather than forcing those who want to do better financially within the school system to turn to administration.

In addition to the salary and career aspect of teacher development, much greater attention is now being paid to a continuation of teachers' own learning processes. Particularly in the physical sciences, larger numbers of public school teachers than ever before are attending special "refresher" courses during the summer months. Larger numbers are enrolled for higher degrees at universities. The enlargement of such activities—with the provision of regular leaves with full pay—

should be an important goal of school administrators. The excitement of learning cannot be imparted to students by teachers who have come to the end of the road. It is rather to be spread by contact with teachers whose minds are themselves engaged in the learning process.

But it would be a very limited viewpoint that separated into two compartments the teacher's teaching ability and his own learning process. The most creative teaching is done by teachers who see their teaching not just as something which takes time and energy away from their studies but *as a positive contribution to their own learning processes.* One of the oldest truths in education (in no way less important because recently "discovered" by psychologists) is that teaching a subject is the best way to learn it. This is true at any level. In the lower grades, in fact, where one has to deal with the most fundamental concepts, the teacher is faced by an even greater intellectual challenge.

The classroom is the teacher's own laboratory for learning about teaching and learning. Here the creative teacher can set out to perfect old methods and develop new ones. He can set out to learn a little more about the ever-varied stream of developing human beings that comes through his classroom.

There is reason to believe that there are vast untapped resources of teaching ability within every public school system. There are the undeveloped or partially developed creative abilities of untold numbers of present teachers. These potentialities can be fulfilled only when administrators can offer an attractive pattern of career advancement, varied opportunities for continuous study and an atmosphere which provides challenge and encouragement to creative activity in the classroom.

A New Approach to Local and State Educational Planning

The concept of administration herein set forth clearly requires long-range planning for all the various educational services that would meet the nation's requirements for more and better education. It requires planning that starts with needs and output, and works back to include the major categories of inputs, the efficient use of such inputs, the investment of resources in the growth of schools and school systems, the development of organizational codes, and a continuing search for more rational methods of instruction and administration.

Above all, this approach implies active participation in planning by all those who will have a role in putting the plans into effect. A local plan will not be worth much if it represents nothing but the views of the school superintendent and the school board. Planning is worthwhile only if teachers, parent-teachers associations, and many other groups and individuals have somehow or other participated in the planning process. Only if developed in this manner can planning be flexible enough to cope with the special conditions in every locality, with changing circumstances and with the very public politics of public education. Only "participative planning" can be truly action-oriented to avoid becoming an academic exercise in preparing documents that are quickly filed and forgotten.

At present, the weakest point in the administration of public schools is the lack of long-range, comprehensive, and participative planning. The little planning that takes place is short-range, segmental or nonparticipative. Few school boards prepare a long-range budget estimate, a practice long since developed by every successful large business. In the budget projections that are prepared the emphasis is too often placed on the funds to be obtained rather than on the educational services to be supplied. When the use of funds is clearly specified, the specificity typically relates not to output but to teachers' salaries and construction. The most detailed long-range planning usually centers around construction programs where the exigencies of land acquisition and building operations leave no choice. The fact that teacher training and development is a still long-range and more complicated process than building has not yet resulted in equally impressive plans on the staff side of the input picture. In part, the weakness of local educational planning is itself compelling evidence to demonstrate the need for a new conception of the school administrator's role.

But local planning cannot proceed in a vacuum. It can develop intelligently only on the basis of a continuing awareness of what is being done in other localities in any area and in a continuing relationship with state educational agencies. This requires a rather general and extremely flexible form of state educational planning.

Even this is not enough. There are certain aspects of public education that can be properly examined only from a national viewpoint. In particular, any serious consideration of the public interest aspects of public education must take into account such matters as the following: (1) the expected growth and distribution of the population by age groups; (2) the expected and the most desirable patterns of change in the composition of the labor force, particularly in the growing proportion of employment in the provision of educational services and in the extension of the period of prework education; (3) future plans of institutions of higher learning; (4) national programs for the promotion of research and experimentation on aspects of the learning process and education; (5) national programs for the promotion of teacher training; (6) priorities in any field of education where shortage of trained personnel may endanger the national interest; and (7) national fiscal policies that may directly or indirectly affect the amount of money available for expenditures on public education.

This does not mean that the federal government should itself formulate a national educational plan or a set of long-range goals, nor endow a citizens' committee with authority to do so. Such efforts, as in the work of President Eisenhower's Commission on National Goals, are too far removed from the agencies with responsibility for planning and program administration.[4]

No educational goals or plans are truly meaningful unless prepared by the persons, organizations, and institutions that will themselves be involved in carrying them out. This is not only a principle of democratic government under the American form of federalism; it is an application of one of the major principles of current thinking on the administration of large-scale organizations.

The U.S. Office of Education, together with other agencies of the federal government, has a major role to play—that of facilitating and promoting the development of local and state educational plans. It can help bring people together. It can supply essential information and initiate or support necessary research undertakings. It can present ideas that will stimulate creative planning. It can therefore make an essential contribution to the democratic planning of public education through the cooperative action of all the many public and private organizations that are concerned. This process might be described as one of "participative national planning" or "mutual adjustment planning" or perhaps even "intergovernmental national planning." The promotion of this process is well within the existing authority of the U.S. Office of Education.[5]

At the national level, unfortunately, the sharp public controversies concerning federal aid to education and racial integration seem to have distracted government officials from other matters of a less dramatic nature. Since it is obviously impossible and undesirable for the federal government to prepare a plan for American public education, federal officials seem to have come to the conclusion that the educational crisis of the coming years can be met without coordinated planning. This position is at striking variance with the attitude of federal officials in relation to other countries. Federal agencies have often stimulated the governments of other countries to develop their own coordinated plans for postwar reconstruction or for economic development and multilateral trade. The federal government has already promoted intergovernmental planning by foreign governments, as with the Marshall Plan, the European Community, and the Alliance for Progress. Why could it not promote intergovernmental planning by public education agencies in the United States?

The answer is that it could and it would if serious proposals in this direction were to be made by the administrators of local and state school systems or by the organizations that represent them. This is the way that any new approach to participative national planning for education can best come into being. Only in this way will it be perfectly clear that the consideration of national needs and goals will be regarded as a stimulus to, rather than a substitute for, local and state planning. If participative national planning starts in this way it will be a hopeful sign that public school administrators are on the road to a more mature concept of their role in serving the public interest through the most effective and efficient use of public resources.

III. The Determinants of School Expenditures

In the United States there is neither central control over educational spending nor are educational standards set by the federal government. Although a great many states do mandate a minimum expenditure per pupil in public schools, no state sets a ceiling on maximum expenditure. As a result there is great variation in expenditure not only from one state to another but also among the school systems within each state. Some of this variation is attributable to cost differentials which require different outlays to provide similar educational services. For the most part, however, expenditure variations reflect genuine differences in the caliber of educational services provided.

The average national per capita current operating expenditures for local public schools in 1959-60 were about $63. Variations among states are considerable; at one extreme, Mississippi, Arkansas, Alabama, and Kentucky spent less than $45 per capita, while expenditures in Wyoming, Alaska, and California were over $83 per capita. Differences in current operating expenditures per pupil enrolled are even more pronounced. The average in 1959-60 was $345 per pupil; Mississippi spent $177 per pupil and Arkansas and Alabama spent less than $220 per pupil, whereas New York spent $484 per pupil, and per pupil spending in California, Oregon, New Jersey, and Wyoming exceeded $400.

Statewide figures, however, are only averages of expenditures of individual local school systems. It is, after all, the amount of these local expenditures which determines the educational services provided to pupils. Data on expenditures within states indicate that variations in local school expenditures differ greatly. In some states such as California, Louisiana, New York, and Ohio the range of variations within the state exceeds the range of average expenditure among states. But in other states, such as Alabama and Massachusetts, the range between the highest and lowest spending districts is quite narrow and falls well within the limits of the observed variation among states.

This chapter is a report on research that seeks to explain the reasons for differences in local school expenditures. The examination of sources of variation in expenditures encompasses both school systems located within a state and those located in different states.

This chapter is based on materials prepared by Jerry Miner.

A satisfactory answer to an inquiry into the determinants of educational expenditures has considerable value for policy purposes. If the effects of demographic, economic, social, psychological, and other factors over which policy makers have virtually no control can be taken into account, policy decisions can be based on clear-cut expectations. Furthermore, such knowledge may make it possible to estimate the net effect of "policy parameters" such as alternative formulas for state aid to education. At the same time, reliable estimates of the effects of non–policy-determined elements (e.g., population growth) reveal the consequences of anticipated developments and make possible more reliable advanced planning.

Knowledge of the trend of current educational developments and of the consequences of specific educational policies must be integrated with concepts of social economy and other social goals if proper policy choices are to be made. Ultimate standards for evaluating particular educational policies are value judgments. But given certain objectives, the social scientist often can evaluate the degree to which different policies conform to the standard.

A Predictive Theory of Public Spending

A positive theory that aims at explaining actual levels of public spending is quite different from the normative theory outlined in Chapter I that considers how much ought to be spent. The positive theory must identify each of the major determinants of public spending and estimate the direction and magnitude of its effect. In statistical terms, the variance of public expenditures must be accounted for by variations in certain independent variables. Also, if implications of cause and effect rather than associative relationships are to be drawn, a further requisite of a positive theory is that the distinction between dependent and independent variables be based on a logical, theoretical structure that explains the distinction.

Attempts to explain the determination of public spending, like most efforts to estimate empirical relationships between dependent and independent variables in the behavorial sciences, are complicated by two factors. First, empirical study of public expenditures cannot use experimental methods. Randomization, a procedure in which variations in the dependent variable are achieved by systematic variations in the independent variables, is the major device for use in empirical study for segregating dependent from independent variables and for avoiding intercorrelation among independent variables. Obviously, it cannot be used in studying public spending or in most other investigations in the social sciences. Instead, a statistical model must be developed which uses nonexperimental data so that inferences similar to those resulting from the use of experimental data can be drawn. A second difficulty in dealing empirically with public spending is that no clear-cut operationally formulated theory has been developed which indicates the crucial independent variables whose effects are to be estimated by empirical study. In public spending, unlike private consumption, economists and other social scientists are just beginning analytic study of the factors associated with behavior.

A representation or depiction of the essential aspects of the underlying behaviors and interrelationships that determine the value of a dependent variable is frequently called a model. Particular models for empirical study of government outlays differ in many ways. Most fundamental are differences in the scope of the dependent variable to be explained. The study of expenditures for a particular purpose (e.g., highways) by a specific government (e.g., a city) is an atomistic approach. A bit more aggregative is the investigation of total spending by a specific level of government (e.g., cities, counties, states). Finally, there is the consideration of total expenditures for a particular purpose by all levels of government, and, most aggregative, the total of all public spending regardless of purpose or level of government.

Aggregative analysis of social phenomena is quite useful, but the "building-blocks" of the behavioral sciences are empirical models based on actual decision-making units. Since total expenditures arise from the actions of individual governments, an explanatory theory of public spending must rest ultimately on an understanding of how various factors influence public decision-making units. At the same time, those searching for regularities in government spending must explicitly recognize the interactions among governments, both at the same level and at different levels. A fully articulated theory of public expenditure would explain the expenditures of one government, not only as a result of conditions prevailing within its boundaries, but also as a consequence of expenditures by other governments. Such a system could only be solved simultaneously for all units. Furthermore, for full generality, this framework for determining public spending would have to be integrated with models for household and business behavior.

Although such an ambitious model cannot be implemented, an examination of its implications is instructive for viewing actual studies of spending in the public sector. Given values for the independent variable, the ideal model would yield estimates of spending for all purposes by each government during a period. Further, year-to-year changes in spending would be estimated on the basis of changes in the independent variables. The study of public expenditures is not sufficiently developed so that a single model can accomplish both of these tasks. Instead, specific approaches aim at explaining either differences in spending among governments at the same time or differences in spending by a government at different points in time. The approach that examines the same unit of government over successive periods of time is time-series analysis, and the study of different units at the same time is cross-sectional analysis. Although the variables that explain changes over time are likely to be similar to those used in cross-sectional studies that explain variations among different units in the same year, time-series and cross-section relationships are different enough so that explanatory models and results will vary.

There is no single "correct" representation for predicting public spending in general or spending for education in particular. The nature of the model depends on the questions asked. In the research here the major interest is in the theoretical and empirical reasons for variations in expenditures for elementary and secondary education by the various governments legally responsible for such expenditures. This study uses an atomistic, cross-section approach based on the fundamental decision-making unit—the school district.[1]

Development of An Operational Model

The formulation of a statistical model of the spending behavior of governments requires the establishment of a set of exhaustive categories into which all possible sources of variation among governmental units can be placed. The categories themselves can most effectively be established by applying the logic of maximization to indicate the relevant factors to be considered in decisions involving public spending. Then, with objective measures for the major elements in each category, the model can be tested.

The analysis here is of educational expenditures during 1959-60 in over 1,100 local school systems in 23 states. Expenditures are studied in relation to data about the schools themselves, the communities and states in which they are located, the interrelationship between state and local control and financing of education, and other relevant factors. The direction and magnitude of relationships are estimated by multiple regression.

This study is a cross-section analysis. It includes both dependent school systems in which municipalities and counties operate schools as one of many functions and independent school districts whose sole function is public education. The individual school system is the focus of the study because it is the decision-making unit. Aggregate levels of state or national expenditures are derived largely as a result of actions taken by the independent school boards and the city and county governments that maintain school systems. Cross-section analysis is used because changing boundaries and lack of year-by-year data for individual school systems make it impossible to obtain a series of observations that is adequate for statistical analysis over time. Further, unbiased estimates of relationships from time series require the dubious assumption of unchanging preferences.

Wide variations in legal and financial arrangements for administering public education among states dictate a procedure in which sources of variation in expenditures within states are distinguished from sources of variation among states. The approach used, therefore, consists of separate analyses of each individual state within the sample to determine the factors responsible for variations in expenditures among different school systems operating under similar state influences, as well as over-all analysis of all school systems in the sample regardless of location in which legal, financial, and other differences among the states are treated as independent variables.

If the maximization of community welfare is taken as the goal of public decision making in economic matters, then the logic and empirical methods used to study private economic decisions are relevant to a considerable extent in explaining government expenditures. The use of economic models of private decision making as a point of departure for an empirical model of educational spending involves three essential aspects. First, the dependent variable or variables must be determined. Second, a set of categories that reflects demand for education has to be derived from factors similar to those used by economists in empirical studies of expenditures for consumer goods. Third, another set of determinants of educational spending is needed that is based on factors which take into account estimates of costs and hence influence supply. In this study the concept of a set of all-inclusive categories of independent variables based on models of private economic behavior underlies the methodology for the estimation of the determinants of public spending.

Selection of Dependent Variables

In choosing the measure of expenditures to use in empirical studies it has been customary to limit the analysis to current outlays. This procedure has been followed here, and may be justified on the ground that capital expenditures are irregular and may not respond smoothly to the needs for facilities. Current expenditures, on the other hand, do respond more quickly to the year-by-year changes in the demand for school services. Related to the decision to omit capital outlays is the further decision to eliminate, from the dependent variable, outlays for debt service—amortization and interest payments. The dependent variable, therefore, is current operating expenditure, which makes up about 75 per cent of total expenditures on elementary and secondary education. Public expenditure on higher education is also omitted.

For present purposes the dependent variable is stated as a ratio. Both per capita current expenditures and per pupil current expenditures are used, the former to permit comparison with other studies of public expenditure where this measure is employed, and the latter to permit comparison with other studies of educational finance. Since local school systems obtain resources for financing current expenditures from both locally collected taxes and from grants-in-aid from state and federal governments, it is also necessary to distinguish the dependent variable in these terms. Spending from all sources is therefore designated *total expenditure;* spending from local resources is designated *local expenditure.* In the analysis four separate dependent variables are thus used to reflect these distinctions: per capita total expenditure, per capita local expenditure, per pupil total expenditure, and per pupil local expenditure.

Selection of Independent Variables

The idea of a unit of commodity or service output in education probably cannot be objectively defined; still, the concept has conceptual meaning and use. The cost of a unit of educational output is the number of dollars it takes to provide educational services per pupil of equal quality in different communities. Larger expenditures attributable to the provision of different educational services represent quality differences and are not indications of higher cost. The quantity of educational services is probably best defined as the number of pupils enrolled in public schools. Although this definition has some drawbacks, in general the more pupils enrolled the greater the quantity of education provided.

Studies of private spending for a commodity or service usually distinguish between those factors that influence demand and those that influence supply. Demand factors determine the number of units taken of a product of specified quality. Supply factors influence the per unit cost of the service or commodity and the differences in cost of products of varying quality. Total expenditures, of course, are equal to the number of units taken times the cost per unit of the particular quality product taken. In cross-section studies of the spending behavior of households only factors that influence demand are included because the cost of products depends on conditions confronting producers and are assumed to be the same for all spending units; the characteristics of individual households have nothing to do with these conditions. However, cross-section study of local spending for public education does require the inclusion of supply as well as demand factors because the local government both produces and consumes public education, and conditions in the community influence the cost of education as well as the demand for it. The explanatory variables used in this study are intended to reflect the underlying determinants of the quantity, cost, and quality of the educational services provided in individual school systems which, in turn, determine levels of expenditures.

Demand Factors. The demand for public education, in this study, is viewed as being determined by essentially the same set of categories that has successfully been used in studies of household demand, although the specific variables representing them are somewhat different. It is believed that all possible sources of variation in demand for public education can be encompassed within this framework. Only variables thought to be important are actually included for consideration, however.

The most appropriate measure of ability to pay for education is probably the total income of the community in relation to its population. The distribution of income and wealth is also important, as is the amount and form of wealth and the place of residence of its owners.

Developing a measure or group of measures of local community ability to pay for public expenditures is more difficult than reflecting the income constraint of a consumer unit.[2] A danger that must be avoided is identifying tax receipts as the measure of ability. The tax-levying authority of a local government is important, but tax collections are generally determined jointly with anticipated levels of expenditures. Ability-to-pay is among the determinants of how much is collected and spent by public bodies while tax collections are a measure of the extent to which ability-to-pay is used and not of the ability itself.

In the state-by-state analysis the variables reflecting positive ability to pay for current expenditures for education are median family income, the percentage of families with incomes of $10,000 or more, and, when available the amount of equalized property value per capita. The amount of school debt service per capita is a measure of funds contractually committed to other purposes and is expected to be negatively related to spending. In the average analysis of school systems, two statewide variables, personal income per capita and equalized value of property per capita, are excluded.

Some studies of public spending have included state and federal grants-in-aid for education as elements in ability to spend.[3] While such funds certainly influence spending, they are not components of ability in the sense that income and property are. Including them in a model does not explain school expenditures because they are, in fact, a component of expenditures. Therefore, state and federal aid are reflected in this study by the effects of explanatory factors, such as property values and number of pupils, which are the underlying determinants of the amount of aid received. Furthermore, the effects of state and federal grants are taken into account by the distinction in the dependent variables between total and local expenditures.

Spending decisions by households depend upon the relative prices of consumer goods and services as well as on family incomes. Getting the most satisfaction from a given amount of income almost always requires that consumers buy more of an item when its price is lower. If education is relatively cheap in one community, more of it will be demanded and produced than in another community where preferences for education and ability to pay for it are the same but its cost greater. The demand relationship between quantity and price is an inverse one primarily reflecting the substitution of cheaper for costlier commodities as spenders attempt to get the most satisfaction from their limited resources. Educational spending can be expected to be consistent with this pattern as communities substitute, to some extent, other public and private goods for education when its price is high in relation to other commodities, and vice versa when the price of educational service is relatively low. The figures shown to represent the price of education in different school systems must, therefore, represent the price of a unit of educational service of uniform quality. While the over-all quality of education varies from one school system to another, it is probably true that the productivity of beginning teachers with undergraduate B.A. degrees is not greatly diverse. If so, an index of salaries paid to these crucial members of the school system is a good measure of educational cost because teachers' salaries comprise about 70 per cent of current expenditures, and salary scales tend to be proportional to beginning salaries. The index of beginning salaries, then, is an approximate measure of the relative price of qualitatively equal educational outputs which confront residents in different school systems.

With given incomes and prices, spending by a decision-making unit for a particular good or service depends upon its preferences. These preferences reflect what are commonly called needs, in the sense that larger families need more pairs of shoes or families with many children need more milk. In addition, the category of preferences encompasses the attitudes that influence choice among commodities that satisfy essentially similar needs; for example, with income and relative prices given, preferences determine whether a family buys a set of home appliances or hires a maid. Finally, preferences influence choices among quite disparate purchases, as when a family decides to forego a vacation to buy a new car. Because preferences cannot be measured objectively, economists treat them as a residual explanatory variable in the theory of consumer behavior.

Preferences for public education are similar in many respects to those for private goods and services. Given the legal requirement that the provision of public education is a responsibility of the state, and with the subsequent delegation of this power to a local government, there is no substitute for local public spending for education. Especially where the state mandates minimum expenditures or service levels in education, it is appropriate to talk of a need for educational outlays measured by the number of pupils to be educated. This minimum level is partly a reflection of statewide attitudes toward education. But the preferences of residents of specific local communities are likely to diverge from the state average. The role of preferences in determining expenditures beyond the mandated minimum depends on attitudes of the members of the local community, not only toward education but also toward other public services and private goods. Strong preferences for education, other things being equal, will raise school expenditures. But strong positive feelings about education must be weighed against such community needs as roads, sanitation, police and fire protection, as well as against needs for private consumption.

Direct need for educational services is measured in this study by the proportion of children under 18 in the population. An estimate for this variable is far more readily obtained than are figures for a more appropriate variable, the proportion of children 6 to 18. The proportion of children in the population is an estimate of total needs for education. The extent to which private and parochial schools reduce the need for public provision requires a second variable, the proportion of nonpublic school enrollment. Also, the per cent attending nonpublic schools may not only reduce per capita public school spending but per pupil spending as well if substantial use of private schools is associated with unfavorable attitudes toward public schools.

A variable included because it is believed to be positively associated with attitudes toward education is median years of schooling. The per cent of nonwhites is included primarily to represent the lack of influence in the decision-making process of Negroes and other nonwhites, but it may also be negatively related to spending because of low relative preferences for education by nonwhites. As a cost factor, however, a large proportion of nonwhites may be associated with higher expenditures, especially in school systems that maintain dual education systems or where delinquency is a concomitant of a relatively greater number of nonwhites.

A final variable that may indicate negative attitudes toward education is the per cent of families that have moved into the school district within the past five years. Recent arrivals cannot vote for some time, often do not own property, and may not plan to be in the community long enough to derive benefits from higher outlays on education. On the other hand, expenditures will be higher if an influx of population reflects preferences for patterns of life in a community that includes a strongly supported local school system.

Supply Factors. A public school system is a governmentally controlled production unit that combines factor inputs to provide educational outputs. The amount of spending in a particular school system depends on the cost of public education as well as on the demand for it. A complete reflection of differences in the costs of inputs among schools would require variables showing the cost of a homogeneous unit of all factors used in providing education. Clearly such a set of variables is out of the question, and some simple measures of differences in the general cost of school inputs are needed. Since teachers' salaries comprise about 70 per cent of all current school spending, an index of the cost of a teacher of uniform skill in different school systems would be a rather good measure of costs. The variable that gives the salary of a beginning teacher with an undergraduate degree but no experience provides the desired index, if it is assumed that all teachers with similar training and experience are equally skilled, and that increments in salaries attributable to increased skills from further education and experience are proportional to initial salaries.

Treating the salaries of beginning teachers as a measure of differential input costs that affect the cost of education should be distinguished from viewing those same salaries as measures of the prices of educational outputs. Unfortunately, it is not possible to separate these salary effects into price and cost influences, since the same variable signifies both elements. The effects of teachers' salaries must, therefore, be interpreted with caution.

Although the cost of teachers is a dominant portion of current expenditures, differences in the prices of other factors can also lead to variations in spending. The proximity of a school system to an industrial or commercial center is likely to necessitate higher costs for many things that schools need. On the demand side, contact with a metropolitan center where the cultural and economic advantages of education are emphasized may have a favorable influence on local attitudes toward support for public schools. It is also possible that greater needs for other public and private goods and services in metropolitan areas act to reduce outlays for local schools. To represent these effects a variable classifying whether or not the school system is located in a Standard Metropolitan Statistical Area is included in the analysis.

Another factor on the cost side is transportation outlays. The amount of spending for transportation depends largely upon the distance covered and the numbers of pupils transported. Density is employed to provide a rough estimate of these varying costs of getting pupils to class.

In addition to these cost elements there are other operating characteristics that may be associated with differences in school costs. One possibility, often investigated but seldom verified, is that economies are achieved once the school system reaches and exceeds a certain minimum size. These economies of scale would occur primarily because increased specialization in larger school units makes possible the use of more efficient division of labor and other cost-reducing methods and equipment. The proper measure of the scale of school operation is not obvious, but over-all average daily attendance is most frequently used to indicate size, and is the one selected to test for economies of scale in this study.

The goods and services purchased by the current expenditures of a school system are not the only productive factors yielding educational outputs. School capital, including sites, buildings, and equipment, contribute to the product. If school capital is productive, it would be possible for a school system possessing a large amount of capital to provide a specified level of educational output with lower current outlays than those of a school system with less capital which must get more of its output from factors paid for out of current expenditures. To test this hypothesis, the insurable value of school capital per pupil is introduced into the regression as an explanatory variable.

The treatment of variations in quality is always difficult in empirical studies of spending, but these difficulties are especially severe for public services where qualitative differences are so hard to specify. In this study, for the most part, variations in the quality of educational product among school systems are explained by the variables that reflect ability to pay and preferences for education. Thus, no variable such as average teachers' salaries is used to specify the quality of commonly provided educational services. Still, however, there is considerable variation in the character of services performed in different schools. The services provided to secondary school pupils are more expensive than those to elementary pupils, and while these differences may be thought of as quantitative, they seem better classified as qualitative. The proportion of secondary attendance to total attendance is used here to represent the higher spending required to provide secondary education.

Another important dimension of quality is the number and extent of auxiliary services provided to school pupils. Services such as guidance, psychological counseling, and medical care are additional qualitative factors that are provided to pupils in some schools and not others. Spending for auxiliary services to other than pupils is excluded from the dependent variable, but failure to take account of those that are provided to pupils would omit a factor responsible for substantial variations in a few schools. To account for these differences, a measure of the number of such personnel per pupil is included among the explanatory variables and is expected to be positively associated with spending.

Legal Constraints. State education laws limit the actions of public bodies that make ultimate decisions about local spending for education. These laws influence spending in two ways. They affect the cost and kind of school services provided by specifying standards of input quality and characteristics of the curriculum. Also, state aid regulations influence the effectuation of demand for education by limitations on the taxing and borrowing powers of local governments. State laws thus determine the capacity to tap local ability-to-pay.

Differences in legal provisions facing school boards or their counterparts in dependent school systems exist within as well as among states. In most states there are several classifications of school systems, and often different legal regulations apply to each type. It is difficult to incorporate into the analysis explanatory variables that reflect differences in legal requirements that affect spending directly, such as grants-in-aid or mandated tax levies, or indirectly by determining the nature of the local decision-making process.

With one exception, differences in legal and decision-making characteristics within states are not treated in this study. The analysis does

TABLE 1
DEFINITIONS OF VARIABLES

Variables	Units	Abbreviations
DEPENDENT VARIABLES:		
1. Total Current Expenditures Per Capita	$	(TE/C)
2. Local Expenditures Per Capita (total current expenditures minus state and federal aid)	$	(LE/C)
3. Total Current Expenditures Per Pupil	$	(TE/P)
4. Local Expenditures Per Pupil	$	(LE/P)
INDEPENDENT VARIABLES:		
Variables Reflecting Demand Elements		
5. Median Family Income	00's of $	(Y)
6. Per Cent of Families with Income of $10,000 or more	%	(Y+)
7. Amount of Equalized Property Value Per Capita	00's of $	(PROP)
8. Amount of Debt Service Per Capita	$	(DS)
9. Statewide Personal Income Per Capita	00's of $	(Y/C)
10. Statewide Equalized Value of Property Per Capita	00's of $	(PROP/C)
11. Salary of Beginning Teachers	00's of $	(SAL)
12. Per Cent of Children Under 18	%	(CHILD)
13. Per Cent of Children in Nonpublic Schools	%	(PRIV)
14. Median Years of Education	Years	(ED)
15. Per Cent Nonwhite	%	(NON-W)
16. Per Cent Moved into District in Last Five Years	%	(MIGR)
Variables Reflecting Supply Elements		
11. Salary of Beginning Teachers (see 11 above)	00's of $	(SAL)
17. Located in Standard Metropolitan Statistical Area	0 or 1	(SMSA)
18. Density	00's of persons per sq. mile	(DEN)
19. Number of Pupils in Average Daily Attendance	00's of pupils	(ADA)
20. Insurable Value of School Capital Per Pupil	00's of $ per ADA	(CAP)
21. Per Cent of Pupils in Secondary Grades	%	(SEC)
22. Number of Full Time Employees in Auxiliary Services Per Pupil	No. per 100 ADA	(AUX)
Variables Reflecting Legal Differences Among States		
23. Dependent or Independent School System	0 or 1	(DEP)
24. State Collected Revenues/Total Revenues for Education	%	(SR/TR)
25. Equalization Aid/Total State Aid for Education	%	(EA/TA)
26. General Purpose Aid/Total State Aid for Education	%	(GPA/TA)

not consider factors such as supplementary taxing powers granted to larger cities in some states, or the ability to borrow without referendum given to certain school districts in a state. The variables included reflect legal characteristics for an entire state and therefore do not vary for intrastate school systems. The sole exception is fiscal dependence or independence. In states where both patterns are found, individual school systems have been classified accordingly and an explanatory variable for this factor is included in the state-by-state regressions.

State grants to local schools are generally classified according to whether they are flat or equalizing grants and whether they are general or specific purpose grants. Equalizing grants often are based on measures of local fiscal capacity relative to the number of pupils enrolled in public schools. Flat grants, on the other hand, are not related to the financial position of the local school and typically depend on the numbers of pupils per classroom. Apart from the criteria for determining the amounts given to local schools, state grants can be mandated for specific purposes, such as teachers' salaries or language and science programs, or the grants can be general purpose ones that are used as the local school sees fit.

Although most states extend all four types of aid, usually one type predominates. To reflect differences in state aid patterns among states, three explanatory variables are introduced into the computations that include school systems in different states. One variable is the statewide ratio of locally collected revenues to total revenues for local schools. The other two are general purpose grants and equalizing grants as percentages of total state grants for local schools. These three variables are identical for all school systems in a given state and are intended to reflect over-all state aid arrangements.

The 4 dependent variables and 22 independent variables are summarized in Table 1.

The Sample

A statistical analysis leading to the identification of major factors associated with variations in spending by local school systems requires data from different systems within a given state and from systems in different states. To be useful for such an analysis the sample must include an adequate number of school systems within a particular state to permit the use of a multivariate statistical technique. At the same time, school systems in a sufficiently large number of states must be sampled so that variables associated with systematic differences in expenditures among states can be identified.

The sampling problems of this study were minimized by utilizing a sample of 8,000 school systems recently prepared by the U.S. Office of Education. Within the resources available for this research it was determined that approximately 1,700 districts, within the Office of Education sample, could be selected. For satisfactory application of statistical techniques it was necessary to secure data for about 50 to 60 districts for each state. Since Office of Education data were supplemented with information secured from a mail questionnaire, it was necessary in view of estimated rates of nonresponse, to select initially approximately 80 for each state.

Twenty-three states were chosen for analysis by stratifying on the basis of both the character of the state aid program and the size of public school enrollment. To maintain uniformity among school systems studied those with fewer than 300 pupils were dropped from the sample. Therefore, the results of this study can be generalized only for school systems with more than 300 pupils, although it may be noted that this omission amounts to only about 4 per cent of all pupils enrolled.

The data for this study come from three sources. As noted, these include information gathered by questionnaires sent to school superintendents, data for 1959-60 gathered by the U.S. Office of Education, and, in addition, information on community characteristics from the 1960 census. These latter required special treatment because the boundaries of census districts are not always coterminous with those of school districts. The principal statistical technique used is least-squares multiple regression.[4]

Results of the Analysis

The over-all analysis of all school systems in the sample encompasses 20 independent variables.[5] Of these, 15 vary among all school systems while 5 are statewide measures that vary only among systems in different states. Among the school systems in this nationwide sample, the variability of per pupil expenditures for public elementary and secondary education is greater than that for per capita expenditures and variability for local spending greater than for total spending. But, as Table 2 shows, regression equations of identical form generally explain a higher portion of variance for the dependent variables that have the largest coefficients of variability. It may be noted that none of the coefficients of multiple correlation is high. The explanatory power of the model is greatest for local expenditures per pupil, but

TABLE 2
CHARACTERISTICS OF THE OVER-ALL ANALYSIS

Dependent Variable	Mean of Dependent Variable	Coefficient of Variability	Multiple Regression Coefficient	Number of Observations
TE/C	$ 64.11	.502	.558	884
LE/C	$ 32.29	.828	.689	880
TE/P	$346.61	.721	.735	1127
LE/P	$189.58	1.057	.780	1041

even here only about 60 per cent of the variation in expenditures is accounted for.

Multivariate Analysis

The results of the multivariate analysis, reported in Table 3, show that the levels of state per capita income are the most important positive determinant of total per capita expenditures.[6] The extent to which the state participates in the collection of revenues for local schools is also significant. Median family income in local communities is, if anything, a negative factor, but the proportion of families with incomes of $10,000 or more and the proportion of children in the population are both associated with higher total expenditures. The proportion in private schools has a negative effect. Among factors that reflect local costs, the proportion of pupils in secondary grades and the salary of beginning teachers tend to raise total expenditures. Location in a Standard Metropolitan Statistical Area and dependent school district organization both have negative effects on total spending.

Local per capita expenditures are negatively related to the extent of state participation in school revenue collections and positively associated with measures of local income. Cost factors are less important for local than for total expenditures, as are location and organization, although both the proportion in secondary grades and the provision of more extensive health and counseling services have a positive influence on local spending per capita.

Auxiliary services are the most important determinant of both total and local per pupil expenditures. There is no evidence that total expenditures per pupil are affected in a systematic way by local demand or cost factors or by state personal income and participation in the finance of local schools, although a larger proportion of general rather than special purpose aid is associated with slightly higher per pupil outlays. Local expenditures, however, respond positively to local variables such as the proportion of families with incomes of $10,000 or

TABLE 3

SIMPLE AND PARTIAL CORRELATIONS AND NET AND STANDARDIZED REGRESSION COEFFICIENTS FOR ALL SCHOOL SYSTEMS IN THE SAMPLE*

DEP. VAR.	INDEPENDENT Y	Y+	Y/C†	PROP/C†	CHILD	PRIV	ED	NON-W	MIGR	SAL	DEN
	SIMPLE CORRELATION COEFFICIENTS										
TE/C	.21	.29	.42	.32	.00	.09	.14	–.22	.05	.39	–.02
LE/C	.43	.55	.57	.42	–.25	.41	.31	–.41	.06	.54	.18
TE/P	.25	.28	.37	.25	–.15	.25	.17	–.24	.01	.35	.19
LE/P	.37	.44	.43	.28	–.25	.42	.25	–.31	–.01	.43	.28
	HIGHEST ORDER PARTIAL CORRELATION COEFFICIENTS										
TE/C	–.05	.13‡	.28‡	.02	.17‡	–.09‡	–.02	.01	–.05	.15‡	–.06
LE/C	.01	.26‡	.06	.03	.03	.04	–.01	.05	–.03	.04	–.01
TE/P	.00	.01	.05	–.03	.00	.03	.00	.00	–.03	.04	.02
LE/P	.02	.15‡	–.12‡	–.01	–.06	.10‡	–.01	.06	–.03	.01	.07‡
	NET REGRESSION COEFFICIENTS										
TE/C	–.07	.53‡	3.48‡	.08	1.16‡	–.25‡	–.30	.03	–.16	1.23‡	–.06
LE/C	.01	.80‡	.52	.07	.17	.08	–.10	.08	–.07	.22	–.01
TE/P	–.03	.16	3.62	–.06	.19	.51	–.32	.02	–.57	2.01	.17
LE/P	.15	2.74‡	–7.11‡	–.18	–1.77	1.39‡	–.50	.66	–.48	.38	.35‡
	STANDARDIZED REGRESSION COEFFICIENTS										
TE/C	–.05	.17‡	.49‡	.03	.17‡	–.10‡	–.02	.01	–.04	.23‡	–.06
LE/C	.01	.33‡	.09	.03	.03	.04	–.01	.05	–.02	.05	–.01
TE/P	.00	.01	.07	–.03	.00	.02	.00	.00	–.02	.05	.02
LE/P	.02	.16‡	–.17‡	–.01	–.04	.09‡	–.01	.05	–.02	.01	.06‡

VARIABLES									
								GPA	
ADA	CAP	SEC	AUX	SMSA	DEP	SR/TR†	EA/TA†	TA†	CONSTANT
SIMPLE CORRELATION COEFFICIENTS									
–.05	.05	.16	.20	.10	–.11	–.26	.06	.08	
.00	–.01	.17	.29	.31	.04	–.60	–.01	–.07	
.01	.00	.16	.71	.20	–.01	–.28	.00	.07	
.03	.02	.19	.67	.28	.06	–.48	–.04	–.03	
HIGHEST ORDER PARTIAL CORRELATION COEFFICIENTS									
–.03	–.05	.10‡	.05	–.11‡	–.08‡	.11‡	.05	.02	
–.02	–.05	.07‡	.09‡	–.05	–.03	–.22‡	.00	–.04	
.01	–.07‡	.04	.66‡	.03	–.09‡	–.02	–.03	.13‡	
.00	–.06	.09‡	.63‡	.05	–.04	–.26‡	–.07‡	.07‡	
NET REGRESSION COEFFICIENTS									
.00	.00	.30‡	.71	–7.44‡	–6.06‡	.32	.05	.03	–125.02
.00	.00	.14‡	1.02‡	–2.79	–1.57	–.48	.00	–.03	11.57
.00	–.02‡	.35	81.79‡	14.14	–43.26‡	–.26	–.19	.98‡	14.25
.00	–.01	.65‡	55.15‡	1.44	–1.40	–3.54‡	–.32‡	.39‡	364.67
STANDARDIZED REGRESSION COEFFICIENTS									
–.03	–.04	.09‡	.04	–.12‡	–.09‡	.19‡	.05	.05	
–.02	–.03	.05‡	.08‡	–.05	–.03	–.34‡	.00	–.03	
.01	–.05‡	.03	.66‡	.03	–.08‡	–.02	–.02	.10‡	
.00	–.04	.06‡	.55‡	.04	–.03	–.34‡	–.05‡	.05‡	

* See Table 1 for an explanation of symbols and a description of variables.

† Variable differs from state to state, but is constant for all school systems within a state.

‡ Significant at .95 level of probability under assumptions of simple random sampling, homogeneous variances, and other conditions for the application of conventional confidence intervals.

more, higher relative secondary school enrollment, and density, and negatively to state personal income and to a greater proportion of revenues for local schools collected by the state.

An imperfect but discernible pattern emerges from the regressions and partial correlation coefficients. Differences between coefficients for total and local expenditures appear to stem primarily from the nature of state provisions for grants-in-aid to local schools. As a consequence of efforts to provide some degree of equalization, such aid generally is granted inversely to local ability-to-pay and directly with conditions that indicate higher costs. These arrangements result in a pattern in which the contribution to educational expenditures by the local community varies moderately in accordance with its ability to pay and the costs of the quantity and quality of the services provided. Total expenditures, however, are affected strongly by grants-in-aid based on various formulas for the equalization of educational services among school systems within a state, thus reducing the influence of local factors. The statistical analysis shows that in contrast to local expenditures, total expenditures vary directly in proportion to the economic capacity of the state, the relative number of children to be educated in local schools, the proportion of pupils in secondary schools, and the salary level of beginning teachers, and are inversely related to density, dependent school organization, and location in a Standard Metropolitan Statistical Area.

Higher local incomes do not have a strong positive effect on total expenditures per capita, but these same incomes are associated with higher levels of local per capita expenditures. Since state (and federal) aid intervene between total and local expenditures, it is logical to conclude that local contributions to expenditures are determined on the basis of local ability, but that state aid acts to reduce the impact of variations in income on total expenditures. Here is an illustration of equalization at work on a nationwide basis. A major mechanism of this equalization process is indicated by the strong effect of statewide personal income on total expenditures, in contrast to the far smaller effect of this variable on local expenditures.

In contrast to the effects of local incomes, the proportion of children in the population and the proportion of pupils enrolled in secondary schools, two factors that raise costs, have a higher association with total per capita expenditures than with local expenditures. Again equalization is in operation because local communities do not bear the major portion of the burden of unusual educational needs. At the same time, educational services are not slighted since total per capita outlays are maintained, probably because of state and federal aid.

Examples from the analysis of per pupil expenditure serve further to demonstrate the differences in coefficients for total and local expenditures. The regression coefficients for total and local per pupil expenditures indicate that larger expenditures stemming from higher salaries for beginning teachers are borne by the state and not by the local community. In contrast, local school systems that have higher proportions of pupils in secondary grades and in private schools and high local incomes contribute more heavily to local than they do to total expenditures. Here the effect of state aid is to equalize total outlays despite local relationships. While such equalization is desirable for income and wealth, its effect is less appropriate for per cent in secondary grades. If more money is raised locally to finance the incremental costs of secondary education, state aid should not have the offsetting effect of equalizing total expenditures regardless of the proportion of pupils in secondary grades. Whether auxiliary health and counseling services should be subject to equalization is a less clear-cut matter. The analysis shows that, for the most part, local outlays are the major source of expenditures for such services, although state and federal aid also serve to increase expenditures associated with this factor.

Demand, Supply, and Administrative Factors

With regard to ability to pay, a major finding is that state personal income per capita has a positive effect on total per capita expenditures, in contrast to its strong negative effect on local per pupil expenditures. While median family income is not important in any of the four equations, the proportion of families with incomes of $10,000 or more is positively associated with expenditures in all equations and an additional per cent in this category raises per pupil expenditures by $2.74. These results are evidence that communities dominated by middle income families do not spend more than required to provide state-mandated or typical levels of education, and that only when there is a high concentration of families at the upper end of the income scale do communities spend more from their own resources for local schools.

As for other factors on the demand side, there is no indication that when these are taken into account more is spent for education in communities in which more highly educated adults reside. Greater nonpublic school enrollments are accompanied by lower per capita expenditures on public schools, but no less is spent per pupil, and local per pupil expenditures tend to be higher. The reduced number of pupils that a local school system must provide for apparently creates a higher local capacity to finance expenditures. As hypothesized, a greater proportion of children in the population is associated with higher per capita expenditures that reflect the greater quantity of services provided. However, despite the burden of relatively more pupils, total per pupil outlays in areas with relatively large school populations are not reduced. The effect of a high proportion of families who have been in the community for less than five years is not great, but it is negative in all cases. Finally, while simple correlations between the proportion of non-whites in the population and the four measures of expenditures are negative, all of the multiple correlations are positive. Perhaps higher costs of dual school systems and their location in states with low per capita incomes explain these differences.

The dominance of auxiliary services in explaining per pupil expenditures has already been mentioned. The high partial correlations of this variable with per pupil expenditures are not solely a reflection of the extra spending which the provision of these auxiliary services requires. Rather, it is likely that school systems which provide extensive health and counseling services also provide an unusual quantity or quality of other auxiliary services and a high quality of regular school services as well. Further, the provision of such services is not systematically and highly associated with levels of local income, education, or other characteristics of the community included as independent variables in the study. The analysis of simple correlations among variables, however, reveals that auxiliary services have about the same relationship to expenditures as do each of the three measures of income, and also are correlated positively with the salaries of beginning teachers. Thus, the analysis of per pupil expenditures has not succeeded, as was hoped, in explaining quality of educational services by indirect measures of local ability to pay and preferences for education. Instead, a measure of auxiliary services appears to have acted as a proxy for cost and demand components of both the quality of education and the quantity of other auxiliary services.

The systematically positive effect of a greater proportion of pupils in secondary grades is further support of an effect well demonstrated in previous studies. A less statistically significant and not previously demonstrated result is the verification of the hypothesized negative effect of higher amounts of school capital per pupil. The small importance of this variable in accounting for variations in school spending, however, makes this finding more a source of theoretical satisfaction than an explanation of educational spending. Density, which was expected to be inversely related to the need for transportation services, has the proper sign only in the regression for per pupil expenditures, and its effect is small. Average daily attendance, introduced to test for the presence of the ever-elusive economies of scale in the operation of public facilities, fails to reveal any such tendencies.

Salaries of beginning teachers, it will be recalled, play a dual role in the analysis. On the demand side, salaries, as an indicator of the price of educational services, are expected to have a negative effect on school spending. As a measure of cost, however, higher salaries, like a higher proportion of pupils in secondary grades, require increased outlays. Coefficients for salary are positive in all four equations. The regression coefficients for teachers' salaries indicate that the higher levels of total expenditures, found in school systems where teachers' salaries are greater, are not accompanied by proportionately larger local outlays; they come instead largely out of state payments to local schools.

Among all relationships between institutional arrangements and spending for local public schools, the effect of fiscal dependence or independence is debated more than any other. The findings of this study indicate that fiscally dependent school systems tend to spend less in all four expenditure categories, and that total spending is influenced more by this organizational arrangement than is local spending. However, since fiscally dependent school districts are predominately located in larger cities, the relationship measured here may simply reflect the general complex of expenditure influences that tend to hold down large city school expenditures. The higher negative coefficients for total than for local expenditures thus reflect the differential impacts of state and federal aid on larger cities.

The intercorrelation between state property per capita and statewide income serves to reduce the impact of property in the explanation of expenditures. The low coefficients for property indicate that, despite the reliance on property taxation for 53 per cent of total revenues for local school spending in 1960, states with relatively low property values utilize other taxes to tap their economic resources and those with relatively high values do not spend more as a consequence. Where the proportion (not the amounts) of revenues for local schools collected from state sources is large, total expenditures per capita are higher, but total expenditures per pupil remain the same and local expenditures are less. An explanation of these results is that in states where the proportion of children is high, and where the state participates in the collection of revenues for public schools to a greater extent, spending per capita is higher as a result of the expenditure of the state-collected revenues. Per pupil outlays are unaffected, however, because the increased spending is spread over more pupils.

Alternative formulas for state aid have produced almost as much controversy as the issue of fiscal dependence or independence. A major problem of equalization formulas is that they are thought to reduce local initiative. This study does find that local per pupil expenditures are lower in school systems located in states that rely more heavily on equalization grants, although local per capita expenditures are unaffected. The estimated reduction of 32 cents in local per pupil spending for each additional per cent of equalization grants as a proportion of total state grants, however, may be an acceptable price for the more equitable burden achieved through equalization. With regard to specific versus general purpose grants, the analysis indicates that higher per pupil outlays take place in those states that make more extensive use of general purpose grants.[7]

Conclusions and Implications

This empirical study of factors associated with public expenditures can be evaluated from several viewpoints. A major concern of the analysis was to test an economic model of government behavior which assumed that the expenditure decisions of local school officials were based on a pattern of rational economic motives. A second interest was the investigation on a comparable basis of simple and multivariate quantitative relationships between local school expenditures and a series of characteristics of communities for a nationwide sample of school systems. A third aspect of the study distinguished the effects of the same determinants on per capita and on per pupil spending. A final element involved the estimation of the influence of state and federal grants-in-aid for education on local spending in school systems in a set of states representative of different grant arrangements. These four aspects of the empirical study are, of course, interrelated; it is the character of the model which determined the specific state and local characteristics used as independent variables. Nevertheless, it is appropriate to evaluate each aspect separately.

The Economic Model of Governmental Behavior

Although a number of the hypotheses that underlie the over-all model of governmental behavior are supported by the statistical analysis, the model as a whole does not have great explanatory power. In the over-all analysis the proportion of variance explained for per capita expenditures is rather low, and the higher multiple regression coefficients for per pupil expenditures are attributable to the unanticipated strong effect of auxiliary services. In the state-by-state analysis, the same basic sets of independent variables revealed widely divergent multiple correlation coefficients.

Several reasons may be advanced for the failure of the estimating equation to achieve a fairly high and regular explanation of variation in spending among local school systems. One possibility is that the fundamental assumption is false and the agencies that determine local school expenditures are not motivated by rational economic objectives. Therefore, local agencies do not respond in similar fashion to similar preference patterns. An alternative possibility is that the basic assumption is correct but that the model, as constructed, is not an effective means of revealing the underlying uniformities. Unfortunately, it is difficult to improve the model to provide a more satisfactory treatment of state arrangements which differ not only among states but among school systems within the same state.

Simple and Multivariate Relationships

The results of the analysis provide a detailed set of simple and partial correlation coefficients between four categories of expenditures for local schools and a variety of factors. There is limited confirmation of long-held notions such as that expenditures are lower in dependent school systems, even when ability to pay and cost elements are taken into account. However, doubt is cast on other equally traditional views. For example, school systems that contain a larger proportion of nonwhites in the population do not spend less when other factors are included. Comparisons of correlation coefficients among states reveal similarities in the effects of variables such as the proportion of pupils in secondary grades and great differences in the effects of others, for example, median family income.

Per Capita and Per Pupil Expenditures

State personal income per capita and the proportion of pupils in the population have strong positive effects on total per capita expenditures and considerably less influence on per pupil outlays. Auxiliary services are of great importance in per pupil expenditures but have little effect on per capita spending. Most other variables have similar effects on both per capita and per pupil expenditures.

Total and Local Expenditures

The dominant theme of the results is the effect of state and federal aid as portrayed by the differences in coefficients for total and local expenditures. These differences show that among local school systems total expenditures are not responsive to variations in local ability to pay but do vary with cost conditions. Local expenditures, however, reflect community income levels but not differences in costs. The detailed pattern of the way in which state aid differentially affects the various factors associated with school spending and the description of the manner in which equalization occurs are among the major findings of this study.

Suggestions for Further Research

A fruitful approach to the solution of some of the unexplained results here undoubtedly lies in an analytic examination of state aid arrangements. A classification based on a study of the responses of local school officials to various aspects of state aid is needed, rather than a classification by statute or by measures of the relative importance of different types of grants. In such a classification it probably will be necessary to go beyond differences among states and to distinguish the various state aid arrangements that apply to different types of school systems within the same state. Small school districts should be included in such an analysis. One possible approach would be first to classify in detail types of state aid programs and then to place a sample of school systems into appropriate categories. Analysis would proceed to determine whether relationships between spending and state and local community characteristics are more regular within categories than among categories. If so, the classifications have explanatory power. An alternative methodology is to search for sets of school systems with similar relationships between expenditures and state and local characteristics, and then to examine state aid arrangements for each of the sets to determine whether there are categories of aid relationships to match the observed similarities.

Another potentially fruitful area for study is to distinguish determinants of demand for education related to consumption benefits from those related to investment or production benefits. Variations in local outlays may stem from differences in the returns to education even when consumption benefits are equally valued. Further studies should attempt to include as an independent variable estimates of the relative economic gains accruing to individuals from higher levels of education in different regions.

Although problems of the definition of the dependent variable, the specification of an over-all model, and the measurement of characteristics in noncoterminous jurisdictions still remain partially unresolved, the crucial requisite for an empirical theory of public expenditures is a method for the treatment of intergovernmental relationships, especially those that involve grants-in-aid to relatively autonomous government units. There is a paradox that emerges from this investigation of expenditures for local public schools. Those variables whose effects are known, such as population growth, percentage of pupils in high school, and state per capita personal income are not subject to manipulation through policy decisions. The major policy variable, alternative state aid arrangements, however, is the factor about whose effects least is known.

There remain some unresolved problems in the specification of demand variables for public expenditures. The preferences of citizens for public education and for other public-sector outlays may be revealed indirectly by measures of income and educational attainment. The research here has attempted to test the extent to which such variables are accurate measures of demand. But decisions about public expenditures are made by administrative and elected officials, not by citizens. Public demands may be imperfectly understood and imperfectly translated by such officials. The political process of resource allocation may or may not reflect accurately, in specific instances, the aggregate of household demands for public services and the additional demands for social benefits that may accrue from specific outlays. At the same time, it is possible that public officials may act on the basis of a different appraisal of the effects of education upon productivity and upon the future earnings of pupils than that held by parents and other members of the community. Under these circumstances, educational outlays would not be closely linked to demand by local households.

Research on the determinants of public expenditures, directed to an examination of the linkage between preferences for public goods and political decision processes, would be helpful in furthering an understanding of the politics and economics of resource allocation.

IV. Cost and Quality

The great educational effort of the past century and a half has been to expand the amount of schooling by increasing the numbers of those attending school and the length of time in attendance. In the next several decades some further expansion in the amount of formal schooling will undoubtedly take place, but a much greater effort is likely to be directed to increasing the quality of schooling provided.

In most sectors of the American economy continued research has been directed toward the increase of efficiency, that is, an increase in the ratio of output to input. The success of these efforts is outstandingly evident in such areas as agriculture and manufacturing where productivity—output per man-hour—has and will continue to increase substantially. In education, however, little systematic research has been directed to attempts to secure a larger return from resource inputs. Part of the reason for this may lie in the fact that educational output itself is so difficult to define.

Viewed in narrowly economic terms, education is both a consumer good and an investment good.[1] As a consumer good, education is desired as an end-product in itself, as a contribution to greater enjoyment of and participation in the cultural existence of the community, and as a contribution to a greater sensitivity to and understanding of society itself. As an investment good, education increases the skills and productivity of individuals and hence adds to total output; education is an investment in economic growth.

Inputs and Outputs

There are other complications in the measurement of output in education. In one sense the student and his knowledge is the output of a school system. But the output of the schools measured in terms of the acquisition of language skills, or mathematical skills, or science skills, does not describe all that the schools contribute to the student and his knowledge. The education of young people is a process of maturation, and the schools are expected to, and do, contribute to this. Education in a mass society also consists of learning to adjust to, work with, and lead organized groups—the much-maligned "life adjustment" goals of education.

Beyond these generalized outputs, which may also be described

This chapter is based on materials prepared by Harold F. Clark.

as the goals of an educational system, numbers of persons and specific interest groups are anxious that the schools organize to produce certain other outputs, such as the inculcation of patriotism, or an exposure to religious education. Still other interest groups are anxious that educational outputs embrace attitudes toward the use of alcohol and tobacco, or skills with respect to driving automobiles, or health education.

The difficulties in defining educational output erect an almost insuperable barrier to a careful analysis of the relationship of inputs to outputs. For present purposes no effort will be made to overcome these barriers by attempts to define proper or optimum output for elementary and secondary schools. Rather, the outputs or goals of the educational system will be accepted as they exist, and emphasis will be placed on doing whatever the schools do in the shortest possible time and at a high level of efficiency.

The concept of input in education likewise poses some difficulties. For some purposes the term is relatively unambiguous; the inputs of an educational system are the resources that it employs to produce outputs. Most of these are measurable in monetary terms—the salaries paid to teachers, administrators, and janitors, and the funds that must be paid for buildings and equipment. But more precise calculations of total input would require the measurement of the cost of student time devoted to education, as was pointed out in Chapter I. In the elementary grades student time would have little value, but in secondary education a complete accounting might require an estimate of opportunity costs—the incomes that might have been earned if high school students were employed elsewhere.

The concept of quality in education is also an elusive one. In industry it is sometimes possible to measure quality and hence physical changes in productivity with considerable precision. The number of man-hours necessary to produce a given quantity of steel ingots to specified standards, or to produce a given number of barrels of cement of specified grade, can be measured and output per man-hour computed. This is possible because the product is standardized. But for education the output cannot be defined and hence there can be no simple measurement of productivity; quality standards are not available. Moreover, in education it is not possible to distinguish the quality of education from the quantity of education. If methods of teaching reading are improved such that third grade students now read at the fourth grade level, is this an improvement in the quantity or in the quality of education? If students of history learn more history in a given year, is this a quantity or a quality improvement?

No attempt will be made here to resolve these kinds of difficulties, and indeed it is by no means certain that they can be resolved. In accordance with popular usage a quality improvement and a quantity improvement in education will be used as interchangeable terms. However, emphasis will be placed here on educational output as the acquisition of knowledge.

Whatever else is expected of an educational system, there is general agreement that competence in language and mathematics and other subject matter fields is desired. The quality of education may be said to be improved if the content and skills or abilities of students are acquired rapidly, and if these skills are pushed to a high level for as many as possible. Thus a high quality education would permit as many people as possible to reach as high a level as possible in knowledge and skill in as many areas as possible. An efficient school system would attempt to accomplish these ends with the minimum use of resources. Whatever additional goals are pursued by a school system, aside from the acquisition of knowledge, should likewise be undertaken with the smallest possible use of resource inputs. An improvement in quality thus means a larger output from any given amount of resource input, whatever that output may be.

Difficulties in defining the nature of educational input are considerably multiplied when the whole educational establishment is examined. The current cost of public elementary and secondary education is approximately $16 billion. Private elementary and secondary education plus public and private higher education add approximately another $10 billion. Education and training in industry may be estimated to cost about $4 billion annually. The cost of education conducted by the military establishment would appear to be at least $3 billion. Self-education by individuals and education and training carried on by voluntary groups may amount to $3 billion annually. All of this would total about $36 billion.[2] If one were to extend the definition of education beyond that provided by formal organizations and self-education, it would be necessary to embrace some of the activities of the mass media. Radio, television, newspapers and magazines carry a heavy load of information and add to the sum total of certain kinds of knowledge of all who are exposed to them.

A further extension of the scope and definition of education is possible by including research activities directed toward the development of new knowledge. Some part of these costs, perhaps $300 to $400 million, are counted in the research activities of colleges and universities, and thus would be included in the foregoing aggregates. Government agencies and private firms may devote an additional amount, probably about $15 billion annually, to research of various kinds. At some level of abstraction it is not possible to separate the discovery and application of new knowledge from the transmission of old knowledge. A complete accounting of resource inputs for education in all of its dimensions would require the inclusion of the costs of new knowledge as well.

Increasing Resource Inputs

One of the possibilities for increasing the total quantity of education and hence its quality is to increase the number of student hours devoted to it. For the nation as a whole in recent years the average school day has amounted to about six hours, with 180 days of school attendance each year. If to this is added, as a rough estimate, one hour per student day of homework, the resulting input in terms of student hours is 1,260 per year. This is probably far below the amount of student hour input that could be secured. An increase in the number of hours per year devoted to education, by way of additional time spent on homework or a longer school day of a longer school year, might increase total hours to as much as 2,000 per year. At some undetermined point between 1,260 hours and 2,000 hours diminishing returns might well set in, but surely the possibilities for an increase in the quality of education simply by way of increasing student hours of input is by no means exhausted.

Another possibility is to encourage students to use their time more efficiently. The provision of better tools and equipment for study would contribute to this end, as would the development of additional techniques for self-education. It may be possible to devise incentives that will encourage students to work more efficiently at their own education.

For elementary and secondary public education, the annual cost of resource inputs for buildings is currently running in the neighborhood of $4 billion a year. The items classified as equipment may amount to about 10 per cent of this total; that is, in the neighborhood of $400 million. However, this will include expenditure on such items as seats for students, desks for teachers, and cabinets for books. The other part of equipment expenditures for strictly instructional and educational purposes, such as outlays for books, maps, tape recorders, television, and motion pictures is a small part of the total equipment expenditure.

Schools in the United States have made very great progress in recent years in the design and installation of school buildings, and in school equipment of the noninstructional variety. There have also been substantial improvements in instructional equipment, but outlays for these purposes have not increased importantly. Fragmentary evidence available on the relationship of expenditures for instructional equipment to total educational expenditures over the last several decades would indicate that the ratio of instructional equipment to the total has remained remarkably constant. In 1890 the average school spent well over 90 per cent of its outlays for buildings and educational equipment on the building itself. The ratios are apparently about the same for schools in the 1960's.

The contrast between these fixed proportions and the striking changes that have occurred in manufacturing industry is illuminating. In 1890 evidence would suggest that about 75 per cent of the total building and equipment outlays by manufacturing firms were devoted to the building, with 25 per cent for machinery and equipment. In the 1960's this ratio is approximately reversed—about 25 per cent of manufacturing outlays for plant and equipment are for the plant itself; equipment expenditures make up the remainder. The very large increases in output per man-hour that have occurred in manufacturing industry since the turn of the century are customarily attributed in large part to the improvements in the tools and equipment available to the manufacturing worker, and hence to increased investment in these tools. The tools available to the student in terms of instructional equipment have not increased in anything like these proportions. There have, no doubt, been many other factors contributing to the rapid increases in output per man-hour in industry, but certainly a major factor has been the enormous increase in the amount and quality of the tools and equipment available to the average worker.

The basic technology of education has not changed in the same fashion. In the 1890's the teacher had a room with 30 students and a few hundred dollars worth of printed books, a blackboard, and some maps. Today there may be rather fewer students and the teacher may have a better blackboard and more and better maps; the science equipment will be improved, and there may be a motion picture machine and a tape recorder. But the instructional equipment has increased very little and the amount of resources devoted to improving instructional procedures has been very modest indeed. The basic input structure of elementary and secondary education has been relatively unchanged in the last century.

When printed books first became available in Western Europe some 500 years ago, the schools and colleges at that time resisted their use. There is, then, a long history of continued opposition to changes in instructional procedures and instructional equipment. Although there is evidence that these resistances are beginning to break down somewhat in recent years, modifications and experimentation have proceeded very slowly. The contrast with other sectors of the economy with respect to recognition of the need for innovation is a sharp one.

The task of introducing innovations into teaching procedures and instructional equipment is made difficult by the widely held view that the concept of efficiency does not apply to education. Somehow there seems to be misapprehension that an effort to increase efficiency necessarily and ordinarily changes the goals of education. This need not be the case. The task is to secure a larger educational output from a given amount of resource input, or a greatly increased resource output from a modest increase in resource input.

Technological Improvements

The introduction of the printed book is undoubtedly the single most important technological improvement in education since the beginning of civilization. Although there were organized classes long before there were printed books, the relationship of teacher to student has probably not been very different since the beginning of formal education. In fact, the introduction of the printed book meant that it was no longer necessary for the teacher to tell the students everything they needed to learn. Students were now able to read and learn for themselves. This, of course, has contributed to very great improvement in the efficiency of the educational process. This should be the goal of other technological improvements in education—to facilitate the self-instruction of students.

Education is in the midst of another technological revolution which may be comparable in the magnitude of its impact to that of the printed book. Instructional machines of varying kinds and varieties can now transmit information and assist in the process of student self-education. No one any longer seriously believes that the printed book will ultimately replace the teacher, and no one should believe that instructional machines will be able to take the place of the teacher.

The technological revolution in educational methods that is now under way includes the use of television, motion pictures, radio, film strips, tape recorders, devices for programmed learning, and many other varieties of teaching machines. At the lowest level of use these machines should further relieve the teacher of the need to convey verbally much of the information that the student needs. At minimum, a substantial part of the time and energy of the teacher now devoted to the transmission of information can be done far more economically by machine technology. Teaching machines open up vast new possibilities for flexibility in instructional procedures. Some machines may be adapted for large class instruction; others may be used on a completely individual basis. Television may reach a thousand or ten thousand students in a dozen different schools at the same time. Teaching machines may be used by a single student. If properly organized and utilized, teaching machines should be able to relieve the teacher of much routine work and thus free up time that can be devoted to doing things that the machines cannot do.

Over the next several decades, the use of machine techniques in education should make it possible to secure a very sharp rise in quality. Initially this may not lead to lower costs for education; outlays for educational machinery may at the outset increase the costs of instruction, but in the long run there surely can be little doubt as to their effects. Properly used, teaching machines should greatly increase efficiency in resource inputs.

The issue may be clarified by stressing that printed books are also teaching machines. The book is a device for learning. Teaching machines similarly are devices for learning.

Specialized Skills

Every economic system, and every component part of an economic system, becomes more efficient as it becomes more specialized. In the process of economic growth those who possess general skills come to acquire special skills; general medical practitioners give way to medical specialists; bookkeepers give way to accountants, and accountants further subdivide into cost accountants, auditors, those skilled in tax accounting, and the like. Specialization brings the increases in productivity that characterize a developing economy.

In elementary and secondary education, in contrast with other professions, there has been relatively little specialization of skills, particularly in the teaching process itself. The failure of elementary and secondary education to develop such specialized teaching inputs gives rise to the suspicion that there has been very little improvement in the productivity of education over time.

If the productivity and hence the quality of education is to improve markedly in the next several decades, it would appear necessary that attention be directed to increased specialization. Since input specialization is the historic accompaniment of productivity increases in all other economic organization, it would seem likely that specialization will bring substantial gains in the quality of educational output.

In the typical elementary school the average teacher spends a large fraction of her time in household chores or in repetitive drills of one kind or another. Studies differ on the amount of time so spent, but there are some indications that from 40 to 60 per cent of the elementary schoolteacher's time is taken up with what are essentially nonteaching responsibilities.

Some communities have experimented with paid aides to do some of the nonteaching chores; other communities have experimented with volunteer assistants for routine duties. Some communities have begun to use parents as aides to teachers, enlisting their assistance on either a paid or nonpaid basis for such chores as reading and grading English compositions. Interestingly enough, before 1900 it was generally accepted as desirable for the student to learn as much as he could at home. Between 1920 and 1950 there were efforts to reduce the importance of parents in educating the child. Recently there has been a return to the approach that the more persons who assist in the process of education the better.

There are some schools now where parents provide a great deal of assistance to the teachers, and this may prove to be an important development in increasing the quality of education. In a large number of American communities parents constitute an enormous reserve of resources that has hardly been tapped for assistance in the educational process.

But the task of specializing resource inputs in education goes far beyond that of reducing the volume of repetitive and nonteaching chores assigned to teachers. The recent experiments with team teaching point the way to an approach to the use of skills in education that offers the possibility for very great improvements in the quality of education.

Team teaching is still in the experimental stage of development and some of its characteristics stir considerable controversy. Some teachers enjoy participating in a team approach; others do not. Some teachers enjoy working closely with their colleagues in the development and presentation of curriculum materials; others prefer the privacy of their own classrooms.

Viewed in terms of the specialization of teaching skills, however, team teaching offers great promise. Teachers who are skilled with large groups have an opportunity to work with large groups; teachers who prefer individualized instruction may do so. One member of the team may specialize in visual aids, another in the preparation of lecture materials. Beginning teachers can work more closely with experienced teachers. Teachers with organizational skills and leadership capacity have an opportunity to develop as team leaders. Moreover, teach teaching offers an opportunity for breaking out of the undifferentiated salary structures that are now based almost solely on experience and formal academic training.

Team teaching will permit salary differentiation in accordance with responsibility and will thus help to raise salary ceilings for teachers. In this regard it should prove to be considerably superior to merit rating, which has not been widely adopted because of the difficulties, within existing organizational structures, of arriving at an objective appraisal of the effectiveness of teaching.[3] Team teaching will permit the establishment of differentials in accordance with the specialization of teaching functions, and may thus make an indirect contribution to reducing teacher turnover and to the retention of men in elementary and secondary teaching.[4]

However, as with all technological change, team teaching has its innovation cost. Specialization in an economic system is accompanied by a higher degree of interdependence, and interdependence means that more time and energy must be devoted to communication processes, to planning, and to organization. Team teaching cannot be introduced without substantial administrative attention to careful scheduling of the use of teacher resources. Team teaching, if extensively utilized, would also require changes in class size, flexible physical facilities, and corresponding adaptations in instructional equipment.

The increased attention to administration that would be required by team teaching would tend to re-orient the attention of school administrators to teaching problems and organization for teaching and learning. This might help to overcome the current preoccupation of administrators with efficiency in the narrowest sense of that term where attention is directed solely to the minimization of local tax costs.[5] Experience to date would indicate that team teaching is not to be undertaken lightly, but that its consequences may be far-reaching in terms of the opportunities for specializing the teaching function, and hence for increasing the quality of education.

Self-Education

In addition to the specialization of teaching skills, the quality of education can be improved by further attention to self-education. Teaching machines and additional homework can contribute to this end. The long-run goal here is to train students to the point where they are capable of continuing their own education throughout their lifetime.

It has frequently been noted in recent years that as a nation we are gradually coming to accept education as a lifetime undertaking not limited to a period of formal schooling. Since World War II business firms have greatly expanded their programs for training and retraining employees at all levels. Earlier programs of on-the-job training have been supplanted by programs for almost continuous reeducation. Management training centers and management institutes have been organized in recent years to meet the demands for the continuing education of executives. Rapid technological changes in both production and office processes, usually described under the general heading of automation, have brought technological unemployment to thousands. Here retraining and rehabilitation are a pressing social concern. The needs for retraining in distressed areas are but a special and acute manifestation of a problem of national dimensions.

All of this places on schools a responsibility for preparing their students to face a lifetime of education, of training and retraining. Within the schools this requires additional attention to processes of self-instruction and encouragement to independent study. Formal education is not now well planned to bring the student to the point where he is able to continue his own education after leaving school, but the widespread application of programs for continuous education will require that somehow student abilities for self-instruction be enhanced. This, of course, should also contribute substantially to an improvement of the quality of education within the formal school system.

A more widespread adoption of techniques of self-instruction will not be easy to accomplish. As with other changes in educational practices directed toward the improvement of quality, increased emphasis on self-instruction must be accompanied by changes in organizational patterns within the school and by changes in attitudes and values of teachers and students. Of these perhaps the most intractable and least susceptible of influence are the value patterns of high school students and their attitudes toward academic achievement and independent study.[6]

Variations in Quality Among Schools

Economic history has been, in good part, a record of effort to find more efficient ways to increase output. In advanced industrial economies these efforts have been very largely institutionalized. In some sectors, as in agriculture and manufacturing, the techniques of change are built-in. Technical research on product improvement and systems analysis directed toward increasing internal organizational efficiency are an integral part of the activities of business firms and government agencies. In the services sector of the economy, however, greater difficulties have been encountered in efforts to increase efficiency. In education, one of society's most important service activities, these difficulties have been considerable.

Large numbers of experiments have been conducted, some dating back to the 1890's, in an attempt to increase the efficiency of education and to establish a basis for judging its quality. All such studies show that school quality varies greatly among different communities. Variations will range from very small differences up to differences of two years or more.

In many cases the differences in the quality of a school are due largely to factors in the community. If parents in one community are well educated, this will have a positive effect on the achievement of children in school. Other community factors, such as income and occupation, closely associated with the educational attainment of parents, are significantly correlated with pupil achievement.

On the other hand, there are very often sharp differences in the quality of education in communities that seem to have the same general socioeconomic characteristics. Studies of agricultural communities reveal large variations in the quality of the school systems. Striking differences will be found among schools in the slum areas of large cities, and among neighborhoods that seem to be similar.

It is not unusual to find differences of as much as two years in achievement in the schools of communities that appear to have about the same socioeconomic characteristics. There are even greater differences in the quality of education among schools that spend approximately the same amounts of money per pupil. These variations would seem to indicate that there are a very large number of factors that can contribute to differences in the quality of education.

It is, of course, obvious that some of these differences are attributable to the abilities of pupils, the attitudes of the community, the education of adults, and the amount of resources devoted to education. On the other hand, it is equally clear that there are great differences in the quality of education in communities that have essentially the same characteristics.[7] Schools vary enormously in quality; they vary in different kinds of communities, and in the same kinds of communities.

There are high expenditure schools that are good schools; there are high expenditure schools that are poor schools; there are some low expenditure schools that are extremely good. This highly confused situation is exactly what one would expect to find where there are a great many things that affect the quality of the school. Many of these influences are independent of each other, and many others are tied together in extremely subtle ways. It is not surprising that a number of factors that are associated with good schools tend to cluster together. Good teachers tend to be attracted to good schools. Good supervision, good administration, and high expenditure levels are associated with good schools. Strong community interest and good schools go together.

It would appear that perhaps one-third of the factors affecting the quality of the schools have some relationship to expenditure levels; but if all schools in the United States had the same expenditure level, there would still be enormous differences in the quality of education. In fact, there are some reasons to believe that quality differences would be reduced very little even if expenditure levels were equated. We are a very long way from a complete understanding of the causal factors that explain variations in the quality of education.

Experiments in Teaching Techniques

Since the turn of the century, both here and in Western Europe, literally thousands of experiments have been undertaken to improve teaching techniques in various subject matter areas. A great many of these experiments have been reported in the professional journals of education.[8] Very often the results from one set of experiments with teaching techniques are in direct conflict with the results from another set of experiments. Moreover, there are fashions in pedagogy as in other phases of human relations. Societal attitudes toward children, the role of children in the family and in the community—all of these things change and attitudes toward them change. It is not surprising that teaching techniques should change and that experiments should be undertaken to justify the alterations. Neither is it surprising, in these circumstances, to find that over the course of several decades teaching techniques in a particular subject matter field will very often turn full circle. A brief review of teaching experiments will confirm these general observations.

There have been experiments in the teaching of reading that put great emphasis upon phonics and the formal structure of language and words. Such experiments will typically indicate a gain of approximately two years in student reading ability. Other reading experiments put emphasis upon the meaning of words and sentences. The children start to read very soon and read a great deal. Little emphasis is placed on phonics, formal grammar, or the structure of language. These experiments show gains of approximately two years in reading ability. An examination of the results and reports of several hundred of these experiments suggests that the gains have in fact actually occurred, even though the teaching techniques are in direct conflict. In most cases the experiments have been conducted with control groups, one taught by previous techniques and another by a new technique. In a very high proportion of cases the experimental technique introduced by the authors of the experiment has turned out to show gains over the traditional technique.

Similar experiences have been reported in mathematics. Some experiments show that students who are drilled in the fundamentals of arithmetic emerge sharply superior in reasoning ability to the nondrilled groups. Other experiments have discovered that instilling in students a personal interest in problem-solving and mathematics experiments is more effective than drill. The findings that emerge from such experiments are typically in diametric opposition. One group of experimenters concludes that drill is the best way to teach arithmetic; another group concludes that drill is an inferior way to teach arithmetic.

Foreign language instruction has likewise been subject to experimentation with resulting conflicts of evidence. Some teachers report that emphasis on reading, pronunciation, comprehension, and grammar brings the most rapid achievement in foreign language. Other experiments emphasize recognition, vocabulary, and extensive reading. In fact, a review of experiments in teaching foreign languages suggests that almost every conceivable method of teaching foreign languages has been employed at one time or another and that large gains are typically reported from experiments with any new technique.

In the teaching of spelling there are likewise contradictory results obtained from an emphasis on phonics and from a deemphasis on phonics. In science and mathematics there are similar conflicting experiments. Here the controversy typically arises over teaching in accordance with "fundamental principles and basic generalizations" or teaching in accordance with emphasis on problem-solving in mathematics or laboratory work in the physical sciences.

For the natural sciences and mathematics much depends upon the educational objectives that are sought. Until very recently in the natural sciences there has been a tendency to require high school students to undertake a great deal of experimental work in the laboratory. This was supposed to be an appropriate approach to the training of students in scientific methods. More recently science teachers have felt that much of the time in the laboratory is wasted, particularly for the able student. Now it is argued that high school students should be taught the great ideas of modern physics and chemistry with a minimum of explanation and laboratory work. It is anticipated that this approach will enable students to move more quickly to the point of undertaking creative experimental work. In all probability the able student has indeed wasted a great deal of time in the laboratory in recent decades. Whether present practices, if continued, will leave the average student with verbal generalizations and no real understanding can only be determined over time. In any event, science teaching is now entering a period when major emphasis is to be placed on improving the quality of education by teaching concepts and generalizations with a minimum of time devoted to the verification of knowledge.

In addition to conflicting results from experiments in subject matter areas, there are frequently conflicting results from experiments with instructional equipment. Some experiments with motion pictures, for example, have demonstrated that the films provide no significant advantage over other motivational approaches used by history teachers. Other experiments conclude that motion pictures alone are almost as effective as conventional classroom techniques and are more effective if films are accompanied by adequate introduction and discussion.

Similar conflicting evidence has been generated in the highly controversial matter of class size. There are a number of experiments that demonstrate that changes in student-teacher ratios within a range of 25 to 1 to 35 to 1 are quite unimportant in explaining differences in student achievement. Other experiments demonstrate with equal force that a 25 to 1 ratio is absolutely essential for effective high quality education. Indeed, some prominent educators have argued that the reduction in class size is the only significant way by which the quality of instruction can be improved.

There is then a wide range of conflicting evidence from experiments in teaching techniques and from the use of instructional equipment. The general explanation of the contradictory findings, however, would seem to lie readily at hand: in most of the experiments there is a strong interest-enthusiasm factor at work. In reading experiments, for example, by the time the teacher has introduced a new method of reading she has probably attained a high degree of skill in teaching. The new method will thus carry considerable emotional overtone, and the teacher will be deeply committed, highly enthusiastic, and energetic. This dedication, energy, and enthusiasm, together with the competence of the teacher, will be largely responsible for the results obtained in the experiment.

Similarly, the children who are in the experimental group will react favorably. This, of course, is the lesson from the famous Hawthorne studies conducted a number of years ago in industry to analyze the relationship between changes in working conditions and increases in output.[9] In these experiments, when better lighting and longer rest periods were introduced, substantial increases in output occurred. When the process was reversed and changes were made to restore working conditions to the prexperimental situation, increases in output also occurred. These experiments have been widely interpreted to mean simply that increased attention to employees' working conditions, regardless of the physical attributes of such attention, tend to increase output.

A classroom situation is likely to produce an even more significant "halo effect" than industrial employment. Children in an experimental group will simply work more diligently knowing that attention is directed to them. This, combined with the energy and enthusiasm of the teacher, will undoubtedly produce important experimental effects regardless of the specific teaching technique that is employed.

This interpretation will also explain the tendency for many of the experiments in teaching technique to be abandoned after a period of time, with a return to the original technique. Gains in educational attainment that are attributable to the enthusiasm of the teacher and of the student may be expected to diminish as time goes on.

The strong probabilities are that almost all the gains from the best experiments in education in the last half century have been brought about by the experimental factor itself. A major effort should now be made to isolate the gains that can be attributed solely to the teaching technique, to the improvements in subject matter presentation, and to the instructional equipment.

In education a great many of the experiments in the improvement of learning have brought instructional gains of from 10 to 15 per cent, or gains in achievement of up to two years in student proficiency. Unfortunately, most of these gains are nonadditive. It has not generally been possible to introduce a second experimental technique and secure an additional two-year gain.

It is extremely important to go on working for the 10 to 15 per cent of educational improvement that may be attributed to a specific new technique, but it is also very important to discover the basic changes in the technology of education that might bring far greater gains that could be added to other gains. This is particularly critical for instructional materials such as television and teaching machines. Thus far schools have not generally been able to capitalize on the potential of these innovations. There has been an inherent resistance to change on the part of many school administrators and teachers; there has been inadequate understanding of the changes in internal organizational structure that must accompany technological innovations in education. Unfortunately, the necessary research on the adaptation of modern communication techniques to elementary and secondary education remains largely undone. If it were simply possible to disentangle the effect of teacher enthusiasm from the results of experiments, this would be a great step forward. It would then be possible to assess with confidence the factors that will generally improve the quality of education in classrooms where teachers are neutral with respect to new teaching techniques.

Increases in Educational Output

A great many of the factors that have a bearing on school quality are beyond the immediate reach and control of school administrators or teachers. The quality of elementary and secondary education could undoubtedly be improved by the assignment of additional homework. Professional educators may take the lead in urging this, but the attitudes of parents toward the importance of education and homework will influence and constrain what educators can do.

Similarly, a lengthening of the school year or more widespread enrollment in summer sessions would increase the amount of education that could be imparted to students. But parents may be opposed to the abandonment of summer vacations for their children.

There remain important areas for the improvement of the quality of education that are more nearly within the scope of decision by professional educators. Many of these possibilities lie in the thorough exploration of all technological devices that are available to assist in recording and transmitting knowledge. These explorations will take many years and must surely be expected to continue indefinitely to accompany anticipated future technological improvements.

In addition, professional educators and parents have a joint responsibility to enlist widespread interest in improving the quality of education. The fact that enthusiastic and dedicated teachers can bring attainment gains of from 10 to 15 per cent in a given subject in a year's time is a matter of greatest importance. It is surely at least as important to capture and hold the enthusiasm and dedication of teachers as to attempt to introduce any other technique for the improvement of educational quality.

Some of the ways for increasing educational output will cost additional money and some will not. An improvement in reading skills by perhaps a grade level of two years may well cost more per pupil, but the unit cost per pupil in relation to grade level may decline. Improvements in course content may not require increases in school expenditure, but may cost additional time and energy of teachers. In general, improvements in school quality and increases in educational output are not likely to be costless in real terms. But the additional resources that are directed to this end are likely to prove to be a good investment.

V. The Politics of State Aid

Education is one of the most thoroughly political enterprises in American life—or for that matter in the life of any society. Yet, ironically enough, school systems and school problems have rarely been studied as political phenomena.

More public money is spent for education than for any other single function of state and local government. No public school in America exists without state legislative sanction. All over the United States school boards are elected or appointed through a highly political process—often most supremely political when called "non-political." Educational planks are increasingly found in partisan platforms at all levels of government. The size, location, cost, looks, and facilities of school buildings are frequently matters of high political controversy. The size, scope, and influence of state departments of education are inevitably conditioned by political forces.

The fact that there have been so few attempts to illuminate the politics of education is in itself worthy of comment. Part of the puzzle is that the profession of political science itself, with a few notable exceptions, has ignored the subject. Academics with an interest in the sociology of knowledge could well address themselves to the question of why it is that the two areas in our political culture which take the biggest slices of public money, defense at the national level and education at the state and local level, have received so little attention from professional political scientists. Political scientists seem to be attracted to subjects for research and analysis in inverse relation to their fiscal importance.

It is perhaps more understandable that professional educators have not made political analyses of their own trade. For generations education has been bathed in an antipolitical atmosphere. The cultivation of the proposition that schools should be "kept out of politics" is itself one of the most fascinating political items of American history. The propagation of the myth by American educators can be interpreted in part as their attempt to protect public education from the naked ruthlessness and corruption of much local and state politics in the 19th and early 20th centuries. But this is too simple an explanation to stand by itself. Our culture is steeped in the notion

This chapter is based on materials prepared by Stephen K. Bailey, Richard T. Frost, Paul E. Marsh, and Robert C. Wood.

that in matters spiritual and intellectual neither the crassness of the market place nor the power-seeking of the hustings should have any substantial influence.

Beyond this there has certainly been a prudential recognition on the part of professional schoolmen that in a system of alternating political parties—or amorphous factions within a single party or community—a close alliance with either a party or a faction might be disastrous to the long-range fortunes of a continuing educational enterprise.

But there has been something else. However understandable the reluctance of political scientists and educators to articulate the politics of education, it is probable that many educators and the lay public have paid something of a price for this lack of illumination. In some states and regions the failure to understand political realities has resulted in a general inability of those interested in education to cope with problems of adequate public support. In other cases, because of the low visibility of educational politics, astute manipulators and single-track reformers have been able to achieve for segments or categories of education advantages which should have been achieved for education as a whole.

Invisible politics is rarely good politics. It may be hoped that some illumination of the politics of education may help to strengthen the cause of public education where it is weak, and to reduce the lumpiness of advantage where school politics is strong.

The subject matter of this chapter is the politics of state aid in eight states in the northeastern part of the United States: Maine, New Hampshire, Vermont, Massachusetts, Connecticut, Rhode Island, New York, and New Jersey. It may be hoped that these states are not sufficiently atypical in their political behavior as to preclude the possibility of generalizing from their experiences. Fortunately for such generalizations, there is reason to believe that the processes by which political power is mobilized in a democratic society group themselves into relatively few patterns of behavior. Nevertheless, the findings here must be read in context. The eight northeastern states are, for present purposes, a region, and no region is completely representative of the universe of all states.

The Common Setting

Today, with approximately one-thirtieth of the area of the entire nation, this eight-state region contains a fifth of the nation's population. It is by all odds the most densely populated part of the country.

Over 80 per cent of its people live in cities. In fact, it has been argued that the ellipse from Portland, Maine, to Trenton, New Jersey, is part of a gigantic metropolis which extends southward to Norfolk, Virginia.[1] Only a small fraction of the income payments in the area are to agriculture (less than 4 per cent). Manufacturing, trade and services, and government constitute the major sources of livelihood. Taken as a whole, the region is blessed with high per capita income: $2,585 in 1961 compared with a United States average of $2,263. And if one ignores for a moment the three states of northern New England, the rest of the area has a per capita income 18 per cent higher than the U.S. average.[2]

Income and population density are only a part of the picture. Of all regions of the country, the northeast is the most polyglot. The interacting elements have been almost too numerous and inchoate to classify; but over the centuries demographic frictions have abounded in all of the eight states. There have been frictions among nationality groups: English, Irish, Scotch-Irish, Dutch, Italian, German, Greek, Slav, French-Canadian, Spanish, Portuguese, Porto Rican, to name but a few. There have been frictions among generations within such nationality groups. There have been religious frictions: Protestants, Catholics, and Jews—there have been bitter struggles within religious denominations. There have been tensions among city-dwellers, country-dwellers, and suburbanites—there have been tensions within each of these categories. There have been partisan political struggles, and struggles among factions within parties. And, of course, there have been racial and economic tensions.

These struggles, frictions, and tensions have been the source of heat for the melting pot. They are an integral part of the stuff of politics—including the politics of educational finance.

The northeastern states share a common political history and common political institutions and customs. The town, for example, remains the significant legal jurisdiction in New England—in contrast to the county and municipality elsewhere in the United States. So New Englanders report their population characteristics to the federal census and so their people identify their homes. Separately or combined, all of the eight states were members of the original 13 American states, and strong colonial influences remain in their basic constitutions.

This Yankee heritage has bequeathed common political overtones which persist in institutions and traditions if not in party alignment. Three of the states—Massachusetts, Maine, and New Hampshire—even retain from revolutionary days their governor's councils as checks on the appointive and contractual powers of their chief executives. Local autonomy is a live, real force in all eight states: except for the largest cities, selectmen are the key local officials and reliance on property taxation is heavy and extensive. In comparison to other states, legislatures tend to be large—embodying revolutionary suspicions of executive action. Indeed, the New Hampshire House of Representatives of 400 members is the third largest assembly in the western world. In every state, acreage is better represented than people.

In short, at the base of the politics of the northeast is a significant historic fact. A heterogeneous, urban, and increasingly non-Protestant population has been superimposed upon an area in which constitutional, representational formulas and political habits were long ago established by forefathers who were over 90 per cent agricultural, Anglo-Saxon, and Protestant.

The generally common development of political institutions in the northeastern states has its counterpart in the institutional development of public education. Massachusetts, of course, was the first colony to require the establishment of common schools, but its special claim to educational fame goes beyond this. In 1642 the colony enacted the "Great Deluder Satan Law" which required, for the first time in the English-speaking world, that all children be taught to read and write.

The other states of the region lagged behind Massachusetts, but by the 19th century all had started along the road of state-mandated education. Public schools had a strong religious orientation in these years, but by the end of the century there was increased institutionalization and secularization of the educational process. Throughout this development, public education in the Northeast remained heavily local and unstandardized, but with common recurring tensions of special relevance to the politics of state aid.

Recurring Tensions

The fact that the history of these tensions runs deep suggests that recent policy struggles in the field of educational finance are, in a generic sense, as old as they are new. These historic issues are (1) religion, (2) control of the state educational apparatus, (3) localism, and (4) urban-rural rivalries.

Religion

In colonial days religion in education was not at issue. Education, in the eyes of New England theocracy, was a vehicle to godliness.

Schools were primarily for religious instruction in the Holy Scriptures, and virtually all colonial schools were church schools, supported with levies against local taxpayers.

This emphasis upon state-supported church schools was the rule well into the 19th century. In the state of New York, for example, during the first quarter of the 19th century Catholic, Baptist, Methodist, Episcopal, Dutch Reformed, German Lutheran, Scotch Presbyterian, and a variety of other denominational schools all received state aid. In Connecticut, in 1818, "an intense battle was fought over the adoption of a constitution which deprived the Congregational Church of its favored position as the established religion of the state."[3] And the reason for this battle was not that the state had no business supporting religious schools, but that certain other Protestant sects wanted to benefit equally from state largesse.

It was internal Protestant controversies and the influx of Catholic immigrants into the Northeast during the early and middle decades of the 19th century that finally brought latent tensions to the boiling point. Protestants were split between those who desired and those who feared further public support to religious schools. Catholics were unhappy about sending their children to ostensibly nondenominational public schools which, in effect, gave Protestant religious instruction. Protestant political majorities were equally unhappy about granting public support to separate parochial schools—especially Catholic ones. Protestants were, in effect, caught between their desire for continued public aid for their own schools and their fear of a militant and rapidly growing Catholic population. As Edwin R. VanKleek has written, "in a word, the Protestants dislike secularism, but they dislike the Pope more."[4]

In 1842 New York passed a law prohibiting the awarding of state school monies to any school in which "any religious sectarian doctrine or tenet was being taught, inculcated, or practiced." This was symptomatic of a growing religious tension throughout the northeast, between Protestant and Catholic and within Protestantism itself.

It is possible to argue by hindsight that all state grants to religious schools—Protestant or Catholic—were in reality unconstitutional from the beginning of the Republic. Certainly the decision of the United States Supreme Court in the Everson Case would so argue.[5] But the fact that this issue was never pressed as long as Protestantism was unchallenged politically, is a point at least of historical interest.

And the struggle continues. The present attempts of parochial school interests—now largely, although by no means exclusively, Catholic—to devolve some of their costs upon the state, and their inevitable involvement in the politics of public education, are but the latest manifestations of a conflict which has gone on for at least four generations.

Control of the State Educational Apparatus

A second area of historic controversy has centered around how the state educational apparatus should be set up and who should control it. Should state educational policy be in the hands of the governor, of a separate board or boards, of a legislature, of a commissioner, of a combination of some or all of these? And to whom or what should educational agents be accountable? A brief look at the history of education in the State of New York may suggest the range of problems faced in different forms and with different intensities throughout most of the northeast.

To the first session of the legislature after the end of the American Revolution New York's first governor, George Clinton, said in part:

> Neglect of the education of youth is among the evils consequent on war. Perhaps there is scarce anything more worthy of your attention than the revival and encouragement of Seminaries of Learning. . . .[6]

The legislative response to the governor's message was the incorporation of "the Regents." The act of incorporation constituted the governor, lieutenant-governor, the president of the senate pro-tem, the speaker of the assembly, the mayor of the city of New York, the mayor of the city of Albany, the attorney-general, and the secretary of state as perpetual regents in virtue of their several and respective offices, places, and stations. Twenty-four additional regents were provided for. As vacancies occurred, they were to be filled by the governor, by and with the advice and consent of the Senate's Council of Appointment. Those regents who were not *ex officio* were distributed geographically among the most populous counties of the state. Interestingly enough, in the light of subsequent developments, the act provided that the clergy of the respective religious denominations might appoint one of their number to be a regent. There is no record that this authority was ever exercised, but it is one of the political realities of the mid-twentieth century that a balance of various religious sects and denominations is always represented in the membership of the Board of Regents.

For present purposes the most interesting aspect of the beginnings of the Board of Regents was the power of the governor and the central role of key politicians in the appointing and managing of the board.

Domination by political executives was explicit. This domination lasted exactly three years. By 1787 a new act reduced the *ex officio* regents to the governor and lieutenant-governor. The number of other regents was reduced to nineteen, and all vacancies by death, removal, or resignation were to be filled by the legislature. In more recent years regents have been elected for overlapping terms. It may be fairly stated that for most of the period since 1800 the regents have been, in many respects, a fourth branch of government—effectively independent in many of their roles of governor, legislature, and even court. What is true of the New York State Board of Regents is true to a lesser degree of the other state boards of education in the Northeast. Although in the other seven states, appointment to the boards is made by the governor (often with legislative consent) rather than by the legislature alone, the effective independence of the boards from direct political pressure and from the political rhythms of gubernatorial and legislative elections is a long-standing tradition.

The desirability of having state school boards as effectively independent as they have become over the years is still a matter of constitutional and political debate. Nothing is more certain to raise the hackles of professional schoolmen and state educational officials than to suggest any diminution of this independence. Just as surely, legislators and governors, and special commissions appointed for the study of administrative organization will periodically propose such a diminution. Since state support for local school finance inevitably involves ultimate determination of policy by governors and legislators, the problem has been less a fractionalization of authority than a special tension within the apparatus of state government in the process of policy formulation. The independence of boards of education and the departments responsible to them from either executive or political disciplines has often given them the semblance of an internalized pressure group set on embarrassing responsible political leadership which must weigh educational interests against a variety of other state needs.

Localism

If the quasi-independence of the educational function from gubernatorial and legislative domination is one of the unifying themes of the political history of education in the Northeast, another has certainly been the unending philosophical and practical political struggle between state and local jurisdictions. There is not now, and never has been, any question about the ultimate power and authority of the state government over educational enterprises. This doctrine, however, has been in constant tension with a widely shared and strongly held view that education was in essence a local responsibility, and that educational policy should be locally determined. For example, in New York State in recent years commissioners of education and various members of the Board of Regents have made a virtual fetish of "local control." The language falls pleasingly on the ears of local school board members, superintendents, teachers, and parents; and it may well be a barrier to arbitrariness at higher levels. But the term "local control"—powerful as it is as a political shibboleth—flies in the face of constitutional doctrine, a variety of legislative enactments, and the fiscal and administrative realities of state and federal grants-in-aid. This struggle between shibboleth and reality is one of the political anomalies of educational finance. In a highly interdependent, technological world the myth of local control of educational policy is increasingly a vast anachronism.

The Urban-Rural Split

Until recently the history of all but one of the states of the Northeast could have been written in part as a struggle between urban and rural interests—or perhaps more accurately between smaller, reasonably homogeneous communities and larger, highly diversified communities.

In Maine, New Hampshire, and New York, this was an upstate rural, downstate urban split. Rhode Island and New Jersey reversed the geography. In Massachusetts, Boston has found itself pitted against the rest of the state. In Connecticut, the traditional struggle has been between the inverted "T" of urbanization in the central and southern portions of the state, and the rural extremities to the northeast and northwest. In Vermont, the absence of large urban areas has almost entirely blunted the issue, although in recent years the interests of Burlington, Brattleboro, and even Bennington and Springfield have begun to make their frustrations felt.

Again, the struggle in its most dramatic form is apparent in the State of New York. Much of the politics of New York has been written in terms of the tensions between New York City and the rest of the state. The reasons for the vast cleavage between upstate and downstate are many and complex. But perhaps at their base has been the unreasoning and ageless fear of the rural and small city dweller that he would be swamped politically, culturally, and economically by the restless, teeming masses of the neighboring metropolitan centers. State politics in Albany—including the politics of education—

can never be understood historically without reference to the upstate-downstate conflict. The same can be said of all other states in the area, save Vermont. Vermont, according to one Vermonter with an instinct for hyperbole, is "51% Republican and 49% cows," and both Republicans and cows live in the country or in small towns.

But the mid-20th century has ruptured the once fairly neat urban-rural dichotomy beyond repair. With the growth of suburbs and the loss of rural populations to metropolitan areas, new forces are at work and strange bedfellows are beginning to appear. In spite of successful attempts to reapportion legislative districts to insure party control, once rurally oriented Republican legislators have been forced to respond to ever widening and more diverse constituencies. In addition, governors and gubernatorial aspirants in both parties need the support of big city voters. Unless they wish to forego executive patronage for all time, Republican legislative leaders cannot afford to ignore big city interests in any of the states where big cities exist. Inequities still exist in the cutting of state fiscal pies as between the big city take and the small town-suburban take; but these inequities are narrowing under the relentless pressure of demographic and political change. No clearer example exists than the decision in 1962 of Governor Rockefeller and his Republican associates in the New York state legislature to increase the fiscal recommendations of the Rockefeller-appointed Diefendorf Commission on School Finance in response to the demands of New York City and various upstate urban areas.

State Aid Patterns

The power of governors over legislatures and parties, the internal discipline of legislature and parties, and the interests and ideologies reflected in these institutions vary from state to state and from time to time. These matters have a substantial effect upon the strategy and tactics of educational finance policy-making and on the resultant patterns of state aid.

Party divisions in the northeastern states are various. In the past, Democratic majorities have begun to appear in both houses of the legislatures of Massachusetts and Rhode Island but this is not the normal postwar pattern for the area. In New Jersey and Connecticut the party legislative pattern has usually been split—Democrats controlling one house, Republicans the other. In the remaining states, New York, Maine, New Hampshire, and Vermont, Republicans have controlled both houses of the legislature. But six of the eight states have had one or more Democratic governors since 1952, the exceptions being Vermont and New Hampshire. In effect this has meant that for most of the time in most states in the area since World War II, party control has been splintered between the governor and at least one house of the legislature. But in terms of the substance of state school aid legislation, party divisions are less meaningful than they might appear. They affect the strategy and style of political infighting; but as isolated variables they seem to have little perceptible influence upon the success or failure of schoolmen or their opponents.

The eight northeastern states have, of course, been subject to the same kinds of economic and educational pressures that have been commonplace in the nation as a whole in the years since World War II. Enrollments have increased, in some cases dramatically. Teachers' salary schedules have been revised upward; per pupil expenditures have risen sharply. The dollar amounts of state aid have increased severalfold; for this group of eight states the increase was from $173.4 million to $1.1 billion from 1946 to 1961. Moreover, although the proportion of state aid to total expenditures remained quite constant in the nation as a whole in the decade of the 1950's, in all but two of the northeastern states (Vermont and New Hampshire) the proportion increased.

State aid patterns differ substantially among these states, both in magnitude and in composition. Almost all have special aid for school construction. In Maine, New Jersey, and New York this is used as an incentive to school district consolidation. Increasingly, special categories of aid have been established—for transportation, health, handicapped children, adult education, and vocational education. But the total amounts involved in construction and categorical aids are small compared with general state aid—the foundation programs.

That each state in the area has a foundation program of some sort is a tribute to many historical forces, but perhaps especially to the creative work of a small group of professors at Teachers College, Columbia University. These men labored in the years immediately after World War I to devise a means for superseding a hodge-podge of patently inequitable state quota grants, and for using state resources to upgrade generally the quality of public education—especially in rural areas. Foundation programs throughout the United States are in large part modifications of formulas developed more than a generation ago by Professors George Strayer, Robert Murray Haig, and Paul R. Mort.

Important as foundation formulas have been in establishing patterns of state aid, they have not been without their inequities, and, in the minds of some schoolmen, they have become an actual depressant upon public spending for education. In recent years particularly, schoolmen have argued that the very establishment of a foundation program has the psychological effect of making local school districts satisfied with a minimum effort. Districts, it is argued, have little incentive to go beyond the foundation program—to experiment, to push towards higher goals. Furthermore, foundation programs have on occasion hurt poor school districts, some of which have been unable to provide sufficient local revenue even to qualify for state aid under the foundation formula. Finally, many schoolmen claim that the needs of rapid-growth areas and of big cities have not been adequately met by existing foundation formulas. It is for these reasons that the northeast is now witnessing demands for revised foundation programs typified by recent developments in the states of Rhode Island and New York.

In 1960, Rhode Island moved beyond the familiar concept of minimum foundation aid to one by which the state shares *all* "approved educational activities of the local school districts." The 1960 Act replaced twelve separate aid programs, and it simplified legal arrangements in the grant procedures. But, from the educators' point of view, its great accomplishment was to authorize state participation not only to insure a minimum statewide level of per pupil expenditures but also to allow state contributions on a constant percentage basis for whatever level of per pupil expenditure a local district chose to establish. A so-called Local Option Program which authorizes state support for kindergarten, transportation, and other approved purposes beyond the mandated minimum now permits local school committees to increase their budgets with the legal assurance that the percentage of state contributions will remain constant.

In short, Rhode Island has embarked on an open-ended program. It has become a model for a vanguard of schoolmen throughout the northeast. In 1962, New York enacted a variant of the Rhode Island formula, and other states in the area can be expected to follow suit in the years immediately ahead.

Schoolmen and Their Friends

For all the eight states, some persistent sources of strength for school aid have been observable and some recurrent types of schoolmen and their allies have been visible. Building upon the fundamental concerns of parents and the citizenry at large for adequate education, pro-school interests can be divided broadly into four groups. First are the educational academics who fashion in the first instance plans for school aid and form the intellectual core of the movement. Second come the officials in state government, sometimes leaders in state departments of education, sometimes officials with other responsibilities, who adopt the school cause. The third type consists of the professional educators—teachers, superintendents, principles—and their lay supporters, school board members, PTA's and school betterment groups, and the formal coalitions which those interests strike. Finally, there are the "surprise" actors, individuals and associations engaged in pursuits not normally aligned with public schools but which for numerous and often subtle reasons make common cause with the schoolmen.

Scribblers and Their Friends

It is impossible to account for the rapid growth in state aid to education in recent decades without reference to the group of dedicated academics who have attached their enthusiasm to their brains and have energized movements for state aid in the entire northeast. The story of state school aid in the northeast starts with the group at Teachers College in the 1920's. The most significant scribbling appeared in two books: George D. Strayer and R. M. Haig, *The Financing of Education in the State of New York*[7] and Paul R. Mort, *State Support for Public Schools.*[8] These two books outlined the need for additional support for education and proposed formulas by which such aid could be equitably administered. The authors, by their writings, by consultancies to public officials and education commissions, by drafting legislative proposals, and by placing their protégés in strategic places in professional associations and state agencies, enormously influenced the course of educational policy throughout the northeast—and beyond—in the forty-year period now ended.

Perhaps of all people Paul R. Mort was the schoolmen's schoolman. Without denigrating in any way the contribution of other powerful academics, it is fair to say that no single person in the 20th century had a more profound effect upon state educational finance than Paul R. Mort. In the northeast alone, his ability to create politically viable formulas, backed with elaborate statistical analyses, influenced the development of educational finance policies in all of the eight states. In the two states of New York and Rhode Island he towered above any other single individual as the mastermind of existing state aid legislation.

The principal companion figure to Mort was Alfred I. Simpson of Harvard, originally a Mort protégé, but subsequently a leader in his own right. Indeed, one long-time school observer, estimating the work of the academics, remarks, "You divide New England states at any rate, into Harvard and Columbia territory. Massachusetts and New Hampshire have been where A. I. Simpson left his mark. Rhode Island and Maine are the scenes of Paul's great victories."[9] And, in New York, Mort was joined by George Strayer and Robert Haig. In New England, Cyril Sargent of Harvard collaborated with Simpson and assumed in large measure Simpson's role upon the latter's death. In Maine, William Bailey of the School of Education at the University of Maine has been influential. And, as the schools of education expand their teaching and research programs in administration and finance, this breed of scholar-activists will almost inevitably continue to be produced.

One other type of consultant needs to be briefly identified: the public relations expert, called in by school people to assist in the promotion of campaigns for better school laws. Serving schoolmen as he does other clients with political problems, the public relations expert is perhaps best regarded as a mercenary and he is by no means universally employed. But in Massachusetts, Eugene Belisle, head of the Department of Public Relations at Boston University, worked side by side with Sargent in promoting that state's great push for a minimum education program in the late 1940's. And the J. C. Jacobs Co. performed similar services in the Maine push for new school laws in the mid-1950's. This participation, if nothing else, demonstrates that schoolmen are keeping up with the political trends of the times.

State Educational and Political Officialdom

If the scribblers and consultants have the crucial role in designing new state aid programs and suggesting strategies for their legislative enactment, they cannot go it alone. They need contact and support from individuals and groups possessing greater political influence than academics and salesmen can muster. Typically, their first couplings are made with officials within the formal structure of those parts of state governments and of state political systems most intimately concerned with educational policy. In short, as proponents for state aid push forward, they soon touch base with state educational agencies. In point of prominence the first of these is the state board of education.

State School Boards. There is considerable variation in the formal responsibilities of state boards of education in the northeast. The range and monolithic character of the operations of the Board of Regents of the State of New York has already been noted. At the other extreme is the complicated maze of educational administration in Massachusetts, in which the Board of Education must compose itself into three overlapping structures in order to do legal business covering collegiate and vocational as well as elementary and secondary education. In addition, the state board must live with autonomous units such as a School Buildings Assistance Commission, a Youth Services Board, a Board of Educational Assistance, and trustees of the Lowell Institute of Technology, which have their own separate jurisdictions. Beyond this, two other technical institutes in Massachusetts have their own boards.

Other states fall somewhere between the administrative patterns of New York and Massachusetts. But whatever the scope of legal power and concern, each state board, by constitutional and statutory provision, has a general mandate to encourage and supervise public education within the confines of the state, and to make recommendations to the governor and the legislature for the improvement of education. However formal and nominal the powers of state boards of education may be in reality, their place in the chain of legal authority makes them significant factors in the institution and execution of state educational policy.

The state boards' political role must be precisely understood, however. They are less independent forces in their own right than sympathetic responders to the executive and administrative officials they oversee. Rhode Island is an extreme case in point. A recent governor and a board member have both complained that the board "rubber stamps" departmental action, and is a passive agent in school policymaking. The general rule, however, is that strong commissioners of education, exercising forceful professional leadership, have a ready sounding-board and supporting officialdom in their state boards.

These observations suggest that as the policy-making—or, at least, policy-sanctioning—state agency for schools, boards are best understood as a statutory link between government and schools. Any official position taken by the commissioner must carry the explicit or implicit stamp of the board's approval. After all, in law the commissioner is the board's executive secretary, acting on its behalf and at its discretion. While practice may construe the relationship differently, statutory formalities are not to be winked at.

But the basic fact is that the visibility of state boards of education as bodies politic is generally low. For the most part they act as sounding-boards for educational ideas and programs rather than as active participants in the political process of consent-building. Exceptions exist. In New Hampshire, the board chairman has recently been so bold as to ask the legislature for 30 per cent more money for state aid—a fruitless, if not quixotic, gesture. In Connecticut, many state board members have testified before legislative committees and have spoken tirelessly before civic and educational groups. But in Vermont, contrarily, public opposition by the State Board to a new aid formula helped to kill whatever slight hopes it had of passage. Most typically, board members can be expected to record on cue their support of the commissioner's program when it comes up for discussion before legislative committees. Members of state boards of education in the northeast do not sit in the councils of the mighty in school politics.

Commissioners and Departments. The key educational official in the state is called commissioner. Except in New Jersey, the commissioner is appointed by the board. In New Jersey he is the direct appointee of the governor. A tradition of professionalism frequently attaches to this office in contrast to the lay backgrounds of state board members. In New Hampshire, for example, strong professional administrators—frequently from out of state—have characterized departmental leadership throughout most of this century.

The commissioner in turn supervises the state department of education, which carries out the various functions which law and administrative rulings mandate. Although departments of education in the northeast vary substantially in size, they all perform certain core functions. A comparison of organization charts of the various departments reveals a recurring list of divisional and bureau titles: Instruction, Vocational Education, Administrative Services, Teacher Certification, Special Education, Higher Education, Finance, and Planning and Research. The peculiar nomenclature in each state reveals the historical development of legislation and of administrative reorganizations. These, in turn, have often reflected the views and recommendations of professional educators from university schools of education, and of professional associations.

In each state department of education there are at least a few individuals, with varying titles and under varying administrative units, who have as their special responsibility research, planning, and administration in the general field of state financial aid to local school districts. It should be noted, also, that in each state department one or more key individuals (sometimes the commissioner, sometimes the deputy commissioner, sometimes the departmental attorney, sometimes others) have as one of their special responsibilities the cultivation of strategic and tactical relationships with the governor (and his staff) and with key legislative leaders concerned with matters of educational finance policy. This is the political role of the department, often working through the mechanism of the board, as in New Hampshire and Rhode Island, sometimes moving through other channels as in New York, Connecticut, and New Jersey.

This "political" orientation of the educational agencies is, of course, not surprising. In spite of the relative independence of board, commissioner, and department of education in each state, there are scores of ways in which the major constitutional instrumentalities of the state impinge upon the activities of the state education agencies. This is most particularly true in the field of educational finance. The amount that a state spends on education is ultimately determined not by the recommendations of the education agencies, but by political decisions taken at the level of the governor and the state legislature. So, although activities of the key officials in the state education agency may be highly relevant to the success or failure of educational finance policies, the final, official, and determinative action is legislative and gubernatorial.

The Political Officialdom. This need for school agencies to engage in a broader arena than their legally independent status would suggest indicates a second linkage made among pro-school interests and introduces another set of actors: political officialdom or, more precisely, governors and legislators. Here the political flavor of the schoolmen becomes even more apparent. Whatever their role as chiefs of state, governors are partisan political figures. However harmonious legislative bodies may be, their capacity to do business and to insure even a modicum of political responsibility is heavily dependent upon the partisan political structure of the state and of the partisan leadership structure in the two houses of the state legislature. This is true even in the states of northern New England in which one-party domination is a long-standing item of state political life.

The cardinal political fact in the region is that partisan political machinery has been fused with a constitutional system of representation which has given inordinate power to rural, small-town, suburban, and overwhelmingly Republican forces in parts of every state legislature save two. This fact produces special tensions in the states of Connecticut, New York, and New Jersey, whose populations are either evenly balanced between the two major parties, or in which a largely big-city, Democratic popular majority feels itself thwarted by the over-representation of suburban, small town, and rural Republican interests in at least one branch of the assembly.

These tensions are heightened by the frequent existence of Democratic governors in these states. These governors, elected of course at large, must somehow develop public policies in cooperation with politically divided or hostile legislatures. The politics of educational finance in the northeast has frequently centered in the executive-legislative struggles of split partisan majorities. This drama is usually personalized in the relationships between key legislative leaders (majority and minority leaders in the upper houses; the speaker and floor leaders in lower houses; and strategically placed committee chairmen in both houses) on the one hand, and the governor and his party stalwarts on the other. Often, the struggle is quite apparent when the governor and the legislative leaders are of the same party: a tribute to the differences in constituencies and historical habits between the two major branches of state governments, as well as to intraparty factionalism which so often builds around competing, strong personalities.

Out of this maelstrom of conflicting partisan and institutional interests, schoolmen nonetheless must co-opt some influential spokesman for their goals. This they do in the northeast in several ways: working on party leaders to have their aims recognized in party platforms, joining hands occasionally with other interest groups, doing staff work for legislative and executive branches alike. But most typically, the procedure has been to persuade governors and key legislators to espouse their cause.

It would distort reality to suggest that leading politicians are always among the staunchest friends the schoolmen have. But the energizing influence of governors and the power and importance of key legislators is of greatest importance. Furthermore, political parties in states where such organizations count have taken important stands on educational policy. Even in those cases where the partisan reaction has been derivative, one must assign credit to the political friends of schoolmen who have given priority to the cause of education.

Special Commissions. Governors, legislators, party leaders, do not always move, of course, in ways the schoolmen desire, and some of their acts of apparent friendship turn out to be ambiguous. A case in point is the use of special commissions as a device favored by politicians for getting themselves off the hook. On inspection, responsible decisions can be found to be politically unpalatable or perhaps enticing political movements may turn out to have irresponsible implications. In instances like these, the study commission has real virtue even if its friendship to schools may be not immediately apparent. The virtue lies both in delaying a commitment and in involving more people—the members of the commission—in reaching a solution. The ambiguity lies in the nature of commission recommendations which, almost by definition, must bridge some political impasse. Study groups may be set up as conscious depressants; others have been conservatively weighted so that strong recommendations for increases in state aid will get somewhere but at the same time will free the governor or the legislature from sole responsibility. School politics by study committee has flourished in just those northeastern states where forces at loggerheads with each other had to find common ground on which to proceed. New Jersey's strongly partisan politics, for instance, beset by keen urban-rural, low tax-high expectation, state-local splits, has for years leaned heavily on research commissions. But in whatever state, if their findings are not always all the schoolmen might hope for, at least they do open ways around political roadblocks.

In states where schoolmen have been weak, one of course can find examples in which the reports of special committees or commissions have been filed away as too radical. But the classic use of the special commission seems to be to construct a conservative countervailing force to the schoolmen which will at the same time provide a rationale for prudent progress in aid to education.

An examination of the personnel appointed to special committees in the various states suggests the conservative bias of such committees. The dynamics of the special committee seems to start from this conservative bias but move toward a more liberal conclusion which is still short of the demands of the schoolmen but which at least presents an entering wedge for further legislative action.

Educational Associations and their Satellites

The sum and substance of school politics is not restricted to inner groups of academics and professional politicians. A broader arena is inevitably involved, and a third set of actors performs the role of uniting the political actionists in government to the laborers in the educational vineyard and to the public at large. The hard core of this group is the professional educational associations, and, to a much lesser extent, teachers' unions, often reflective of the split personality of an occupation still unsure of its status. In these states, the more professionally oriented associations claim by far the majority of teachers as members, around 90 per cent. These have professional staffs, at least an executive director and a research (figure-gathering) person, and are active at their respective state houses. Minimum salary laws, teacher retirement plans, and teacher dismissal laws occupy the attention of professional associations year in and year out. So does the publication of journals, the holding of conventions and workshops, and the organization of committees. The unions are limited to the large cities and are likely to be oriented more directly to such bread-and-butter issues as single salary schedules for elementary and secondary school teachers, higher pay without regard to differences in educational attainment, and better working conditions. Except in New York, the unions rarely figure at the state level except in a line of witnesses before a legislative committee. More typically they snap at the heels of associations, encouraging them to more hardboiled stands on benefits and privileges to keep the membership rolls intact. In New York, however, the United Federation of Teachers works intermittently with organizations like the United Parents Association and the Public Education Association in developing legislative policies, and it has a full-time legislative representative in Albany.

Between the teacher groups and the state educational officials are the "hierarchical" associations of superintendents and sometimes principals. These may best be classified as administration-oriented, for their concern is for education as a going enterprise. They keep the local school staffs together, meet payrolls, schedule school bus arrivals and departures, speak to parents, oversee school plants, keep school doors open, make budgets and present them to school boards. Unlike the teachers, they are sure they *are* professionals, in careers which, when duty, advancement, or better pay calls, can take them out of their districts, out of the state or even the region, to new positions. Theirs is the broader horizon and the greater sophistication, for their problems are not so much with day-by-day concerns of teaching but with the management of schools and school systems, and their recognition of the importance of state action is clear and unwavering.

Following those for whom education is a livelihood come the more diverse assemblies of laymen who for one reason or another are drawn into school affairs. The distinction is perhaps a Weberian one: they live for the schools in their public lives and not off of them. True, in the case of school committeemen, the local popularly elected officials charged with the legal responsibility of determining local school policies and perhaps ultimately accountable for their quality, the line may be blurred. Especially in a large city, a position on the local school board is often a stepping stone to a grander political career. But local school board members do not belong to the professional ingroup, and not infrequently they part company with the professionals on matters of salaries, the dismissal of superintendents, teacher qualifications, merit plans for promotions, and curriculum.

Less ambiguous are the roles of the Parent-Teacher Associations and the councils of citizens, variously named, organized for "school betterment." Here the distinction is the lack of any official responsibility for the conduct of school affairs and the absence of paid staffs or a permanent budget. As between the two groups, the difference is in orientation: the first are parents, discharging the age-old concern of how Johnny is actually faring, whether he can read, and whether the school product satisfies the customers. The second group, the citizens' councils, are engaged in what they consider a "higher" calling. For them the schools are an agent in the national life, a prime source of strength in our worldwide battle with the Soviets, the underpinnings of our economic system—in short, a national resource. But both groups share the frustrations of amateurs. They are uncertain as to whether or not in the eyes of the Internal Revenue Service they can lobby without losing a tax-support status. They are not clearly informed as to the details of how the school enterprise functions. They cannot commit major portions of their time and political capital to the cause and they are sporadic in their attention.

Supplementing these groups whose pronounced aim is better schooling are other civic associations which encompass education in their general agenda. School bills sometimes become the pets of organizations not exclusively concerned with education. While state Leagues of Women Voters from time to time back school legislation, they are not the only ones to do so. State branches of the American Association of University Women, Federations of Women's Clubs, Library Associations, Leagues for Mental Health have all been found involved with educational campaigns on occasion. Each with its own style—often social—and at its own best level—usually local—these groups and others like them can rouse considerable political influence for matters they care about. And professional politicians know it.

The Coalitions

Given such a diverse array of actors in the twilight zone between officialdom and public, it is not surprising to find in most of the northeastern states a striving for some form of collaborative endeavor. The coalition may express itself in formal permanent organization; it may be a strategic device of a state department of education, as appears to be the case in Rhode Island and possibly New Hampshire, or it may be an *ad hoc* one-time affair as in Massachusetts. But the need is obvious and the trend toward cooperative action unmistakable. The New York Educational Conference Board, the New Hampshire Joint Committee on Needs of Education, the New Jersey "Princeton Group," the Massachusetts Association for Adequate State Financing for Public Schools in the late 1940's, the Connecticut Legislative

Coordination Committee, the Maine Advisory Board, the Rhode Island Liaison Committee are all representative of the urge to coalesce.

New York State Educational Conference Board. Far and away the most impressive of these coalitions is the New York State Educational Conference Board. Superficially the conference board is an alliance of the major educational interest groups in the state: New York State Teachers Association, New York State School Boards Association, New York State Congress of Parents and Teachers, Public Education Association of New York City, New York State Citizens Committee for the Public Schools, New York State Association of District Superintendents of Schools, New York State Council of School Superintendents, New York State Association of Secondary School Principals, and New York State Association of Elementary School Principals. In reality, however, the conference board is an effective front for the deliberations of an inner core of schoolmen.

The New York State Educational Conference Board was created in 1937 by the then secretaries of the New York State Teachers' Association and the New York State School Boards Association. The board was almost precisely modeled on the New York State Conference Board of Farm Organizations, which had been created in 1918 in an attempt of a half dozen farm organizations to reach unanimous agreement on broad questions of agricultural policy which involved state legislative action. The farm conference board had pooled its impressive lobbying power with extraordinary success.

The obvious area of possible cooperation between school boards and school teachers was additional state aid, which could help satisfy teachers' demands without imposing impossible fiscal burdens upon local school boards. The solution seemed to be for the State Teachers' Association and the State School Boards Association to form a united group of all statewide organizations concerned with the betterment of education, to strive for policy unity on the single subject of state aid, and to present a united front to the Board of Regents, the legislature, and the governor.

Over the years since its founding, the educational conference board has looked to the secretariats of the major associations and to research staffs in the state Department of Education, and at Teachers College, Columbia, as the strategic and tactical core of the conference board's interests.

The "Princeton Group" in New Jersey. The second best example of the coalition is in New Jersey. When the present commissioner of education was appointed in 1952, he felt the necessity for a regular, informal communications device among the schoolmen in the state. The result was the "Princeton Group," so named merely because the Princeton Inn in the college town 11 miles north of Trenton was a pleasant and conveniently central place for all to meet.

There are five member groups in New Jersey which attend meetings called four or five times a year. They are the state Department of Education, New Jersey Education Association, New Jersey Congress of Parents and Teachers, State Federation of District Boards of Education, and the School Superintendents Association. Each group is entitled to send four officials to any conclave of the group. Meetings are called "in turn" by the respective members, but actually it is the Department of Education or the New Jersey Education Association which decides when it is appropriate to get together. Only the high-ranking officials go to the Inn. For example, the typical delegation from the State Department includes the commissioner, the deputy commissioner and two assistant commissioners. The character of the meetings is wholly informal, as these people have worked together in overlapping capacities for a long time. For example, all the departmental officials in attendance had been members of the New Jersey Education Association working committees when they were teachers, and still work with New Jersey Education Association committees as state officials.

The group is more of a clearing house than a decision-making body. Here the schoolmen determine where they will agree and where they will disagree—the state federation opposes raises in minimum salaries not supported by new state money. Here also are discussed tactics, general strategy, planning, and execution of various campaigns for school improvements, and here intelligence on the political climate and possibilities for forward motion are pooled.

The role of the state Department of Education in the Princeton Group has always been a little self-conscious. The officials have found it a very helpful device, but in the last year or so they have been pulling away from leadership in it rather than become identified as a prime mover. The organization has sub-units in several of the more important countries—little "Princeton Groups" generally brought together under the impetus of NJEA rather than of the department.

This self-effacement by the New Jersey commissioner indicates his recognition of several important developments in his political sphere. The first is that the "Princeton Group" has become a going concern and no longer needs to lean on the initiative and prestige of the department. Educational officialdom will unquestionably continue to pull their own weight in the coalition, but as participants, not leaders. Furthermore, the now-established dominance in New Jersey politics of the governor, the only state officer elected at large, and his appointed "cabinet," of which the commissioner is a member, prohibits the latter from seeming to lead a special interest. Common sense and prudence agree that the commissioner must play the governor's game. What some observers interpret as shrinkage of visibility can be more accurately described as political sensitivity. New Jersey seems to have achieved a flexible and comprehensive alliance of key schoolmen. The other states in the area have, or have had, similar coalitions, although their life, visibility, and effectiveness have varied substantially.

Other Political and Economic Forces

Schoolmen have not only willing allies; at times they have strange allies—with help from interest groups which on first inspection one would not expect to be in education's camp. Generally, this support occurs when the aims of schoolmen coincide with the objectives of those concerned with the structure of state finance, and especially state-local tax relations. Associations of municipal officials seeking tax relief and sophisticated taxpayers' federations often have deemed it in their best interests to shift school financial loads to the state.

The guardians of the public purse are not always aligned against schoolmen. In the complicated world of public finance, school aid legislation may help to readjust state and local tax burdens and provide relief for particular taxpayers and particularly hard-pressed areas. A tax group working in a public atmosphere of conservative political ideology may, on occasion, be something for educators to regard with fear and trembling. But this is not always the case. A tax group swimming upstream in a welfare state may become an important and powerful ally. And business groups other than the well established tax federations can prove sympathetic.

The constellation of business interests is often blindly tagged as antitax at all levels of government, and on occasion they are. But they are certainly concerned not only with the total tax levy, but its distribution. What these interests oppose is state or local taxation which is thought to discriminate excessively against business, and very often this means local property taxes. What is favored are statewide sales taxes. A heavy property tax on a manufacturing concern will raise costs and make the firm's competitive life difficult; a sales tax does not appear to the business firm to have such adverse effects. This is not to say that all business associations are against the property tax or local governments. What they dislike is taxation that they feel discriminates against their membership—and tax discrimination, they feel, is often characteristic of local taxes whose only base is real property.

Given such broad-based state taxes, state and local chambers of commerce and associations of manufacturers have not proved unduly restive about the rising costs of school government. In Maine, for instance, a prime mover in the long and difficult campaign for greatly increased and sound financing of state school subsidies was vice-president (now president) of the Bangor Hydro-Electric Company and a director both of the Maine Chamber of Commerce and of the Electric Council of New England. A student of New Jersey state politics recently observed that he foresaw only token opposition from the state's business groups to more money for state school aid so long as the funds came from a sales tax. Connecticut's tax-minded groups feel they have already gone pretty far in shifting taxation to the state, and they claim local schools have not suffered from the shift. Responsibility and competence, not cost, are frequently the considerations of the tax-minded.

On balance, it is hard to defend the proposition that tax-minded groups are implacable enemies. At specific times and places, business groups oppose taxes which appear to them discriminatory or irresponsible. When and where broad-based state taxes for school support are concerned, many business associations have been no more than passive. At times they have been forces for improvement.

Depressants: Imagined and Real

In view of the steady increase in general state aid to education in the northeast since the end of World War II, it may be argued that depressants have been singularly unsuccessful. On the other hand, most schoolmen would contend that state legislatures would have gone much further than they have in state aid had it not been for both overt and invisible opposition.

The political process involves dynamic tensions. There are people for something. There are people against something. In the case of state aid, most of the schoolmen are highly visible even when they are unsuccessful. The problem of identifying and analyzing the schoolmen's opposition is, on the other hand, a complex and difficult exercise.

No responsible citizen ever says he is against schools—especially public schools. On the other hand, responsible citizens can and do argue that at a given time and at a given place something else is more pressing. And many citizens—responsible or not—argue that education should be kept local and that increased state financial involvement in local education is a threat to cherished principles of local autonomy. But the true depressants in the area of school aid seem to transcend identifiable individuals and groups. Political and economic conservatism in large sections of the northeast is a pervasive climate of opinion which conditions the actions and reactions of men in authority. The task is not only to examine the organizations and institutions opposed to the demands of schoolmen for increased state aid, but to identify some of the intangible attitudes which permeate all decision-making at the state level.

The Roman Catholic Church

What first comes to many minds as a possible depressant on state school support is the only large-scale, across-the-board competition public schools have: the Roman Catholic educational system. School for school and level by level, the church is parallel with the state. There are parochial grade schools and high schools at the local level; diocesan high schools at the regional level; Catholic colleges and universities at the level of higher education. Nor is the similarity with public education institutional only. In most parishes attendance at the church's schools is as compulsory as the hierarchy and existing facilities can make it. And so are levies and tuitions against parishioners requested by the church to pay for these schools and their operation.

It would be easy to jump to the conclusion—as many people have—that self-interest would dictate a massive and uniform opposition of loyal Catholics to increased spending for public schools. Not only do Catholics subject themselves to what they sometimes refer to as "double taxation" for education, but any substantial advantage given to public schools in the form of higher salaries for teachers increases the competitive disadvantage of parochial schools in attracting qualified staff to teach in Catholic schools.

Logical inference in this case is, however, not supported by empirical evidence. Certainly there have been times and places in which assumed or real attitudes of the Catholic populations and of leaders of the church have had a depressant effect on local public school finance. But there is no evidence whatsoever that this has been the result of a conscious policy on the part of the Catholic hierarchy. Local priests and local politicians have often responded negatively to demands for increases in local public education budgets out of sensitivity to the "double burden" placed upon Catholic voters. On the other hand, there have been scores of examples of Catholic laymen,

Catholic members of local school boards, and Catholic politicians taking the leadership in promoting the cause of public education in heavily Catholic districts.

But even if it could be proved that Catholicism by and large is a depressant upon local spending for public education, no evidence could be found in this study to support the proposition that the church has used its influence to hold down the level of state aid to public education. There is plenty of evidence to document the church's interest in increased state services for parochial school children—in transportation, health, welfare, etc. There is also evidence to indicate that Catholic interests can be affected by the nature of state aid formulas. The most explicit example of this was in Massachusetts in the late 1940's, when the Bishop of Fall River stated that a projected state aid bill would be the most iniquitous bill the state had ever passed. But the "inequity" in the bill, in the bishop's mind, was the fact that state aid was to be apportioned on the basis of a census of public school children. The Massachusetts General Court, responding to the bishop's statement, dropped the word "public" from the phrase "public school children." The effect of this deletion was simply to increase state aid to localities with a heavy parochial school attendance. This meant in turn that all taxpayers in the area—including of course Catholic taxpayers—would pay a lower percentage of the total public school cost, with a lower local tax. Local priests would obviously find it easier to raise parochial school money than if the local tax were higher.

But an interest in the nature of a state aid formula is a far cry from opposition to state aid. For those who argue that increased state aid to public education decreases the competitive advantage of parochial schools, Catholic spokesmen can and do argue back that state aid eases the burden on local property taxes, that it provides additional income to Catholic communicants who represent the majority of public school teachers in at least half the states of the northeast, and that it improves the quality of education for the hundreds of thousands of Catholic pupils who attend public schools. Furthermore, the number of instances in which Catholics have performed leadership roles in increasing state aid to public schools is impressive.

Rhode Island adopted the most open-ended state aid formula in the northeast with a Roman Catholic priest as chairman of its state board of education and a Roman Catholic commissioner of education. Maine's Protestant legislature passed the most liberal state school subsidy in its history with the strong and active backing of a Catholic governor. Connecticut, certainly not one of the backward states in terms of state aid in the area, also has a Catholic commissioner of education. The pioneering attempts to create state aid formulas in the entire northeast were undertaken in the state of New York in the 1920's. The governor was Alfred E. Smith. Throughout the northeast, school aid bills have been passed by legislatures most of which are overwhelmingly Catholic in at least one of their two houses.

In short, there is no evidence whatsoever to suggest that the Roman Catholic church has been a depressant upon state aid to public education. Neither is there any evidence to suggest that the church hierarchy has taken leadership in the struggle for additional state aid, although there is substantial evidence that individual Catholic laymen have provided strong, if intermittent, leadership for the achievement of break-throughs at the state level in granting additional financial assistance to local school districts. Whatever may be true of the church as a depressant upon local and federal public school spending—and even here the story is mixed—the church cannot be reasonably accused of being a depressant at the level of state aid.

Tax-Minded Business Depressants

Certain tax-minded business groups were previously identified as uncommon bedfellows of the schoolmen. But this is far from a universal phenomenon. The first of the real depressants is the inclination of many such groups to oppose at every level of government taxes which strike them as discriminatory or assessments which they feel are disproportionate to postulated social gains. Even when increased taxation is deemed necessary or inevitable, many business groups fight additional taxes until they are satisfied that the incidence of taxation is relatively favorable to business interests.

In New Jersey, for example, conservative business groups have begun to soften their opposition to a broad-base state tax—but only on condition that the tax is a sales tax. This single-mindedness is at loggerheads with a growing conviction among many political leaders—especially in the Democratic party—that an income tax would be more equitable and efficient. As long as these two influential groups stand in opposition over the kind of broad-base tax to have, campaigns to get any new major state tax will be protracted. This in turn has inevitably a depressant effect upon additional state aid to education.

In some states tax-minded business interests have gone far beyond arguing over the nature of new state taxes. They have flatly opposed new state taxes of any kind. For years on end, in the state of New Hampshire, the railroad lobby led the fight against any sort of broad state taxes. In recent years the place of the railroad lobby has been taken by the Paper and Pulp Association. These forces have been so consistent and insistent in their effect upon legislative behavior that they surely must be considered one of the prime reasons why New Hampshire ranks at the bottom of the list of all states in the union in the field of state aid to education.

Localism

The most pervasive and persistent of depressants on state school subsidies is rural localism. These stalwarts are emphatically not against good schools. Their main concern, however, is to oppose, and, if possible, to thwart, the pernicious growth of the power of state government. On their side they have, in this section of the country, three hundred years of tradition as well as the support and intensity of their own parochial mode of living. Occupied for the most part as farmers or as primary extractors of natural wealth, they are tied to fixed locations and bound by their own local preoccupations. Their legislative frame of reference begins—and all too often ends—with consideration of their own community's advantage. They grapple with law-making by applying the only standards they feel sure of—home-town benefit. Since their rooted existence, if not their manner of enterprise, is akin to that of the 18th century, they can speak to modern legislatures with the hallowed tones of their forefathers, venerable and well-tested.

These good and sincere Jeffersonians never really examine how much autonomy their schools have. At best, their address is negative; their aim, opposition to increasing state power in education. They are devoted to the antique Yankee rule of thumb that every tub should stand on its own bottom, but they do not define their terse and tidy terms. Their devotion to elementary schooling is complete and unrestrained—if their children can come home for lunch and if bus transportation is neither expensive nor long. They cherish high school education—if their youngsters are not needed at home or in the fields. They want good teachers—if their salaries, by local standards, are not plutocratic. (A Maine legislator recently felt compelled for this reason to oppose a minimum starting salary for teachers of $3200.) They flatly oppose large modern school buildings as extravagant and lush. Rural legislators find schooling on these terms expensive, different from their own education, and incomprehensively remote. Indeed, they care too much. Schooling is the major effort of their local governments, a level of operation they love too intimately and manage too handily to delegate.

There is nothing venal in this posture. It enjoys all the respect of long and widespread usage. It is almost never espoused by legislators considering personal gain. It has philosophical roots at least as old and as positive as the Kentucky and Virginia Resolutions. It handles the routine vote-getting at election time. It is consistent. It continues to affirm the American faith in grassroots democracy. What it lacks is sympathetic and thorough examination—and translation to modern circumstances. Without this redefinition, modern rural localism with the best of good intentions works against increasing state school aid.

Conservative Politicians

Conservative, tax-minded legislators are both an effect and a cause of a conservative ethos in the political life of a state. Bolstered in their attitudes by editorial support from a generally conservative press, often elected with the active support of powerful business interests from one-party districts, many legislators in the northeast in turn become articulate spokesmen for frugality and localism in government. Their words are news, and a reinforcing cycle is established.

Appropriations committees, as watch-dogs of the state treasury, are often foci for such conservatism. Such committees usually take a proprietary interest in the funds they allocate. In session after session in state after state, house and senate appropriations committees rank at the top in seniority and prestige—and consequently in power. Their caution is not selective. Their axe is not aimed at school subsidies alone. But appropriations committees have a role to play, and this is often antagonistic to the spending recommendations of outside groups or of other legislative standing committees, including education committees. The priorities of education committees and appropriations committees legitimately differ in accordance with their separate responsibilities. The difference often shows up in amounts recommended by the former which are cut by the latter. A case in point occurred in Massachusetts in 1949 when a school aid bill reported out of the education committee of the legislature called for a $28 million increase. The appropriations committee cut the amount by $14 million. The original $28 million had been chopped in half by the simple expedient of dividing the proposed distribution formula by two. Tax-conscious leaders in the legislature had performed a routine operation. The pattern is sufficiently familiar not to need further elaboration.

Education is not the only item on the agenda of a state's budget. At any one point in time, the demands for additional appropriations for highways, welfare, conservation, prisons, police courts, or any of the other responsibilities of state governments, may be insistent. The very competition for state money is frequently, at a given time and place, a major depressant upon additional state aid to education. Even when a governor and a legislature are reasonably friendly to the cause of education, the essence of governance is the allocation of resources to a variety of functions of which education is only one. The more sophisticated and insistent the demands for increased state spending for noneducational purposes, the more difficult the problem for the schoolmen and their allies.

In more northeastern states than one this prudence has basked in explicit and decisive executive support. Vermont, New Hampshire, Connecticut, and New Jersey have all recently had governors who for one reason or another have opposed or seriously slowed down increased state spending for education. And here again the prohibition has not been selective; any other item of growing state expense would have been as dispassionately discouraged. In each of these states, the chief executive has felt compelled to hold some fiscal line or another—state expenses, state taxes, the value of the dollar. In Vermont, in 1961, Governor Keyser flatly opposed any increase in state spending for school assistance, regardless of the hopelessness of correcting inequalities without it. In postwar New Jersey, both Governor Driscoll and Governor Meyner placed executive blankets upon demands for increased school aid. In New York, in 1948, Governor Dewey set a flat amount of money he was willing to consider as a reasonable increase for general state aid. This was determinative, although far below the demands of the schoolmen.

This is essentially a kind of tax-mindedness located where it counts most. Any governor has great political power on his side. He is a hard man to fight, especially when he wants to hold the line on state finances. There is nothing pejorative in this conclusion; it is a cold fact of political life. Responsible, experienced, powerful, and tax-minded governors, and their budget officers and political advisers, have on occasion acted as real depressants on state school aid in the northeast.

The Splintered Schoolmen

Frequently schoolmen themselves have made their own programs easy to oppose. Far and away the most common handicap to increasing school subsidies in the eight states has been the inability of schoolmen to work and speak as one for a responsible general school aid bill.

Public education is almost endlessly organized. In every state there exist at least four kinds of official educational agencies—the state board, the state department, local boards, and local departments. And local boards commonly have their own independent state association. These official agencies rarely act in common. The real proliferation, however, is on the private and professional side. Every state has its education association, sometimes at war with a teachers union in a major metropolitan area. There are statewide associations of school principals and of school superintendents, of guidance counsellors, of teachers of vocational education, of coaches and teachers of physical education, and of classroom teachers. The public joins in the Parent-Teachers Association and has its own councils and other groups working for better schools. Associations for mental health and for retarded children represent special educational interests in many northeastern states. Furthermore, many members of these groups really care about the organizations' impact, and their officers work hard at representing the real or divined wishes of the membership. Each of these public and private groups has its own pet concern and its special momentum. The number of special educational interests stirs up a vast—and often infuriating—buzzing in a lawmaker's ears. The wily lawmaker finds it easy to ignore educators disunited—or to play one educational group off against another.

The root difficulty is that too few states have a permanent forum where ardent schoolmen can organize their interests and coordinate their activities into orderly, clear political campaigns. More than once school groups have lined up publicly on opposite sides of the same bill. Unfortunately, it is no easy thing to get schoolmen to agree on state aid allocations. Indeed, educators in the northeast can be found in a variety of distinct camps. There are backers of general state aid: state subsidies for local operating expenses, to be allocated as the local jurisdiction wishes. There are also backers of general, unrestricted school construction assistance. These two are across-the-board financial programs with few strings attached. Far and away the bulk of state school aid is of this sort, but schoolmen differ on which is needed most at a particular time.

But these general "aiders" are frequently at war with the defenders or sponsors of more limited categorical aid. Under categorical aid, funds go for special education of some variety or even for special schools—for the deaf, the blind, the crippled; for Americanization, for veterans or their orphans; for home economics or for agriculture. By and large, the amounts currently devoted by states to these restricted programs is only a very minor portion of state aid, but categories could logically be multiplied to include almost every facet of schooling. While the over-all cost of general aid as opposed to the totality of special aids might theoretically be the same, the political and institutional implications differ radically. General aid implies that schoolmen can and should stand or fall together in legislative campaigns. Categorical aid implies professional independence for every special educational interest and the devil take the hindmost. There has been no explicit comparison of the political strength of these two approaches. Universally, however, the northeastern states have moved away in the last fifteen years from bundles of categorical subsidies to general programs except for schools for handicapped children. The question is insistent, however: would not general state aid have moved faster and farther if the depressant of categorical aids—with all of the divisiveness therein implied—had not to be negotiated?

Another major division among schoolmen splits the professionals and the trade unionists. Where strong teachers' unions have been formed, hard-headed militance is the order of the day, but this style of unionism is offensive to the so-called "professionals" in education. Teachers' unions charge professional associations with prissiness and company unionism. Professional educators accuse educational trade unions of crass self-seeking, and of demeaning the white-collar character of the teaching profession. In New York State, where the issue is hottest, the incapacity of teachers' unions and educational professional associations to work in common cause has had an inconclusive effect upon state aid. It is fair to say, however, that until December, 1961, when the United Federation of Teachers was voted the sole bargaining agent for teachers in the New York City school system, the internecine warfare in New York City among union-minded and non–union-minded educators (and even within these respective groups) seriously limited the capacity of New York City schoolmen to influence state aid policy. The first state legislative session following the resolution of the bitter struggles within New York City saw the most pronounced advance in state aid for urban areas in the state's history; and even if the prime cause for this was a shift in Educational Conference Board policy, a consolidated teachers' union in New York City provided a unity of metropolitan support lacking in previous years.

In sum, all too often, political activity by schoolmen in the northeast has been amateur politics, with all the zeal and disorder the phrase conveys. On balance, this lack of political sophistication and discipline among schoolmen assumes major proportions in depressing state assistance. Many lawmakers would respond favorably to financial appeals that schoolmen can make when they agree on common goals. Most legislators, small-towners or not, find it difficult to withstand coordinated pressure from their grassroots. Special pleading by splinter educational groups stirs up an uneasy suspicion of excess among responsible statesmen, whether legislators or governors. Governors may honestly disagree with responsible schoolmen on school finance, but the schoolmen's case, if orderly and well organized, cannot be brushed aside. In many northeastern states, schoolmen have handicapped their own political success by their failure to understand, develop, and use political machinery available within their own ranks.

The Political Matrix of Educational Finance

Levels of educational finance for public schools are not determined by the fiat of professional educators or the hopes and expectations of parents and teachers. State aid to local school districts is the outcome of extended and highly complex political struggles which involve the interaction of group interests; parties; boards, commissioners, and departments of education; governors; legislative leaders, and followers; courts; academic scribblers; opinion leaders in the mass media; and a host of lesser individuals and institutions.

Each state in the northeast has responded to this complex in recent years according to political and cultural forces peculiar to itself. Policy entrepreneurs in the field of education have had to tailor their strategies to accidents of leadership, unique patterns of party organization, historical political habits, and private and public institutional characteristics peculiar to the state in which they operated. The success of schoolmen has been directly related to the sophistication of their understanding of the political instruments available to them.

It seems clear, however, that certain kinds of political contexts make the work of the schoolmen easier than other kinds. Strong executive and legislative leadership, active and well staffed departments of education, disciplined political parties, elastic and broad-based state revenue laws, vigorous and coordinated educational pressure groups, and the existence of rapid-growth factors in metropolitan areas appear to create a favorable context. Conversely, where traditions of localism are strong, where political parties are lop-sided and internally fragmented, where educational interest groups are divided, where populations are heavily rural and relatively stable, where tax-minded businessmen with the help of a conservative press create a strong ethos against state spending and state action, where executive and legislative leadership is weak and uncommitted, where state boards and state departments of education are inadequately staffed and divided, where state revenue systems are rigid and unviable, schoolmen find rough sledding.

In most of the eight states under review, these structural, cultural, and political strengths and weaknesses have been found in almost random mixture. In such situations, the success of schoolmen has stemmed from their capacity to exploit the strengths and to correct or overcome the weaknesses which have existed. This capacity, in turn, has depended upon the quality of the schoolmen's leadership, their sense of the complex texture of decision-making in their particular political society, their sense of timing, and their sophisticated handling of the institutions and devices which had to be negotiated in the furthering of a policy objective.

There is a highly differentiated leadership within the ranks of the schoolmen themselves for the furtherance of these policy objectives. Four kinds of leadership have been identified here: (1) intellectual, (2) private interest group, (3) bureaucratic, and (4) political. Individual schoolmen have frequently performed more than one of these leadership roles; but the roles themselves are, for purposes of analysis, separable. All four leadership roles must be successfully performed if schoolmen are to realize their goals.

Intellectual Leadership

In every state in the northeast the translation of inchoate public need into specific policy proposals has been the function of intellectual leadership. Successful political activity begins only after a need has been recognized and a formulation of concrete policy proposals has been attempted. This intellectual leadership has come from a number of sources—but most commonly from academic scholars, interest group staffs, special commissions, and the staffs of state departments of education. Oftentimes, the intellectual leadership has been a cooperative endeavor—drawing its strength from a variety of sources. But in every case the function has been the same: canvassing and elaborating the need; studying existing laws and policies; formulating general goals; testing optional programs in terms of possible benefits and disutilities; and preparing legislative language designed to implement in specific terms the goals set forth and agreed upon.

Private Interest Group Leadership

However significant the contributions of intellectual leadership to the schoolmen's success, there must be strong leadership in private interest groups. In fact, the financing of intellectual leadership itself is frequently one of the most important functions of private interest groups. Without the financial support of the New York State Teachers Association and the Central School Boards Association, the intellectual work of the Educational Conference Board and its subsidiaries could not have been performed. The same is true of private interest groups in relationship to intellectual leadership in most of the other states of the area.

But private interest groups perform a variety of functions beyond the support of intellectual leadership. They mobilize consent within their own organizations; they develop linkages with each other in an attempt to build a common political front; they fertilize grass roots; they exploit mass media, and develop mass media of their own; they build fires under lethargic officialdom; they lobby and cajole legislators and governors; they provide a continuity of energy and concern in the face of temporary defeats and set-backs. Sometimes they work at cross purposes; but when they work together under strong and coherent leadership, they perform an indispensable function in the political process.

Bureaucratic Leadership

The notion that departments of the executive branch of government are limited in their function to the routine execution of policies developed elsewhere and legitimatized by legislatures, courts, and chief executives, is a widely held and stubborn myth. In the northeast the creative and energizing—and even lobbying—role of state departments of education is of greatest importance. Often working in close conjunction with private interest groups, sometimes working separately, state departments of education help perform functions of intellectual leadership and political strategy. The quality of leadership of state commissioners of education has often proved critical to the success of state aid programs. With built-in research and statistical services; with a knowledge in depth of educational needs; with the aura of semidetachment from partisan politics; with the symbolic and sometimes the active support of state boards of education; with symbiotic associations with key legislators and key executive staffs in the gubernatorial entourage; state departments of education have been inextricably involved in all phases of state educational finance policy.

Political Leadership

Finally, of course, the success of state aid to education in the northeast has depended upon the quality of gubernatorial and legislative leadership. In part, political leadership is derivative; that is, it is responsive to effective, intellectual, private interest group, and bureaucratic leadership. But political leadership is also an independent force. Governors and legislators have been sponsors and energizers of specific proposals; they have built consent behind educational policies among their own partisans; they have worked across party lines on behalf of state aid; they have defended education's cause in the face of insistent demands for increased state appropriations for other state functions; they have taken leadership in increasing the state revenue base—often with additional support to education as their major goal; they have sponsored special committees and commissions to study educational needs with full knowledge that the recommendations of such study groups would inevitably push up the cost of state aid to education; they have developed support for education through messages, speeches, press releases, and party platforms.

It is, in short, evident that political leadership is the keystone to the arch of state educational finance policy. Political leadership establishes the effective climate within which intellectual, private interest group, and bureaucratic leadership operates. It is for this reason that schoolmen cannot ignore the ballot box if they wish to move their cause ahead.

For those who believe that state governments must share an even larger burden of the cost of public education in the years ahead, the lesson is clear. The road to increased state aid is political. Those who would travel that road successfully must understand the political process in all of its ramifications. They must develop intellectual, private interest group, bureaucratic, and political leadership capable of defining goals and of mobilizing effective power for the realization of those goals.

VI. Governments, Schools, and Suburbs

Public schools are educational institutions but they are also agencies of government. The professional educator, quite naturally, looks at schools in their educational context. The political scientist looks at them in their governmental context. It is the latter approach that will be employed here, with particular attention to school government patterns in the suburbs, where an increasing proportion of children will be educated in the decades ahead.

Examination of patterns of relationship between schools and other governments requires at least a brief look at history, in this case the history of the tradition of separation. In this tradition public schools have come to be regarded as a unique branch of government, operating independently of and frequently beyond the influence of other state or local government agencies, or of organized political parties. Important and useful as this separation may have been in the development of public education in the United States, it will be argued here that the tradition has now outlived its usefulness. One of the most important ways in which both state and local governments and public education can be strengthened is by further integration of education with the rest of government, not by further separation.

It need hardly be mentioned that this is not a popular thesis, either with professional educators or with professional politicians. Nevertheless, there is considerable evidence that increased urbanization and suburbanization will bring the integration. All government—federal, state, local, and interlocal—is becoming increasingly interdependent. More and more public programs are operating across traditional governmental boundaries.

The Public School Tradition

Education is among the most firmly ensconced of all governmental functions, and at the local level its primacy is unchallenged. There has never been a time when a majority of Americans did not consider education basic to the proper functioning of a democratic society.

In colonial times the reasoning regarding education rested on theological rather than temporal considerations, and the church played an important part in both founding and supporting the early schools.

This chapter is based on materials prepared by Roscoe C. Martin.

Educational organization and practice varied from colony to colony, depending primarily on prevailing religious beliefs. Thus in the southern colonies education was held to be the responsibility of the church and the home, hence the concept of a widespread system of education was slow to take hold. In New England, by contrast, the settlers early arrived at the conclusion that at least a rudimentary education was necessary for all who aspired to salvation; and since all did (or should) so aspire, the doctrine of general education available to all gained ready acceptance. So, in time, did the corollary doctrine of public responsibility for education; wherefore the towns early moved into the educational arena, and schooling by a natural and evolutionary process became public schooling.

Initially, decisions regarding the school in New England were made by the town meeting, as were decisions regarding other matters of common concern. As the towns increased in population and school problems became more demanding, the town meetings named school committees to assume special responsibility for the schools. Thus was germinated the modern concept of education as a separate and special function of government. Further, with the growth of new settlements, some of them some distance removed from the central village, the town meeting found it expedient to establish districts for the local administration of the schools. So was born a second major feature of the modern school system, namely, administration of the schools through special school districts.[1]

In the beginning, schools were of necessity local institutions; the need for schooling asserted itself in the towns and villages. That's where the demand was, and that's where both school patrons and available resources resided. And as long as school problems proved manageable locally, there was little disposition to recognize a higher authority and even less to seek outside assistance. At the same time, public education was (or soon came to be) recognized as a *public*, not just a local, responsibility, which meant that sooner or later a higher government would assert an interest in it.

The time came, early in the last century, when it was clear that local districts needed help, if only to the extent of assisting them toward achievement of minimum standards and thus toward some measure of uniformity. The response by the states, exploratory as it was, for many years consisted of taking two steps forward and one backward: of naming a state superintendent (or commissioner) of education, then abolishing his post; of designating an already preoccupied state official to serve *ex officio* as superintendent of education; of making brave sounds about a state educational organization, but providing so little support as to leave it an empty shell. In the course of half a century, however, this Sisyphus-like progress eventuated in a department of education in most states. The state organization ultimately came to rest (typically) on a board of education, usually appointed but sometimes elected; a superintendent (or commissioner) of education, usually elected but sometimes appointed; and a professional staff ranging in size from fewer than a dozen members to more than 500. Even so, the states were loath to assert their suzerainty over the local schools. Only need demonstrated over a period of years would bring the states into the local school arena, and then its activities commonly would be limited to the steps necessary to rectify long-observed ills.

Notwithstanding a general reluctance to do so, the states have assumed more and more active roles in public education since (about) 1850, and there has been an acceleration in this movement during the last four decades. In general, state-local educational relations have been affected by three major developments. The first witnessed the setting by the state of minimum standards in the domain, first, of teacher certification. Next the states undertook to influence the selection of textbooks in the interest of standardization, sometimes supplying the books outright but more often establishing eligible lists from which textbooks were to be chosen. Finally, increasing control came to be exercised over the subjects taught. Having established standards over the course of decades, the states then created a system of supervision to ensure that the standards were met. In these moves the hands of the states were greatly strengthened by the development of state financial aid to the public schools, so that the charge of dictatorship was blunted by the largess of the state and those speaking for it.

Public education presently is characterized by two conflicting drives in matters of centralization and decentralization. The first, reflecting the public school's traditional preference for local autonomy, is toward variety; the second, manifesting the recent reassertion of the state's interest in public education, is toward uniformity. To some, the persistence of localism represents an individualizing force, the resurgence of state concern, a socializing tendency. However denominated, the trend toward uniformity is unmistakable; and if the state has not yet forced all public schools into a common mold, it has at least made substantial inroads on the anarchy which prevailed in 1800.

Suburbanization

This chapter is concerned with the relations between school and other governments in the suburbs; some general background is in order.

In many important respects the history of the United States is the history of urbanization and its recent manifestation, suburbanization. The phrase itself connotes economic development and change—industrialization and specialization. The phenomena that may be embraced under these broad headings affect all of the social, economic, and political characteristics of the nation.

The data are too familiar to require repeating; the suburban ring clearly represents the growing edge of the nation's population. New and complex social and governmental problems arise here, and among these, supplying and paying for governmental services is not the least. Within the range of government services, public education will take front rank, as it almost always has in all American communities of whatever age, kind, or condition.

Suburban communities differ among themselves as much as do places of human habitation in general. Nevertheless, aggregate data reveal how close suburbia comes to the prototype of popular thinking. Thus the suburban population is overwhelmingly white—82.2 per cent in 1960. Suburban dwellers are comparatively youthful, with a smaller proportion over 65 and a larger proportion under 18 than in central cities. There are fewer unmarried persons in suburbs; the median years of schooling is higher than in central cities; there are fewer women in the labor force; median family incomes are higher.[2]

As for the characteristics of suburban dwellers that relate to schools, the following general propositions would seem to be warranted. First, by and large the suburban family is oriented toward the public school: any number of observers have cited superior schools as a prime reason for the exodus from the central city to the suburbs. Second, because of larger and younger suburban families the public school task is quantitatively greater in relation to population in the suburb than in the core city. Third, the constant need for rapid expansion aggravates the suburban school problem. Fourth, the absence of substantial commercial developments in many suburbs, and of industrial properties in most, deprives the suburban areas of a tax resource sorely needed for the support of an effective school program. Fifth, the stronger emphasis on family life, the larger number of children of school age, the greater percentage of home ownership and of residence in the community, and the higher income level combine to provide the suburban school with a more solid cliental base than that enjoyed by the core-city school system. Sixth, the suburban public school is "closer to the people" than its central-city counterpart, and from the combination of factors just noted one might anticipate more active participation in school affairs by suburban school patrons than by those of the core city. Seventh, the boiling point for factionalism is low, particularly in the newer and more volatile communities. Finally, the school problems associated with the suburbs may be expected to mount in both number and severity for years to come, for there is in prospect no abatement in the trend toward the suburbanization of the American people.

The dominant characteristic of government organization in the suburbs is its multiplicity. The 1962 Census of Governments reported 212 Standard Metropolitan Statistical Areas embracing 18,442 local governments. This number included 4,142 incorporated municipalities, an average of 20 per metropolitan area. Included also were 5,411 special districts—an average of 25 per area—discharging duties with respect to such functions as water supply, sewage disposal, fire protection, and street and road improvement, and 2,575 townships—an average of 12 per area. The metropolitan areas embraced 310 individual county governments. To this potpourri of local governments public education contributed 6,004 independent school districts and 601 dependent systems, representing an average of 21 school systems per area and more than 35 per cent of all local governments.[3] This is grass-roots government with a vengeance; it is one of the oddities of American democracy that little government finds such generous representation in the standard metropolitan areas.

In governmental organization, the suburb offers little that is novel. Most suburban cities have small councils which are elected, either by districts or at large, by popular vote. Virtually all have mayors, who normally serve as the city's chief administrative officer. An exception is found in the case of the council-manager city, whose number has increased rapidly of recent years. At present approximately one-third of all council-manager cities are found in metropolitan areas; of these, 15 per cent are in central cities, 85 per cent in suburbs.

A number of features of suburban city government may be singled out for brief mention. First, suburban government is reasonably effective government, particularly in the larger cities. Exceptions will spring at once to mind, but further thought will reveal that these are not representative. Members of the city council are held responsible through periodic election by the people. The mayor, who serves as the focal point for the city's government, likewise is subject to control through popular election, and to a considerable degree of council control as well. In this connection the growth of the council-manager plan is especially significant; for if the mere existence of the manager plan does not guarantee good government, it remains true nevertheless that the cities (particularly those small-to-medium in size) which enjoy reputations for good government more often than not will be found to operate under the council-manager plan. As a single illustration, ten out of eleven of the "All-America" cities for 1961 were council-manager cities.[4]

Second, suburban government—again with notable exceptions—tends to be amateur government. If all suburbs, small and large alike, be considered, the preponderance of villages and small cities makes for government by nonprofessionals. There is at the same time a tendency toward the bureaucratization of municipal services, particularly as the communities increase in size. As in the case of the public schools, municipal bureaucracy and all it entails are a function of size and specialization.

Third, a substantial majority of suburban cities recognize the rule of nonpartisanship in local elections. This does not mean that the suburb is nonpolitical. As the term is employed here, indeed, it would be impossible to remove municipal government from the arena of politics. In some suburbs the "great game of politics" is played vigorously and openly: Dearborn, Michigan, is a case in point. In most cases, however, nonpartisanship is employed to suppress overt political action, and politics is thus reduced to backroom negotiation. Personal or factional bargaining on an informal basis is substituted for open contests between political parties at the polls. One consequence of nonpartisanship is that, in the absence of political parties to build up and defend opposing positions on public questions, the issues brought before the electorate tend to want significant program content and the campaigns to lack zest. A second consequence, which flows directly from the first, is that the voters, failing to find any particular interest at the polls, stay home in large numbers.

The place of the public school district in the panoply of suburban government is a generally understood and not uncomfortable one. On the one hand, the independence of the school district from other local governments gives the schools a special position and the school people a unique sense of security and well-being. On the other, schoolmen understand the organization and method of operation of the city's government, particularly that of the smaller city, very well. In machinery of government, the municipality and the public school are in many respects comparable, and this is especially true of the school district and the council-manager city. Schoolmen also understand nonpartisan politics, for they are the country's prime practitioners of nonpartisanship. Concerning the trend toward bureaucracy in the municipal services, they have witnessed the triumph of professionalism in the public schools and so find nothing remarkable in the decline of amateurism.

From the point of view of the suburban city, the independence of the public schools is universally understood and almost as widely accepted. The needs of the schools, insofar as they concern the municipality, are generally thought to be two. First, the school must have certain services which local government is in a position to render, and which it has supplied without serious discommodation or complaint in the past. Second, the school requires financial support above and apart from that accorded the standard municipal services. Such support, insofar as it is derived from local resources, must come from the same tax base as that employed by the municipality. These two considerations, together with the continuing drive to rationalize government within the metropolitan areas, may ultimately necessitate a new look at the problem of relations among local governments, including the school districts.

The typical suburbanite is education-minded. He moved to the suburb in the first place to secure better education for his children, and once there he lends the educational enterprise his support. Here are to be found the "lighthouse" schools, with the most recent educational programs and the best equipment. Here the schools are a point of local interest and pride. In the sociological study of Crestwood Heights it was reported:

> The community of Crestwood Heights is, literally, built around its schools. . . . In the absence of industrial development and of any large commercial center, the schools (and the houses) assert the community as a physically organized entity, as a psychological reality, and as a social fact.[5]

It is to be expected, and available data support the expectation—suburban school systems have smaller classes; teachers are better paid than in nonsuburban systems of comparable size; per pupil expenditures are higher. For example, in 1955-56, the most recent year for which comparative data are available, the median annual salary of suburban teachers was $4,785, that for all city schools was $4,605, and that for all schools was $4,156.[6] In suburban school systems in 1955-56 per pupil expenditure in average daily attendance was $342. In nonsuburban cities of comparable size the figure was $305; for all United

States cities in the same size class it was $313. Moreover, expenditure per ADA increased more rapidly in suburban city school systems between 1951-52 and 1955-56 than did expenditures in other systems.

School Government

The essentials of public school government, in suburbs and elsewhere, emerge from five basic propositions:

1. Education is a state function whose administration, however, is vested primarily in the local school district, which by state action has been created as a unit of government.
2. The people of the district elect the members of the board of education. The board is the district's primary governing body; this assures ultimate control of local schools by the people.
3. The school board assumes responsibility for the basic decisions in managing the affairs of the district and hence for major school policy.
4. To assist it in its deliberations and to secure the advantages of professional leadership to the schools, the board employs a chief administrative officer, commonly called the superintendent of schools. Appointed by the board, the superintendent is also subject to discharge by that body; and this ensures that he will be held accountable to the board and ultimately, through that agency, to the people.
5. The superintendent's role is a dual one: looking upward, he makes recommendations to the school board concerning policy; looking downward, he is responsible for implementing the policies fixed by the board. He is, therefore, both a policy person and a manager, though long-held doctrine emphasizes his managerial role.

It is not without interest that general government has a closely congruent set of concepts in the doctrine which surrounds the commission-city manager plan. There is little in the literature to indicate that the school superintendent provided any substantial (or recognized) inspiration for the city manager, who apparently was conjured into being without significant reference to the history of the public schools. This is the more remarkable when it is remembered that by 1910, the approximate time of beginning of the city manager plan, the system above summarized had been in existence (or in process of evolution) for not less than half a century. The important thing, however, is that all school districts and a large and growing number of cities operate under systems which are comparable in many important respects. A further striking parallel is found in the fact that, like their counterparts in education, students of municipal government until quite recently have been content simply to describe the manager plan and extol its virtues. Only recently have studies appeared which subjected the system to critical examination. That the students of public education and city government might learn much from cross-analysis would seem so obvious as to require no documentation.

The School Board

Data for an adequate description of the suburban school board are available from the Office of Education's recent survey of local school board practices.[7] The questionnaires cover schools of all sizes, though they concentrate on systems in the small-to-medium range. The mode is the size group 1,200-2,999, and 67 per cent of the systems covered have pupil enrollments of less than 6,000.

Of the school boards included in the sample 97 per cent were chosen by popular vote, usually in a separate school election. For well over half of the boards candidates are nominated by petitions signed by qualified voters; for one-third, candidacy is declared by individual announcement; for 16.5 per cent nomination is by caucus, and for 12.5 per cent it is by primary election. For a small fraction (less than 6 per cent) nomination is by annual school, town, or other similar meeting, and for an even smaller fraction it is by convention. The prevailing methods of nomination, then, are by popular petition and individual announcement.

The most common term served by a school board member is three years; this category accounts for more than half of all boards. Next is the four-year term, which accounts for another 25 per cent. The remainder are divided almost equally between five-year and six-year terms. The modal board size is five, with the seven-member board next in popularity. Six-member boards account for 12 per cent, and nine-member boards for somewhat more than 11 per cent. Boards which have seven members or less comprise 87 per cent of the total number. Of the school boards under survey, 51 per cent have no women members, which is perhaps not so surprising as the fact that 49 per cent *do* have women members.

As for the education of school board members, 89 per cent of all suburban boards have one or more members who are college graduates. The modal number of college graduates per board is five, and 67 per cent have from two to five members who are college graduates. Seventy-four per cent of all school boards have some members who are high school but not college graduates. The occupational backgrounds of board members fall in line with this educational pattern. Eighty-two per cent of all boards had some members who represented professional and technical services, and somewhat more than 82 per cent had members from the ranks of managers, officials, and business owners. About 40 per cent of the boards contained some housewives but more frequently one than two such members.

Thus the anatomy of the suburban board of education. What of its physiology? One may tell any story one wishes to tell about the manner of functioning of the school board, for the chronicles of public education afford bountiful documentation for almost any interpretation. There are, of course, countless success stories, but there are also many horror stories. The purpose here is to examine the board as an operational agency, in an effort to arrive at some judgment both of its effectiveness and of the doctrine which supports it.

Concerning the method of choice of the school board, several subjects suggest themselves for attention. First, the nominating process is so free and easy as to appear to open the door to candidacy for almost any qualified person who might decide to make the race. In practice, however, the guarantees of access sometimes turn out to be window dressing. Local imperatives frequently add requirements concerning class, status, color—and political affiliation—which are unknown to the law. A recent survey by an NEA commission of inquiry tells how in Indianapolis (a city of almost half a million) nominations for election to the Board of School Commissioners were controlled for 30 years by a self-appointed citizens committee of fewer than 200.[8] The report is not explicit on this point, but the implication is clear that the committee represented powerful financial and commercial elements. In a suburban city in an upstate New York metropolitan area nominations were controlled for a like period by the single major industry which dominated the economic life of the community. In both instances the slates normally ran unopposed, and never during the 30-year period was there serious challenge of the ruling clique in either city. Evidence is not available as to the extent of such practices. It may be hoped, though not expected, that these are isolated instances.

A second feature of the public school electoral process which warrants attention is the practice of holding school board elections separately from other elections. From the point of view of the schools, separate elections make possible the concentration of energies and resources on educational affairs. They permit candidates to announce and run their campaigns as custodians of the schools, and to propose issues and choose sides within that limited framework. They emphasize the independence of the schools, setting them apart from any and every other public activity. But separate elections also emphasize the cliental nature of public education, in that they bring to the polls mostly citizens immediately and directly interested in the schools—that is, parents with children in the public schools. Moreover, they render the whole electoral process—choice of candidates, selection of issues, management of the campaign—more subject to control by school officials than if the drama of school politics were played on a larger stage. One result of the system appears to be lack of public interest and small voter turnout. Not uniformly, of course, but often a school board election takes on the appearance of a managed production, a *pro forma* observance with little of content to whet the public appetite. One observer reports evidence that the school administrators favor a small and mannerly election, finding in nonparticipation a sign of public satisfaction with the conduct of the schools. "This arrangement," he concludes, "while it has had the advantage of giving the choice of school board membership over to those persons most interested in and friendly toward the school, may not be an unmixed blessing."[9]

A third feature worthy of note is the school election's professedly nonpartisan character. The whole public school system, indeed, is characterized broadly as nonpartisan, and so it is in the sense that, for the most part, it proscribes political party labels. A particular school system likewise may be nonpartisan in that candidates normally do not announce as Republicans or Democrats, nor are they elected nor do they serve as such. But partisanship does not consist only in public profession of allegiance to this or that political party; on the contrary, partisan issues (sometimes party issues as well) often arise in their most virulent form in overtly nonpartisan systems. Moreover, the organizational leadership-and-responsibility vacuum resulting from nonpartisanship often is filled by factions which are as odious as the old-style political machines the schoolmen seek to avoid.[10] Skimpy budgets have been approved, low tax rates maintained, textbooks banned, library holdings purged, subjects for classroom discussion screened, and loyal administrators and teachers fired for allegedly subversive activities by "nonpartisan" school boards. Vincent Ostrom years ago demonstrated that, with respect to the Los Angeles Board of Education, nonpartisanship was a myth whose single achievement was the removal of political party names and symbols from the school electoral process.[11] A survey of mayors queried for this study, persons accustomed to seeing nonpartisanship (and partisanship) for what it is, bestowed the label of nonpartisan on no more than 60 per cent of the school boards.[12] To them, 22 per cent of the boards appeared to have Republican majorities, 18 per cent Democratic majorities.

In the central New York suburb above referred to, a local politician was accused of having introduced politics into school board elections. He not only confessed his guilt, but boasted of his achievement. His rationale was persuasive. "What I did," he said, "was to throw out a company-controlled school board in favor of a board elected by the people. I substituted a real contest for the mock contest which had prevailed for thirty years. I introduced *public* politics into a system where *private* politics had been the rule." Partisanship in school elections is deserving of more searching examination than it has received.[13]

The exclusively educational orientation of the public school system brings in its wake two consequences for democracy which, though unanticipated, are nonetheless grave in their portent. The first arises from the public school's cliental base: from the fact that, serving as it does a particular segment of the total population (i.e., parents with children of school age), it associates itself primarily with that segment in all its undertakings. The school's reason for being is the child, and child and parent are of course inseparable. An earnest effort is made to justify public education in more inclusive terms—as a program in training for citizenship or for adjustment to society, for example—and so to broaden its popular base; but when all is said and done the most effective tie which the school has is that with the parent. It goes without saying that this is a two-way street; for if the schools are basically dependent upon parent support, the parents on their part recognize a deep and lasting debt to the schools.

Public education, then, is in essence a special government program run by and for and with the valiant support of that segment of the population comprising parents with children of school age. The populace at large is keenly conscious of the limited and special character of educational service. Time and again respondents to the citizen questionnaire employed in this study replied in this vein: "I am single and have no interest in the schools." "I used to take an active interest in the schools, but my children are all grown now and I haven't paid any attention to school issues in years." "I have two children in parochial schools, but none in public schools. No interest." The implication of the proposition that the schools are the basic concern of parents with young children is, of course, well understood by such parents. It is also accepted by them. In the citizen questionnaire completed and returned, a much larger percentage of parents with children in school professed a familiarity with school affairs and participated actively in those affairs than of persons without children. Of parents with children in the public schools, 66 per cent voted in their communities' last school board election, compared with 44 per cent of those without children. Of parents with children, 71 per cent voted in the last school bond issue; 55 per cent of those without children voted. A considerably higher percentage of parents with children attended school board meetings than of parents without.[14] The testimony suggests that the schools are considered to belong to families with children, for the obligations of school citizenship normally are left to, as they are assumed by, those families.

All this may be thought good by some but certain problems arise when one activity in the total public enterprise is raised to a level scarcely approached by any other activity. Concentration on the needs and desires of the school district cliental group tends to divide the population into two groups: those who are served by and who are concerned with the public schools and those who are not.

Creation of a special and sharply defined public school clientele results in both advantages and problems; for if the school's public is thereby isolated and its "community relations" target clearly delineated, by the same token an active element of fluidity is injected into the clientele and the target is converted into a moving one. The arithmetic of it is that, in a typical school system, there will be a turnover of one-twelfth in the parent group each year. But simple arithmetic does not tell the story accurately, for the "freshman class" of parents is much larger than the "graduating class," since incoming pupils typically outnumber those departing. Thus is the ever-present task of citizen education, difficult in any case in a democratic system, additionally complicated for public education.

Politics and Politics

In order to discuss the subject of citizen participation it is necessary to examine the term "politics," which is among the most slippery of words. Unfortunately, the term is employed with such reckless abandon that it has lost all semblance of precision in popular usage, and hence has meaning only in a specific context.

In one of its commoner senses the word is employed to characterize the activities of the big-city political organization, as in the phrase "machine politics." In this instance it is used very largely for pejorative purposes, for in nontechnical writing or conversation one almost never speaks well of machine politics. It is necessary forthwith to reject this concept of politics as practiced by such notorious operatives as Charles Murphy of Tammany Hall, Big Bill Thompson of Chicago, Thomas Pendergast of Kansas City, and Boss Hague of Jersey City; for "politics" and its various derivatives are misused when employed to characterize the conduct of men active on the near edge of crime.

These men and others like them normally were extreme partisans who professed fealty to the Republican or the Democratic organization as circumstances required or convenience directed. Through their activities they helped to create the model of politics which schoolmen loathe, but to concede that they were politicians in any allowable sense of the word is to submit to perversion of a term basic to the democratic lexicon, one necessary and wholly proper to analysis of the democratic process. Politics as the legacy of the big-city machines of an earlier day is not the appropriate definition for present purposes.

In another sense politics means the manipulation of human relations to achieve institutional goals, or mayhap personal preferment or profit. Here invocation of the term may be legitimate, for it may be used to describe what goes on not only in a quite literal but in a technically accurate sense as well. Its common employment, however, to cover a wide and heterogeneous range of activities scarcely makes for responsible usage. Moreover, as in the first instance, the word is commonly used here in a depreciatory sense: seldom is one complimented to hear his activities or those of his organization characterized as politics, and seldom is compliment intended.

In yet a third sense, the sense in which the word is used here, politics is nothing more (nor less) than the contest which develops around the control of policy. "Policy" is itself, of course, a term with variable meaning. It may be applied to private as well as to public undertakings, hence there may be said to be church policy or industrial policy or union policy, and so church or industrial or union politics. Obviously the concern here is with policy in its public connotation, and in that broad domain public school policy—and public school politics. The political system is the framework or pattern of arrangements through which politics is conducted. As in the case of politics, the political system concept is applied in the present context to the public schools. To define a term is not, of course, to endow it with fixed significance for all time and every place, but only (or chiefly) to indicate its changing meaning with varying circumstances. The phrase continues to offer at best a moving target, its meaning affected —indeed sometimes determined—by the context in which it appears.

Under the broad definitions proposed above, it is obvious that every undertaking where important issues of policy arise has both its politics and its political system. Of public education, indeed, it may be said that the management of the public schools in a significant sense *is* politics; for politics centers on the principal foci of decision-making, and public school administration is fundamentally a process in which decisions are arrived at and implemented. Politics therefore may be said to be essentially a way of looking at the public school system and its management. With this view of politics most schoolmen might be expected to agree, for they are well aware of the political nature of much of public school administration, particularly of the policy decisions made there. The politics they reject is that practiced by (or in) other governments, quite specifically the "political" politics of the city. This suggests the possible usefulness of distinction, from the point of view of school spokesmen, between internal politics, or politics as practiced within or by the schools, and external politics, or politics as practiced in other agencies and units of government. The concept is covered by the terms "school politics" and "general politics." One senses that the politics anathematized by the schoolmen is that of the big-city machine of yesteryear, whose ghost continues to haunt municipal democracy long after death has departed the archetype. This is to perceive politics in the worst of the three senses examined above; it is, moreover, to give currency to standards of public morality long since discredited and by now almost universally rejected. The habit of thought among schoolmen which places school politics on one level and urban politics on another and lower level is deserving of careful reappraisal.

The term politics as defined here may embrace (1) the process of governance within the schools, (2) the process by which schools are controlled and held responsible to the citizenry, and (3) the process of decision-making as it relates to other governments. It is politics in this third sense, that is, general politics as practiced in and by other governments, and particularly by urban governments, that so often arouses the antagonism of schoolmen. Any contact between urban politics and the schools is held to be destructive of sound educational practice. And since the city is conceived to be dominated by politics, it is natural and easy to bring it within the interdiction. This bitter and denunciatory attitude of professional educators toward urban politics inhibits the development of patterns of relationship between school government and other general government. In addition, traditional hostility toward urban government and urban politics may well be translated into student attitudes, with future generations made hostile to urban government and urban politics.

Citizens and Schools

The issues which excite citizen concern over public schools may be classified broadly as perennial or episodic. The evidence at hand suggests that in the former group fiscal affairs rank uppermost. In the questionnaire survey conducted as part of this study, League of Women Voter presidents and Chamber of Commerce officials were asked to rank public school issues. Both put the school tax rate in first place, school building and expansion programs second, bond issues to support such programs third, and the school budget fourth. Teachers' salaries ranked fifth. The respondents indicated no particular interest in curriculum, textbooks, subversive activities, personalities, athletics, race relations, or independence of the schools. These are apparently the episodic issues. Thus the curriculum is not a matter for perennial concern but a particular textbook under a special set of circumstances may be a public issue. Subversive activities are not a perennial issue but a teacher who assigns for reading a piece of UNESCO literature may become a public issue.

The agencies through which citizen concern finds expression range from political parties to *ad hoc* committees. The former are generally banned under the tradition of nonpartisanship; beyond identification the latter require no attention. The community groups with a typically continuing interest in education include the League of Women Voters, service clubs, taxpayer groups, the Chamber of Commerce, and on occasion organizations of school alumni and religious and patriotic groups. Replies from the survey questionnaire indicated that trade unions seldom take a continued interest in public education.

The most frequent method for the expression of interest is recourse to the board of education. Direct appeal to the superintendent is much less frequently employed, and recourse to the teachers ranks third. If grievances are not redressed through these normal channels of protest, then mass meetings, petitions, and, in rare cases, taxpayers' strikes may be employed. Appeal to higher authorities, such as a state department of education or a state legislature, may result in challenges at the polls as a remedial measure, although processes of what might be termed community conciliation tend to resolve most issues of intense citizen concern. Unfortunately, the superstructure of machinery and procedure to permit the expression of citizen interest and influence does not always elicit vigorous citizen response. In the survey questionnaires employed in this study, half of those replying did not know how long their school superintendent had served; well over half could not name the president of their school board; two-thirds did not vote in their community's last school board election. Although greater interest was exhibited in connection with bond issues with nonvoters averaging only 29 per cent, even so 26 per cent of the citizens whose opinions were solicited did not know whether or not the bond issue was approved.

The findings of other studies corroborate this testimony. A survey by the Stanford University Institute for Communication Research found that about half of the voters "show no evidence of any participation in school affairs and no interest in such participation." No more than a third took part actively in school affairs, and the extent of knowledge about the schools was reported to be "only slight." "This is not an encouraging picture," the study concluded gloomily.[15]

Some school systems have undoubtedly achieved a good working model of democracy in terms both of the internal conduct of school affairs and of effective public responsibility, but it would be difficult to argue that the schools excel in this regard. There is certainly no reason to believe that public schools are uniformly more democratic in terms of citizen participation and public accountability than either central city governments or suburban city governments.[16]

The Role of Bureaucracy

The separation of school government from other government is perpetuated by the educational bureaucracy—the administrators, classroom teachers, and miscellaneous professional employees that may generally be lumped together into the category of professional educators. To describe professional educators as a bureaucracy is to note a condition, not to levy a charge. All government is staffed by bureaucrats, which is but another name for civil servants. Public school administrators, teachers, and other professionals as government employees are therefore both civil servants and bureaucrats whether they wish it or not. But in popular parlance, the terms "bureaucrat" and "bureaucracy" suggest an introversion which places the interests of the service group above the interests of the group served. Bureaucracy in this sense seems to be an almost natural concomitant of professionalism. The most advanced professions are those most affected by the bureaucratic spirit—the certitude of the rightness of any professional course or stand, impatience with a contrary view, and suspicion of all criticism. Who is so rash as to challenge the admirals on naval affairs or the doctors on hospital care? Professional education, like other professions, has developed over the last century by closing the doors to intruders, producing powerful professional associations, generating a pride in workmanship, and building a confidence in and respect for the calling. These are the same developments, unhappily, that produce an advanced spirit of bureaucracy. In the last century the task of professionalizing education included the necessity of closing the doors to the politically appointed teacher. There is at least this much historical justification for the antipathy of professional educators to the political process.

The central assumption in this professionalization was that public education is a unique function of government. The corollary was, and is, that as a unique public function education must be accorded separate and special treatment. In the extreme manifestations of this point of view professional educators alone are to be responsible for education. Citizen and parental concern is to be channeled through and controlled by professional educators.[17] The fiscal manifestation of this point of view is a continued quest for financial independence; that is, the separation of school finance from all other general government budgetary authority.

The role of the superintendent, the chief of the public school professional staff, is crucial in an appraisal of the nature and significance of the educational bureaucracy. This role has changed in two important respects in recent years. First, the superintendent has emerged as the leader rather than as the servant of the school board. His is no journeyman's job, and he is no handy man merely to do the bidding of the board once policy has been established. On the contrary, he is at least as much a policy maker as he is a manager in the narrow sense; for he enjoys an expertise, a professional reputation, and a community position which combine to give him an almost irresistible voice in school affairs.[18]

The school superintendent has also emerged in recent years as an influential politician in the popular understanding of that term. Every successful superintendent, particularly in a rapidly growing suburban community, must be skilled in "community relations," a synonym for the consent-building process so familiar to executives and legislators who must periodically submit to the verdict of their fellow citizens in the polling booths. A successful superintendent is almost by definition a skillful politician in the popular sense of the term. Schoolmen are strangely loath to concede this proposition, although the annals of public education are filled with incidents which testify to its soundness. Interestingly enough, these recent developments in the role of the school superintendent are paralleled by comparable trends in the city manager profession. There, too, the manager has emerged as a master bureaucrat on the one hand and as a master politician on the other.

School Programs and Government Programs

Although professional educators have generally insisted on maintaining a tradition of aloofness and hostility toward general governmental processes, it must be allowed that those who are concerned with local government in its broader context have done little if any more than their educator counterparts to associate the public schools with other government. The American Municipal Association, which represents thousands of cities in state leagues of municipalities, conducts an annual municipal congress. Among the subjects considered by the congress in its last five meetings were "Human Needs in the Changing City," "City-Federal Relations," and "Intergovernmental Cooperation." It would seem a difficult feat to avoid mention of public education under one or all of these rubrics, but the mayors managed it: they passed by the schools as dexterously as the schoolmen pass by the cities in their professional conclaves.

The same story may be told of the International City Managers' Association, which in its annual conference never discusses the public school as a municipal problem. Both mayors and managers regard the school districts as local governments, even as the schoolmen do. Moreover, they agree that the public schools pose many not insignificant problems for the cities. "Schools and cities are only now beginning to scratch the surface . . ." of the fruitful interrelations inherent in their common interests and concerns, as a local official stated in a recent letter; nevertheless, it is obvious that the practitioners of general government are no more minded to scratch than are the school people.

Nor have academic students of local government been energetic in attacking the dragon of school aloneness. An early and still notable effort was made by two University of Chicago scholars, one a professor of political science, the other a professor of education.[19] Their work, though promising as an exploratory excursion into city-school relations, has had distressingly few emulators. Chancellor Thomas H. Eliot of Washington University has written a recent perceptive article on the subject.[20] His comments, and more especially his bibliographic citations, emphasize the poverty of the political science literature on the subject of the schools and local government.

The relations between the school districts and other local governments, and specifically between the schools and the cities, therefore remain largely unexplored; for if the schoolmen have maintained an air of aloofness, the mayors have cultivated an attitude of diffidence. One group thus has not recognized, or has not been willing publicly to acknowledge, the existence of problems, while the other has been loath to raise them on its own initiative.

As things now stand, there are problems in abundance in the program relations between schools and other governments, particularly in metropolitan areas. One of these arises out of the simple fact that school districts are special districts of government. As students of government have long noted, all special districts contribute to the further fragmentation of local government structures, give rise to a series of special publics based on cliental interests, and absorb the residual energy and interest for common problems; that is, those of general government. Such fragmentation, by setting up a series of competing centers of attention, reduces the visibility of governments. A prime requisite of enlightened citizen action is a structural government in which the loci of decision-making can be readily identified by the voter and held steadily in view. Although the number of school districts nationwide is continually reduced, the processes of reorganization and consolidation within metropolitan areas proceed much more slowly than in the countryside, and suburban area reorganization seldom brings congruity between school district boundaries and other municipal lines.

The areal discrepancies between school districts and other units of local government, together with the traditional separation of schools and general government, make for some unhappy programmatic consequences. It is most difficult for rational or concerted programs to emerge from the independent deliberations of half-a-dozen individual and tenuously related decision centers. For example, school building plans and city development programs, such as urban renewal, cannot be fitted together to best advantage as long as school district and city proceed without reference to one another. Coordinated land use planning is a collateral casualty of fragmented local government.

A generally prevailing fiscal independence of suburban schools in metropolitan areas adds further to programmatic difficulties. School districts, like other special districts, are in constant competition for the public revenue dollar. Although the evidence is very much in conflict, there is at least some experience to suggest that school support suffers more than it gains from fiscal independence.[21] Of perhaps even greater importance is the untoward effect of school independence on fiscal planning. Such planning, whether for current programs or for capital outlays, obviously is impossible where a number of autonomous units make separate and individual decisions about financial matters. Fiscal independence may result in a more or less generous support for the schools, depending on the relative strength of the contending publics and the comparative skills of their negotiators. But surely fiscal independence will not eventuate in sound fiscal planning for public resource use.

There are, of course, many operational relationships between public schools and municipal government, notwithstanding the traditional pattern of independence. Municipalities render the schools such services as police and fire protection and sewage disposal almost as a matter of course. The practice of exchange in use of such physical facilities as libraries, playgrounds, gymnasia, swimming pools, and auditoria likewise is widespread, although the intergovernmental use of such facilities may by no means be taken for granted. In the domain of fiscal management, as distinguished from fiscal planning, the picture is spotty. Municipalities frequently assess property for school purposes and collect taxes therefor. But in the custody and disbursement of funds only a very small number of schools utilize the facilities of constituent general government, and in the field of purchasing and auditing programmatic interrelationship is almost nonexistent. A beginning, but only a beginning, has been made in the joint sharing of data processing equipment. In such service areas as these, the relationships between schools and municipalities could be pushed forward to the advantage of the public at large.

Integration of the municipality and its school system and the development of closer working relations between the two are, of course, quite different things. The first is debatable and may be expected to be debated increasingly in the years ahead; the second is not arguable in terms of logic or reason, nor is it assailable on the basis of experience. There is no good reason for the present failure to get on with the improvement of operational relationships; no statute inhibits such development. What is required are certain personal qualities on the part of the mayor and city council or the supervisor and the town board on the one hand, and the superintendent and board of education on the other—the imagination to identify opportunities for and the good will to work toward constructive arrangements. The secret to positive relations between municipalities and schools is not legal mandate but personal commitment.

Future Prospects

Certain prospective developments in the relations between public schools and general governments may be identified with some assurance; others remain in the realm of speculation. Among the former, the first prospect is that the tide of centralization, which for half a century has seen a gradual growth in state control over local districts, will continue to run. A number of major centralizing devices may be readily identified.

First, the local schools in all likelihood will be subjected to an increasing number of statutory stipulations, including, in particular, laws designed to effectuate uniform standards in curriculum. Second, the state's growing interest in education, following a line of development witnessed in other functional areas, very probably will manifest itself in increasingly close administrative supervision over the schools. Already such supervision is substantial. Third, many public school spokesmen, despairing of drastic local action looking toward the consolidation of school districts, have demanded that the states take an increasingly firm hand by encouraging, or even mandating, district consolidation. Fourth, the rejuvenation of the county and its emergence as a unit of general government in all likelihood portends growing activity by that unit in the domain of education. The county is of course already active throughout much of the South as the basic district for the administration of local schools; it may well come to play a similar role elsewhere. The prospect, then, is that local school districts will suffer a further decline in autonomy in the face of the state's increasing interest and activity in the field of public education.

A second prospective development is that the trend in school district reorganization is likely to continue. The movement toward school district consolidation, which has seen their decline in number from 108,579 in 1942 to 35,082 in 1961, is quite dramatic; yet many thousands of districts remain which serve no significant purpose. As the school districts decrease in number they of course increase in size, with consequences in the de-personalization and formalization of the schools.

A third prospective development may well see the closer integration of the school districts with the units of general local government. This trend is not as clearly established as the two previously examined; indeed it may be questioned whether developments of trend porportions are yet to be discerned. At the same time there are many, prominent educators among them, who foresee the growth of closer relations between the schools and other public activities. Reller has commented to this effect:

> Education will be closely coordinated or integrated with other services such as public health, housing, social welfare, land use, recreation, employment and assistance with youth, and library. The growth in population and the concentration of population with the attendant problems will require that education be related more significantly to the lives of children and youth and to other organizations which bear upon them. This integration may take place through coordination of the efforts of various governmental agencies or through some changes in legal structure which may facilitate a broad, common attack on the problem.[22]

Elaborating on this theme, Reller suggested that educators take cognizance of emergent developments and adapt educational practice to new needs. Among the other steps, he recommended that some prospective school administrators be elected for training from among general public administrators, including "assistant city managers, assistant directors of planning, and junior administrators in various public service areas." Expressing similar concern for the relationships of schools with other governments, Lonsdale has proposed that an assistant superintendent be appointed with primary responsibility for representing the school district in metropolitan area programs.[23]

The closer relations which are visualized may come about in any or all of four principal ways. First, in the process of rationalizing school district boundaries the limits of the enlarged district may be made congruent with those of the municipality. This would permit the synchronizing of education with other governmental activities at any of several levels of cooperation. It could proceed directly into the second major device for collaboration, found in the outright assimilation of public education to the activities of urban government. The integration of school and city governments is opposed by virtually all educational spokesmen, yet it is a possibility which cannot be dismissed lightly. If, as is widely agreed, it is desirable to bring the public schools into the purview of other important activities, integration offers a quick and effective way to achieve that goal.

Third, both cities and schools might profit materially from fiscal collaboration between the two. The integration of the school district with the city, which would represent the logical extreme in fiscal cooperation, would also destroy one of the schoolmen's most prized possessions, fiscal independence. The value of this possession may, however, be subjected to increasing question with the passing of time.

A fourth way by which school system and city might be brought into closer working relationship would entail nothing more drastic than program collaboration. Involved here would be such municipal programs as health, recreation, and planning—all activities with a high content of interest and usefulness for education. Many other municipal programs also have significance for the schools. For its part, the school system likewise is equipped to render some services that would be useful to the city. Indeed, some educational programs reach out into the community even now in a way which identifies them as in effect joint school-city undertakings. Chief among these is the adult education program. The growing community college movement may be expected to provide impetus toward a more active spirit of cooperation. Concerning programmatic collaboration, there is every reason why school system and city should get together in a series of agreements for the benefit of both, and no important reason why they should not. Schoolmen understand this simple but central fact more and more clearly with the passing of time, and there is cause to believe that they are ready to move into an era of much more active cooperation with regard to programs. Mayors and city managers are reticent to speak on this subject, but they have not often held back on proposals for cooperation in the past.

Schools are a community enterprise. Professional educators readily accept this proposition as do students of government, but it means substantially different things to the two groups. To schoolmen a community is an aggregation of people residing within a given area; to political scientists a community becomes real only when its people recognize the legal authority of a unit of general government. For schoolmen the community achieves fullest and richest expression through its public schools. Political scientists tend to think of the community in corporate terms, and so to emphasize government administration and politics.

The traditional views of public educators contain an inherent paradox in attitudes toward democratic government. The problem may be stated in the form of a dilemma. On the one hand, the success of democratic government depends on an informed and responsible citizenry whose development is a prime task of the public schools. The public schools as the builders of an informed citizenry are, therefore, the cornerstone of democratic government. But on the other hand, general government, the principal agency through which democracy is achieved and safeguarded, is a rough and tumble affair. As an organism primarily and directly concerned with the realization of the aspirations and welfare of the citizenry, the city, in particular, is deeply involved in general politics which is anathema to schoolmen. Public education, therefore, shuns urban government, its institutions and its works, preferring to go it alone as a public program entirely separate from other local government. Thus the public school rejects the political world in which democratic institutions operate.

This dilemma will not be resolved by abrupt action but only through gradual softening of educators' attitudes toward politics and government. The imperative need is for wider understanding among schoolmen of the nature of the democratic process and the contribution of cities to the practice of democratic government. Movement toward that goal would result from improved relations between the schools and other local governments. Fortunately there are some signs of hopeful prospects for closer collaboration.

VII. Suburban Values, Decisions, and Taxes

There are no major defects in public education that can be remedied by providing less money with which to run the enterprise. Rather, the evidence presently available consistently supports the claim that the quality of education, by almost any sensible measure, is likely to be higher where expenditure per student is higher. If education is to be improved, more resources must be channeled to its support.

This chapter is a report on research on community attitudes and decision-making structures that affect local tax support of public education in suburban communities. The findings are of particular relevance for those partisans of public education—school leaders and citizens—who are faced each year with the task of organizing additional fiscal support for education in their communities.

Theoretic Expectations

For each school district in the world of suburbia there is a limited range of alternatives of locally determined tax support for the public schools. The upper and lower limits of that range are set by such hard facts of life as the number of children who attend school, existing personnel and physical plant, taxable resources, state laws establishing minima for educational systems and various types of economic aid, and entrenched traditions about what amounts and kinds of education will be made available. These change through time, but usually not very rapidly. The actual support level established within this range of potentialities by each district each year is critically affected by the perception and evaluation of these facts of life and of various aspects of the school system's performance by those in the district who establish and implement school policies—in effect, by all those whose participation in the decision-making process has some noticeable impact on the final outcome.

Who participate most directly in such decision-making? Much of the time they are individuals or groups who have more than a spectator's concern for and opinions about school support, who are willing to commit some of their own time, energy, and other resources to efforts to shape such decisions. For some this may be an official

This chapter is based on materials prepared by Warner Bloomberg, Jr., and Morris Sunshine.

obligation because they hold positions vested with authority in this area of action; for others it may be the result of belief that school decisions significantly affect their own well-being. At elections, of course, many people manifest an interest in school affairs by expending the small amount of time and effort required to attend an annual district meeting or to vote at a polling place. This is a very attenuated form of participation, and only the cumulated decisions of many individuals determine the outcome. Moreover, their range of choice has already been severely limited by the actions of those involved directly in determining what to submit to referendum. The rest of the decisions are administered ones—quite small numbers of people exercise authority and influence to establish from among a much wider variety of alternatives the policies, practices, and consequent budgets of the school system.

Considerations of this sort suggest a typology of power and interest. There are those who have both an interest in school decisions and the power to back up that interest; and there are those who have no active concern for school affairs nor any significant power resources to utilize. Between these two types are those who have power but lack interest and those who have a manifest concern but lack the power to implement it. These two types represent decision-making potential. If the interests of those who do have power in the community should shift to the sphere of public education, they might well become significant figures in educational decision-making. Similarly, should those who have lacked the ability to pursue their interest in this area achieve the power resources they need, perhaps by organizing with others who share their values, they too might become decision-makers. That is why these last two types constitute a decision-making potential.

The relative dispersion of the population among these four types should, according to available theory, have a significant effect on school tax levels. Thus, local taxes for schools would move toward the upper limit of the range of alternative levels as those individuals and groups who perceive and evaluate the public school system in ways most favorable to increased expenditures commit substantial power resources to the support of this interest. That tendency would be reinforced if in addition those who were unfavorable either lacked power resources or were unwilling to commit them to this sphere of decision-making. Differences between districts in level of local financial support should be explainable in terms of differences in patterns of perception and evaluation, of interest and commitments, and in the distribution and allocation of power resources—taking account, of course, of differences in the range of alternatives open to each district.

Finally, the perceptions and evaluations of the general adult population in each district must be taken into account, not only because budgets and bond issues must be submitted to referenda, but also because the officials and influentials who make the administered decisions try at times to take into account the desires and criticisms of these complex and often diffuse publics. If attitudes favorable to high support levels are widely distributed among the population of the district, the administrative leadership, formal and informal, obviously will have an easier time—other things being equal—in maintaining or raising expenditure levels than if they face an ambivalent or resistant electorate. In the latter case they must seek either to change prevailing attitudes or else to reduce their relevance for decision-making in the sphere of local tax support for the schools.

From a research standpoint this theoretic model of suburbia is thus highly complex. Yet it may seem much too simple and abstract to those who have been caught up in the day-to-day realities of school district decision-making—to those who must live with the inevitable surprises, pleasant and bitter, that accompany involvement in the political process. Nevertheless, very substantial research tasks must be accomplished just to examine those aspects of reality incorporated into this model. For each school district the model requires that research establish:

1. The range of alternative levels of local school financial support open to the community.

2. The actual level established within that range of possibilities for a period of several years.

3. The patterns of participation in community decision-making.

4. The power potentialities of those who do and those who might make school decisions.

5. The perceptions and evaluations of the school system (a) by participants in school decision-making, (b) by the adult inhabitants of the district who only participate in decisions submitted to referenda, and (c) by those with manifest power resources committed to other than school interests—that is, participants in other areas of community decision-making.

If these formidable tasks were accomplished, districts could be compared to see if the real world behaved in the way expected—to see how much events in actual suburbs could be explained by propositions which explain everything about the mythical suburbia of theory.

Research Design

For purposes of measuring community values and power structures four suburban communities were selected for intensive research. It is, of course, apparent that data concerning differences among four school districts are not adequate to justify acceptance or rejection of any generalized explanation of the factors affecting local tax support for schools. Nevertheless, if events in four suburbs did occur as would be expected from the analysis of a hypothetical suburbia, then, at least, there would be some justification for confidence in the theory.

In choosing the places to study, attention was focused on upstate New York, where some eighty suburban school districts were examined. The four chosen for specific study represented an optimum compromise among six criteria:

1. The area should be large enough to be interesting in terms of possibilities for structural complexities.
2. Each suburb should have a rapidly expanding population, with a consequent press on the resources of the school system.
3. The school district should contain at least one central settlement—a village, incorporated or otherwise—of substantial size relative to the total population.
4. The area should have enough of an identity, organizational life, and round of associations among its inhabitants to be clearly separable as a settlement from the central city.
5. Two important different metropolitan areas should be represented—in effect two suburbs should be studied in each of two metropolitan areas.
6. The four suburbs should vary significantly in terms of characteristics indicated in theory and in the literature generally as being important for school support.

The places selected on the basis of these criteria differ with respect to size, the complexity of their boundaries, wealth, ethnicity, religion, school revenues raised by local taxes, and so on. Two, Wonandota and Centerville, are in a metropolitan area with a population of about half a million, and the other two, Leland and Winston, are in an area with somewhat more than two million inhabitants. (These names are fictitious.) The larger metropolitan area is much more industrial and, in terms of property values, wealthier than the smaller.[1]

It was then necessary to devise an index for local tax effort to arrive at a reasonably objective measurement of the supportiveness or effort of each district. This index would measure the relationship between needs and resources in each district and permit comparisons among the districts under study and with other suburban school districts in New York State.

For this purpose the New York State Department of Education's estimate of each district's full value of property per student was taken as an index of that locality's total tax resources available for public expenditure in relation to the need of the school system. The higher a district stood in an array based on this ratio the greater its taxable wealth for each unit of need. The 770 upstate New York school districts were then ranked and an index number assigned to each, to indicate its relative resource potential.

Each district's school tax rate per $1,000 of full value was taken as the index of the actual commitment of available resources to the public school system. The position of each district in the total array of districts indicated its relative resource utilization. A comparison of relative resource potential with relative resource utilization permitted the computation of an index of the district's relative expenditure. The principle operating here is similar to that embodied in the assertion that the poor man who gives $1.00 to a charity may sensibly be considered to be as supportive of that purpose as the rich man who gives $10.00.

The procedure followed thus establishes the rank of each district in terms of relative fiscal effort. Each of the four districts studied was then established as the median case in an array of eleven districts most similar to it in terms of relative resource potential, and the range of these districts for relative expenditure was taken as an estimate of the upper and lower probable limits for the median district. The rank of the district in terms of relative expenditure in this array of eleven districts was taken as an index of its "tax effort," and that level of effort is what the research sought to explain. To eliminate deviant behavior that might be associated with a single year's tax-expenditure experience, patterns were examined for the four year period 1956-57 to 1959-60. This made it possible to characterize the four suburbs under study in terms of their relative supportiveness. One suburb—Wonandota—emerged as a poor area which, during the four year period, was pushing toward the upper limit of relative expenditure for comparable suburbs. One suburb—Winston—is best characterized as a very well-to-do district tending toward the lower limit of relative expenditure for suburban areas with similar resource potential. One suburb—Centerville—oscillated in the array from year to year, while the remaining district—Leland—continually established the upper limit of relative expenditure for suburbs with comparable fiscal resources.

The basic data for the research were derived from interviews with a randomly selected sample of inhabitants at least 21 years of age in each suburb. This group, designated as the random sample, consisted of 80 inhabitants in Wonandota, 100 in Centerville, 87 in Leland, and 97 in Winston.[2]

In addition to the random sample of inhabitants, community decision-makers were likewise selected and interviewed. Interviews were first conducted with especially well informed persons in each community who were asked to identify important community decisions over the preceding five years affecting both schools and other community matters. Informants were interviewed from all institutional sectors of the community. A second much larger round of interviews made it possible to identify participants in a selection of these decisions. After collating and checking the results of these interviews it was possible to identify 99 decision-makers for 20 decisions in Centerville, 76 decision-makers for 20 decisions in Winston, 113 decision-makers for 21 decisions in Wonandota, and 59 decision-makers for 17 decisions in Leland. These decision-makers included both official authorities and informal influentials.

For each community the decisions selected by this interviewing process could be then classified as a school district decision, a town or village decision, or a private or mixed decision. The latter group was made up of such actions as the formation of a united Community Chest, the construction of nonpublic schools, or major private real estate developments.

In order to obtain some measure of individual favorableness to increased school taxes, each person interviewed was asked to indicate which, if any, of a list of school system functions and activities he would be in favor of supporting through a larger local school tax out of his own income. Individuals could then be compared with respect to both the total number of items for which they indicated a willingness to pay taxes and the functions and activities designated by those items. In addition, each person interviewed was asked to rate the various school functions and activities for their basic importance—very important, moderately important, or not very important—without regard for their own tax willingness or the immediate needs of the school district. For these purposes a list of functions and activities presented to each respondent was compiled in terms of 14 specifics, ranging from the construction and maintenance of buildings, to curriculum, to administration, to special classes and extracurricular activities. Each of these also was characterized as an area in which "enough," "not enough," or "too much" was being done, or an area about which the respondent felt unable to make a judgment ("don't know").

From each respondent, both for the random sample and for decision-makers, detailed information was secured on social characteristics, including occupation, home ownership, ethnic background, community involvement, income, geographical mobility, and family background. Thirty-four specific social characteristics were included in the interview schedule.

The principal statistical technique employed in the analysis of this mass of interview data was factor analysis. This technique permits the delineation of clusters of responses from a large number and variety of observations. A factor consists of a set of empirical variables that fit together statistically and that can be designated in terms of a single more abstract variable. Factor analysis thus permits the measurement and description of groups of responses.[3]

Not all of the results from the analysis of this very large mass of data can be reported and discussed here. Therefore attention will be directed only to those community characteristics and leadership patterns that are most closely related to local fiscal support for education.

Strategic Alternatives

Alternatives of strategy open to partisans of the public schools involve a consideration of three variables: (1) the power resources of school leaders relative to others involved, and how efficiently this potential is employed; (2) the values and goals of school leaders—how favorable their attitudes are with respect to seeking greater local tax effort; and (3) the attitudinal favorableness of citizens at large. By means of a mechanical metaphor, illustrated in Figure 2, the policy import of the relationships among these three variables can be explicated in a convenient, if overly simple way. The figure shows relationships among these three variables and the relative expenditure of a district, which locates it somewhere between the top and bottom alternative levels of relative expenditure for districts of that resource potential and thereby establishes its status for tax effort. The ends of the lines making up the figure are tagged with a plus and a minus to signify favorable and unfavorable directions. The ball on the incline represents current tax assessments on full property value relative to the size of the school enrollment. The higher the ball on the incline, of course, the closer this utilization of local resources is to the pragmatic maximum tax effort for districts of that level of property wealth.

FIGURE 2
DETERMINANTS OF LOCAL TAX EFFORT

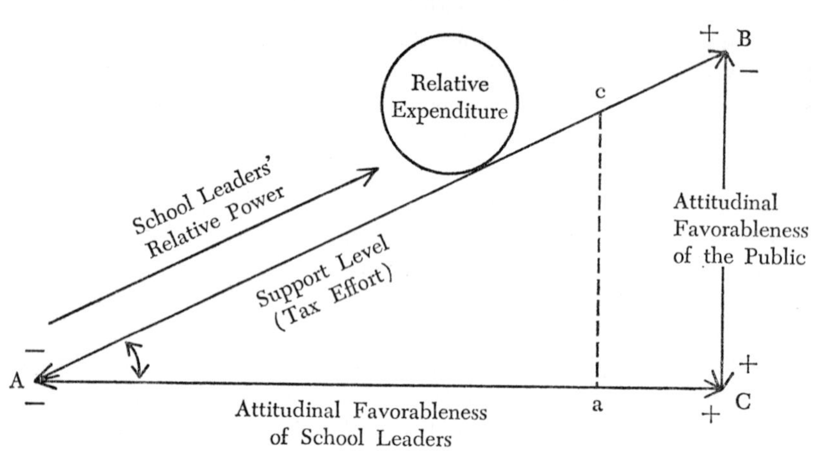

The line ac indicates that the attitudes of the school leaders, to be located for favorableness on line AC, serve to set a limit on how far along the tax effort continuum the district could be pushed if there were no resistance whatever to the power of the school leaders. It also shows the "distance" between their aspirations, as indexed by attitudinal favorableness, and the actual level of relative expenditure. The length of the line AB represents the total distance between top and bottom alternative levels of relative expenditure, indexed as described above. The slope of the line portrays the resistance faced by school leaders, which is determined essentially by the attitudes of the public, represented by the length of the line BC. This mechanical analogy makes it clear that the amount of power required to move the tax ball is a function of the angle BAC, or, more simply, the length of the line BC. If the citizens of the district have very unfavorable attitudes, line BC is lengthened, thereby increasing the slope and increasing the amount of power which school leaders would have to be able to apply to boost school taxes.

The contents of this metaphor, of course, do not exhaust all the strategic possibilities open to supporters of the public schools. For example, a district might significantly improve its educational quality by focusing most of its efforts on the efficient employment of its available funds rather than by pressing for more tax dollars. Or efforts might be made to shift more of the local school costs to state or federal budgets. Finally, school leaders whose power is limited might try to deploy their power more efficiently. All of these possibilities are not conveyed by the figure. Moreover, the identification of optimum strategies, given the variables under discussion, is made difficult because one cannot speak with certainty about the relative manipulability of the variables, nor say with certainty which variables will have long-run rather than short-run consequences.

It is possible that in the short run school leaders might well try to increase their power by seeking more active support from other community leaders. But this apparently simple proposal proves to harbor hidden complexities. First, it may prove quite difficult to involve those active in local village and town politics because these individuals may not believe any laurels are to be won in the educational sphere. Second, it is not safe to assume that nonschool leaders are always more favorable toward schools than the average citizen. Thus, closer affiliation poses some risks as well as offering opportunities. Co-opting such influentials might improve their attitudes and the coupling of power resources could be beneficial. On the other hand, if they are less favorable to increased tax effort than the public to start with, and remain so, to mobilize their interest in the local schools would be to create a resistive faction within the ranks of school decision-makers.

Moreover, in contemplating possibilities for increasing power potential the question must always be raised: What power base is to be expanded with what anticipated consequences? Would the recruiting of nonschool leaders into the ranks of the active partisans of the school system extend control over the information reaching the public or increase the acceptance of the official view of the revenue needs and tax resources of the district, or would it be a means of reducing the likelihood that opposition to increased tax support would become effectively organized? In addition, would not those who presently specialize in participation in making school decisions then be obligated to involve themselves in efforts to enlarge support for the other branches of local government? Such questions, unfortunately, are in an area of inquiry where little validated knowledge exists. All strategies for increasing informal power resources by adding to the ranks of school partisans those who have the appropriate social characteristics are at present highly speculative. The social science literature dealing with techniques for increasing either power bases or the efficiency with which power resources are used has yet to prove itself an effective substitute for the doctrines and intuitions of those actually involved in decision-making. However, such variations in power resources as were delineated by this research, other than the authority of school decision-makers among the four suburbs, had no relationship whatever to the suburb's rank for local tax effort.

There is one type of power, however, which is somewhat more amenable to assessment—authority. School leaders, as either short-range or long-run strategy, might try to increase the authority they have to determine local taxes. Of course, such a suggestion has serious implications for the whole philosophy of local democracy in school districts. There are practical political problems, since school board authority in large measure is prescribed by state laws and administrative regulations. Strategies for increasing the power of school leaders relative to the rest of the community thus seem either extremely uncertain in any cause-and-effect sense, or extremely unlikely.

A second element in strategy considerations is the level of local tax effort sought by the school leaders and the consequences of that goal in each district. In Leland, school leaders, deeply concerned about high taxes and believing they faced extensive community resistance, were unwilling to press for higher taxes. At the same time, they had not been able to find acceptable ways to reduce the level of tax effort. In Centerville the administration was not willing to attempt to sustain a high level of effort, not because it sensed resistance, but because it didn't want to spoil a good thing. The administration had the most favorable public with respect to taxes and even overestimated its favorableness, but preferred a slow, long-run gain in tax support not likely to reduce that supportive mood. In Wonandota, on the other hand, the school leaders apparently felt that the district had accepted a heavy tax burden for too long, that people were school-tax-weary; they shared with the public and the nonschool decision-makers a desire for a rest. Indeed, during the four years indexed, the district's relative expenditure increased less than in most suburbs of similar property value so that they slipped downward a little in tax effort. In Winston, on the other hand, school leaders faced a well-to-do community that rejected their efforts to bring its school tax burden up to the level typical of suburbs of that wealth. Not even the public in Wonandota is as resistive in its attitudes toward tax increases for the schools as that in Winston.

What can be said of these different policies, each considered in its own setting? Should the leaders in Leland stop trying to get down from the top rank for tax burden in suburbs of its class just because the public is not as unfavorable in its attitudes as they thought? This public, though sustaining more favorable attitudes than in Wonandota and Winston, nonetheless expressed frustration at its tax burden by voting out two administrations in six years. How long should the leaders go on trimming down the tax effort in Wonandota? How should they balance a professional view of school needs against a politically wise sensitivity to community attitudes? Has the Centerville leadership been oversensitive on this score? Perhaps they should risk a somewhat heavier tax press on the community, given its unusually receptive attitudes toward tax increases. And what of Winston? Should school leaders there reduce their official aspirations for local revenues for the school system until they finally get them down low enough to satisfy the public? What kind of a cut-rate budget might secure such contentment when the citizens in this suburb already perceive a lower than typical tax effort as extremely burdensome?

No research whose results have thus far been made public provides a basis for objective answers to these difficult questions. What can be provided, however, is some additional detail on the sources of the attitudes of the public. And such information is important for policy and for strategy on two grounds. First, any long-run improvement in attitudes toward local tax effort will, to return to the mechanical metaphor, reduce the slope of the plane representing the resistance against which school leaders must deploy their various kinds of power resources. Such a gain is especially desirable since it means that less over-all effort would have to be devoted to overcoming community resistance, facilitating a greater and more secure preoccupation with educational issues *per se*. Second, in attempting to bring about any long-run improvement in attitudes school leaders must know what they are up against. Are the values of a community merely reflections of its social structure, and thus likely to change only as underlying economic and demographic factors are altered? Are tactics which worked well in one suburb likely to be equally effective in another, or must each school district have its own unique strategy?

There are three relevant questions that can be examined here: (1) To what extent are an individual's attitudes toward the local school system likely to be predetermined by his social characteristics? (2) How critical are the differences in attitudinal patterns and their determinants among the four school districts? (3) What are some salient possibilities for changing attitudes?

The Social Determinants of Educational Values

That differences in opinions are associated with variations in such social characteristics as age, sex, occupation, income, education, and the like has been demonstrated by countless surveys. General explanations of these patterns are, on the other hand, both rare and incomplete. The needed theory of the social determinants of values will not be set forth here, but it will be made clear that existing value patterns are not tightly bound into the social structure and therefore appear to be amenable to deliberate change.

To explore these relationships the social characteristics of both leaders and the random sample were correlated with attitudinal dimensions for each of the four suburbs. The thiry-four social characteristics described above were employed for this purpose. Two attitudinal dimensions were used—judgments about the importance of school functions and willingness to pay taxes.

These correlations did not reveal any overarching patterns of association between social characteristics and attitudes. The values of the public are not extensively or consistently predetermined by income, education, religion, number of children, or similar characteristics. Moreover, there is no apparent relationship between a school district's rank for relative expenditure or tax effort and the extent to which social characteristics and attitudes are correlated. Suburbs can vary substantially in the extent to which educational values are influenced by social characteristics, and this implies that care should be taken in generalizing to particular communities. Moreover, it is clear that it is inaccurate and misleading to speak about the correlation between social characteristics and willingness to pay higher school taxes. A much more complex pattern must be specified by taking into account the particular social characteristic, the type of program for which the taxes are to be spent, and the special characteristics of the school district.

This analysis provides general support for the argument that connections between the facets of the social structure dealt with in this research and educational attitudes are weak. This provides some basis for optimism about deliberately trying to change such attitudes.

An additional statistical technique (analysis of variance) provides an answer to this question: are attitudinal differences associated with community of residence, occupational prestige, and participation in community decision-making processes, and do these three predictors operate separately or conjointly to produce attitudinal differences?

The application of this technique reveals that tax attitudes are more predictable, in terms of these variables, than attitudes toward the importance of school functions. Occupational prestige, the best single indicator of social level, turns out to have very limited effectiveness as a predictor of underlying values. The analysis shows that there is more of an overarching consensus about what is most important among a public school system's functions and activities than about what should be supported by more taxes. However, school leaders are most likely to consider the central teaching function very important, followed by nonschool leaders, and then by the general public. School leaders also are most likely to view auxiliary teaching services as very important, with nonschool leaders and the public rating them in about the same way. Individuals with blue-collar occupations are more likely than the white-collar person to regard the nonteaching services and functions as of top importance.

The only other basic attitude affected by occupational prestige is willingness to support modern educational services through higher taxes; individuals with blue-collar occupations are more opposed to increased taxes for this purpose than those with white-collar jobs. This dimension of tax attitudes also is affected by community of residence and by participation status, with school leaders once again most supportive. They are also most willing to support through more taxes the basic school functions, another attitudinal dimension along which the four suburbs differ significantly. Variation in tax willingness for school-provided community services is associated with the interaction of all three predictor variables. This kind of interaction between variables also is found with respect to willingness to pay for auxiliary school services.

Some of the results of the analysis of variance could have been anticipated from preceding analyses, especially the effect of the community of residence variable. Once again systematic community differences in commitments to higher taxes are established. However, the rank order of the four communities for tax willingness is not uniform across the four tax factors, and the community of residence variable sometimes operates in concert with occupational prestige and participation status. These complexities defy theoretical explanation at this time, emphasizing the hazards of the transition from data to broad generalizations about policy. The same can be said of the effects associated with occupation and participation.

In general, then, the analysis indicates that social characteristics operate quite unevenly in determining attitudes. They do condition tax willingness judgments more often than judgments about the basic importance of school functions.

While these data clearly are not unequivocal in their implications, three conclusions would seem to be in order: first, the frequent assertion that educational values are directly derivative from individual social traits is both oversimple in form and incorrect in content. Social determinants of educational values can sensibly be discussed only if sufficient particulars are taken into account. This does not mean they can be disregarded. While attitudes appear to be subject to extensive change within any given social structural context, strategies for bringing about such changes must take into account whatever degree of constraint on attitudes that may obtain in each district because of the social characteristics of its citizenry.

Second, the data underscore the presence of district peculiarities. From a policy standpoint, this means that local school leaders should carefully assess the potentialities and obstacles present in their own districts rather than relying on general formulations or doctrines for action, or on case studies of other districts. It is not too difficult or expensive to regularly sample school district opinion, and such information could provide a sounder basis for effective strategy.

A third conclusion which is consistent with this analysis is that direct involvement with school matters promotes favorable fiscal attitudes. This argument derives from the fact that school decision-makers regularly had more favorable attitudes than nonschool decision-makers or the general public. Even if school leaders were more favorable to start with—a point on which no data were available—involvement would sustain and strengthen such attitudes. This suggests that school leaders might seriously consider trying to expand the ranks of school decision-makers in their own district, with school boards developing policies promoting more of a participative than a merely plebiscitarian form of school district democracy. This means broadening participation in administrative decision-making, not just in elections. The formation of a lay advisory committee and activation of the PTA are only small steps in this direction. The problem is not one of instituting more bake sales, or increasing the size of the regular school reports from two to four pages, or establishing more committees to receive and transmit board policy to the general public. What needs to be done is to find new ways to engage many more local citizens and local nonschool leaders in school matters.

Each of the random samples in the four districts was examined separately in order (1) to determine more precisely their underlying attitudes toward school functions, and (2) to establish the extent to which there were clusters of like-minded people, or "publics," within the general public. Specifically, an assessment was made of the average person's judgment about the importance of school functions, his judgment of the current adequacy of school programs, and his expressed willingness to pay higher taxes.

Two procedures were employed to identify underlying value patterns and attitudinally similar groups in each district that could be thought of as publics with potentially different responses to school issues likely to arise in most districts. The first procedure was factor analysis, with each district analyzed separately. The underlying attitudinal structures of the four districts were then compared. The second procedure involved the use of a scalogram board. This is a device which permits display of the responses of individuals to test items. The columns of the board are the items, and the rows are individuals. Each row consists of fourteen squares (plastic cubes) whose colors indicate the individual's response to each item (school function). By a judicious shifting of columns (guided by the factor analysis) and rows the board is progressively organized so that individuals with similar attitudinal profiles are adjacent to each other. The result is a graphic portrayal of the attitudinal configurations of the district.

These analyses reveal how extensive is the opposition to higher taxes, whatever the underlying attitudes and environmental pressures may be. Only one-third to two-fifths of the respondents (the exact proportion varies from district to district) express a willingness to pay higher taxes for more than one of the fourteen functions and activities of school systems. Only about 10 per cent in each district see themselves as willing to support with higher taxes as many as three or four items. Among these most supportive individuals there are few clear-cut publics in the sense of consensual clusters.

In every district noticeable segments of the population expressed a willingness to support by higher taxes just one school program. In Leland such individuals most frequently favored special classes for the retarded and for the most talented, or the upgrading of teachers in terms of training and experience, or the development of recreational facilities. In Wonandota such persons were most likely to approve of recreational facilities or the construction and maintenance of school buildings; special classes, the training of teachers, and buildings were items which cracked the otherwise solid antitax barrier in Winston; and in Centerville special classes were most likely to be approved by those indicating willingness to pay higher taxes for one item only.

These detailed analyses of the value patterns in each district emphasize the magnitude and complexity of the problem of determining how best to work with or to attempt to change established value patterns. The findings appear to have these important implications:

1. If by a public one means a group of persons agreeing on what is important, needed, and worth paying for, such publics hardly exist among those inclined to have the more favorable attitudes toward the schools in the four suburbs studied. The only large number of individuals displaying such across-the-board consensus are those who consider relatively few functions to be very important, who see little or nothing about which more needs to be done, and who don't want to pay another nickel in taxes for anything connected with the schools. For the remainder of the population, the structure of values seems to lack coherency and articulation.

2. Speaking generally, it appears easiest to build up a supportive public around the importance of the basic functions, but as auxiliary and other school services are added, more and more people begin to "get off," their getting-off place being determined by the location of psychological boundary lines in terms of what is absolutely essential to education, what is highly desirable but not essential, and what is neither especially desirable nor essential. The data for all four districts tend to confirm the belief that most people have, by comparison with contemporary professional standards, a rather narrow conception of essential educational services.

3. The lack of any sizable groups who agree on improvements that ought to be made in the school system is evidence of the general inadequacy of the efforts of school leaders to make their case for the needs of the district known and accepted. The magnitude of this attitudinal gulf between the professional educators and their school district constituencies can hardly be exaggerated.

4. The frequency of favorable judgments received by any one specific school function or activity tends to be associated with the nature of the basic underlying attitude. For example, in Winston any program which is perceived as a part of a package of school-provided community services is not likely to be rated as very important.

The import of these similarities for strategies aimed at sustaining or increasing local tax effort will be considered below. First, however, it is important to examine one especially salient implication of the differences among the four districts. These differences fall into five categories: variations in number of people who have favorable attitudes, variations in the popularity of particular school programs, variations in the extent to which "publics" are identifiable, variations in basic underlying attitudes, and finally, variations in the way specific school programs are linked with underlying attitudes. All of these district-to-district variations are underscored in the data. Even if general lines of attack on the problem of attitudinal resistance are possible, the district-to-district differences suggest that they would have to be adapted to what is particular to each district.

This means that school system partisans must make more systematic and extensive efforts to locate the social and individual determinants at work in their own communities. The research that can be mounted by suburban school leaders, either by themselves or with professional guidance, may be limited in some respects, but it could improve substantially the information on which they could base the development of policy and strategy. Comparative studies can provide guidelines for action by indicating important variables and their probable relationships. But the application of any generalization to the particular case requires knowing the magnitudes of those variables and their relationships in the particular district.

Attitudes and Programs

School leaders need such information in making decisions involving three interrelated elements of strategy. In the long run they should seek to sustain favorable attitudes and to improve them where they are unfavorable. In the short run they must seek to obtain the best level of local tax support that existing attitudinal patterns permit and facilitate. Finally, they must consider the impact of short-run strategies on the long-run goal of developing and maintaining a more favorable attitudinal climate in the district. These three aspects will be considered one at a time, but their interdependence is also significant.

Many studies of attitudes have produced evidence showing that the presence of one attitude predisposes the individual to a second attitude, and that attitudes are frequently interrelated and form clusters. For example, people who strongly advocate restricting government expenditure usually prefer local to national governmental action and oppose extension of governmental services into any areas previously preempted by private enterprise or voluntary associations. Here specific attitudes are clearly interrelated. This interrelatedness, however, can usefully be thought of as deriving from a basic underlying attitude—conservatism. With respect to school support, it follows that successful long-run strategy for increasing willingness to pay higher school taxes must take into account how this attitude is dependent on other specific attitudes and on the basic underlying commitments of the individual to particular complexes of school functions and activities.

The findings here suggest that people tend to find inadequate performance among those items they consider to be very important, and that if they express a willingness to pay higher taxes at all, they tend to select for more tax support from among those functions and activities where more needs to be done. As might be expected, there is a tendency for a much larger proportion of those with the more favorable combination of attitudes to be willing to accept greater tax burdens.

This suggests how important it is for school system partisans to have systematic knowledge of the attitudes of their fellow citizens. If a substantial majority believe that major items in a school budget are very important but that enough is being done, campaigns should concentrate on the latter point. On the other hand, pleas for more to be done with respect to one or another function are likely to be premature if that function is considered to be of high importance by only a small segment of the general population. Indeed, by underscoring a gulf between the values of school leaders and those of the general public, such a campaign could boomerang and activate latent discontent and frustration. Thus, in contemplating possibilities for improving the attitudinal climate, school leaders must anticipate a two-stage process: first, less favorable dispositions must be changed into more favorable ones; second, the transformation of favorable dispositions into actual acceptance of tax burdens must be strengthened where it is weak.

How can attitudes best be affected in ways strengthening local receptivity to school taxes? This is a mysterious realm replete with prejudice and propaganda, which so many have tried to explore and yet which still remains largely unmapped terrain. Nevertheless, some observations are in order.

It would appear that the general public tends to perceive school functions and activities in terms of a few broad categories rather than with respect to discrete items, and that particular functions and activities tend to be viewed as elements of such categories. Also, the favorableness of a group toward a particular item will usually reflect its evaluation of the underlying variable.

Evidence from these four suburbs shows that over-all there is greatest expressed willingness to support basic school functions and modern educational services with more taxes, least willingness to support school-community services. It should also be noted that basic and modern school functions encompass items which generally rank higher for the number of people evaluating them as being very important and in need of greater accomplishment. However, the theory that the proportion saying "yes" to higher taxes for a given program is a simple function of the underlying attitude (factor) which that program ties into is not a perfect one, for these proportions vary considerably within factors and there are percentage overlaps between factors.

This qualification to the notion of underlying attitudes as determinants of tax willingness has implications for both long-range and short-run strategies. If in a rapidly expanding district school leaders foresee the need for a substantial increase in administrative personnel, a psychological foundation can be laid, not by focusing on each particular, immediate need for this or that kind of additional supervision, but by emphasizing the implications of administration for the carrying out of basic school functions. Clearly, people tend to view teachers as much more relevant to the basic educational activity of the schools than administrators, who may still be captives of traditional stereotypes of the custodial function.

More tangible than the portrayal of the components of a school budget is the actual distribution of school revenues among the various functions and activities. The low value placed on community services suggests that a well publicized deemphasis of these least favored items could do much to placate some of the frustration and hostility which is often widespread among suburban taxpayers. This strategy may mean a long delay in further expansion of the school as the central institution of suburbia, but the alternative may be budgets which, though models of certain professional aspirations, become victims of very refractory political and psychological realities.

While long-run strategies may seek to revise the attitudinal profiles of school districts, the problem in the short run is how best to operate within the existing attitudinal environment. Of course, each campaign can have an important impact on the continuing emergence of community values, and that by-product should not be forgotten. Short-run campaigns can be thought of as embodying mainly one of several types of strategy:

1. School leaders can press for an "all or nothing" response from the public. In this instance, the whole school program as developed by the existing decision-makers can be made *the* issue. Individuals then are either for or against in an unselective way. Given the number of largely satisfied individuals inclined to support at most only

one or two functions with more taxes, this strategy would seem to maximize the likelihood that tax increases, even for undoubtedly excellent programs, would be defeated.

2. Partisans of the school system can emphasize fulfillment of immediate needs on a one-at-a-time basis. For example, major campaigns can be mounted on behalf of one and then another particular function or activity—special classes one year, increased teaching staff another, buildings a third. Such a concentrated effort might succeed in any one year in putting over even a less favored proposal, although opponents have all too frequently managed to defeat budgets by using the same strategy, focusing attention on some one item to which resistance was already evident.

3. A third alternative is to build each year's campaign around the concern for underlying attitudes and the attitudinal profiles of various "sub-publics." This means that school leaders must first ascertain the basic evaluative frameworks around which public opinion tends to be constructed. The rhetoric of the campaign can then be cast in terms which reflect these orientations in the community. This strategy, more than either of the preceding two, facilitates the development of optimum compromises between professional goals and community preferences. First, by focusing commitment on broad areas of school function it would reduce irrational preoccupation with particular components of the total budget. Second, by forcing school decision-makers to examine the place of each major budget item in local attitudinal configurations it would facilitate judgments about the degree of opposition likely to be generated by pressing for one or another program.

Such an approach also promotes efforts to direct messages to the identifiable consensual clusters within the community, addressing each in terms especially relevant to their attitudinal profiles. For example, those with white-collar occupations are likely to hold nonteaching services and functions less important than will the blue-collar category, but the latter appear less willing to pay more taxes for modern educational services than the former. Again, attempts can be made to persuade each sub-public built up around support for one particular function to see it as but one item inseparably linked into a complex of interrelated functions. This is analogous to the efforts of parents who attempt to cultivate cosmopolitan food tastes in their children by urging that the one who enjoys chicken chop suey and the other who likes egg foo yong both realize that these are but specific instances of "Chinese" food, and that they should go on to appreciate many other dishes in this category. If successful, in time one can cultivate a generally receptive approach to foreign foods. Thus, to those who assert a willingness to pay higher taxes for more teachers, but nothing else, campaign materials might well present this sort of argument: (1) the one big reason for hiring more teachers is to provide each child with a sound basic educational experience; (2) such an adequate number of teachers cannot be put to proper use unless each teacher has a room to teach in, and the kind of room which facilitates rather than impedes the instruction of the children; and (3) only with effective administration can all of these necessary teachers go about their work with maximum efficiency. In sum, to hire the needed number of teachers and then to reduce their productivity by inadequate working conditions both wastes the taxpayer's money and defeats the purpose of those willing to pay more taxes to employ more teachers—namely, a sound education for the children, the basic function of the school system.

Obviously, efforts should be undertaken to develop this third approach. It dovetails nicely with the proposals for a long-range program to improve the attitudinal climate at the same time that, in the short run, it maximizes favorable values and seeks to minimize and evade the consequences of unfavorable values. The pay-off of such an approach should compensate for the many problems and difficulties which accompany it. Of these, the costs and complexities of the requisite research should not be too difficult to overcome. If individual districts worked collaboratively with the research arm of the department of education in each state and with interested universities, there is every reason to expect that satisfactory instruments to delineate underlying attitudes and consensual clusters could be developed and continuously improved. Data analysis also could be the function of organizations with the requisite facilities, such as state departments and universities, while each district would take responsibility for gathering the data at regular intervals and deciding upon the implications of the findings for future action.

There is another very important point which school leaders should take into account when formulating strategies to work for local tax support within the existing attitudinal milieu and at the same time to seek to improve it. It appears that opposition to increased taxes for the schools is part of a general opposition to allocating more local resources to local government. All respondents were asked to evaluate fourteen functions of town and village government in the same three ways that school system functions and activities were judged. As willingness to pay more taxes for town and village government increased, so did willingness to support in this way the local school system. Examination of the data for leaders and nonleaders within each community revealed that this linear trend was fairly consistent in each population. Thus, it would seem that those who seek more local tax support for the public schools should not think of themselves as in competition with the partisans of town and village government; both groups are in the same not very secure boat. The problem, properly understood, is not how to cut the pie, but how to make the total pie bigger. The development of coordinate strategies for both short-run and long-run improvements in local tax effort for both schools and town and village governments is indicated.

One problem confronting any effort to utilize or alter existing attitudes is the difficulty of controlling the reception and interpretation of the messages which school system partisans must issue in trying to inform and persuade the various audiences (consensual clusters, sub-publics). Many studies of the various mass media and of both political propaganda and consumer marketing campaigns have revealed that those on the receiving end are selectively attentive, disregarding much of what they hear and see, that they are capable of reinterpreting to the point of extensive distortion the messages they receive, and that they tend to adopt the views current among their informal associates, especially those who hold the status of opinion leaders, in spite of the flow of argument and information directed at them. This does not mean that campaigns have no impact; it does mean that the magnitude and exact direction of the effects of efforts to change attitudes are difficult to predict.

It is somewhat ironic that partisans are always their own best audiences: Democrats and Republicans listen most attentively and least critically to the spokesmen of their own parties. It is therefore not surprising that the analysis here reveals that the most favorable groups from an attitudinal point of view are those involved in making school decisions. Those who are favorable are likely to become involved; those who become involved are likely to become more favorable in their attitudes. In fact, there is some evidence to suggest that even those who become involved because of hostile attitudes tend to become somewhat more favorable after continued participation.

Involvement is thus emphasized, not merely as an antidote to apathy, but as an educational process. People who are sympathetic to the school system thereby discover that they are not alone. They also learn that knowledge must be coordinated with sympathy to institute intelligent action. As long as educational theory and institutional doctrines continue their rapid development, it is unlikely that anything less than regular contact with the school can enable a person to evaluate alternative lines of action realistically and sensibly.

It is not reasonable to expect that the addition of another dozen or two dozen individuals to the decision-making ranks will affect generally held community values. Minor variations in number of school decision-makers among the four suburbs were not correlated with rank for tax effort. Participation appears to offer an effective means of changing values if—and only if—some kinds of major institutional innovations are made to vastly increase the numbers directly involved in decision-making. Obviously, it is not possible to devise practical arrangements whereby thousands could participate in administrative decision-making; but it is possible to so contrive this decision-making process that those directly engaged would number in the hundreds. The existence of such a cadre of informed, involved, attitudinally committed citizens, many able to serve informally as opinion leaders among their friends where school affairs are concerned, could have a profound effect on the attitudinal environment of the school district.

The program of continuing research into local attitudes can itself serve as a form of citizen participation. The conversation between interviewer and respondent, in which the former takes the latter seriously and which requires that serious attention be given the subject at hand, is an ideal format for stimulating involvement in local school affairs. The kinds of questions asked, the areas of school activity pointed to, the regions of ignorance revealed, the vague opinion clarified—all of these aspects of an interview could aid school system partisans in their efforts to reduce the attitudinal resistance of the community to pressure for greater revenues for the schools through local taxes.

Some Speculation on Alternatives

This research on four suburban school districts does not, by any means, answer all the questions that could be asked about community attitudes and school support. In fact, more questions have been raised than could be disposed of. Nevertheless, this research does suggest a variety of possibilities for action and innovation.

First, important changes in the power structure should not be neglected as a possible approach. The suburbs studied here did not vary significantly in this regard and yet displayed major differences in their levels of relative expenditure and tax effort. This may be interpreted to mean that small adjustments in the local power base of school partisans, such as a wider representation of school personnel in civic clubs, or a more comradely relationship between the superintendent and the district's businessmen's groups, are not likely to be of much consequence. Giving the school board legal authority to develop and implement budgets without the consent of the local electorate would be an innovation of significant magnitude. So would placing the determination of district tax rates in the hands of the state legislature. And so would the proposal that school decision-making processes be modified in ways that would engage as direct participants hundreds instead of dozens of citizens.

A second kind of change involving power relationships is indicated by the suggestion that some strenuous reappraisal be undertaken of the school's involvement in those functions which are regarded most negatively by a large proportion of the local citizenry. The question here is not whether such functions should be met by government, but whether or not the school system should be used to meet them; supporting unfavorable activities may so weaken the attitudinal favorableness of large parts of the citizenry as to prevent the fulfillment of the major obligations of the school system. Suburban schools especially have tended to take on more and more functions, partly because of the inadequacies of local village and town governmental structures and leadership, partly because of the philosophy, espoused by some educational professionals, that views the school as the central institution of the local community. There is reason to believe that expansion of school budgets might be looked upon with greater favor if leisure time were provided for by a recreation commission—be it village, township, or county; if public health were attended to by an agency with that one function—which might well have its personnel service the schools; even library facilities might be maintained by a system that could share in the space of each school building but not in the school district's budget. Though the total dollar savings for the school system might be relatively small, the resulting assurance that all locally raised revenues voted for the schools went to educational activities *per se* might well diminish some of the existing attitudinal resistance to increasing tax demands.

Many school leaders resist all such suggestions on the grounds that previous experience demonstrates that the quality of the fulfillment of the function will be lowered, sometimes drastically, if it is placed in the hands of other governmental agencies. Unfortunately, they seldom consider how the school system, with its professional staff and resources, could aid in the strengthening of the other branches of local government in suburbia. This approach would also lead to an interpenetration of concerns and decision-making activities by school and nonschool leaders, which would appear to be highly desirable. It also should be noted that such innovations do not require any immediate major restructuring of local government. They can be accomplished in largest part without "metropolitanizing" or otherwise remapping the territorial distribution of obligations and authority. Obviously there would be difficulties and dangers in this approach, but the difficulties and dangers of the status quo are, if anything, increasing.

Improved internal practices, better "human relations," more rational organization, and more accurate perceptions of the environment all undoubtedly have some desirable consequences for the effectiveness with which an organization performs its tasks at present, but there is no convincing evidence that such accomplishments have any sort of direct impact on the evolution of community values. In the course of this research the extent to which the school board and its superintendent within each district displayed consensus with respect to the importance and effectiveness of school functions and how well they could predict the responses of the general public were both examined. Though there were interesting variations among the four districts, they did not correlate with either differences in values or levels of tax effort. Meanwhile, there is danger that one or another nostrum will have enough appeal to stimulate illusory efforts which prove to be digressions from, rather than attacks on, the main issues. For example, in a district that is relatively starved for sheer fiscal wherewithal, an emphasis on the nonmonetary aspects of educational quality may be illusory, for many of the techniques for maximizing quality simply require something more than a bargain-basement budget.

Nevertheless, the difficulties of all these lines of action emphasize the attractiveness of any possible gains in educational productivity—of means for obtaining greater quantity and quality in public school task performance with available revenues. Awareness of the necessary revenue base for improving quality does not detract from the desirability of such efforts.

Finally, there is an apparent need for better scientific theory about human conduct. Perhaps what appear to be the most critical determinants of local tax support—community values—may turn out to be as refractory to efforts to reshape them as they have been to efforts to describe and analyze them. Nevertheless, research is too important to be left entirely in the hands of professionals. It is a kind of action in which school and nonschool leaders, professionals and laymen, public school educators and university personnel can all collaborate and from which each can gain useful knowledge. The conduct of such research in a community can focus the public's attention on relevant school problems. If the research were a survey, both interviewers and respondents might be stimulated to consider questions which otherwise might pass them by. And the publication of many locally performed studies can provide springboards for action in each district, as well as contributing data essential for broad generalizations.

VIII. State and Local Tax Support

The history of the public finances of the United States suggests that, short of major depressions and wars, patterns of intergovernmental fiscal relations and the character of tax structures change but slowly. The depression of the 1930's did, of course, bring a redefinition of the national government's fiscal role. World War II brought a sudden and dramatic increase in the importance of individual and corporate income taxes in the total tax structure. For over twenty years military outlays have dominated national government expenditures. But in times of relative peace and stability fiscal patterns are modified slowly. The structure of taxation and the division of fiscal responsibility among levels of government have remained relatively stable since the end of World War II.

As for the fiscal support of public education, the stability of intergovernmental patterns is illustrated in Table 4. The decade of the 1920's, for example, brought no changes in the relative roles of the three levels of government. The depression and war years did increase the relative role of the states, but between 1950 and 1960 state support of public elementary and secondary education was virtually unchanged. The recent heightened concern over the adequacy of education, typically dated from the Sputnik launching of 1957, has not contributed to stronger proportionate fiscal support of public education by the states, only to modestly stronger national support.

TABLE 4
Governmental Support for Public Education
(selected years)

	(Per cent of Total)		
School Year Ending	Federal	State	Local
1920	0.3	16.5	83.2
1930	0.4	16.9	82.7
1940	1.8	30.3	67.9
1950	2.8	39.8	57.4
1960	4.4	39.1	56.5

SOURCE: U.S. Bureau of the Census, *Historical Statistics of the United States* (Washington, 1960), 208; preliminary data for 1960 from Office of Education, *Biennial Survey of Education, 1959-60* (from correspondence).

Since fiscal change comes slowly, it is not reasonable to anticipate that tax structures to support public education will alter drastically in the immediate future. Even if the Congress should enact a program of general aid to public education, the amounts involved for a number of years ahead are likely to be modest in relation to total outlays. Therefore, in all likelihood, there will be continued heavy dependence on both general state revenues for state aid to education and on local revenues derived predominantly from the property tax.

No fiscal revolutions are in sight. The economic, political, and social forces that will establish patterns of public need and shape attitudes toward taxpaying are very largely those forces now in being. Urbanization will continue to dominate local government finance, and the states and the national government will adapt their programs belatedly but continuously to encompass urban needs. Tax bases in metropolitan areas will continue to be fragmented by a multiplicity of separate governments. Competition among these governments and among state governments for fiscal advantage will prevail. Business firms will persist in their efforts to shift tax burdens toward other segments of the community. Trade unions will oppose sales taxes; homeowners will oppose property taxes. The nondefense public sector will continue to increase modestly as a proportion of total economic activity. These are the forces that shaped and structured state and local public finances in the 1950's and early 1960's, and they are likely to dominate for the remainder of this decade.

This chapter necessarily centers major attention on the property tax—a tax which continues, year after year, to bring in the major portion of revenue needed for the support of local governments and hence for the support of public education. An examination of the recent and remarkable behavior of the property tax is of central concern here. There are two other general sources of state and local support for public education which will be examined in less detail. The first of these is general state revenue—the source of support for grants-in-aid to local school districts. The second consists of local nonproperty taxes which have offered some incidental revenue support to public education in recent years.

The Property Tax

The property tax is a complicated affair. Its economic effects are difficult to measure; its administration is frequently haphazard; its future, as a part of state-local revenue structures, is often questioned. Nevertheless, this "backbone of local finance" continues, in the nation as a whole, to be the most important source of revenue for the aggregate of counties, municipalities, school districts and other special governmental units.

The relative importance of the tax varies greatly among the states. In 1958, for the 48 states, the property tax provided 88 per cent of all local taxes, but in Alabama this ratio was 57 per cent and in Connecticut it was 99 per cent. Local taxes, of course, are not the whole of local revenue, since the latter includes state and federal aid. In 1958 the property tax for the aggregate of states made up almost exactly one-half of all local general revenue (borrowing excluded), but in Alabama the ratio was only 18 per cent and in New Hampshire it was 82 per cent.[1]

Character of the Tax

The property tax varies among states in the base subject to tax. Fifteen states have a partial classification system that applies a low tax rate to intangibles; five states have a "comprehensive" classification system with specified rates applied to several classes of property. About thirty states have no classification system but differ in the extent to which types of property, such as intangibles, are included in the base. Utility and railroad property is also subject to widely differing assessment practices.

The property tax base is not related in any straightforward fashion to significant economic magnitudes. The total of real property subject to tax, for example, is not a simple function of past or current levels of economic activity or of the volume of past or current private investment. Tax rates are subject to a pattern of influence different from those that affect the base. Property tax revenues are the resultant of a complicated interaction between private economic activity and public policy. There are, however, patterns of regularity; these are explored below.

Burden

There is an unfortunate tradition in public finance that emphasizes the burden of taxes in isolation from the benefits of public expenditures provided therefrom. It is easy to understand that this approach may be encouraged by those on whom the burden of taxes is heavy and who may feel that they enjoy a relatively small share of the benefits of expenditures. But a great many who ought to know better have been caught up in this tradition. Fortunately, in recent years, there have been a few who have begun to establish a broader perspective. But it still seems to be very difficult to get a hearing on the proposition that a high-tax, high-expenditure community may provide a volume of public services that make that community a desirable place in which to work and live—or, specifically, that higher taxes within a community may provide a volume of government services of such kind and variety as to actually reduce the cost of doing business.

The efforts to define some kind of limit, either for specific taxes or for the tax system as a whole, are representative of this long and unfortunate tradition in public finance. Nowhere have these efforts been more widespread than with property taxes. The assertion that "the property tax has reached its limit" has very often been a rallying point for those who would curb government expenditures. In some cases the assertion is made by the same persons in the same community over a period of fifty years.

In some circumstances there is a legal limit to the property tax set by constitution or statute, and a municipality or school district may indeed reach this limit. But this is not an economic limit in the sense that no further revenue could be expected from this source; the constitutional or statutory limits could be altered. There is probably only one experience in American history when, in a great many jurisdictions, the property tax reached its economic limit. This occurred in the 1930's as community after community found that increases in the tax rate produced not an increase in revenue, but an increase in tax delinquency. In these circumstances the economic limit was reached but not because of any inherent characteristic of the property tax. The limit was reached because the level of community income was depressed. Since that time there have been almost no communities in the nation characterized by a rising spiral of property tax rates and property tax delinquency.

It is not possible to define a limit for a specific tax nor for a tax system as a whole. Neither is it possible to analyze with precision the total economic effect of any tax and its accompanying government expenditure, given the present state of knowledge about the benefits of public expenditures and the relationship between benefits and burdens. The best that can be done is to look at a number of indirect relationships. For the property tax these are (1) the relationship of the tax to the aggregates of national income, (2) property tax revenues in relation to market values, and (3) the burden of the property tax by income class.

Property Taxes and National Income. An examination of historical trends shows that the property tax, in terms of fiscal significance in relation to the total of state and local taxes, was stable from the turn of the century until the early 1920's, then declined consistently until the decade of the 1950's. Since that time the tax has held its own. As a proportion of national income, the property tax moved steadily upward from the turn of the century until the 1920's; the depression brought further increases in the ratio. At the end of World War II the property tax was at its low ebb as a proportion of national income. Revenues have increased greatly since that time, but in 1960 the burden of the tax, measured in national income terms, was about one-third less than in the 1920's.

Property Taxes and Market Values. One of the ways of looking at the burden of the property tax is in relation to the market value of property. This approach implicitly assumes that the property tax is not shifted forward but that the incidence is on the owner. McLoone has recently assembled data on revenues and property values for the period 1902 to 1958 to illustrate this relationship.[2]

With the 1927 figure as a benchmark the trends are not very different from those of the property tax as a proportion of national income. The tax in relation to estimated market values was high in the later 1930's and declined thereafter during World War II and the immediate postwar period. The proportion rises after 1948 but in 1958 is still less than in the later 1920's. Nonfarm property tax burdens, on this measure, increased nearly twice as much as burdens on farm property in the years 1948-1958. The fact that property tax burdens are thought by many farmers to be excessive is a reflection of the level and trend of farm income, and not a reflection of disproportionately heavy increases in taxes on farm property.

State-by-state estimates of similar data show that the ratio of property taxes to market valuations varies widely.[3] In 1957 the average for the nation was 1.3 per cent, but the range was from .4 per cent in Alabama, New Mexico, and South Carolina to 2.8 per cent in Massachusetts.

This kind of evidence, however, tells very little about tax burden. The computations of effective rates rest on some questionable assumptions concerning incidence. The property does not "pay" the tax; the tax is paid out of income and burden must be judged in relation to either the income from the property, the income of the owner of the property, or the income of whoever bears the ultimate burden. Neither does the fact that the ratios of property taxes to market values are high in some states and low in others suggest that the high-ratio states are approaching a limit or that the low-ratio states could tax property more heavily. In some states firms doing an interstate business may be successful in shifting property taxes to out-of-state consumers. Furthermore, two communities may have identical preferences for taxpaying, but one community may prefer its taxes in the form of levies on sales and income and the other may prefer them in the form of levies on property. All taxes, with the possible exception of death duties, must be related to current levels of economic activity—from the income produced during a period of time. Property taxes do not differ from income and sales taxes in this regard.

Burdens by Income Class. Any effort to relate tax burdens to family income is fraught with great difficulty. Such analysis must rest on necessarily arbitrary assumptions about the incidence of the tax in widely varying economic conditions. Estimates must be expressed in terms of averages which necessarily obscure wide variations among states and among jurisdictions within states. To complicate matters further, the property tax is deductible for federal income tax purposes. Therefore, a taxpayer in the 70 per cent marginal federal tax bracket pays his property tax with 30 cent dollars. A corporation with more than $25,000 in taxable income finds the burden of its property tax payments reduced by 52 per cent. But an individual whose income is below the exemption limit receives no advantage from deductibility nor does a corporation with no net taxable income. This, however, is not the end of the complications. The rental value of owned homes, although an element of real income, is not taxable under the federal personal income tax. Therefore, the homeowner may be burdened by local property taxes, but is given favorable federal tax treatment.

In spite of these and other complications, a number of economists have put together some reasonable estimates of the burden of taxes by income class. The most frequently cited study is by Musgrave, who finds that families in the lowest bracket pay about 30 per cent more in property taxes in relation to their income than families in the highest bracket.[4] If deductibility were taken into account, the degree of regressivity would be further accentuated since tenants may not deduct against the federal income tax and since deductibility is of greater value to upper than to lower bracket taxpayers. A good deal of the regressivity is attributable to the part of the tax that rests on housing. This, in turn, is explained by two factors: families spend a smaller proportion of income on housing as family income rises, and there is some tendency for assessment practices to be regressive. In many communities the ratio of assessed to market value appears to be higher for lower-priced homes than for higher-priced homes.

A finding of regressivity is not, however, sufficient grounds on which to condemn the property tax. Regressivity and its presence or absence is an important criterion by which to judge a tax, but the regressivity of a specific tax may not be a serious matter if the over-all tax system is progressive in its impact. Benefits financed by the expenditure from property tax revenues may also partially or wholly offset the regressivity.

There is one class of cases, however, where concern over the regressivity of the property tax—and other taxes as well—may be especially important. Retired homeowners, or homeowners generally whose incomes are fixed and who have no opportunity for income supplementation, will feel the burden of increases in taxes with particular severity. Moreover, the additional tax-provided expenditures, as with public education financed from the property tax, are unlikely to bring any immediate benefit to many such fixed-income families.

Justification of the Tax

Judgments about the place of the property tax in the fiscal system, and specific judgments about the tax as a source of support for public education, should be grounded on a careful examination of incidence. Ideally, one should be able to analyze the extent to which the property tax is shifted forward in the price of products, and the extent to which it affects the returns to factors of production such as labor and capital. Then some reasonably definitive conclusions would be possible. Unfortunately, the present state of incidence theory does not permit this kind of analysis; no effort will be made here to review that theory or its imperfections.[5]

If the property tax were a general net wealth tax on individuals it could be justified on grounds of ability to pay. But the property tax in this country is far short of a general wealth tax. It is directed to specific properties, not to the aggregate net holdings of individuals. The unevenness of its base, the wide variations in rates, and the imperfections in its administration probably make its impact such as to move the tax system as a whole away from, not toward, ability to pay. Although property tax revenues correlate very highly with personal income in a given county or region, the correlation among individuals is very imperfect.

If a justification of the tax is needed on grounds other than revenue availability, it must be found in some kind of crude benefit terms. Local expenditures, by and large, and on the average, must either make the property more valuable by an amount roughly equal to the capitalized value of the annual tax payment, or property owners must derive benefits from governmental services approximately equal in value to the tax payments. The possibilities of ascertaining the relationship of tax costs to benefits from government expenditures are most limited, since this requires not only studies of incidence by areas, but, in addition, the allocation of benefits by area and by economic groups within areas.

A general view of these relationships would suggest that property tax costs in relation to benefits are far more haphazard in older, central cities than in suburban areas. Where neighborhoods are deteriorating and property values are shifting, and where the benefits from local government expenditures are very imperfectly correlated with property tax payments—here the tax may have unfortunate economic effects. In predominantly residential suburbs, however, the property tax comes closer to being a true benefit tax and is a far more equitable fiscal instrument than in central cities. In a residential community the behavior of the tax will be determined primarily by the income of families and by family willingness to support local government services from the levy.

Property Tax Elasticity

In the early 1950's there were few students or practitioners of public finance who would have wagered very heavily on the future of the property tax as a source of finance for local government. The tax had behaved badly in the 1930's, and the immediate postwar years did not bring major improvements in property tax administration. In a number of states, notably Pennsylvania and New York, there were significant developments in the local nonproperty tax field that offered the possibility of replacement levies. As of 1950 it would have seemed safe to predict that the property tax was entering a period of significant decline and that important new sources of local government revenue would be found.

But the tax revived dramatically during the decade of the 1950's. Property tax revenues held their proportionate importance in the total tax structure of state and local governments and the tax proved to be highly responsive to the needs of growing communities, particularly suburban communities. Revenue from the tax increased proportionately more than the increase in personal income.

An appraisal of the future productivity of the property tax must rest on careful examination of recent experience. This can best be analyzed in terms of the concept of elasticity, which has its origins in the economic theory for market demand for goods and services. As applied to public revenues, elasticity measures the rate of change in a revenue source in relation to the rate of change in income. If a source of revenue has an elasticity of unity this means that a proportional increase in income is associated with an equal-proportional increase in revenue. Revenues that increase less than in proportion to income are said to be relatively inelastic; revenues that increase more than in proportion to income are said to be elastic.

Increases or decreases in property tax revenue are the product of changes in the base, that is, in taxable real and personal property assessments, and changes in rates. The property tax base itself may have an elasticity of less than unity, which would mean that, as income increased, taxable property did not increase proportionately. But an increase in the base may be accompanied by increases in rates, so that revenues may have greater than unit elasticity.

The analysis of the elasticity of property tax revenue is, in a sense, the analysis of the elasticity of local government expenditures. As expenditure requirements increase, unless offset by intergovernmental transfers or nonproperty taxes, local property tax revenue will rise; either the base or the rate must increase. State-mandated increases in teachers' salaries, for example, will increase local school expenditures and local property tax revenue. Expenditure requirements force revenue increases. The inability to separate the determinants of local revenue from the determinants of local expenditure does not make for conceptual clarity. However, this interdependence of revenue and expenditure is inherent in local public finance and attempts at separation would be artificial.

The elasticity of the property tax base has not been neglected by economists who have attempted to project the future of state-local revenues.[6] Estimates of the responsiveness of the property tax base to increases in income have ranged from .8 to 1.2. However, the elasticity of property tax revenues is a product of changes in both the base and the rate, and recent experience, in almost every property tax jurisdiction, is that both have increased. The growth of income has been associated with a greater or lesser degree of growth in taxable property, depending on the complex of relations between income and property. Property tax rates have increased under the pressure of expenditures so that the combination of the growth in the base, the reassessment of old property and the increase in rates has produced an increase in property tax revenues that is much more rapid than the increase in income. For example, for the nation as a whole from 1950 to 1960, the average of annual percentage changes in revenue to changes in personal income was approximately 1.43.

As a part of the research underlying this report, a detailed analysis was undertaken of the elasticity of property tax revenues in New York State counties for the years 1949 to 1959.[7] County personal income, by place of residence, as estimated by the New York State Department of

Commerce, was used as the measure of income. The five New York City counties were excluded, not only on grounds of lack of comparability with the remainder of the state but also because constitutional limits have set effective ceilings on tax rates and tax revenue in New York City in recent years. In the analysis both revenue and income are expressed in per capita terms.

Data were secured on total property tax collections, including special assessments, for each of the 57 counties for each of the years 1949 to 1959. The rate of growth in property tax collections is thus the numerator in a fraction in which the rate of growth of income is the denominator:

$$\frac{\text{year to year rate of growth in property tax collections}}{\text{year to year rate of growth in income}}$$

This ratio, for each county, is the coefficient of revenue elasticity for the period 1949 to 1959. In effect, this treats time series data as if it were a cross section for the period as a whole. The coefficient is the dependent variable for the analysis. An elasticity coefficient of 1.0, for example, would indicate that for every 1 per cent increase in county income there is a 1 per cent increase in property tax revenues.

The revenue elasticities were estimated statistically with income lagged one year behind revenue: for example, 1958 income is associated with 1959 property tax revenue. This makes sense from the standpoint of property tax administration, where it may be assumed that current levels of community income influence property assessments and the setting of tax rates by public officials and that the levies are then paid out of the income of the following year.

The computed revenue elasticities range from .89 to 3.37. The median elasticity is 1.61 and the mean 1.67; 29 of the 57 counties have elasticities that fall in the range from 1.40 to 1.82.

To analyze the socioeconomic variables that are associated with differing patterns of property tax behavior, the elasticity coefficients were made dependent variables and a number of possible independent variables were examined. Some variables were rejected because they appeared to be intercorrelated with other variables; some were rejected because their explanatory power was limited. The following were selected for multiple correlation largely on grounds of their institutional relationship to the determinants of local fiscal behavior. Where possible, "dynamic" variables were chosen, that is, relationships were expressed in rates of change over time. In some instances, however, available data did not permit this. The computed coefficient of multiple correlation corrected for degrees of freedom was .715.

X_2 —— per cent increase in population, 1950-1960*
X_3 —— per cent change in ratio of population over 65 to total population, 1950-1960*
X_4 —— per cent change in ratio of public school average daily attendance to total population, 1950-1960*
X_5 —— average per capita income, 1949-1959†
X_6 —— per capita nonproperty taxes, 1959†
X_7 —— per cent increase in full value tax rate, 1955-1959†
X_8 —— average equalization ratio, 1955-1959
X_9 —— per cent increase in proportion of households with incomes over $7000, 1955-1960
X_{10} —— per cent increase in service trade employment, 1950-1960
X_{11} —— density of property value per square mile

* Significant at .01 levels: † significant at .05 level.

The relationship of each of the independent variables to the dependent variable was analyzed by means of multiple regression.[8] The pattern that emerged suggested that, at least for New York State, property tax behavior is not erratic and random and that revenues respond to definable economic magnitudes. Revenue elasticity is positively and significantly associated with increases in population, and with the increases in the proportion of school children to the population. The tax responded most favorably in rapid growth counties, but in stable growth industrial counties elasticity approximated the median response for all counties. Elasticity tends to vary inversely with the yield of local nonproperty taxes. The level of assessment—the ratio of assessed to full (equalized) value—does not influence the responsiveness of yields.

On the whole, the statistical findings support the conclusion that the property tax is a far better fiscal instrument than most of its critics would allow.[9] There is reason to believe that it will continue to hold its relative fiscal importance in state-local public finance structures. This will be accomplished by increases in the base of property subject to taxation and by increases in the rate of tax.

This moderately optimistic conclusion with respect to the property tax rests, of course, on a projection that the state-local fiscal future—in the 1960's and 1970's—will be more like the 1950's than the 1930's or 1940's. This means that wars and depressions are ruled out and that economic development and income distribution patterns will continue very largely in accordance with recent trends. If the forces of urbanization, suburbanization, population growth, and increases in personal income continue in this fashion, the property tax should respond as well in the future as it has in the last fifteen years.

Administrative Patterns

It has been appropriately said that, in spite of its patent disadvantages, the case for the property tax is essentially the case for local government.[10] Unfortunately, it is sometimes difficult to make a strong case for local government in the United States, at least in terms of its efficiency, vitality, and administrative excellence. Neither does the property tax typify the best of local government administration. Far too often, although perhaps less often than is commonly supposed, assessors are poorly trained and poorly paid, basic assessment records are kept in a slipshod fashion, the review of assessments is full of favoritism, and collection procedures are antiquated. To a considerable extent the same kinds of descriptions can be applied to many other local government administrative patterns, starting with comments about poorly paid and poorly trained personnel. But there seems to exist a general feeling that administrative malaise is more characteristic of property tax administration than of other mechanisms in local government.

There are a number of curious paradoxes here. Since its beginnings in colonial America the property tax has always been subject to a high degree of administrative ineptitude. Reform has lagged far behind needed improvements. Yet the voices for reform have always been strong. For the last hundred years competent students of property tax administration, state tax commissions, citizen groups, commissions of legislative inquiry, and official and nonofficial agencies of all kinds and varieties have set forth proposals for improvement in property tax administration, but very little comes of this activity.

A second paradox is that, in spite of the widespread failure to achieve improvement in administration, the tax itself has responded vigorously to local government needs in the last decade. One might expect that an increase in effective property tax rates would bring forceful citizen demands for an improved assessment administration to eliminate inequities. With rare exceptions, this has not happened. The high degree of interpersonal inequity that is inherent in the tax has imposed no apparent limit on its productivity, nor has this led to effective political expression of the need for greater equity in assessments.

The long-standing failure to effect improvements in property tax administration, particularly in the assessment process, suggests that students of public finance may not understand the patterns of political behavior that bring administrative reform.

Certainly the forces that oppose reforms in property tax administration are strong in almost every community. Real estate brokers and developers will very often prefer to negotiate assessments with local government officials rather than submit to the forces of impartiality in assessment. Beneficiaries of special exemptions, such as veterans and homeowners in a number of states, will oppose assessment reform that raises the level of assessed value to market value and thus destroys a part of the real value of their exemptions. Industrial firms that have secured favorable tax treatment as a part of negotiations for locational advantage will oppose reassessment. Moreover, many property owners are lulled into a state of apathy regarding the inequities that exist because of the prevalent tendency to assess at a small fraction of current market value. A homeowner who has purchased a residence for $15,000 and is confronted with an assessment of $5000 is likely to feel that he has been gently treated. If he took the trouble to inspect the assessment rolls he might discover that similar property was assessed for $4000.

Unfortunately, one community interest group that has a stake in improved assessment administration is too far removed from the scene to be effective. This is the interest that supports more adequate financing of public education. Local boards of education generally rely on assessment rolls prepared by other governmental agencies; that is, the board uses the roll but has no authority to improve its quality. In a great many communities in the last ten years the bulk of property tax increases have come by way of increased school taxes, but the public support for such tax increases does not carry over institutionally into support for strengthened tax administration, in part because of the separation of schools from other government. It is difficult to be optimistic. A reform in assessments is typically so unpopular that it occurs only as part of a general local government reform movement swept along in the wake of other programs that have stronger appeal.

An examination of state-local patterns of political and fiscal behavior does not suggest that improvements in property tax administration will automatically emerge from state capitols. The gradual withdrawal of state governments from a share in property tax revenues has been accompanied by a gradual withdrawal of interest in the assessment process. State government administrative agencies, such as tax commissions, have no reason to press for administrative improvements in the property tax. Their responsibility is for improvement in the administration of levies important for state purposes, such as income or sales taxes. Neither is there very good reason for state legislators to become promoters of reforms that are unpopular in their home districts. Nor can a state governor be expected to provide leadership in such matters when there will be no resulting gains in strengthened state programs and when powerful local opposition exists.

Nevertheless, if there are to be reforms in property tax administration, and particularly in assessment, state intervention is necessary.[11] Somehow state administrations and state legislators must become convinced that a strengthened property tax at the local level is important to statewide concerns. State governments are unlikely to have much enthusiasm for sharing the burdens of local administration. There must be benefits to be shared, political or fiscal, before state action is likely to be forthcoming. Perhaps at some point state officials will become convinced of what is in fact reality—that a strengthened property tax is an alternative to additional state aid.

But, as in most areas of public policy, such convictions on the part of state officials do not come easily. There must be some prior understanding on the part of local citizenry and local officials that the property tax will be increasingly utilized for the support of both public education and other local government functions, and that its future productivity depends heavily on improving its administration. In particular, those who favor increased support for public education should recognize that the property tax is a fiscal friend and not an enemy.

State General Funds

The ability of a state to keep its fiscal house in reasonably good repair, and to assure that state revenues are responsive to the growth of income and economic activity makes possible a more generous grant-in-aid system for the support of schools and other local government activities.

Ideally, every source of state revenue could be made available to meet any and all state expenditures, including education. State governments could merge all revenue sources, channel them into the general fund, and charge all appropriations against this general fund. But such unitary and comprehensive budgeting is almost unknown among American states. Many revenues are earmarked for specific functions; special funds are established by constitution or statute and may not be diverted to other governmental purposes. Such arrangements are not, of course, inviolable. Constitutions could be amended and statutes enacted to establish a true general fund. But the immediate outlook is very far short of this kind of budgetary comprehensiveness. Specific programs will continue to be financed by specific levies. Highway funds, in particular, are not likely to be mixed with general funds.

Earmarking and grants-in-aid introduce rigidities into state budget structures that make for extreme difficulty in any analysis of state revenue potentials. A state's revenue for the support of any specific function, such as public education, is limited at any one time by constitutional and statutory provisions that establish the budget pattern, by the constraints imposed by federal grants and, of course, by the interest groups that support existing arrangements. It is somewhat unrealistic to argue that a state could substantially increase state aid for public education in the next biennium when, in fact, this could be done only by diverting funds from constitutionally segregated motor vehicle receipts. It is similarly unrealistic to argue that state aid can be increased when this would violate a governor's campaign pledge for "no tax rate increases."

Therefore, any attempt to project the future of state revenue sources in terms of aggregates, and to argue that these aggregates may be made available for the support of specific governmental functions, is not wholly realistic. Nevertheless, such a projection, unrelated as it may be to immediate possibilities within any one state, is not without its value. The behavior of state revenue structures in the decade of the 1950's may be at least a rough indication of expectations for the 1960's.

There are some general characteristics of the states' fiscal behavior that should be noted before examining recent experience with revenues. As pointed out above, state support of public education, for the nation as a whole, held its own during the 1950's. Local shares dropped slightly while the federal government's proportionate support increased slightly. But public education has been relatively favored by the states. When other governmental functions are taken into account it turns out that the states have barely held their relative fiscal position. State tax revenues were the same proportion of state and local spending in 1960 as in 1950 but declined from the middle to the end of the decade.

The fiscal decline of the states, particularly since the middle of the 1950's, and the proportionate increase in the fiscal importance of local governments, measured in terms of the tax support of local expenditures, may be attributed in part to shifts in population from rural to urban areas.[12] These shifts have not brought increased proportionate state support of government programs associated with urbanism—the health, education, welfare, transportation, and air and water pollution problems of metropolitan areas. State programs, including grants-in-aid, have had no important expansion in these fields. Local governments derived 30.1 per cent of their general revenue from state governments in 1950. This had declined to 28.5 per cent in 1960. With only modest grant-in-aid support from the national government, local governments have been required to assume heavier fiscal burdens.

Comparisons of the importance of state and federal aid in metropolitan and nonmetropolitan areas are further indicative of probable growing fiscal burdens at the local level.[13] In 1957, the only year for which details are available, state and federal aid as a proportion of local general expenditures was substantially smaller within each large metropolitan area than in the rest of the state that contained the metropolitan area. Unless state aid practices are altered, the continued growth of metropolitan areas would appear to bring an almost automatic decline in the relative fiscal contribution of the states.

Responsiveness of State Revenues

The functional relationships between changes in income and changes in property tax revenues were examined above as a basis for prognosis about the future of the property tax. However, a comparable exploration of the relationship between changes in state personal income and state tax revenues involves conceptual difficulties even more formidable than those encountered in the examination of property tax revenues.

The assumptions that are necessary in the analysis of the behavior of state revenue systems are very much the same as with property tax revenues. Income and changes therein are the primary measures of economic activity, and hence the base or source of state revenue. The fraction of a state's income which will be channeled into the state treasury is the resultant of a number of forces which include, but need not be limited to, (1) the composition and distribution of income within a state, (2) the pressure of needs for expenditures, and the strength of interest groups and citizenry in expressing these needs, (3) the responsiveness of governors and state legislatures to political forces that urge higher expenditures, and their responsiveness to political forces that favor leaving a larger fraction of resources in private hands.

However, a state's fiscal system is only a part of the state-local fiscal system within a given state. The responsiveness of state revenue systems will necessarily differ in accordance with the division of fiscal responsibility between the state and the local governments. Where, as in New Jersey, custom and tradition have dictated that the state's fiscal responsibility is limited while local government's fiscal responsibility is extensive, response patterns will differ as compared with states that have a more centralized fiscal system. Moreover, states levy a wide variety of taxes, with greater numbers of levies than either the national or local governments. This will lead to variations in the responsiveness of state revenues.

As a measure of responsiveness the ratio of state tax revenues to state personal income is thus an awkward conglomerate. Nevertheless, there is little choice; this is the variable whose behavior must be explained insofar as possible. However, since the analysis of the behavior of this ratio for state revenue systems is even more imprecise than the analysis of the behavior of the ratio of property tax revenue to personal income, the terms "responsiveness" and "sensitivity" will be employed here rather than the term "elasticity."

Attention will be centered on the behavior of state revenue systems during the decade of the 1950's, with emphasis on changes between 1950 and 1960. Any projection of this experience into the decade of the 1960's and beyond thus assumes implicitly that economic conditions and the reaction to these conditions by taxpayers, beneficiaries of government expenditures, governors, and state legislatures will be similar to the behavior patterns of the 1950's.

The responsiveness of state tax revenues for the aggregate of the 48 states in relation to changes in national income was examined for selected years from 1927 to 1960.[14] Over this whole period state tax collections increased nearly two and one-half times as much as national income. For the decade of the 1950's, the growth in state tax revenues was about one-and-a-half times as much as the growth in national income. State revenues tend to be somewhat more stable than national income. In the recession year 1954 national income declined by 1.2 per cent, but state revenues increased by 5.1 per cent. In the recession of 1958 national income was virtually unchanged, but state revenues increased by 2.7 per cent. The measure of responsiveness shows extremely erratic behavior, even when computed with tax collections lagged one year after income. However, with the exclusion of two deviant years—1955 and 1959—there is an average with some meaning. The remaining eight observations for the years 1950 to 1960 show an average annual responsiveness of state tax revenues to national income of 1.11.

A part of the explanation for the inconstant response of state revenues to national income undoubtedly lies in the fact that a number of state legislatures meet biennially. Furthermore, state tax rate increases do not react smoothly to either income or expenditure needs. Most governors would prefer to propose rate increases early in their term of office rather than late in the hope that adverse political reactions will be forgotten before the voters return to the polls to elect an incoming state administration. And there seems to be a tendency to patch up state revenue structures only periodically with small rate increases that have limited revenue potential.

State revenue structures, of course, differ widely. In 1960, for example, 34 of the 50 states levied general sales or gross receipts taxes. These brought in 23.9 per cent of the total of state revenue. States that employed sales taxes raised about one-third of their revenues from this source, but the range was considerable. The state with the lowest proportionate dependence on this levy was North Carolina, where sales tax revenues amounted to 19.2 per cent of total taxes. At the other extreme was the state of Washington where the sales tax brought in 56.8 per cent of the total.

The responsiveness of total state revenues to changes in state personal income also varies widely. In the years from 1950 to 1960, one state—South Dakota—had a responsiveness of 0.60; two states—Georgia and Montana—had a responsiveness exceeding 2.0. The median for the 48 states was 1.28.

Surprisingly enough, the differences in revenue responsiveness among the states are not attributable to gross differences in their tax structures. It might be expected, for example, that motor vehicle revenues would have a different response pattern to changes in state personal income than other sources of revenue, and that states with a large proportion of motor vehicle receipts in their revenue structures would thus have different behavior patterns. Analysis of general fund revenues, exclusive of motor vehicle revenues, however, demonstrated that this was not the case. Motor vehicle revenues are approximately as responsive to changes in state personal income as are other sources of state revenue.

It might also be expected that states levying personal income taxes would have a more responsive tax structure than states with sales taxes, but neither does this pattern obtain. In 1960, 33 states levied individual income taxes.[15] These levies brought in 12.3 per cent of the revenues of all the states. In the years from 1950 to 1960, personal income tax states had a median revenue responsiveness of 1.30.

The number of sales tax states is about the same as the number of income tax states—34 in 1960—and, of course, the two categories are not mutually exclusive since some states have both. Sales tax revenue, however, bulked larger—23.9 per cent of the total of all state revenue.

The median responsiveness of the revenues of sales tax states for 1950 to 1960 was 1.29, virtually identical with the responsiveness of income tax states. No doubt the reason for these similarities in response patterns lies in the fact that state personal income taxes tend to have relatively high personal exemptions with rate structures that are graduated only moderately. This dampens down the sensitivity of the tax to changes in personal income as compared, for example, with the federal personal income tax. On the other hand, the decade of the 1950's was characterized by high and rising patterns of consumer expenditures, and there was only moderate resistance to increases in sales tax rates. States that depended heavily on sales taxes were thus able to capture for their tax coffers as much of the increase in economic growth as states with income taxes.

Revenue responsiveness among the states does, however, differ systematically with respect to growth rates. For any one state, an increase in population is highly associated with an increase in aggregate personal income. Therefore, the analysis of either of these variables is sufficient as a rough measure of growth. For present purposes the states were divided into four growth groups in accordance with percentage changes in state personal income between 1950 and 1960. The median revenue responsiveness for each group was then computed. The quartile of states with the highest growth rates showed a median responsiveness of 1.12. The second quartile was 1.36; the third, 1.30, and the quartile of lowest growth, 1.57. That is, rapid income growth was associated with low revenue responsiveness and vice versa.

The differences between the highest and lowest growth groups are significant and disturbing. States with low growth rates must continue to finance public expenditures; tax revenues rise more rapidly than the increase in personal income. On the other hand, states with more rapid growth do not succeed in capturing very much more than a proportional increase in revenue as income expands. The states that are growing in population and income are the states where the rate of urbanization is highest. The relative unresponsiveness of state revenues contributes to the lag in state fiscal support for government expenditures in such urban areas.

The Outlook for State Revenues

Economists have made a number of projections of state and local government revenue and expenditures for the years ahead.[16] These projections, when arrayed against experience of the 1950's, permit some reasonable guesses about the future. L. L. Ecker-Racz has made such comparisons and concludes that if the economy grows at 3½ per cent annually in the 1960's to achieve a gross national product in excess of $700 billion by 1970, the yield of all state and local taxes could be expected to increase about 45 per cent.[17] Since most of the projections suggest that state and local expenditures, given foreseeable patterns of need, will increase by from 50 to 60 per cent by 1970, this would leave a gap of approximately 15 percentage points. The recent behavior of the property tax would suggest that this source of revenue can be counted on to hold its own in the total of state-local revenue. State tax rate increases would therefore be required to absorb approximately half of the gap; that is, to increase by 7 to 8 per cent.

This would be a modest attainment and one within the scope of reasonable expectations. In 1959, for example, two-thirds of the states increased rates for one or more major tax sources. In recent years state sales tax rates have generally gone up and the base subject to tax has been broadened in many jurisdictions. Two states—Texas and Wisconsin—have added the sales tax to their structure of state revenues. The personal income tax has been less popular than the sales tax, but one state—West Virginia—joined the income tax states in 1961, the first such addition since 1937. A rather large number of the older income tax states have introduced source collection for personal income; 24 of the 33 income tax states now have such provisions. This, of course, adds substantially to the productivity of the levy. In addition, almost every state during the decade moved to increase excise tax rates on gasoline, cigarettes and, in some cases, alcoholic beverages.

None of this was accomplished without considerable stress and strain. The age-old controversy over sales versus income taxes continues in many states, although probably with abated fury. A sales tax with food included in the base is indeed a regressive levy, imposing heavy relative burdens on low-income families and on middle-income families whose food expenditures are a high proportion of family income—which is the case in large families. But a sales tax with food and drugs exempt is not heavily regressive. In fact, it is generally proportional through most of the range of family income. This is the levy that is likely to win acceptance in the remaining non-sales-tax states over the next several years. The general outlook is that within a decade virtually every state will have a sales tax and more states will have personal income taxes. In states with both levies there is always the possibility of relieving the regressivity of the sales tax by providing expenditure credits under the income tax.

Since no state likes to get very far out of line with its regional competitors, strengthened and expanded state revenue sources are likely to proceed in a kind of state-by-state lock step. Wisconsin's new sales tax will encourage Minnesota to adopt the levy. Personal income taxes will come more slowly, but pressures already mount in states like Washington and Michigan, where sales tax burdens are high in relation to neighboring states.

There will, of course, continue to be opposition to state tax increases. In an era when almost every state has an official agency charged with responsibility for industrial promotion and when in every state there are dozens, if not hundreds, of local groups anxious to attract industry for economic growth, it is reasonable to expect that the views and attitudes of business firms will have the greatest impact on the structure of state revenues. Since the business community generally favors sales rather than income taxes, no particular political acumen is required to prognosticate that the growth-minded states will move slowly in both the corporate and individual income tax fields. Although it can be forcefully demonstrated that the shift in a state tax structure from business taxes to sales taxes on consumers may not bring an increase in a state's economic welfare, such demonstrations may avail little against the argument that industry is leaving the state.[18]

The forces that will contribute to higher state-level taxes are very nearly inexorable. Population growth, urbanization, state commitments to established programs, and pressures for new programs will certainly continue. The needs of public higher education, for example, are immediate and pressing. The proponents of assistance for elementary and secondary education are now and will increasingly find themselves competing with higher education for a share of the states' tax resources.

State grants for public education can be expected to increase, probably in proportion to the increase in expenditures for elementary and secondary education. But it would be unwise to project that state grants-in-aid will provide important relief to local property taxpayers. There are too many other claimants on the state dollar.

Local Nonproperty Taxes

In a survey of state and local taxes for the support of public education some attention must necessarily be given to local nonproperty levies, if only for the sake of completeness. However, such revenues have been important for the support of schools only in a replacement sense—in the same way that a federal grant-in-aid program for urban renewal may indirectly free up local tax resources for the support of education. Local nonproperty taxes may provide for a modest strengthening of the general sources of local revenue, particularly in urban areas. In only one state—Pennsylvania—are they widely used for the direct support of public education. New York State permits some access by school districts to nonproperty taxes but utilization is most limited. Increased reliance on such levies is likely to be significant only in the larger cities, and only if new administrative arrangements can be devised for their imposition on a metropolitan area basis.

Local nonproperty taxes have a thirty-year history. The first was New York City's retail sales tax, introduced in 1934 and followed by a similar tax in New Orleans in 1938. Philadelphia experimented with a sales tax in the 1930's, but adverse local reactions led to adoption of a flat rate tax on earned income in 1939.[19] The State of California authorized supplementary local sales taxes in 1945 and 1946; Toledo was permitted to impose a local income tax by the Ohio legislature in 1946—the first medium-sized city to employ the levy.

In 1947 Pennsylvania, and to a lesser extent New York State, took the lead in permissive tax legislation. The Pennsylvania law was particularly sweeping with an extension of taxing authority to municipalities and school districts to "tax anything" not then subject to state levy. New York's statute was much more restrictive, authorizing counties, or cities with a population of more than 50,000, to levy (1) sales taxes, (2) gross receipts taxes, and (3) a package of levies on hotel rooms, restaurant meals, and admissions, at rates and bases specified by the legislature.

In New York State the development of local nonproperty taxes has been modest in terms of the number of levies. In 1962 five counties, five cities, and one school district had permissive sales taxes and some additional jurisdictions employed other local levies. Only Monroe County (Rochester) attempted a gross receipts tax, and authority for this levy was later withdrawn by the legislature. In Pennsylvania the reception has been more enthusiastic. There are more than 800 cities, boroughs, townships and school districts that have imposed flat rate income taxes at rates of one per cent or less.[20] In the last fifteen years 5,000 new and separate local taxes have been enacted.

In addition to the Pennsylvania development of local income taxes, a few other states authorize this levy for some or all cities. St. Louis, Missouri, has a local income tax, as have Louisville and eight other Kentucky cities. In Ohio the tax has extensive use. As of January, 1961, 42 cities and 13 villages imposed the levy.[21] In 21 of these Ohio cities the local income tax was more important than the property tax, but it should be noted that Ohio does not have a state tax on personal income.

Although the aggregate of local nonproperty tax revenue stabilized at about 12 to 13 per cent of local tax collections in the decade of the 1950's, this development has been significantly important in some states. In 17 states in 1960, local nonproperty taxes were less than 5 per cent of total local taxes, but in New York State they were 23 per cent of the total; in Pennsylvania, 25.9 per cent; and in Alabama (local sales taxes) they were 43.7 per cent. Moreover, these levies are important for cities with population of more than 1,000,000. With the recent addition of Detroit, all of the nation's five largest cities now have local nonproperty levies.

It is difficult to be enthusiastic about local nonproperty taxes except perhaps for large cities. Such levies deserve the appellation "nuisance taxes." The jurisdictions that impose permissive levies are frequently too small for effective tax collection; administrative costs are high; in most communities these are imperfect substitutes for additional local property taxes or state grants-in-aid financed from uniform statewide levies.

The rationale for locally imposed and locally collected taxes, particularly of the Pennsylvania variety, is difficult to establish. In other states, however, such as Illinois, California, Mississippi, and New Mexico, where local taxes take the form of supplements to a state-collected sales tax and where no additional local collection machinery is necessary, the resulting administrative patterns may not be especially unhappy. In every case local nonproperty taxes are viewed by governors and state legislatures as alternatives to a strengthened state tax structure accompanied by additional grants-in-aid. Looked at in this way, local nonproperty taxes may simply reflect an abnegation of state political and fiscal responsibility.

For large cities the justification for local nonproperty taxes has very often rested on an effort to reach the commuter, who is thought to impose additional public service costs on the city of his employment. A better justification would regard local nonproperty taxes imposed by central cities as contributions to defray the costs of urban congestion. However, only the city earned income tax fits either justification. A sales tax in the central city will very often be avoided by the nonresident commuter by trading outside the taxing area or by purchasing in the central city free of sales tax when the goods are shipped to outlying residential communities. Even the "commuter burden" rationalization for local income taxes fails in Pennsylvania where the community of residence (except in Philadelphia) is given priority over the community of employment in the imposition of the levy.

Locally imposed income taxes have probably brought few distortions in the patterns of location of retail trade and employment, simply because rates are sufficiently low as to be generally unimportant in decisions to locate employing firms. Local retail sales taxes, however, may have contributed, along with a great many other factors influencing patterns of suburbanization, to the outmovement of retail shopping centers, although evidence on this point is most difficult to isolate. Beyond doubt, one of the most unfortunate consequences of the local levies has been their contributory influence to the general state of apathy regarding improvements in local property tax administration.

Low-rate earned income taxes or local sales taxes, if imposed over the whole of the metropolitan area, would not produce appreciable distortions in the location of economic activity and would have the advantage of reaching taxable attributes not otherwise available to local governments. However, most metropolitan areas are now very far from attaining intergovernmental solutions to the most pressing of areawide problems such as sewage treatment, water pollution, air pollution, and transportation, to say nothing of land use planning and zoning. An agreement to impose common areawide local nonproperty taxes is even farther from sight.

From time to time specific metropolitan areas will undoubtedly introduce additional nonproperty levies. Proposals for multidistrict levies for school purposes, for example, have recently been advanced for three counties contiguous to Detroit. But there is no evidence to suggest that levies of this type will be proportionately more important in the future of local finance than they have been in the past, and there are no grounds for concluding that they are superior, as fiscal devices, to strengthened state revenue systems and concomitant grants-in-aid.

The Outlook

Social scientists may take some comfort in the fact that their research inquiries are very often directed toward large and important questions. But social scientists must also be painfully aware that their ability to answer large and important questions is very often most limited.

Certainly the question to which this chapter is addressed is one of major significance. The future of public education in the United

States, and therefore the future of our ability to strengthen societal values that are the fabric of our well-being, depends heavily on the availability of fiscal resources for the support of education at state and local government levels. At the same time, the answers to questions of resource availability tend to fall into one of two categories. Either they are obvious and hence trivial, or the answer depends on assumptions whose validity may be questioned.

For example, in one sense it is quite apparent that over the next decade state and local resources for the support of education will be adequate to meet levels of community expectations. As long as the decision processes that control the provision of resources are reasonably responsive, this must necessarily be the case. General community aspirations for public education may be lower than are needful for the satisfaction of the educational preferences of some sectors of the community. General community aspirations may also be higher than necessary to satisfy the preferences of some other sectors of the community. But if governors, state legislatures, and local school boards are reasonably responsive to the whole range of aspirations, some average preference pattern will be satisfied.

An equally obvious answer can be given to the question, "Will state and local resources be adequate to satisfy the aspirations of all sectors of the community with respect to the whole range of public and private goods?" To this the answer must necessarily be "No!" Affluent as certain sectors of society may be, the total public and private wants of the community will always exceed available resources. There is, then, no precise analytical technique available for judging whether resources are adequate for any particular public or private purpose in the absence of knowledge about the future dimensions of the entire range of preferences for the goods and services that may be produced by a society.

In this chapter an effort has been made to appraise the three general sources of state-local support for public education: the property tax, state aid from general state revenue, and local nonproperty taxes. The findings are conservative; the immediate future is very likely to resemble the immediate past. The fiscal support of elementary and secondary public education will depend heavily on the property tax and it may only be hoped that this traditional levy can be strengthened by administrative reform. The states are generally lagging in their fiscal responsibilities; grants-in-aid for elementary and secondary education are not likely to increase as a proportion of total expenditures. Local nonproperty taxes appear to have settled down to a reasonably constant fraction of local revenues; they are more likely to be of assistance to other local government programs, and of only indirect help to public education.

The outlook for state-local revenue sources depends heavily on national government programs for economic stabilization. All levels of government draw support from a common source—the taxation of current levels of economic activity. The effectiveness of national programs for the stabilization and growth of such activity will determine in substantial measure the ability of states and local governments to capture tax resources for education and for other state-local needs.

The system of fiscal federalism that characterizes the public finances of the United States has responded slowly down the years, but has nevertheless responded positively, to the forces of economic and political change. There is no reason to believe that it cannot respond with reasonable adequacy to the needs of public education as well as to other public needs in the decades ahead. There is no absolute limit to the ability of state and local revenue structures to support public education and other governmental services. We live in a high tax society whose tax limits are constantly being extended. The ingredients of such extension are, as they always have been, a citizen awareness of public needs, a political leadership that is effective, and an organizational pattern for merging the two.

IX. State Aid Patterns

State grants for public education are intended to serve a number of objectives, at least four of which have been historically significant. First, grants are intended to stimulate local spending on the schools. In particular, it has been hoped that the availability of state funds for education will encourage the more progressive school authorities to raise expenditures to high levels. The districts in which such spending occurs can demonstrate to other communities the efficacy of advanced practices. This is a process under which general improvement can occur under a decentralized structure of public education.

Second, grants are intended to provide a greater degree of equity among the households of the state. That is, both the distribution of educational services and the distribution of the school tax burden are to be brought more closely in alignment with some criterion of fairness. As a minimum goal, students of all districts are to be assured of reasonably adequate educational opportunities, with the financing of these opportunities so arranged that the combined state-local levies do not fall with undue severity on any group of taxpayers.

Third, the grants are expected to promote efficiency in expenditures, both with regard to the choices of type of educational outputs and with regard to the choices of methods to be used in producing them. The state may seek to exert control over the content of the school program, as in recent efforts to strengthen instruction in mathematics and science. Alternatively, the state government may seek to encourage consolidation of school districts that are too small for the efficient use of resources, or it may promote, even, the more rapid introduction of educational innovations, such as team teaching and teaching machines. As a minimum, the state will seek to have at least some of the financial burden of inefficient operation fall strictly on local taxpayers, and, likewise, some of the financial gains of prudent control.

Fourth, the grants are to provide local tax relief, a term which is widely used, but not often defined. Clearly, "tax relief" as used in the context of discussions of state aid refers to relief of an "excessive" level of local taxation that is judged to exist in a large number

This chapter was written by Charles S. Benson, Lecturer, Graduate School of Education, Harvard University, who is indebted to Edgar L. Morphet for valuable comments on an earlier draft.

of districts. From here there are three possible meanings. (1) The term may imply that a local school district will undertake to reduce its levy by a proportion of the additional state aid. This may be termed "absolute tax relief." (2) The term may refer to the situation where the state's share of educational expenditures is constant, either for the districts taken one by one, or for the total of expenditures of all the districts. Since the state payments would increase in proportion to total expenditure, this might be called "relative tax relief." (3) Finally, the term may refer to the condition where local tax rates, on the average, are held approximately constant. Rather than tax relief, this may be called "tax stabilization." Under these circumstances the state's share must increase wherever school expenditures are rising more rapidly than the size of local tax bases.

These four ends are to be served, further, under the constraints (a) that a proper degree of local autonomy in the administration of the schools is preserved, and (b) that there is no serious distortion in the allocation of resources among the whole group of local public services.

School authorities, legislatures, and the interested public may give a different ranking to the several ends and may view the objectives with different intensities of feeling. It is also likely that there will be disputes on the distribution of authority between the state and the localities with regard to school policy and on the extent to which school aid warps the distribution of local spending among competing public activities. The conclusion appears to follow that any plan of state aid designed to yield maximum results for any one of the major objectives is almost certain to be unacceptable. Compromises are inevitable.

Suppose, for example, a state embarks on a scheme to maximize local spending. In the short run, it would necessarily seek to exploit differences in demand for educational services. Under the reasonable assumption that demand for elementary and secondary schooling is functionally related to household income and to the educational attainments of parents (those two factors are known to be highly intercorrelated), the single-minded pursuit of the stimulation objective would probably preserve—and possibly enhance—whatever inequalities of educational opportunity existed. This is likely to be true even if there is some diffusion of educational benefits from the high spending districts (presumably the rich ones) in behalf (eventually) of the student population of the nonfavored districts, since such diffusion is a long run process. Further, the nonparent who may receive general but not specific benefit from the expenditure and who happened to live in a high spending district would appear to be placed under an onerous tax levy. Thus, extreme concern with the stimulation objective seems to run afoul of the equity goal.

In addition, extreme stimulation would place the state in a passive role with respect to raising efficiency. Should the state mandate certain types of educational outputs, or should it direct the use of certain processes, some districts would respond by offering fewer local dollars for the state money than they would if they could have the funds *carte blanche;* hence, the opportunity to use such mandates would be severely limited. Next, those who give priority to tax relief—local taxpayers' associations, for example—would not be inclined to offer their support to a strong stimulation scheme. Finally, extreme stimulation would probably result in a harmful degree of distortion of resources among the various locally administered public activities. Public health, recreation, and other services might suffer as public education advanced.

The same kind of consequences would follow from the single-minded pursuit of other major objectives. For example, an overriding concern with equity in the short run would probably shift policy toward the use of very large state grants and a high degree of state control. This would even out the discrepancies in resources in relation to needs that persist among districts. However, those persons who feel it important to preserve local control of education would be offended at such a shift. And so on.

Fortunately, the objectives of state aid plans are not wholly exclusive, and there exist other means than cash grants to accomplish at least some of them. It is, then, the task of the student of school finance to point out the implications of choosing one kind of plan over another, to the end that some acceptable balance among the several objectives is obtained, a balance acceptable to the voters of a state. However, the analysis of the consequences of choosing one type of aid scheme over another can be done in only a general way because certain information is lacking. In particular, measurements of local needs, resources, and demand are imprecise, as are measurements of the real costs of inputs and the real volume of outputs. The measurements are imprecise not only with regard to educational services but with regard to local public services generally. Nonetheless, certain conclusions can be drawn.

In this chapter it is intended to consider three recent developments in state aid practice: (1) the revival of interest in general purpose, percentage equalization grants that involve state sharing of all district expenditures, (2) the search for solutions to the school finance problem of the great cities, and (3) the concern about the "excessive" level of debt service in some districts. Before turning to these developments, it is appropriate to examine a scheme of classification of grants and also to summarize the features of the major types of general-purpose subventions. This will help to place the discussion of recent developments in better perspective.

Classification of Grants

In 1957-58, 48 states used 389 distinct programs of aid for education.[1] To avoid getting lost in the detailed provisions of such a large number of educational grants, some scheme of classification is necessary. A taxonomy is useful also in making judgments on whether the whole group of state educational grants is weighted toward some objective or other and how such weighting has changed from one time period to the next.

The U.S. Office of Education distinguishes among grants on two criteria: (a) whether the grant is "general" or "special" purpose and (b) whether the program is "equalizing" or "flat." A grant is general purpose if the funds are "allocated to boards of education with very little instruction as to the use to be made of the funds."[2] Special purpose grants, on the other hand, may be expended only on designated objects (rehabilitation of school buildings, textbooks, etc.) or on designated functions (adult education, school lunches, and the like). Grants are designated as equalizing or flat depending on whether a measure of local resources is used in determining allocations among the districts. The most commonly used measure of local resources is equalized value of taxable property per public school pupil.

The distribution of grants under this taxonomy is familiar. The larger number of grants—284 of 389—were special purpose. However, the larger volume of dollars was paid out under general purpose aids ($3.7 billion (82 per cent) of the total distribution of $4.5 billion). Among the 105 general purpose grants, 49 were classed as equalizing and 56 as flat, but the larger dollar volume ($2.3 billion or 63 per cent) of the general purpose money was allocated in equalizing form. In short, using dollar measures, the states have shown a strong preference for general purpose aids and, within this category, a preference—though somewhat less strong—for equalizing measures.

It does, of course, make a difference just how local resources are taken into account in an aid formula, as will be pointed out below, but the distribution, as it stands, between equalizing and flat tells this much at least: of two programs that are otherwise similar in all important respects, the one which incorporates a resources measure will meet the equity objective in greater degree than one which does not.[3] To ask more of a classification on this particular topic requires substantial refinements in taxonomy and considerably more data from the states.

It appears, nonetheless, that an improvement in the classification is in order. Presently, the taxonomy yields no useful information about how local needs are determined. Such distinctions are especially important with regard to the stimulation and equity aspects of grants, and they also have, in themselves, a bearing on efficiency considerations. Accordingly, it is suggested that a taxonomy such as the following might profitably be employed.

Taxonomy of Grants:

I. Use of Proceeds
   A. General Purpose
   B. Special Purpose

II. Resources Measure
   A. Equalizing
   B. Nonequalizing

III. Needs Measure
   A. Unit Costs
      1. Fixed
      2. Variable
   B. Percentage of Local Expenditures

Under this classification, the terms "general purpose" and "special purpose" stand as defined by the Office of Education. A grant is equalizing if a measure of local resources is taken specifically into account in the allocation formula; otherwise, it is classed as nonequalizing. The distinction here is the same as that made by the U.S. Office under its equalizing-flat-grant dichotomy.[4]

With respect to needs, the essential distinction lies with whether the grants are based on unit costs (dollars per pupil, per teacher, per classroom, etc.) or are based on a percentage of local expenditures. Under the unit approach, the state government undertakes to decide, in effect, how much various types of educational services "should" cost, with estimates generally adjusted for size of district and sparsity of population. On the other hand, the percentage formulas rely upon a local determination of need.

It is necessary to make a further distinction under the unit cost approach. The cost measure may be absolutely fixed by the state or it may be variable, within limits, by local choice. For example, the state may grant x dollars per teacher (the number of credited teachers being related to some count, perhaps average daily membership—ADM— of pupils) or it may grant x dollars for each teacher with the A.B., y dollars for each one with an M.A., and z dollars for each one with six or more years of training. In this latter case, the amount of state aid a district receives increases as it hires more highly trained teachers. Normally, this would mean that high-spending districts get more aid per pupil than low-spending ones, which is to say that the variable unit cost plan and the percentage distributions are similar. Yet, there remains a significant difference between the two approaches.

From data published by the Office of Education, the distribution of general purpose grants in 1957-58 is estimated to be as follows under the foregoing taxonomy:

	Number		
Equalizing			49
Unit		48	
Fixed	28		
Variable	20		
Percentage		1	
Nonequalizing			56
Unit		56	
Fixed	51		
Variable	5		
Percentage		0	
Grant Total			105

The most common form of general purpose equalizing grant was the fixed unit type, usually described as the "Strayer-Haig" form. However, 20 states made use of a variable unit equalizing grant. There was a marked regional influence in the choice between these two instruments. The Strayer-Haig form was more heavily used in New England, the mideast states, the Great Lakes region, and the far west. The variable unit type was popular in the southeast, southwest, and the Rocky Mountain states. (The Plains states were rather equally divided.) Only one state, Wisconsin, could be said to be using a general purpose equalizing percentage grant. More recently, however, this form has been adopted in Rhode Island, to some extent in New York, and has been under serious consideration in Maryland and Delaware.

In the general purpose nonequalizing category, the overwhelming preference was for fixed unit grants. Those states that used variable unit grants were ones, such as Delaware, North Carolina, and Tennessee, that finance a very large share of their school expenditures from state tax sources.

There are two other possible criteria for classification. One is based on whether grants are conditional. The conditions take at least three forms. (1) To receive state aid, a district may be required to meet a certain educational standard such as holding school for a minimum number of days or maintaining an "enriched program." (2) The condition may be fiscal in the specific sense, i.e., in terms of levying a minimum rate of local tax or meeting a state-mandated salary schedule. (3) The condition may be fiscal in the automatic sense, i.e., in cases when state aid is proportional to local expenditures.

Lastly, grants may be given in cash or kind. Examples of grants in kind are subsidies for teacher training, state-financed educational research activities, and the services of state-employed curriculum specialists. The question of whether some particular state interest is better served through cash or kind grants is an interesting one in fiscal relationships and one that has not received thorough exploration.

The Major Alternatives

Authorities in school finance have generally taken the position that general purpose grants are to be preferred to special purpose.[5] It is held that the special purpose aid is likely to be anti-equalizing, in effect, since the richer districts (which is to say, in many cases, the better informed districts) are quicker to respond to offers of state funds. Second, it is held that special purpose grants lead to a misallocation of resources in the local districts, the implication being, of course, that judgments of local authorities on allocation are more likely to be correct ones than judgments of state authorities.

Among the possible forms of general purpose aid, there is likewise a strong preference for equalizing grants. While recognizing realistically that even with state support of education, some children may receive schooling vastly superior to that offered to other children who live in other districts, the school finance experts have been unwilling to advance schemes of state support which would have the effect of reinforcing local differences in level of expenditure—unwilling, that is, to see the state take a position which says that some children "should" receive greater opportunities than others. Equality of opportunity, of course, may require that some children receive the benefit of more expensive programs than others, but the differences in cost of program should reflect the pupil's needs and aptitudes, not geographical accident of birth.

The Fixed Unit Equalizing Grant (1)

The amount of subsidy received by a school district is the difference between a dollar estimate of needs and a dollar estimate of the reasonable local contribution for schools. Both estimates consist of two parts. The needs figure is a product of a measure of attendance—say, average daily membership (ADM)—and a state-mandated expenditure per pupil. If a district has 1,000 pupils in ADM and if it is determined by the state that expenditure per pupil should be not less than $400, the needs estimate in that district is $400,000. In symbols the number of pupils in the 1st district will be referred to as N_i and the mandated expenditures level as u. Then, the needs estimate is N_iu.

The estimate of local contribution is the product of a tax rate—call it r—times the tax base in the district, Y_i. That is, the local contribution is rY_i. Ordinarily, the tax base is the equalized value of taxable property. In the example just above, the district has needs of $400,000. Suppose the district has a local tax base of $12 million and suppose further that the state has decided that a reasonable rate of local contribution is 10 mills. Then the state grant is

$$1000 \text{ pupils} \times \$400 - .01 \times \$12{,}000{,}000 = \$280{,}000$$

which is to say that the district can provide an education for its children of $400 per child at a local tax rate of 10 mills. The local contribution in dollars is $120,000. The local contribution in dollars at the same expenditure level will be higher in richer districts and lower in poorer ones.[6]

Now, the "net grant" to a district will be the difference between the state subsidy and the amount of state taxes levied in the district to finance the school aid program. For simplicity, let it be assumed that both the localities and the state make use of the same tax base, which would be the case if the state relied exclusively on the property tax or if both the localities and the state relied exclusively on an income tax. In such a case, the state tax base is the sum of the local bases, ΣY_i. The rate of state tax is the ratio of the total of subsidies, ΣA_i, to the state tax base, i.e., $\Sigma A_i/\Sigma Y_i$. If we make the further (reasonable) assumption that the state tax is levied in a proportional fashion among the districts, then the amount of state levy in the ith district is $\Sigma A_i/\Sigma Y_i \cdot Y_i$. Accordingly, the net grant in the ith district, V_i, is the algebraic sum of the amount of the subsidy and the amount of state school taxes raised in that district.[7] The net grant, of course, can be positive or negative. In general, it will be positive in districts where the local resources per pupil are meager and negative in districts where they are high.

One particular type of fixed-unit equalizing grant has received by far the largest amount of attention, namely, the type proposed by George D. Strayer and Robert M. Haig in the Report of the Educational Finance Inquiry Commission (New York), in 1923.[8] In the Strayer-Haig form, $r = N_i u/Y_i$, where N_i and Y_i refer respectively to the number of pupils and taxable resources in the richest district of the state. As the Strayer-Haig form is commonly used, a local tax rate equal to r must be levied as a condition to receiving any general purpose aid from the state. The figure for u is sometimes referred to as the "foundation program," i.e., the level of expenditure per pupil in all the districts of a state that is deemed minimally acceptable. The Strayer-Haig scheme is often called the "foundation program plan" of state aid.

Certain features of the Strayer-Haig form should now be noted. (1) The value of u (the mandated expenditure level) becomes the minimum expenditure per pupil in all districts. (2) All districts provide the minimum expenditure level per pupil at the same rate of local taxation; if state taxes are assumed to be proportional, the burden of state and local taxes to provide the mandated expenditure per pupil is proportional among the districts. (3) Given the number of pupils and the distribution of resources per pupil in the districts, the amounts of state and mandatory local taxes levied will both increase in proportion to an increase in the mandated expenditure level. (4) The relative shares of state and local support are determined by the distribution of resources per pupil in the districts.

The Variable Unit Equalizing Grant (2)

In present practice, the variable unit form of equalizing grant is quite similar to that of the fixed unit form. The subsidy in the ith district is the difference between a closely defined measure of need and a measure of a reasonable local contribution. Let us take the matter of the determination of the local contribution first. As before, this is a product of a local contribution rate, r, times an estimate of local tax base, Y_i. The rate, r, is theoretically determined by the ratio of the cost of a standard program in a rich district to the value of tax base per pupil in that place. Y_i is either some measure of taxable property in the districts or a synthetic measure based on retail sales, motor vehicle registration, etc.

The difference between the fixed unit and variable unit grant is found in the treatment of the foundation program, u_i.[9] In the variable unit scheme, the expenditure per pupil toward which the state will grant support is allowed to vary within limits, depending on the quality of educational resources that the local district chooses to purchase.[10] (Superficially, of course, the fact that u_i can vary within limits poses a difficulty in the exact determination of r, but r is seldom determined exactly anyway.) As we know, the fixed unit plan uses one value of the foundation program for all the districts of the state.

The basis for the variability of u, i.e., of the local expenditure level toward which the state provides support, is normally the characteristics of teachers: how many have advanced degrees and how many are highly experienced. If a district has only inexperienced teachers with the B.A. degree, it may be credited with, say, $4,000 per teacher for purposes of determining its aid. If a district has only teachers with ten years or more of experience, all of whom have the M.A., it may be credited with the maximum figure of state support, say $6,000 per teacher. Most districts would have some inexperienced and some experienced members on their staffs, as well as some with advanced training and some without it. In computing u_i, each teacher would be listed at an appropriate figure drawn from a state salary schedule. Ordinarily there is a maximum number of teachers that a district can count, perhaps one for each 25 students.

The Percentage Equalizing Grant (3)

There are only two basic features of the percentage equalizing grant as it is used in education. First, the state pays some share of locally determined school expenditures in the given district. Second, the state's share is larger in poor districts than in rich.

How is the state share for a particular district determined? There are several steps in the process. First, it is necessary to calculate the ratio of tax base per pupil in the ith district, y_i, to state tax base per pupil, y. The relative economic standing of the ith district is thus established in the form y_i/y. Next, this ratio is multiplied by an arbitrary constant, call it x, which normally has a value between 0 and 1. (As a first approximation, the value of x can be taken to represent the local share of educational expenditures in the state, i.e., the local spending of all districts taken together.) Finally, the product of x times the relative economic standing of the ith district, that is,

$x \cdot y_i/y$, is subtracted from the numeral 1. The resulting figure, ordinarily a fraction, is the state share of support in the ith district.[11] Since y_i/y will have a relatively low value in poor districts, the state share in those places will be correspondingly high, and the converse applies to rich districts. The process can be described in various ways in state law, but the essential elements of the scheme are uniform. What we have laid out is the only major type of open-ended aid that has received serious consideration in educational circles. Hereafter in this chapter it will be described as the "basic percentage-equalizing formula."

To see how the formula works, let us consider the case of a district of average resources. Suppose that such a district has equalized valuation per pupil equal to \$30,000, that it has 1,000 pupils, and that it spends \$400 per pupil on education. Suppose further that the state wishes to meet 50 per cent of school costs in that district. This means we set x = .5 in the formula so that it reads

$$A_i = \left[1 - \left(.5 \frac{\$30{,}000}{\$30{,}000} \right) \right] \cdot \$400{,}000 = \$200{,}000$$

Clearly, the state subsidy is \$200,000, or 50 per cent of expenditures. Now, let us take a poor district, one that has a per pupil valuation of \$15,000, but let us say it also has 1,000 pupils. Keeping x at .5, the formula will read

$$A_i = \left[1 - \left(.5 \frac{\$15{,}000}{\$30{,}000} \right) \right] \cdot \$400{,}000 = \$300{,}000$$

The state share in this poor district is 75 per cent of expenditure. As the reader can readily verify, the state share in a district of \$45,000 per pupil valuation will be 25 per cent. Each of the three districts could provide a program costing \$400 per pupil at the same level tax rate: 6.7 mills.

In the general case, this formula works as a "resources equalizer." That is, any two districts that spend the same sum per pupil on education have equal local tax rates for schools.[12] As long as x has a value equal to or greater than zero but less than 1, then the expression (1 — x) indicates approximately the share of educational expenditures that is financed from state tax sources. (This follows, incidentally, from the earlier statement that x is a measure of the *local* share.) These points need brief amplification.

First is the matter of the size of the state share. If all districts are included under the aid program, (1 — x) will indicate the size of the state share, provided the average expenditure per pupil is the same in all districts. If per pupil expenditure is not the same in all districts, then $(1-x)$ will still indicate precisely the size of the state share if the sum of the weighted deviations of per pupil expenditure in districts below mean income is equal to the sum of weighted deviations above the mean. Most commonly, one would find that high income districts spend more per pupil than poor; hence, the size of the state share will usually be somewhat less than $(1-x)$.

Next, the size of the state share applicable in a locality decreases as a district is richer. As one moves up the income scale of districts, the state share at some point may fall to zero. For example, if $x=1$, the district of mean income will have a zero share. If $x=.8$, it will be a district whose income per pupil is 25 per cent above state average. For $x=.5$, it will be a district of double the state average, and so on. As x approaches one, it becomes increasingly likely that some districts will be excluded from the grant program. Should this happen, there is no longer the possibility of relating $(1-x)$ to the size of the state share, since the expenditures in some districts will fluctuate independently of state aid.

But there is a more serious consequence of excluding some districts from the grant program, namely that districts no longer will have equal local tax rates for equal per pupil expenditures. In particular, the rich districts will be able to finance any given level of expenditure at a lower tax rate than all the other places that are included in the grant scheme.

There is a way, however, to preserve both the resources equalizing effect and the relation between $(1-x)$ and size of the state share: to recognize negative values of the state shares in particular, i.e., rich districts, negative values, specifically, $\left(1-x\frac{y_i}{y}\right)$. Suppose in district A, this expression has a value of —.2. Then A should tax itself at 120 per cent of its educational expenditure and turn over the extra 20 per cent to the state for distribution to poorer districts. Such a device is obviously of no practical significance, and it is thus in the short-run fiscal interests of the rich districts to seek to obtain a value of x high enough to exclude them from the grant program.[13]

The state share of educational expenditures under the distribution can increase over time (a) as x is deliberately set at a lower value, (b) as lower-income districts increase their expenditures at a higher-than-average rate,[14] and (c) as the inequality of income among districts falls, with the result that a larger proportion of the state's school population is included under the distribution plan. The absolute change in state-financed educational expenditures will reflect both changes in size of state share and fluctuations in local expenditures.

As the percentage equalizing plan has been used in education and in the forms in which it has been proposed, there are three special features worthy of note. (1) It is customary to set a minimum level of expenditure in the aided districts. The figure is commonly thought of as the expenditure level below which the state will suffer a serious loss of social benefit.[15] (2) When differences in necessary costs are easily measurable, they are incorporated into the aid formula. That is, Ni (which is used to compute y_i) is adjusted for proportion of secondary pupils, sparsity, density, etc. (3) The state funds are distributed on a reimbursement basis. This provision can be said to fall with severity on the poor districts, since these places may find it difficult to meet the year's incremental costs solely from their limited resources.

Evaluation of the Alternative Schemes

It is now possible to reach some conclusions about how well the major plans of state aid meet the four objectives listed earlier: stimulation, equity, efficiency, and tax relief.

The Fixed Unit Plan (1). With respect to stimulation, the effects of the fixed unit plan, once established, would appear to be minor. Local expenditures in any district will be $N_i\ (u + l_i)$, where l_i is the "voluntary" rate of local taxation per pupil. All expenditures above the "foundation program," i.e., above u, fall on the local tax base. Local resources per pupil vary widely among districts. It follows that a rich district can advance its expenditures farther at a given increase in rate of local tax than a poor one, but, even so, there is no sharing of high per pupil expenditures in districts, poor or rich.

Now, it might appear that it is possible to provide stimulation by raising u (the mandated expenditure level). In practice, it has been difficult to set u higher than the state average expenditures. If a figure substantially higher than the average is picked, some of the low expenditure districts may find it difficult to make wise use of the additional funds in the short run, given the limitations that exist on the supply of educational resources (mainly personnel) at any point in time and on the possibilities that exist for making use of such higher quality resources as can be found. Also, if mandated expenditures are raised sharply, so too is the mandatory rate of local taxation. Since the property tax (which is the main instrument of localities) is at least mildly regressive, some of the poorer households in the state might well find the burden unusually onerous.

Suppose that a state adopts a new tax instrument and finds that it can raise the state support of education by one third. If it seeks to keep to strict Strayer-Haig distribution of aid (assuming no change in number of pupils and distribution of income among the districts), it will have to raise both u and the mandated local levies, i.e., r, by one third. This would probably be out of the question, so the device of providing "tax leeway" is employed. Tax leeway is given by setting r at a lower level than is determined by the ratio of foundation program to tax base per pupil in the richest district. When this is done, the state aid is, in effect, split in two parts: one, an equalizing portion and two, a nonequalizing portion, equal on a per pupil basis to the state aid to the richest district, divided by the number of pupils in that district. The range of expenditure among districts would be expected to widen as the richer places used at least part of their nonequalizing grants to raise their own levels of spending. Under the Strayer-Haig formula, stimulation, as expected, appears to be bought at the price of slighting the equity objective. The question is whether the price is too high.

The equity criterion, however, poses a more serious objection to the Strayer-Haig approach. This distribution plan offers very limited possibilities for taking differences in "necessary costs" into account.[16] Necessary costs are expenses which—in the short run at least—are beyond the control of the local school district, as, for example, in the purchase of labor inputs. An applicant for a teaching position will take into account both the monetary and nonmonetary advantages offered by a particular district. A number of the nonmonetary advantages, such as location, characteristics of the student body, opportunities to engage in experimental work, and career advancement are not subject to control by that district in the immediate period. (Differential advantages of location, of course, are fixed for an indefinite time.) It would be foolish to deny the existence of the nonmonetary rewards, but it is presently impossible to establish the monetary differential that would serve to offset them. The measurement of teacher quality and the payment of corresponding salary differentials is not possible at the present time. Accordingly, corrections for this major source of differences in necessary costs cannot be incorporated in a fixed unit formula. The practical results are either that the pupils in poor districts suffer from an inadequate program or that the taxpayer in such districts bears an onerous burden. The former is the more likely result.

With respect to the promotion of efficiency in expenditure, the fixed unit type of grant would appear to be effective, insofar as any general purpose grant can be effective on this score. The costs of inefficient operation fall on local taxpayers for the most part. The gains from improving the efficiency of operation, whether taken in the form of higher quality service or reduction in local tax burden, are enjoyed mostly by local people. If, however, a particular district has very low costs of operation and a very low demand for educational services, the mandating of a given expenditure level may encourage it to use resources wastefully.

If the mandated expenditure level (u) is adjusted periodically to the average level of expenditure in a state, then the Strayer-Haig type of grant program would appear to offer relative tax relief. That is, the share of state support of education should remain approximately constant. (It is not unknown, however, for u to lag considerably behind average expenditures.) The tax relief effect may be spread quite unevenly among districts, nonetheless. If tax leeway is provided, some rich districts may use part of their state funds for tax relief, especially if they happen to have low real costs. On the other hand, some poor districts may have high real costs and feel the necessity to supplement the full amount of the state grant with a high rate of local taxation.

The Variable Unit Plan (2). With respect to meeting the objectives of efficiency and tax relief, there appear to be no major differences between the fixed unit and variable unit plans. There are, however, differences in regard to stimulation and equity. In summary, the variable unit scheme offers greater stimulation but it appears to have some particularly undesirable results under the equity criterion.

To see why this is so, some extreme assumptions are necessary. Suppose that the state credits each district with $4,000 for a beginning teacher with the B.A. and with $5,000 for a beginning teacher with the M.A. Assume, for simplicity, that there are no experienced teachers in the state. More important, assume that teachers' salaries correspond exactly to the figures ($4,000 and $5,000) at which the state offers support. If there are no teachers with the M.A. available to any district, the use of a variable unit plan will yield results similar to those of a fixed unit plan.

Now, let a small number of M.A. teachers move into the state.

Any district can exchange the services of a bachelor's degree teacher for the better trained person as a free gift. That is, local taxes will not increase and, while state taxes go up, they will go up in just the same amount whether one's own district obtains these services or whether they go to some other school system. Probably the better trained teachers will distribute themselves among the richer districts because of the nonmonetary advantages these places offer. Since, then, the rich districts are the ones who receive the free gift, an element of inequity exists. In this case, there is stimulation of expenditure but not of local expenditure.

Now assume, more realistically, that teachers' salaries stand at a higher level than the figures under which the state gives credit. That is, B.A. salaries are higher than $4,000 and M.A.'s get more than $5,000. At this point, it is likely that stimulation of local spending is introduced. In effect, the state grant reduces the price of higher quality educational inputs in all districts. If all districts had access to the teachers' market on equal terms, the reduction in price would be the same in all districts. The rich districts by definition are better able to take advantage of the "bargain." But to say that equal access exists is a heroic assumption. The variable unit scheme does relatively little to handle the problem of expected differences in necessary costs of personnel. Teachers can be expected to consider both monetary and nonmonetary advantages offered by the districts. If a poor district has to offer more dollars than a rich one to obtain equal quality in teaching personnel, this extra monetary inducement will fall as a cost solely on the poor district's resources. It can be claimed, however, that the value of the stimulation is worth whatever degree of inequity is imposed.[17]

The Percentage Equalizing Grant (3). Under this type of grant the degree of stimulation would appear to depend mainly (a) on whether local expenditures are viewed in terms of tax rate or tax bill and (b) on whether the level of state taxes is taken into account by citizens when judging the level of local expenditures. Point (a) will be considered first.

If local expenditures are weighed in terms of tax rate, percentage grants would appear to have a relatively minor stimulating effect. Unless the constant x is set very low, the major result of the operation of the grant scheme is to allow all communities to finance schools at approximately the same tax rates as rich communities have been accustomed to. On the other hand, should the people in a community consider only the local tax bill for education as the proper criterion for judging expenditures, the stimulation effect could be quite powerful, especially in the poorer communities. For example, some of them might be in a position to say, "We can get an additional $100 worth of school services at a price to us of $10." This might well appear to be a very great bargain. Probably some persons would take the tax rate view and some the tax bill, with nonparents leaning toward the former and school authorities (and possibly parents) the latter. If the percentage grants come to be more widely used, such a hypothesis should be subject to test.

If judgments about short-run changes in state tax burden are taken into account in weighing local expenditures, it might be expected that rich districts would seek to have themselves excluded from the distribution by way of taxes and expenditures. However, such exclusions do not accord with conventional attitudes and practice. State tax burdens per capita usually can be influenced in only small degree by local decisions and attitudes. For any one district to protect itself from exploitation by others, its only recourse is to secure a larger grant, which it can do first, by seeing that it is eligible to receive aid and then by raising the level of its local support of education. This is stimulation of a defensive character.

Of course, the willingness of a district to increase its expenditures will depend in part on the judgment of school authorities of the productivity of different types of educational programs at a given time in the district. Incremental spending may take the form of purchasing higher qualities of conventional inputs, of adding new products, or of changing one or more processes (eventually, these new processes may allow a reduction in expenditure levels through the higher average productivity they afford, once installed). All districts, but especially the poor ones, could be expected to respond to the service opportunities more readily under state sharing of costs. One of the prime advantages of the percentage grants is that their use allows the state to share the cost of innovation even when the change in a given district cannot yet be expressed in standard (unit) costs per pupil.[18]

With regard to equity, the percentage scheme, as noted, serves as a resource equalizer. As it does so, it reduces absolute differences in necessary costs. Suppose a favored district can obtain a teacher of a certain competence at $4,000, while another less favored district must pay $5,000 to obtain his services. If both districts are receiving state grants at a rate of 50 per cent, the difference in necessary cost is cut from $1,000 to $500. This may be the strongest feature of the scheme. However, it should be noted that differences in necessary costs are not fully eliminated.

It is sometimes held that a percentage equalizing scheme can have anti-equalizing effects. That is, the rich districts may be sufficiently stimulated by state matching, even though it is at a low rate, to expand their educational activities to the point where children in the poorer districts suffer greater discrimination in opportunities, relatively speaking, than before. This can be a real danger if the supply of educational resources is relatively fixed. Otherwise, high spending by the rich districts may provide returns that are very widely shared in the state. First, the demonstration effect may lead most districts to raise their educational aspirations, which would be especially important if the whole state has been lagging in its school support. Second, the expenditures in the rich districts may provide external economies in the other school systems. The financing of the in-service training of teachers and educational research particularly, are likely to yield such benefits. Third, some graduates of the superior programs may be helped by their education to make contributions of inestimable value to society; i.e., the social benefits of well-established systems may be very large.

The percentage grants are probably weaker than the unit type with regard to the efficiency objective, since the costs of inefficiency are no longer borne solely by the local community but are shared with all the taxpayers of the state. This argument, however, needs to be examined with some care. If it should be discovered that taxpapers view school expenditures in terms of tax rate, then a resources equalizer does nothing more than allow, in essence, the poor districts to be as little concerned with the efficiency of expenditure as rich districts have always been. Further, programs that absorb a large part of local budgets have, simply by their size, a visibility that promotes a concern with fiscal responsibility. Education clearly falls in this class. The tax bill for education will be prominent in almost all districts, even under a percentage equalizing formula. Finally, the reimbursement feature serves the objective of fiscal responsibility.

These counterarguments, nonetheless, bear mainly on increases in expenditure. If technological advances occur in education so that methods to raise productivity become available, will districts be as eager to adopt them and to reduce their expenditures under a percentage scheme as under unit grants? Probably not. A tax rate once set is likely to become generally accepted (the pressure against raising taxes is greater than that to lower them), so under either plan the argument on the basis of tax rates is weak. If residents look at school expenditures in terms of their tax bill, the inducement to efficiency is obviously stronger under unit grants. Only the reimbursement feature of the percentage grants can be said to give any strong inducement to adopt money-saving methods.

On the side of tax relief, the percentage plan automatically provides a large measure of relative relief. If tax stabilization is desired, then the state share will need to be adjusted up or down, depending on whether educational expenditures advance less or more rapidly than the value of local taxable properties in the state.

Two further notes should be added. It is probable that the wider use of percentage equalizing grants would be associated with an increase in the effective power of state departments of education, because the scheme appears to be relatively weak with regard to efficiency objectives. It is by no means clear that this movement would need to be carried to the point where there was any serious loss of the values of local control.

More damaging, the use of the percentage grants appears to lead to a misallocation of local governmental resources. Whether local expenditures are viewed in terms of tax rate or tax bill, the subvention of this one service can be expected to distort local spending decisions toward the schools at the expense of other needed public activities. A number of points can be made to show why such distortion should, nonetheless, be accepted. (1) Social benefits are more clearly characteristic of education than other types of local expenditures. (2) Under the social ethic, a greater weight should be given to the goal of equality of opportunity than to the maximization of returns from local public services. (3) The demands for noneducational services may be relatively constant at any one time, hence, the increase in school spending may result primarily in a shift from private to public consumption, with relatively little effect on the growth of the whole group of local public activities. (4) Education as a local public service is peculiarly labor intensive. This means (a) that differences in necessary costs among districts are likely to be large and (b) that the possibility of obtaining advances in productivity are relatively slight. Point (a) argues for the use of percentage grants, while (b) tells us that the loss of the other services will be less than the dollar magnitude of the distortion, could it be measured, would indicate.

Percentage Equalizing Grants, Adopted and Proposed

In December, 1961, the New York State Joint Legislative Committee on School Financing recommended the adoption of a percentage equalizing type of grant, to replace the Strayer-Haig formula then in use and also to replace most of the rather large number of special purpose grants.[19] Since New York has long held a position of leadership in school finance, the serious consideration of a general purpose percentage grant by that state calls for a look at the actual operation of the plan in those states that use it. This is rather easily done, for there are only two: Wisconsin and Rhode Island.

Wisconsin Experience

The Wisconsin plan was adopted in 1949. In its original form, it used, essentially, the basic percentage equalizing formula, where the measure of local income is equalized property valuation per public school child. The formula provided equalization of resources up to the state average valuation per child. In addition, "flat grants" of $25 to $35 per child were offered, but a district could not receive both the equalization and flat grant aid. Rather than present the aid plan in terms of a percentage formula, as above, the school authorities in Wisconsin speak of a "guaranteed valuation." When first adopted, then, the guaranteed valuation was equal approximately to the state average, i.e., $17,000. By 1959-60, it had been raised to $33,000, which was some $5,000 above the state average. This is equivalent to reducing x in the formula given earlier in this chapter from 1 to roughly .85. (One reason for reducing x will be noted shortly.) As x is lowered, a larger proportion of the districts come under equalization aid. Whereas in 1953-54, the flat grant portion was 2¼ times as large as the equalizing ($13 million flat and $5.8 million equalizing), by 1959-60 the equalizing portion had risen to a size 2.5 times larger than the flat part ($36.1 million equalizing and $14.4 million flat). It remains true, nonetheless, that only about half of the pupils in Wisconsin attend schools in districts that receive equalization aid.[20] The flat aid districts are in a highly favored position: not only is there no attempt to withdraw their excess resources, but they actually receive grants from the state which are independent of their level of expenditure.

In 1960-61, the plan worked in approximately the following way. Let a district have an equalized valuation of, say, $20,000 per pupil. Let its current expenditures net of special purpose state and federal grants be $400. The per pupil support, $400, divided by the guaranteed valuation of $33,000, equals a "required operating (tax) rate" of 12.12 mills. State aid per pupil would be 12.12 mills x $13,000 (i.e., $33,000-$20,000), or $158, in the succeeding school year. Any district that had a valuation of $33,000 or less could provide $400 per pupil at no higher rate on equalized valuation.[21]

Now, actually, the figure of $33,000 as guaranteed valuation applies only to "integrated" school districts, grade K (or 1) to 12. (These districts included approximately 75 per cent of the public school population in 1960-61.) Wisconsin makes a qualitative distinction among school districts, with those classified as "integrated" meeting certain standards on minimum size, range of course offerings, in-service training of staff, etc., while those classified as "basic" are affected only by the typical conditions that states impose on districts, such as holding school for 180 days a year. The guaranteed valuation for basic districts is lower than for integrated: for example, the figure for a basic K-12 district in 1960-61 was $24,500.

The Wisconsin plan of state aid is often described as an "incentive" plan. The major incentive element would appear to be in the higher level of aid offered to districts that raise themselves to integrated standards, not in the matching provisions of the percentage grant itself. Thus, the Wisconsin plan offers the same kind of incentive to spend state and local funds as the variable unit type of plan, but with one important difference, namely, that the state shares with the districts the burden of meeting necessary costs in those systems where such costs are high.[22]

There is one more feature of the Wisconsin plan which is worth special comment. For integrated districts there is a local tax rate limit of 15 mills on equalized valuation for current school expenditures, which is a high limit, relative to the rates of local taxation actually imposed in most states. Districts may spend above 15 mills, however, and, as they do so, the state pays 100 per cent of the school costs.[23]

The Wisconsin plan has been well accepted by state and local school authorities and by the public, as indicated by the revisions in the scheme since its adoption. Between 1949-50 and 1960-61, the guaranteed valuation for integrated K-12 districts was raised by 94 per cent. That for basic districts and also the flat grant per pupil were increased, but not by as much. Also, when first voted, the plan had a 9 mill limit on state matching, which meant, of course, that between 9 and 15 mills the districts were on their own. This 9 mill limitation was removed by the 1955 legislative session. Lastly, the state legislature has in its last two sessions adopted a biennial rather than an annual appropriation for education aid, which serves to forestall the necessity to prorate funds to the districts in cases of inadequate appropriation.

By objective measures, education in Wisconsin has fared rather well under the percentage equalizing plan. With respect to stimulation of local spending, the results must necessarily be somewhat inconclusive, since the state has deliberately sought to provide tax stabilization for the districts. Total expenditures, state and local combined, have advanced rather remarkably, however. Between 1947-48 and 1957-58, educational expenditures rose 1.75 per cent for each 1.0 per cent increase in state personal income, while the national average was 1.66 per cent.[24] In 1960, the expenditures per pupil in Wisconsin were 19.67 per cent of per capita income; nationally, the figure was 17.68 per cent. The response of educational expenditures in Wisconsin to increases in state income should be viewed in the light of this fact: between 1948-49 and 1957-58, the number of school districts was cut from 6,038 to 3,500 (the figure for 1961-62 is 1,700!). Since many of the districts that disappeared were of an inefficient size, the total volume of educational services must have risen handsomely.

The results in terms of equity are fairly startling. It is commonly found that educational expenditures per pupil are highly correlated with the resources of the district. It is not at all unusual to find simple correlation coefficients between per pupil support and valuation (or income) in excess of .8. Such a relationship does not exist, apparently, among the districts included in the percentage grant in Wisconsin. In 1960-61, there were 154 integrated K-12 districts. One hundred twenty-one received equalization aid, and 33 received flat grants. For the 121 equalization districts, the coefficient of multiple correlation of equalized valuation per pupil and size of district on local tax rate for current school expenditures is .104, which is not significantly different from zero. (In this instance, local tax rate and per pupil expenditure stand in a one-to-one relation, since all the districts under state aid have the same guaranteed valuation per pupil: $33,000.) On the other hand, the 33 flat grant districts show a simple correlation of .633 of valuation on expenditures per pupil, which *is* significantly different from zero.

For districts receiving equalization aid, then, size is not an important determinant of expenditure. Here, however, it should be noted that the group of 121 districts did not include any very small or very large places (the smallest had 760 pupils and the largest, 7,481.) More important, income (as measured by equalized valuation) is not a significant variable. There was a substantial range in income in the group: $6,538 per pupil to $28,421. Both rich and poor districts were in the high expenditure category and both rich and poor were to be found in the low. If the differences in expenditure that one finds among the Wisconsin districts reflected variations in necessary costs, it could be concluded that a remarkable degree of equality of opportunity had been attained. Unfortunately, the information to make such a judgment is lacking.

On the question of the efficient use of resources in education, the sharp drop in the number of school districts has already been mentioned. Further, the integrated districts must meet a more stringent set of quality standards than is imposed by most state authorities. The per cent of public school children in integrated districts has risen from 68 in 1949-50 to 86 in 1959-60. These apparent gains are not a necessary result of the use of percentage equalizing grants, but they serve to show that the goal of efficiency is not inconsistent with its use, provided the districts are willing to sacrifice a measure of local autonomy.

Tax relief is a stated objective in Wisconsin. "It is the purpose of the state aid formula . . . to cause the state to assume a greater proportion of the costs of public education and to relieve and reduce the general property of some of its tax burden." (*Wisconsin School Law*, 40.69.) At the same time, the aid program, particularly insofar as it offers a higher level of aid in districts that meet the "integrated" standards, acts to stimulate local taxation. The inconsistency has been resolved by raising the level of state aids, e.g., by raising the amounts of the guaranteed valuations, to the end that the average local tax rate on equalized valuation has been stabilized at about 10 mills. In particular, an attempt is made to adjust the guaranteed valuation up to the point where a 10 mill levy will yield the current average expenditure per pupil. This has required a small increase in the share of state support (19.3 per cent in 1953-54 to 23.6 per cent in 1959-60). At the same time, the reduction in the number of very small districts in itself has probably served to reduce the extremes in local taxation.

The Rhode Island Program

The percentage equalizing plan in Rhode Island has not been in use long enough to provide clues on its effectiveness in meeting the various objectives of state aid, but its features are worthy of note. The method of determining the state share of expenditures in a district is written in the law of rather complex form, but what it comes to is the basic percentage equalizing formula, with x equal to .8625. However, the state share of total current expenditures is not approximated by 1 — .8625 = .1375, because (a) the value of x is so large that many places would nominally be excluded from receiving grants and (b) the further stipulation that the state contribution shall not fall below 25 per cent in any district. When the plan was introduced in 1959, there were 17 of 41 districts at the minimum percentage.[25]

The Rhode Island plan thus gives even more favorable treatment to rich districts than Wisconsin. Excess resources are not withdrawn and the aid granted is a percentage of locally determined expenditures. (In Wisconsin, of course, the rich districts were restricted to a flat grant.) Just as the city of Milwaukee fell into the favored category in Wisconsin, so Rhode Island's large city of Providence receives the special treatment in that state.

Three other features should be mentioned. (1) Unlike Wisconsin, Rhode Island has no local tax rate limitation. (2) School districts in Rhode Island are fiscally dependent. It is provided in Section 11a of the act (Chapter 27, *Laws of Rhode Island*) establishing the percentage grant that, should a city or town fail to meet the state minimum teachers' salary schedule or should it fail to spend $300 per pupil, the state will withhold such deficiency from its noneducational grants due to the place and allocate the sum specifically for education. This would appear to place the state in a fairly active role with respect to the control of resource use in local government. (3) The law provides for an "education improvement fund," under which the state can make appropriations for research and development.

There is as yet insufficient experience to judge the response of the richest school districts to a percentage grant. Thus, an interesting question will be faced in the revision of the Rhode Island plan, at such time as funds are available, that is, for its extension. Should x be reduced from .8615 or should the minimum percentage be raised to, say, 30 or 35 per cent? The former presumably would serve the equity objective but the latter might provide greater stimulation.

Maryland and Delaware Proposals

As noted, the percentage grant has been recommended for adoption in Maryland and Delaware. The Maryland proposal has these distinctive features. (1) It would be fully operative, in the sense that all districts would be included at their precise state shares under the formula. The present level of state support and the distribution of income among the county districts of Maryland would make such a program feasible. (2) In the 1961 recommendation to the legislature, the districts' tax contribution would not be affected by the receipt of federal funds under the federally affected areas program (P.L. 874). This was to be accomplished by deducting such grants from the state's share rather than from the district's contribution. (3) Equalized valuation as a measure of local resources was adjusted to take account of the following kinds of differences in necessary costs: secondary pupils, special classes, kindergarten, junior college students, sparsity, and transportation. (4) The particular form of brake on expenditure was to give state sharing on increments on only $20 per pupil. For example, if expenditures in a district were $400 per pupil in year 1, $440 in year 2, and $460 in year 3, the state would share in only $420 of the expenditures in year 2, but the full $460 in year 3.

The Delaware proposal is interesting mainly in that it shows how major revisions of state aid plans must bend to the heritage of past practices. In 1959-60, the state provided approximately 89 per cent of school funds in Delaware, taking account both of current expenses and of capital outlay. Many districts levied very small amounts of local taxes and some none at all. On the other hand, a few places had taxed themselves relatively heavily for schools. By and large, these were the richer ones.

It was proposed at first that the present system of state aid be retained in full (essentially, a variable unit, nonequalizing type) and, second, that a supplementary percentage equalizing formula be used, with $x = .50$, but the formula was only to be applied to a dollar amount of $40 per pupil in the first year. Each year an additional $40 per pupil was to be added to the percentage grant plan. Districts which already were taxing themselves in any substantial amount would have received the additional money from the state without making any extra local effort. In some cases, the present effort was enough so that they would not have had to raise local levies per pupil to share fully in the plan for four years. Such was the price felt necessary to reward past efforts in school support, in a state where any substantial local effort was a rare thing.

It is not to be implied in this section that only those states that are using or are considering the use of a percentage equalizing scheme stand in virtue. The more conventional plans can be so designed as to yield progress toward meeting the major objectives of subvention of local districts. Further, some states, such as California, Utah, and Alaska, have given thought to the use of combinations plans, i.e., plans which embody aspects of the foundation program and percentage aids. The objective here has been simply to deal with some aspects of one of the new developments in school finance.

The Problem of the Cities

In the early days of school grants, it was the economic difficulties of small towns and rural areas that stood as the prime justification for subventions and, further, that caused certain provisions of the aid to be written in favor of such districts. Now, it is from the larger cities that one hears the call for special treatment. With regard to the measure of resources commonly used in aid schemes, namely, property base, the case is made that valuation per capita represents an overstatement of the ability of the cities to support schools, since cities have extraordinarily high noneducational municipal costs. That cities do face such high costs has been amply documented and needs no discussion here.

What of school costs themselves? There are several cost-increasing factors that exist in cities. First, their payments for salaries per teacher are high. In 1960-61, the median salary of a classroom teacher in urban school districts of 500,000 population and over was $6,422, while the figure for urban districts 10,000 to 29,999 (essentially suburban places) was $5,318. The median in the cities was thus 21 per cent higher than in the smaller systems. The difference can be explained on various grounds. Large systems probably cannot be as effective in screening recruits as small; hence, they offer higher starting pay in compensation for their (relative) nonselectivity. Large systems have many older teachers (44 per cent over age 50 in Chicago in 1960), which teachers are likely to be at (or near) maximum salary. The cities offer the teacher the opportunity to change from one school to another; hence, various frictions can be relieved without the necessity of leaving the district to get a change of scene. Further, appointment to an administrative post is more likely to come to a person who has a good bit of seniority within the system. These factors contribute to higher salary costs in city systems.

Second, site costs for schools in the cities are vastly more expensive than in less populated areas. Third, certain costs that are "fixed" in the middle-run time period may be high because the population of the cities is highly mobile. That is, as population drops in one attendance area and rises in another, the school in the declining area may become unavoidably overstaffed by principals, assistant principals, and custodians. For example, some schools in Boston operate at less than 40 per cent of capacity. It has been estimated that savings of $90,000 a year could be made on salaries of principals and assistant principals in the City of Boston under school consolidation. Fourth, pupil turnover is high, and costs are attached to the induction and withdrawal of children in the schools. Fifth, the size of secondary schools in the cities is generally large and often determined by factors other than close consideration of the relation between size and plant operating cost. There is some evidence to show that the most economical size of plant is in the range 700-900 pupils.[26] Since many city secondary schools exceed this figure, the large urban districts may be committed to a (slightly) uneconomical size of plant. Sixth, there is the factor which has drawn much attention recently, namely, the cost of special programs. It is estimated that 12 of our largest cities spent $57.1 million in 1960 on programs for maladjusted and culturally deprived children. For these 12 cities, it is estimated that these costs will rise to $125.5 million in 1965.[27]

Finally, the composition of the student population is such as to impose high per pupil costs on the cities. By and large, the cities have relatively large parochial and private school enrollments. The greater number of male secondary students in parochial and private schools take the college preparatory program. This leaves the public system with a relatively strong weighting toward technical and trade education, and these latter programs have high per pupil costs. The points can be illustrated in the case of Boston. In Massachusetts, approximately 22 per cent of the population ages 5 to 16 is enrolled in private or parochial schools; in Boston, the figure is 35 per cent (as of October 1, 1959). The largest single group of nonpublic students is found in church-supported institutions. Among the male graduates of these institutions in 1961, 62 per cent entered college. The figure for public schools in 1960 was 44 per cent. Only 11.5 per cent of the graduates of church-supported schools had received technical or trade education; for the public schools, the corresponding figure was in excess of 30 per cent. The per pupil cost in Boston Technical High in 1960 was $148 above that of Boston Latin (a college preparatory school of no mean reputation); likewise, the per pupil cost in Boston Trade High was $52 above Boston Latin, after deduction of state vocational aid.[28]

On the other hand, there are certain factors which serve to reduce the cost of education in the cities. Density leads to lower transportation expenses. Size should allow economies in purchasing and record keeping, particularly with the availability of modern data processing equipment. Relative stability of staff means lower expenditures on inducting teachers.

The percentage equalizing type of grant can be of substantial assistance to the large cities. In Wisconsin and Rhode Island, the cities, along with all other places of high property valuation, are placed in a favored position, this serving to offset, at least in part, any understatement of resources available for schools in the giant systems. It is, of course, hard to defend this arbitrary treatment on grounds other than expediency. But more important, a percentage grant serves the general purpose of reducing absolute differences in necessary costs to the local taxpayers. Moreover, pupil measurement in the grant formula can easily be adjusted to take account of the numbers of children who need special programs. For example, it has recently been suggested in New York that children in the culturally deprived category should have a weight of 2.[29] Similarly, pupil measurements could be adjusted to take account of relatively large numbers of students in technical programs.

Beyond this, there is the unsettled question of the role of the cities in education. It would appear logical that these districts should be engaged in the further development of the staff, techniques, and instruments for schooling. Assume that the state offered significant special purpose grants for in-service training, for research, and for the development of materials. It is not unlikely that the largest part of the funds would flow to the cities. This would meet no immediate needs, but the long-run consequences with respect to recruitment and retraining of staff and with respect to the more effective use of resources in general might be substantial.

What, then, of the use of a general density correction in a state aid formula, corresponding to the sparsity corrections that formerly were so popular? The problems are not mechanical. By and large, the treatment of differences in necessary costs should be ordinarily such that the size of cost differentials cannot be subject to favorable manipulation by a recipient. The prime element of cost in education is teachers' salaries, and teachers in cities are often represented by a single bargaining agent. Hence, a density correction may encourage collective bargaining with the state carrying a large portion of salary increases. The desirability of this outcome would have to be decided on grounds other than state aid formulae. This is a different order of problem from any that may hold in using a sparsity correction, since the values introduced in a formula are based on the average cost of a large number of small districts in a given state.

Special Aid for Capital Outlay

In spite of their general disapproval of special purpose grants, school authorities have long supported subvention of school construction. Like payment of teachers' salaries, building schools is a major and obvious type of expenditure. The customary separation in school accounting practice between current operations and capital outlay allowed the grants to be made with minimum requirements for audit of the local books. Hence, there has been great fear of state control under this type of special purpose aid.

In the postwar period, school construction costs have advanced more rapidly than the average of all public construction costs. This may be deplorable, but it is a condition largely outside the control of any single school district. Since 1953, interest rates on municipal bonds have fluctuated in the 3 to 4 per cent range, whereas they hovered between 1½ to 2½ per cent in the 30's and 40's. Higher construction costs and higher interest rates have combined to raise debt service charges to extraordinary levels in some districts. For example, one can find cities and towns in Massachusetts where payments on long-term school interest alone exceed 10 per cent of the levy on property, this levy supporting both school and nonschool municipal expenditures. Similar cases exist in other states.

By and large, the districts that face extraordinary debt service charges are ones that have a low bond rating (or no rating). The low-rated places have poorer-than-average success in judging the timing of the market, and the market for municipal bonds is notoriously unstable. With respect to interest charges at least, it appears that the poorer districts face a substantial differential of necessary costs.

To protect school districts against the distortions in school expenditures that such differentials might cause, some of the newer plans of state aid contain special provisions that the state will assume the burden of extraordinarily high debt service charges. For example, in Rhode Island, the state pays 75 per cent of the net cost to the community of debt service above a 3 mill levy on equalized valuation. This provision is supplementary to a percentage equalizing grant for school construction. A similar feature of payment for excess charges is incorporated in the 1961 recommendation of the New York State Educational Conference Board.

The objective is laudable, but the mechanism may be open to serious question. There is no organized exchange for municipal bonds. Further, the districts that are likely to require special aid often receive very few bids on their issues. The way is open for local authorities to take a cavalier attitude toward the height of the interest rate they receive, in a situation where competition in making offers is limited and where current information to justify refusing all bids is not easily available.

It may be preferable to restrict the excess cost aid to interest payments alone, and to require all districts that may apply for such assistance to market their bonds under the advice of a state fiscal officer. A plan of this kind was used in New York in 1959. In spite of technical problems, it appeared to have much merit. For subvention of debt service, the emphasis should be placed, it would appear, not only on efforts to save communities harmless against excessive local burdens but also on efforts to reduce differentials in necessary costs of interest. There is, after all, only one quality of money.

Further, it would appear desirable that states distribute a larger part of their funds for construction in the form of lump sum payments. There would be some equalizing effects and savings in interest would be substantial. Local borrowing capacity would be preserved to meet future enrollment increases and to meet needs to renovate plant to reflect technological changes in education.

Summary

In the past few years there has been an increasing concern with the differential costs of providing educational services. Among school districts, differences in costs stem basically from the fact that the districts do not have equal access to the market for teachers' services. At the present time it is not possible to put a monetary measure on the variations in necessary costs that arise from this source. Percentage grants—in contrast to ones of the unit type—offer advantages in dealing with this problem.

The use of percentage grants does not solve all problems, however. Even when the more open-ended aid schemes are employed, the large cities remain in a disadvantageous position. It appears appropriate to incorporate in the grant formulas corrections for the extra costs of certain programs, such as technical education and education of the culturally deprived, toward which city districts show a relatively heavy weighting. A general density correction is an embracing solution, but open-ended grants may permit manipulation of cost differentials by the recipient; accordingly, there is reason to believe that the use of a general density correction could be risky. Further, percentage grants are not appropriate (a) when differential costs are subject to fairly close measurement and (b) when a reasonable objective is to obtain a reduction in such a cost. The example that has been cited in this chapter is interest costs on school construction.

Percentage grants also serve the objective of stimulation. However, stimulation of local spending for schools will produce some distortion in resource use among the range of local public services. The social benefits of education and the central role of education in preserving social mobility argue that some distortion is tolerable if stimulation results. Nonetheless, should percentage grants come into wider use, as it appears likely they will, the distortion effects should be a matter of serious concern. Other public services, in addition to education, are important to community welfare.

X. National Politics and Federal Aid

The federal government today constitutes what is probably the last major untapped source of revenue for public school education in this country. Federal grants have been made for limited and specific purposes, as in the National Defense Education Act of 1958. Endowments of land have been given to the states for educational purposes, the most famous being the grants made under the Articles of Confederation through the Ordinances of 1785 and 1787. Emergency allocations of funds were made to local school systems by the federal government in the depression days of the 1930's. Under the Morrill Act of 1862 and later legislation, higher education has been encouraged through the establishment and support of lang-grant colleges for agriculture and the mechanical arts. Areas especially affected by federal government activities have been assisted under the Lanham Act and subsequent legislation. But no long-term, general federal aid program for elementary and secondary education has yet been approved.

Inevitably, attempts have been made to secure such a program. This chapter is concerned with the question of why such efforts have failed. No attempt will be made to appraise the validity of the case for federal aid or to argue the form it should take. The focus will be upon the proposals made for general federal aid programs for operating expenses, for school construction, or both; the only answers offered will be suggestions as to why these proposals have failed of enactment by Congress.

Certainly it has not been for lack of trying. During the 1948 floor debate over federal aid, Senator Lister Hill (D., Ala.), one of the bill's sponsors, told his colleagues:

> Mr. President, bills similar to this one have been before the Senate for many years. Volumes of hearings have been taken. If we were to bring into the chamber from the Committee on Labor and Public Welfare the many volumes of hearings, they would be piled high on our desks. . . . Year after year, the committee has spent weeks considering the bill, attempting to reconcile differences, attempting to wipe out inequities, attempting to bring forth the best possible bill to provide Federal aid, with the primary responsibility for education still continuing in the states.[1]

This chapter is based on materials prepared by Frank J. Munger and Richard F. Fenno, Jr.

Senator Hill's statement did not exaggerate the amount of time that had already been given to the subject of federal aid. Yet since his statement the Senate has formally debated federal aid bills five additional times. During that period the relevant House and Senate committees have conducted hearings whose published record, by conservative estimate, runs to over ten thousand pages and includes more than six million words of testimony.

In the extent to which it has occupied the time of Congress and congressmen, federal aid to education is clearly one of the major issues of American politics today. As such it is intrinsically worthy of detailed study. But the length of time through which the debate has been carried on in American national politics suggests a broader framework for analysis, an examination of the process by which consensus is created for new departures in government policy. One of the most striking features of the issue has been the failure to secure such consensus; this study will attempt to suggest some of the reasons why.

Ninety-Four Years of Controversy

A full account of the proposals for federal aid to education would have to begin in the 19th century. The first major federal aid bill was the Hoar bill of 1870, providing for the establishment of national schools in all states where the state government failed to provide adequate public school instruction. Although no measure seriously considered since has been as far-reaching in its terms, the debate over the Hoar bill opened a period of two decades that has been described as the first phase of the federal aid struggle.[2]

The Early Phases: 1870-1943

Congressional action taken on the proposals of this period—as of the years since—is summarized in Figure 3. Although the bill introduced by Representative George Hoar (R., Mass.) was denounced by educational groups as unwarranted federal interference in public school education and withdrawn, it was followed by others, and bills were passed by both houses of Congress at one time or another—by the House once in 1872 and by the Senate four times. Unfortunately for the proponents of the legislation, the same bill was never passed by both houses in the same Congress. A federal aid bill came closest to success in 1880 when the Morrill bill was approved by the Senate, and the House Committee on Education offered a motion to suspend the rules and accept it. The House refused the motion, however, and though the Senate three times subsequently approved versions of the

FIGURE 3

CONGRESSIONAL ACTION ON GENERAL FEDERAL AID TO EDUCATION BILLS FROM THE 40TH (1867-69) TO THE 87TH (1961-63) CONGRESS

HOUSE			CONGRESS	SENATE		
Passed House	Passed House Committee	House Bill Introduced		Senate Bill Introduced	Passed Senate Committee	Passed Senate
			40			
	—	—	41	—		
—	—	—	42	—	—	
	—	—	43			
	—	—	44	—	—	
		—	45	—	—	
	—	—	46	—	—	—
	—	—	47	—	—	
	—	—	48	—	—	—
	—	—	49	—	—	—
		—	50	—	—	—
	—	—	51	—	—	
		—	52			
			53			
		—	54			
			55			
			56			
			57			
			58			
		—	59			
		—	60			
			61			
			62			
			63			
			64			
		—	65	—		
		—	66	—		
		—	67	—		
		—	68	—		
			69			
			70			
		—	71	—		
		—	72	—		
	—	—	73	—		
		—	74	—		
		—	75	—	—	
		—	76	—	—	
		—	77	—	—	
		—	78	—	—	
		—	79	—	—	
		—	80	—	—	—
		—	81	—	—	—
		—	82	—		
		—	83	—	—	
	—	—	84	—		
	—	—	85	—		
—	—	—	86	—	—	—
	—	—	87	—	—	—

Blair bill for federal aid, none of the three passed the House. The only legislation to win approval from Congress was a measure concerning higher education, the second Morrill Act, passed in 1890 and augmenting the federal assistance provided to the land-grant colleges.

With the defeat of the last Blair bill in the Senate in 1890, the struggle to secure general federal aid died. After a lapse of only a few years, however, Congress renewed the concern with educational legislation in a new guise. In the first two decades of the twentieth century Congress concentrated on problems of vocational education. From 1906 to 1917 bills for federal assistance to state programs for industrial, agricultural, or domestic education were continually before Congress. With the temporary disposition of the question by the passage of the Smith-Hughes Act in 1917, the way was cleared for the resumption of the general aid fight. Reconsideration of the issue was encouraged by World War I. The discovery by the draft boards that close to 25 per cent of the draftees were illiterate, that surprisingly large numbers did not speak English, and that the great majority of the one-third who were physically unfit suffered from defects that could have been remedied if identified at school age, precipitated a demand for action.

Occasional federal aid bills had been offered before, but late in 1918 Senator Hoke Smith (D., Ga.), one of the sponsors of the vocational education law, introduced two bills into the 65th Congress, one to establish a Federal Department of Education, the second the so-called Americanization bill. The following year, in the first session of the 66th Congress, a new bill, the Smith-Towner bill, was introduced incorporating features of both; it provided for the establishment of a cabinet-level Department of Education and made appropriations for the removal of illiteracy, for the equalization of educational opportunities, for Americanization programs, for physical education, and for the preparation of teachers. Similar measures were introduced into the 67th and 68th congresses and the issue of federal educational policy was actively pending before the Congress continuously from October 10, 1918, to March 4, 1925.

Despite endorsement by President Woodrow Wilson and support by the National Education Association and numerous women's organizations, none of these bills was even reported out of committee. With this failure the proponents of federal action for education turned to more limited goals. The Curtis-Reed bill in the 69th and 70th congresses and the Capper-Robinson bill in the 71st Congress all proposed the establishment of a Department of Education but were shorn of provisions for equalization funds, teacher education, and the like. Still no bill was reported from committee.

At President Herbert Hoover's direction, his Secretary of the Interior, Ray Lyman Wilbur, within whose department the Office of Education was then lodged, in 1929 appointed a 52-member committee to study the federal government's relations to education. The report of this National Advisory Committee on Education, published in 1921 as *Federal Relations to Education,*[3] although favorable to a program of general federal grants for educational purposes, spelled a kind of finish to the agitation of the twenties. The coming of the depression terminated concern for a permanent federal policy of aid to education by forcing immediate consideration of an emergency program of temporary aid.

As local school financial problems multiplied, the 72nd Congress, meeting from 1931 to 1933, was urged to amend the Reconstruction Finance Corporation Act to authorize loans to states and municipalities for educational purposes. This effort was renewed by Senator Walter George (D., Ga.) in the first session of the 73rd Congress, but it was not until the second session in 1934, when the public school systems in many states were near collapse, that the rush of bills came. Twenty-five to thirty bills were introduced providing for aid in one form or another, usually on an emergency basis.

Much of the steam was taken from the drive for emergency aid at this time by the fact that the federal government was already assisting in the problem out of general relief funds. At House committee hearings in February, 1934, Harry Hopkins, Federal Emergency Relief Administrator, estimated that 40,000 teachers were being paid from relief funds. Many of these were employed to teach in adult education or in rural schools. Hopkins estimated that from $2 million to $3 million was being spent each month for federal educational relief work. The Congress eventually set aside $48 million of relief money to employ unemployed teachers and authorized the Reconstruction Finance Corporation to allocate $75 million for loans to meet overdue teachers' salaries. No direct aid to education on either a temporary or permanent basis was voted; money was to be provided either on a loan basis or in payment to individual teachers in the form of relief. School systems as such were not to be helped.

The 74th Congress, meeting from 1935 to 1937, again saw numerous bills introduced concerning education. The House Committee on Education held hearings, but the only bill passed was another RFC loan bill. In addition, direct aid was provided to needy students through the National Youth Administration and a portion of federal relief funds earmarked for the employment of unemployed teachers. An unsuccessful effort was made by Senator Matthew Neely (D., W.Va.) to attach an allocation for school construction to the relief appropriation bill.

The return to a strategy of seeking long-term federal aid legislation was signalized by the introduction of companion bills by Senator Pat Harrison (D., Miss.), and Congressman Brooks Fletcher (D., Ohio), in the second session of the 74th Congress in 1936. The Harrison-Fletcher bill proved to be the first in a long series of bills providing for a permanent policy of federal grants-in-aid. No action was taken, but a similar bill was introduced into the 75th Congress, and hearings were held before the Senate Committee on Education and Labor in 1937. The bill was reported out of committee unanimously, but withdrawn by its sponsors after an advisory committee on education appointed by President Roosevelt brought in a recommendation for a combination of general and specific educational grants to the states. Through an amendment offered by Senator Elbert D. Thomas (D., Utah), the bill was rewritten to conform generally to the Committee's recommendations and again approved by the Senate Committee. But the Harrison-Thomas bill, as it was now called, remained upon the Senate calendar and in the House Committee on Education.

The federal aid fight was renewed in the 76th Congress with the principal proposal, largely unchanged, now called the Thomas-Harrison-Larrabee bill. Congressman John R. Murdock (D., Ariz.) informed his colleagues in the House: "Because I have been a schoolman and am now in the national legislature, some of my school friends regard me as a 'watchman on the tower.' They are saying to me: 'Watchman, how goes the battle?' "[4] The answer was: not so good. The Senate Committee again approved the bill, but the House Committee pigeonholed it, refusing even to hold hearings. The only major educational legislation approved at this time was the Lanham Act providing funds for schools in areas sharply affected by federal activities, a measure made necessary by the rapidly expanding national defense effort.

History was repeated in the 77th Congress as another federal aid bill was introduced, approved by the Senate Committee, and died. In the following Congress, however, for the first time in over fifty years, a federal aid to education bill was debated and acted upon in the United States Senate. This was the Educational Finance Act of 1943, introduced by Senators Thomas and Hill. After extensive hearings before the Senate Committee on Education and Labor, it was approved by the Committee and taken up for consideration by the Senate in October of 1943. The bill was debated for four days but, after the addition of an amendment requiring an equitable distribution of state funds for segregated schools, it was recommitted as its southern supporters deserted it. The House companion bill was never acted upon.

The Postwar Struggle: 1945-1952

The setback in the Senate in 1943 proved only temporary, and new federal aid legislation was soon before the Congress. Since 1945, in fact, federal educational legislation of some sort has been pending almost continuously. Figure 4 provides a more detailed account of the treatment given these various bills by the two houses of Congress during these years. The separate stages of committee hearings, committee reports, floor debate, and floor approval are identified on a year-to-year basis. The fact that additional entries are required for action in the House of Representatives testifies to the greater complexity of the parliamentary procedure in that chamber, an important factor in explaining action—and nonaction—during this seventeen-year period.

During the first of these sessions, 1945, two major federal aid bills were offered to the 79th Congress when the principal sponsors of the measures—the National Education Association and the American Federation of Teachers—split in their approach. The most dramatic change of front occurred, however, within the subcommittee appointed to attempt to reconcile the two bills. Senator Robert A. Taft (R., Ohio), one of the principal opponents of the 1943 bill, changed his position and joined his name as sponsor to an amended version of the NEA bill, called the Thomas-Hill-Taft bill, which was then approved by the Committee. Although no further action was taken in the Senate in 1946, another version of the same bill, with Senator Taft again as co-sponsor, was introduced into the 80th Congress, reported out by committee, and approved by the Senate in 1948. Even the U.S. Chamber of Commerce, long the principal antagonist of federal aid, hesitated briefly in its opposition.

The Senate action came too late in the session to secure parallel action in the still recalcitrant House of Representatives, but after the 1948 elections returned the Democratic party to majority status in Congress, enthusiasm ran high among the proponents of federal aid. A federal aid bill had failed to clear the House Committee in the 79th Congress only by a single vote and it was expected that favorable action could now be secured. Selective service rejections during the war had emphasized continuing illiteracy, and the postwar teacher and classroom shortage further dramatized the demand for federal action. The Senate Committee pushed a new bill, S. 246, to the floor

FIGURE 4

Congressional Action on General Federal Aid to Education Bills from 1945 to 1961

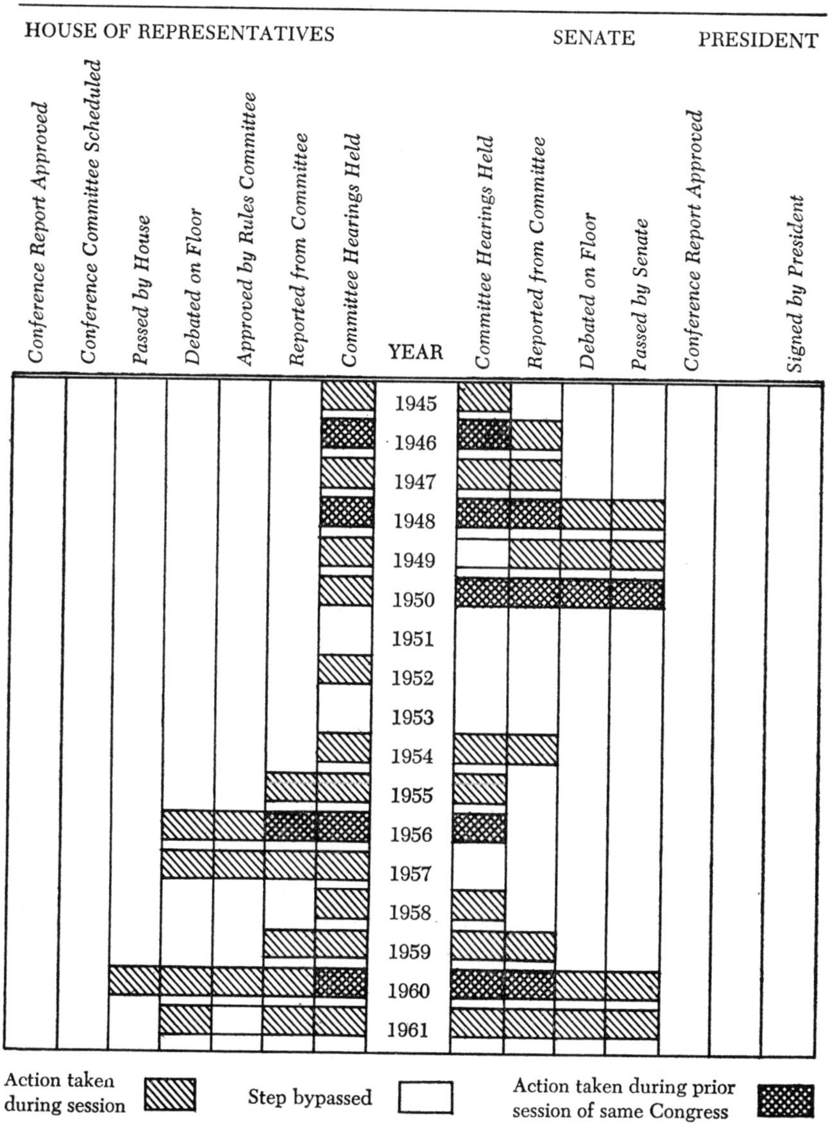

HOUSE OF REPRESENTATIVES

Conference Report Approved

Conference Committee Scheduled

Passed by House

Debated on Floor

Approved by Rules Committee

Reported from Committee

Committee Hearings Held

YEAR

SENATE

Committee Hearings Held

Reported from Committee

Debated on Floor

Passed by Senate

Conference Report Approved

PRESIDENT

Signed by President

1945
1946
1947
1948
1949
1950
1951
1952
1953
1954
1955
1956
1957
1958
1959
1960
1961

Action taken during session

Step bypassed

Action taken during prior session of same Congress

without hearings, and Senator Hill, a longtime proponent, opening the debate, expressed confidence that it would be approved by Congress.

The confidence proved misplaced. The Senate approved the bill early in the session on May 5. Once more, however, the House proved to be the obstacle. A subcommittee of the House Committee on Education and Labor under the chairmanship of Graham A. Barden (D., N.C.) conducted hearings, rejected the Senate measure, and reported the so-called Barden bill. Since this bill explicitly prohibited any sort of aid to private schools, including the use of federal funds for transportation to parochial schools where this was permitted by state law, it was violently attacked by Catholic groups. A resolution of the Knights of Columbus, for example, described it as "the worst and most objectionable Federal-aid bill ever approved by any Congressional committee." The controversy exploded into dramatic national headlines when Mrs. Eleanor Roosevelt criticized Francis Cardinal Spellman of New York City for precipitating the religious conflict and the Cardinal replied: "Your record of anti-Catholicism stands for all to see. . . ." and described her newspaper columns as "documents of discrimination, unworthy of an American mother." The bill never emerged from the full House Committee.

By 1951 the fervor of the push toward federal aid was declining. Although President Truman endorsed it in a message to Congress, fewer federal aid bills were introduced and none emerged from committee in either House or Senate. The heat of the religious controversy discouraged congressmen from acting further and for the next several years the movement for federal education support turned in other directions.

One such direction was the enactment of more permanent legislation for assistance to schools in the so-called impacted areas of heavy federal employment. During the 1950 session Congress passed two laws in this field, P.L. 815 for construction grants and P.L. 874 for operating costs "in areas affected by Federal activities."[5] The laws providing for the expansion and continuation of the same kinds of educational support begun under the Lanham Act, but as the number of communities assisted increased, the impacted areas program served as a substitute for general federal aid insofar as the affected communities were concerned.

A second change of direction involved an effort to secure funds for education through the use of income from the tidelands oil fields. After a Supreme Court decision vesting title in the federal government, efforts were made in Congress to secure legislation to transfer ownership to the adjacent states, but such attempts were frustrated by presidential veto. Following a suggestion originally made by Secretary of the Interior Harold Ickes, a bill introduced in 1949 proposed to use the federal share of the oil revenues for grants to all the states for educational purposes. In the subsequent 82nd Congress the proposal was actively taken up by Senator Hill, but congressional support for a quitclaim bill proved too strong. In 1952 another bill was passed transferring title to the states, and again was vetoed by President Truman.

The most significant shift in 1950 in the direction of the movement for federal aid was the beginning of a concerted campaign to secure federal grants for school construction. Such an alternative had been proposed during the 1949 Senate debate by Senator John Bricker (R., Ohio), who had offered a substitute bill, authorizing appropriations of $250 million a year for five years for school construction. After a very sketchy debate, the amendment was defeated overwhelmingly, but subsequent hearings by a Senate Subcommittee on Construction of Educational Facilities, chaired by Senator Hubert Humphrey (D., Minn.), began the task of compiling a record to justify school construction legislation.

School construction bills were also pending in the House, and in 1950 a subcommittee of the House Committee on Education held hearings on one of these. The legislation was supported by the same general groups that had supported the federal aid bill, but all were insistent that construction funds should not be a substitute for general aid. U.S. Commissioner of Education Earl J. McGrath testified: "I do not regard financial aid for school construction as in any sense a substitute for Federal financial aid for current expenses, particularly since such aid will be essential in attracting additional teachers to man the additional classrooms. Both types of Federal financial assistance to the States are desperately needed."[6] Spokesmen for the American Association of School Administrators, the CIO, and other groups echoed this sentiment.

From the objections made to the exclusive emphasis on construction, it seems clear that the decision to switch to an approach to federal support via school construction was made largely by the congressmen themselves. Various reasons could be and were given for the shift, but it seems obvious that the principal reason for the change was to avoid the religious issue. If such was the purpose of the strategy, it proved successful, for when a school construction bill finally reached the House in 1956, no amendments were presented relating to private schools. Although the bill failed, the primary causes lay elsewhere.

Despite their original opposition to the shift to school construction as the focus for attack, the executives of the NEA came to accept the change through most of the next decade. By late 1954 the NEA had moved so far toward emphasis on construction that an NEA witness was embarrassed by a question at a House hearing as to her personal opinion of Federal aid for teachers' salaries. A friendly chairman ruled the question "not germane to the purpose of the hearing." A similar question to an NEA representative at a Senate hearing the same year produced the answer that the NEA had not given up hope of federal aid for teachers' salaries eventually, but also hoped that assistance for construction might release local funds for teachers.

The Eisenhower Period—Race and Other Problems

The final factor confirming the new emphasis on aid to construction was partisan—the change in administration that followed the 1952 election. Insofar as the Eisenhower administration was willing to support federal aid for education at all, its preference was for construction assistance.

The initial position taken by President Eisenhower after his election was that no action of any kind should be taken until the newly appointed Commission on Intergovernmental Relations had prepared its report and until the White House conference on education, scheduled for 1954, had met. Neither the NEA, the American Federation of Teachers, nor the senatorial supporters of federal aid were willing to wait so patiently and a school construction bill was prepared and sent to the Senate floor in 1954. There it died.

Following the unexpected victory of the friends of federal aid at the White House conference on education, President Eisenhower proposed a school construction program in early 1955. The presidential proposals were relatively complicated in character, involving three possible forms of assistance—purchase of local school bonds, federal backing for the bonds of state school building authorities, and, where nothing else would work, federal matching grants. The NEA and other educational groups objected to the form of the administration bill, protesting both that it provided too little federal assistance and that it imposed too many conditions on the aid authorized. Accordingly, the mid-fifties witnessed a series of annual struggles among the supporters of different kinds of school construction bills.

The central arena for this struggle, however, shifted to the House of Representatives. In large part because of the impact of the school segregation decision on the southern senators, the Senate, previously the leader in seeking federal aid for education, now abandoned the stage to the other house. Although the Senate Committee conducted hearings in early 1955, no bill was reported to the floor. Instead, for the first time since the emergency Douglass bill of 1934, the House Committee gave its approval to a federal aid bill. This was the so-called Kelley bill which was reported from committee late in the 1955 session and brought up for debate in 1956 in the first formal House debate on a federal aid bill in the 20th century.

The Kelley bill was a compromise, combining some of the elements of the original Eisenhower administration bill with some of the counterproposals of the NEA and similar groups. Unfortunately for its sponsors, the coalition of support that had brought it out of committee fell apart on the floor. Supporters of the administration approach broke away during the debate to push their own substitute, while the opponents of the bill combined with some of its proponents to attach the Powell Amendment restricting aid from segregated school systems. Shorn of all southern support and deserted by most administration Republicans, the bill was killed by a 30-vote margin.

The next year saw a repetition of the debacle. After another set of hearings a new House bill, H.R. 1, was reported out, debated, and defeated. Again the attempt was made to compromise with the administration proposals and the Democratic congressional sponsors insisted they were now going 70 to 85 per cent of the way with the President. Some administration Republicans accepted the argument and the bill; others, including Charles Halleck (R., Ind.), the party whip, did not. After the adoption of the Powell Amendment again imperiled the bill, the Democratic floor managers promised "to cross every 't' and dot every 'i' " and accepted a substitute that incorporated every particular of the Eisenhower plan. Before this substitute could be voted upon, a preferential motion by Rep. Howard Smith (D., Va.) to strike the enacting clause from the bill was adopted 208 to 203 as many Republicans refused the offer to join in support of the Eisenhower bill.

With the failure of a second successive school construction bill in the House, the proponents of federal aid began another reappraisal of their strategy. Such a reconsideration was further encouraged by the decision of the Eisenhower administration to withdraw its support from the school construction measures it had proposed in 1955, 1956, and 1957. Decreasing administration enthusiasm had already been evident in 1957 and had helped to explain the defeat of the bill.

The revised position of President Eisenhower was now formalized. According to a letter from the acting Secretary of Health, Education, and Welfare, Elliott L. Richardson, to House Committee Chairman

Barden, May 1, 1958, the administration still recognized the existence of "a serious shortage in school housing which adversely affects the quality of education," although it believed local and state construction programs were "keeping abreast of the rapid increase in enrollments" and making slow progress in remedying the backlog of need. The principal reason given for the withdrawal of support, however, was the need to concentrate attention on "other needs and deficiencies in our educational system" which were "brought into sharp focus" by "the events of the past year."[7]

These circumlocutions were references to the Soviet breakthroughs in space, which, by 1958, had begun to frighten and alarm Americans. One reaction was the passage of the National Defense Education Act, providing federal educational grants for a variety of specific programs, primarily connected with instruction in science.[8] The concentration of interest on NDEA had the indirect effect of diminishing the interest shown in a general federal aid program. Hearings were held on general aid in both houses, but no new bills were reported.

The proposals made at these hearings were significant, however, for after a lapse of eight years the NEA now revived the question of federal aid for teachers' salaries as well as that of construction costs. In the form of the Murray-Metcalf bill this program was put before Congress again in 1959. An alternative to it was offered by the administration; after a year of silence the Eisenhower administration proposed another school construction bill, but on a sharply restricted basis due to budgetary stringencies. Although both education committees cleared bills, it was not until 1960 that either came up for floor action.

In 1960 the House passed a federal aid bill—for the first time in seventy-five years. Unhappily for its proponents, however, the bill approved by the Senate the same year differed materially. And, when a conference between the houses became necessary to compromise the differences, the House Rules Committee refused to provide the necessary permission to appoint conferees.

The Kennedy Period: The Religious Issue Returns

There were three characteristics of presidential action in the 1950's. Eisenhower favored federal aid only for construction, he favored only a very limited construction program, and he gave only limited support even to that. All three of these characteristics came under review during the 1960 presidential election. The Democratic candidate, Senator John F. Kennedy, sought to make federal aid to education a major issue in the election, criticizing the limited support given by President Eisenhower, criticizing Vice-President Nixon for proposing aid for construction only, and calling for federal aid for teachers' salaries as well as for buildings. Although reluctant to intervene in a presidential campaign, NEA statements made note of the fact that the Democratic candidate's policy accorded with NEA policy.

It seems fair to say that in the long history of federal aid to education proposals, John F. Kennedy was the first president to make aid a major element in his domestic program and to give it vigorous personal support. By the time he took office, President Kennedy's position was clear-cut. His campaign statements plus his legislative record on federal aid as a senator had already filled in most details of his program. After receiving a task force report, he submitted to Congress legislative proposals calling for $866 million a year in federal aid for construction and teachers' salaries. This measure was coupled with renewal of the federally affected areas program in an effort to broaden its base of support; the package bill was then identified as a key part of the administration's domestic legislative program. President Kennedy's principal addition to his earlier statements was to reiterate in increasingly strong language his opposition to federal aid for parochial schools.

The nearness of victory in 1960 produced the same contagious optimism in 1961 that had been so deceptive twelve years before. Once more, as in 1949, the proponents of federal aid felt confident of success. With the strong support of a new president, it seemed inevitable that the near victory of 1960 would be turned into real victory in 1961. Federal aid to education bills were cleared promptly out of the Senate and House committees, and the Senate gave its approval soon after.

Not every impact of President Kennedy's support was, however, favorable to the cause of federal aid. The incentive to accept the bill because the President had asked for it was diluted in part by the narrow margin of Kennedy's election-day victory, and in part by the administration's greater interest in pushing other legislation. One great advantage of vigorous presidential leadership was its effect in spotlighting one particular proposal as the federal aid bill to be taken seriously. In this way at least a part of the tangle over multiple issues was cut away; the President's bill, for better or worse, was the bill that Congress must approve or reject. Within a short period of time, however, this asset was partly dissipated by HEW Secretary Abraham Ribicoff's reiterated willingness to consider modifications. Even the position of opposition to aid for parochial schools was weakened as the administration promised to consider a compromise that would make available increased funds for private schools by appropriate amendment to the then pending extension of the National Defense Education Act. In practice these concessions meant reopening to every congressman the possibility of a federal aid bill just a little more to his own taste if only he could succeed in strangling the bill at hand.

In addition the involvement of federal aid as a major issue in the presidential campaign created for the first time a situation in which the President of the United States actively identified his entire administration with the struggle. By making federal aid a partisan issue in national presidential politics, the 1960 campaign hardened the position of the two parties in Congress. Passage of a bill with aid for teachers' salaries would be a Democratic victory; a bill with aid for construction would be a Republican bill.

Once more, it was the House of Representatives that disappointed the proponents of federal aid. And once more it was the House Rules Committee that exercised the veto. Despite a Kennedy administration victory early in the session that had expanded the membership of the Rules Committee, an 8 to 7 division tabled action on federal aid. The pivotal vote in opposition was provided by an advocate of federal aid to parochial as well as public schools as the religious issue was raised once again. When a truncated federal aid measure was brought to the House floor late in the 1961 session by a parliamentary maneuver that bypassed the Rules Committee, the bill was decisively beaten. With this defeat general federal aid appeared to be dead for the duration of the 87th Congress and—probably—for some time to come.

An Interpretation

This chronological account of the history of federal aid legislation in Congress from 1870 to 1962 serves to suggest several characteristics of the controversy. It provides clear evidence for a frequently cited proposition—the importance of social crisis in encouraging government action. Repeatedly, it has been the emergence of some crisis that has forced consideration of action concerning federal aid to education.

More than any other single cause, the rate of selective service rejections produced the demands for federal aid in 1918. Strengthened by other forces, the repetition of the same events in the World War II draft produced the 1943 Senate debate on federal aid. The depression forced emergency aid to education in the 1930's. The severe postwar teacher shortage stimulated the federal aid proposals of the late 1940's. The baby boom of the 1950's—abetted by suburban sprawl—generated the school construction bills of the same decade. Legislation for federally affected areas followed one national defense crisis while the

NDEA was called into existence by the cold war crisis that followed the launching of the Soviet Sputnik. Apparently, no crisis as yet has been big enough to justify general aid to education.

Reference to federally affected areas legislation and to NDEA suggests, however, a second characteristic of the federal aid debate. For the purpose of this analysis primary attention has been given to general federal aid proposals rather than to such special purpose grants as these, but in practical political terms it is impossible to make a clear separation between the two types of educational assistance. In fact, both the area legislation and the NDEA appear in large measure to be the products of the general federal aid fight.

The adoption of these two programs followed periods of maximum legislative pressure for general aid, P.L. 815 and 874 in 1950 succeeding the struggles of the 1948-49 legislative sessions and NDEA in 1958 following the 1956-57 school construction controversy. Each bill served the purpose of satisfying a major part of the demands of some of the most active proponents of federal aid. This pattern, in which a specialized program serves as a lightning rod minimizing the pressure for general aid, seems in 1963 destined for repetition. The efforts made in 1960 and 1961 for general aid will apparently produce not a general aid bill but new measures of federal support at the college level.[9] It may well be that it takes the impact of an all-out struggle for general federal aid to generate sufficient support to secure approval even of such limited programs.

A third comment also seems justified. Mention has previously been made of the significance of the effort to win support for federal aid as an illustration of the problems faced in building consensus for any new program. The difficulties attending advocacy of federal aid for education are in this sense comparable to those faced by the proponents of any new governmental service, although they are exaggerated by the magnitude of the service involved—education—and the magnitude of its total cost.

A glance at the history of the federal aid struggle, however, raises the real question whether the effort to build consensus for federal aid has made any headway whatsoever. Rather than a steady progression toward greater and greater evidences of strength, the federal aid movement betrays a cyclical character. For almost a full century efforts have been made to secure such legislation, but in each phase of the struggle support has been mobilized only to be lost again. Then, after a delay, the effort is renewed once more.

In any study of this kind a constant danger exists—an unwarranted assumption of the ultimate inevitability of federal aid. Certainly, sponsors of education bills have often explicitly made such an assumption. During the Senate debate on the Educational Finance Act of 1943 Senator Lister Hill (D., Ala.) assured his colleagues:

> Whether the bill shall pass or not, its enactment is as inevitable as that the day will follow the night.
>
> The longer we live, the more our country develops, the more complex becomes our civilization, the greater and more compelling becomes the need, the absolute necessity for the Federal government to meet its duty, accept its responsibility, carry out its obligation, and play its part in the training and the preparation of the citizenship of America.[10]

Such certainty may be consoling in defeat, but is not necessarily accurate as prophecy. The scenario for a Hollywood production must have a beginning, a middle, and an end; there is no guarantee, however, that such will be the case in a story of the making of public policy. For close to a century the federal aid story-line has run on without a break, rather in the manner of a daytime television serial. There is no particular reason to assume the end is now in sight, and some good reasons to suspect that federal aid will not be approved within the immediate future.

The Problems

On several occasions a federal aid bill has appeared to stand on the verge of passage. Each time some unanticipated difficulty has arisen to prevent final approval. So frequent has been this sequence of events that Douglas Price, in his study of the federal aid bills of 1961, has suggested that the measures should be regarded as "politically accident-prone" and, presumably, given prohibitive insurance ratings.[11]

Many of the reasons for the difficulties faced by federal aid bills have been implicit above; they may be summarized briefly here. One of the most important is directly related to the notion of passage of a federal aid bill of some kind as the final act in a story; congressmen believe—correctly—that passage of a bill will not be an ending, but a commencement. Subsequent sessions of Congress will not find the issue settled. Instead they will be confronted with educational groups seeking higher support levels to meet the continually rising costs of the educational establishment. This has been the experience of state legislatures with state aid programs, and would undoubtedly be repeated at the federal level.

To conservative congressmen this is a frightening prospect. And contemplation of this probable future helps explain what otherwise appears inexplicable, the vigor of the opposition shown by the U.S. Chamber of Commerce to what is, after all, a paltry sum by the standards of present-day federal finance. The Chamber and its allies assume that an appropriation of $300 million a year—or even a billion—will be only a small beginning toward the total cost of the most expensive domestic service provided by government within the United States. This is one of the principal themes in the writings of Roger Freeman on the subject, and helps explain his popularity among economy-minded congressmen.[12]

To justify such a risky commitment the Congress finds little in the way of public pressure to act. Opinion surveys show widespread popular support for federal aid, but only mild interest in it. The NEA to the contrary notwithstanding, few congressmen consider their chances for reelection endangered by the failure of Congress to approve federal aid. One answer to the lack of success of education bills was suggested at a 1955 House hearing by John Burkhart of the U.S. Chamber of Commerce, quoting in turn from an NEA official:

> Why, then, has this prodigious, long-sustained battle of NEA not yet attained the hoped-for goal? Perhaps the chief reason was discovered years ago by NEA Legislative Director Charl O. Williams who reported:
>
> "It no longer makes any impression on Congress to have your secretary appear at a hearing and present a very fine statesman-like statement . . . which they say has been endorsed by a million or more men and women. Congressmen immediately want to know how many of these men and women believe in the legislation under consideration, how many of them made it their own, how many are willing to stand by it, how many are willing to fight for it in their respective congressional districts."[13]

Another of the significant obstacles to approval has been the skill in maneuver shown by its opponents, both within Congress and without. On the Senate side the federal aid cause profited for a number of years from the personal prestige of its sponsor, Senator Robert Taft (R., Ohio), but within the House of Representatives the bill's managers have never been able to match in agility such astute parliamentarians as Representatives Graham Barden (D., N.C.), and Howard Smith (D., Va.).

The comparison is not altogether a fair one, however, for the rules of the game are rigged to the advantage of the opponents of change. There are serious institutional obstacles to achieving legislative consensus for new departures in policy. The most serious consists of the large number of hurdles over which a bill must pass—action by two House committees, one Senate committee, two legislative chambers, and one president. Final approval of legislation, in practice, even requires a second decision by the House Rules Committee to permit a conference, a procedure so obscure it ordinarily is not mentioned in the textbooks, but which has nonetheless been used successfully to block action on federal aid. All this means that the legislature is favorable terrain for the opponents; without broad agreement on the need to act it is impossible to secure the separate majorities needed at each step of the road. If federal aid legislation has proved "accident-prone," it is, in part, because it travels a dangerous highway.

The "broad agreement on the need to act" so necessary in making the legislative system work is the consensus that has been the focus of this study. It would appear, however, from the chronology above that the most important barrier to such consensus has been the multiplicity of conflicts concealed within the single label of "federal aid to education." Such a proliferation of issues is inevitable in a society in which education deals with all aspects of human values, but in a very real sense it doubles the task of the proponents of aid. First, they must break down resistance to the novel idea of federal financing for education. Second, they must eliminate these multiple controversies so that legislators may ultimately be led to line up for or against some single identifiable program. It may be suspected that the federal aid advocates have passed the first test; they remain baffled by the second.

Indeed, it seems plausible that the difficulties faced by a federal aid bill have multiplied within the past few years and seem likely to increase in the immediate future. That conclusion emerges from a review of the principal issues dividing the proponents of federal aid.

Race. In the early federal aid proposals of the 20th century, race was a divisive issue due to the unwillingness of the southern sponsors to write in guarantees of an equal division of funds between white and Negro school systems. With the acceptance of such a provision in the late 1930's, however, the racial issue no longer divided the proponents despite its tactical use by the bill's opponents in 1943. Following the shift in NAACP policy at mid-century to uncompromising opposition to segregation, the racial issue has again become divisive. Confirmed by the Supreme Court decision of 1954, it effectively prevents the full mobilization of support by the advocates of aid.

Optimists might predict the waning of the racial education issue as the Supreme Court decision is implemented and segregation ended in the South. Such an outcome seems unlikely, however. Even if integration is formally accomplished in the southern states in the near future, it seems certain that the racial issue will express itself in new ways. Federal aid policy may then be proposed as a weapon to force the change from token integration to general integration, a proposal that would make it controversial in many *de facto* segregated school systems in both North and South. There is little reason to anticipate the banishment of the civil rights issue from the debate over federal aid.

Religion. The 1949 federal aid debate was a breaking point as far as the racial issue is concerned; less change has occurred regarding involvement with the issue of parochial schools. Before 1945 Catholic groups opposed all aid. Since that time the official position of the Catholic hierarchy has been one of acceptance of federal aid if, and only if, some aid to religious schools is incorporated. Since a congressional majority for a general aid bill of this kind has never been visible, the sum and substance of the situation has not changed. Catholic influence has been exerted against the only type of bills public school educators are willing to accept.

Even a prophetic look into the future provides little reason for optimism. The most likely alteration in the situation would be for a movement of the Catholic hierarchy toward direct support for a federal aid program that would include religious schools. Such a change in front is conceivable as financial pressures upon the parochial school system mount. Increasing support for legislation of this sort may also come from Jewish and other groups committed to religious day schools. The opportunity provided by this shift would pose a difficult choice to public school educators forced to weigh their relative preferences for no aid against aid to both public and private schools. It is difficult at the present time, however, to conceive of such a coalition producing a federal aid bill in the foreseeable future.

Federal Control. The issue of federal control has likewise displayed a continuing ability to divide the advocates. Hopefully, it might be expected that the lengthy debate over federal aid would have clarified the subject, losing some support for aid among those unwilling to accept the minimum of necessary federal standards, while consolidating support for a defined program. This has not occurred; a substantial part of the blame probably belongs to the debaters who have consciously obscured rather than clarified the issues. Whatever the cause, the issue remains fundamentally unchanged.

Equalization. Similarly, the interminable disputes over the formula to be employed in the distribution of funds have been constant through the years, dividing the supporters of one aid bill from the supporters of another. Spokesmen for wealthy states, particularly strong in the House of Representatives, have insisted on a flat grant formula that will provide some aid to all states. The Senate, on the other hand, has tended to prefer bills that maximize aid for the poorest states.

This, however, constitutes one area in which change is taking place. The sectional disparities in income within the United States have been declining. And as the differences in regional income become less, the differences in the impact of the various formulas grow less also. In specific terms, the changing economy will eventually make agreement on a flat-grant formula easier to secure. Unfortunately for the proponents, however, the impact of the change is double-edged; since the principal argument for federal aid has always been the need to equalize regional disparities in income, the Chamber of Commerce has been quick to point out that the alleged basis of the need for aid is steadily disappearing.

Construction and Salaries. The most important shift in the capacity of other issues to fractionalize the pro-aid coalition has concerned the purpose for which federal funds should be used. Although the efforts of the AF of T to secure guarantees for teachers' salaries divided it from the NEA in the late 1940's, there was little evidence of significant division among the legislative supporters of federal aid at that time. And when the shift to a strategy of construction grants occurred, it was a shift mutually agreeable to all parties concerned.

In the late 1950's, however, the friends of aid for construction and the friends of aid for salaries began to draw apart. This separation was confirmed by the partisan use of the issue in the 1960 presidential campaign. The line of cleavage hardened and was largely responsible for the lack of Republican support for federal aid in 1961.

These facts together suggest that the prospects for broad agreement on a single federal aid bill were probably at their height in the late 1940's. Such issues as federal control, religious schools, and the formula to be used were present, but the others were quiescent. After 1950, divisions over race were added to the controversies already plaguing the managers of the bill. In the decade of the 1960's a new issue has emerged with heavy partisan overtones, that of the purpose for which federal funds are to be employed. This issue complicates the task of securing agreement on a single bill. The managers of federal aid legislation are not to be envied their jobs.

The Possibilities: Strategies of Substance

Faced with these problems, the bill's advocates have not, however, thrown up their hands and thrown in the towel. The principal strategic problem confronting them has been twofold: to maximize support for federal aid by minimizing the conflicts among its supporters, and to marshal their support at the critical points in the legislative process. Accordingly, their strategies have been of two interlocking kinds: strategies of substance concerned with the content of the legislation to be proposed, and strategies of approach defining the manner in which the aid bill should be advanced.

In their efforts to secure approval the supporters of federal aid have made use of every conceivable argument. After World War I the need for federal aid was portrayed as part of a war against illiteracy. Then it became a part of the struggle to Americanize the immigrant. Other proponents presented federal aid as an essential step to prevent the bolshevization of America, since ignorant citizens could not see through the appeals of communism. In the 1930's aid to the schools was a depression measure to solve the temporary fiscal emergency, to deal with unemployment, and to accelerate economic activity. During the war federal aid became a national defense measure that would help to mobilize more men for military service. As the immediacy of the issue of selective service rejections faded after the war, the bill's proponents turned to the gap between performance and need in school construction. Then in the late 1950's the national security argument was revived when it appeared that the Soviet Union was outdistancing America in some fields of scientific research. And so forth. There are substantial grounds, however, for suspecting that these changes in the style of the debate are fashions only, and that the new arguments convince only the same, already committed supporters. The principal variations in the content of the bills actually proposed have been of a different order.

The Necessary Compromise. The first problem facing the sponsors of any federal aid bill has been that of threading a way among the multiple conflicts earlier described. Most decisions concerning the provisions to be included in a specific bill are tactical in character, that is, they have been calculated in terms of what appears most likely to secure the most legislative support. As estimates of the political situation have changed, the measures to be proposed have been modified. When the principal educational groups have estimated the politics of the legislative situation differently, rival bills have emerged. But whether the educators are united or divided, they still face the same problem in each session: to secure a majority vote for what appears to be the most feasible compromise bill.

One effect of this strategy of compromise has been to multiply the inconsistencies in the record of the supporters of federal aid. Speaking for the American Federation of Teachers at the 1945 Senate hearings, Selma Borchardt derisively reviewed the past:

> Through the years, supporters . . . of federal aid have changed their reasons for wanting the legislation on practically every point involved. First, the supporters of this legislation made the request for a Department of Education; then they dropped it. Next they dropped their original request for State fund-matching programs; and then they condemned this formula. They dropped, picked up, and dropped again provisions for specific levels and kinds of education.
>
> They urged the allocation of funds on a basis of school population, on a basis of total population, on a basis of need, on a basis of weighted formula combining the other methods; and then they dropped this formula. They first ignored the need of protecting the Negro's right to share in the benefits of a federal program; then, they opposed the right on a basis of state's rights; then they supported it halfway; then opposed it; then supported it.
>
> They have supported bills including the present set-up for vocational education, and they have deleted it. They have included, excluded, and included provisions for school-building programs. At first they ignored the question of aid to Catholic schools. Then they opposed the principle. Then they tacitly accepted it. Then they opposed it again. It is to be observed that this principle was most ardently opposed while many of these same opponents were endorsing WPA educational programs which aided private groups, and while they were urging support for NYA which made direct grants to Catholic schools. . . .
>
> The vast majority of the supporters of the principle of federal aid have adhered to a policy which has been vacillating in principle, opportunistic in tactics, and fatal in practice. As a result, the program has actually not advanced one bit while the teachers have been told that the legislation is on the way—for the last 25 years.[14]

Miss Borchardt's criticism was expressed in 1945; it is still applicable 18 years later. To a considerable extent it is an inevitable by-product of the necessary strategy of compromise; some of the testimony given on the religious issue by AF of T witnesses at the same 1945 hearing might be reduced to the summary: "I can argue that either way." It seems probable that the advocates of aid have injured their cause by making their strategy too obvious, and might have accomplished more by preparing one proposal and standing by it, but much of the inconsistency reflects a consistent willingness to compromise in order to get federal aid.

This is not, however, the only strategy that has been employed in the effort to prepare an acceptable aid bill.

The Very Modest Proposal. Another strategy recurrently employed has been to seek to disarm the opposition by the modesty of the sum sought. As HEW Secretary Arthur Flemming expressed it in 1959, urging Democrats to support the Eisenhower administration's bill:

> The only thing that I am impressed with as of this present time is that in order to get those 75,000 classrooms constructed we can get more support for this kind of approach as contrasted with the general grant because when we go to the general grant we are asking people not only to take one step in the direction of the federal government being of help on this classroom construction, but we are asking them to take a second step.
>
> I would like to see us take a step which would get us off dead center and get the federal government into the business of helping these school districts construct classrooms.[15]

In accordance with this strategy of what might be described as one-sixteenth of a loaf, the proponents of federal aid have scaled down their requests, and asked only for small appropriations. The only difficulty with this strategy of "a first step first" is that it is totally transparent. The opponents of federal aid recognize that the sums sought are only fractions of the total costs of education in the United States, assume that the first step will be followed by others, and fight vigorously against letting the camel's nose come under the tent.

The Outrageous Proposal. As a result, some proponents of federal aid have at times abandoned the limited approach and instead asked for sums and programs far larger than they expect to get. The billion-dollar-a-year aid bill of the late 1940's was such a measure; so too was the Murray-Metcalf bill. The clearest example of this strategy, however, was the 1962 proposal by the American Association of School Administrators of $8 billion a year for federal aid. The reasons for suggesting such measures are various. The intention may be to emphasize the importance of the problem or the seriousness of purpose of its advocates. The proposal may be intended to establish a bargaining position from which further negotiation can be carried on. Or it may be hoped that it will frighten some of the bill's opponents. Or again, such recommendations may be born of simple frustration.

Trading Stamps. A somewhat different strategy was employed during the 1961 effort for federal aid, a strategy which was a variant of the ancient legislative device known as logrolling. In an effort to broaden the base of support, the Kennedy administration tied renewal of the federally affected areas educational program to its general grant bill. Wayne Morse (D., Ore.), the bill's manager in the Senate, accurately described the area allocations as "the little green trading stamps" of the federal aid bill. The strategy proved unrealistic in the outcome, however, since the federally affected areas program was too popular to be denied renewal. Confident that it would be approved in any case, its supporters could not be forced to accept general aid as the price of renewal.

The Subtraction of Conflict. The combination of the two bills in 1961 might be described as a strategy of addition, an effort to join together the advocates of two separate kinds of educational programs. At the same time, the bill's sponsors tried to pursue the strategy of subtraction, dropping off controversial features of the bill to minimize opposition. This they did by offering separate bills to provide grants for public schools and to renew and expand the National Defense Education Act, which included benefits for private schools. It was hoped that both could be passed, each supported by overlapping but distinct majorities. The strategy proved too clever as the mutually suspicious friends of the two bills deadlocked the House Rules Committee and blocked action on both.

The strategy is an old one and has been tried often in the past. Federal aid bills have been divided and subdivided in the effort to increase their palatability; the shift to construction grants was one such effort. In many ways the most ingenious attempt was Senator Hill's proposal of "oil for the lamps of education" in the early 1950's. By substituting a measure to apply to educational purposes the revenues from federally owned tidal oil lands for a quitclaim bill to turn ownership over to the states, Hill sought simultaneously to secure the support of opponents of the quitclaim and to disarm the arguments of those who insisted aid for education must come from increased taxes. Unfortunately for Senator Hill, the substitution added more opponents than supporters and, like all the other trick proposals, failed.

The Possibilities: Strategies of Approach

All the strategies so far mentioned have one characteristic in common; they concern the content to be included within a specific federal aid bill. A second type of strategic question also faces the proponents: whose sponsorship shall be sought for the bill and under what circumstances should it be presented? During the past two decades the advocates of federal aid have tried every conceivable strategy to manage their bill to legislative victory. Almost the only legislative strategy not employed was one that was unavailable: the attempt to slip "a quiet little bill" through Congress with a minimum of attention and controversy. The federal aid issue has been too widely publicized to permit such a procedure to work, and the opposition has been too alert to overlook any major educational proposal.

Congressional Leadership. The first choice of strategy was made for the advocates of federal aid by the presidents of the United States from Warren G. Harding through Franklin D. Roosevelt. Their indifference to federal aid made it necessary to build strength in Congress. And the internal structure of Congress made it almost inevitable that the leadership for any successful legislative drive must be bipartisan. From the decision of Senator Taft to support federal aid in the late 1940's down to the late 1950's primary reliance was placed upon bipartisan congressional leadership. In many ways this is one of the most interesting features of the federal aid controversy. In a political system in which presidential leadership in law-making has been constantly enhanced, aid to education has been treated almost exclusively as a decision to be made by Congress.

The Appeal to the People. The failure of Congress to act, however, compelled the educational groups to devise other strategy. Their first response was to seek to go beyond Congress, to take their case to the people, and to mobilize such popular support that congressional action must follow. To some opponents of federal aid, this was not playing the game. As early as 1948 Representative George Schwabe (R., Okla.), lamented:

> Pressure groups have been organized and propaganda has been inspired and broadcast among the members of Congress in an attempt to force us to vote for federal aid to education. Some have even written letters threatening to vote and work against the reelection of present members of Congress unless we support the pending measures. Of course, such letters are beneath the dignity of what we have a right to expect of the teaching profession.[16]

More serious than the suggestion that such strategy is undignified has been the fact that it has been proved to be unsuccessful. Interest in education is widespread among the public. Support for federal aid is extensive. But the depth of involvement in the issue by the general public has been insufficient to coerce recalcitrant congressmen into supporting a bill for federal aid. And as long as the educational system appears to be reasonably satisfactory, this situation is likely to be perpetuated.

The Sense of Crisis. Concluding a study of federal aid legislation written in 1953, Anne Gibson Buis prophesied:

> The records reveal that the Congress has seriously considered federal aid to education bills only during periods of national stress when teacher shortages have forced school doors to close. Judging from the past, another teacher shortage threatening to close the doors of the schools will have to recur before the Congress seriously considers a federal aid to education bill again. The fact that teacher qualifications may continue to fall will probably have no influence as long as the doors of the schools do not close and excite the "constituents" to prod inert legislators to action.[17]

Since such total disaster in American education seems unlikely under present circumstances, the conclusion is a pessimistic one (pessimistic at least from the viewpoint of proponents). Efforts have been made, however, to promote lesser crises into convincing evidence of the need for federal aid. Unfortunately for the advocates of general grants, the fright that followed Sputnik was turned to use in the NDEA rather than in the type of bill they sought. And subsequent events have largely diluted its impact on popular attitudes. On a different level of political behavior this is what Richard F. Carter found in his study of voters and their schools. Reporting his findings, he wrote:

> Within a few weeks after planning for this research had begun, American education faced a seeming crisis—Russia's Sputnik. Critics fell on the schools, questioning whether an education valued for its ability to give citizens a knowledge of and an occupation in our society could continue to serve the country's needs without drastic change and re-emphasis. Those critics still hold forth, and their listeners were found among the voters interviewed in this study. Has anything changed? Could the needs of a nation be installed as the wants of its people? Are these new values for education? To these questions the answer is *no*. The concern expressed about the schools, and particularly about curriculum, appears to have been absorbed into previously determined value positions. The arguments have changed, but the values have not.[18]

In the absence of any continuing concern over the scientific threat, the only crisis left for the advocates of federal aid to cite is the shortage of classrooms. And this produces an unhappy, if mixed, reaction. Some congressmen have come to disbelieve in the shortage, convinced or brought to neutrality by the contrary statistics of the U.S. Chamber of Commerce. Other congressmen, while accepting the figures of the NEA and the Office of Education, have simply heard the argument too often. It is difficult to believe in the importance of a crisis which has demanded remedial action for a decade and a half, but has got along without receiving it; the position may be an illogical one, but the passage of time has dulled the sense of immediacy surrounding the problem.

Presidential Leadership. With all the other strategies tried over and over without success, the educational groups in 1960 tried a gamble by seeking to mobilize through presidential action the support they were unable to secure by themselves. When Congress balked at an aid bill including teachers' salaries, the NEA clearly expressed the preference for making federal aid into a 1960 campaign issue rather than seeking to salvage a compromise bill. Without expressing an open endorsement of either candidate, widely circulated NEA literature during the fall of 1960 made it clear that the Democratic presidential candidate's stand on federal aid was in agreement with NEA policy while the Republican candidate's was not.

In the short run this frankly political strategy appeared to pay off. In contrast to his predecessors, President Kennedy became an enthusiastic champion of federal aid. In the outcome, however, the presidential endorsement did not bring success and federal aid was defeated once again.

The reasons for President Kennedy's failure are significant since they form the principal evidence by which the effectiveness of future presidential action in support of federal aid may be estimated. To the extent that the factors leading to the president's defeat were peculiar to Kennedy's situation in 1961, they may be disregarded as guides to future events. For example, Kennedy's identification as the first Roman Catholic to occupy the presidency made it singularly difficult to bargain flexibly on the crucial issue of private schools. His narrow election-day victory made it harder for him to claim a popular mandate for his campaign promises. Mistakes were made, as in the expressed willingness to consider reasonable compromises, which further weakened the administration by opening again the Pandora's Box of alternative proposals.

To the degree that these causes for defeat might be avoided in future presidential action, even future action in this administration, they do not necessarily indicate the bankruptcy of this strategy for securing federal aid. More serious are the indications of two weaknesses in the presidential position intrinsic to any presidential action. The first of these is the problem of partisanship. All of the above evidence suggests the impossibility of creating a strictly partisan majority for a federal aid bill under the present conditions of American politics. Yet forceful, vigorous presidential leadership on a domestic issue of this kind is almost inevitably accompanied by a tightening of party lines. To the many other conflicts already surrounding the bill is added a new symbolic conflict—which party will secure the credit for passage.

The second limitation upon presidential action might be summarized as lack of time. As Douglas Price has emphasized in his study of the 1961 federal aid fight, President Kennedy consciously refrained from committing his full resources of time and effort to the struggle for federal aid. With only limited reserves of strength, the president chose to hold back a part of his influence for subsequent efforts to impose his will upon Congress. Some of the future efforts might concern such domestic legislation as tax reform and medical care for the aged; most especially, however, the president was conserving his limited resources of power to secure his program objectives in the fields of foreign policy and national security.[19]

It is exciting to speculate on what might happen if the cold war were to be brought to an end. One of the incidental results would be an unleashing of presidential capacity for leadership in the field of domestic policy-making. But barring such an unforeseeable eventuality, it seems likely that future presidents will face the same problems as John F. Kennedy and find it necessary to sacrifice domestic program objectives for the immediate concerns of foreign policy and military security.

The Prospects

On several occasions the advocates of federal aid have considered their struggle to be won; each time they have been frustrated. It would be as reasonable to expect that when the future seems blackest, hope may be greatest. But apart from such perverse logic, the argument of the preceding pages leads to a pessimistic conclusion concerning the prospects for federal aid to education in the immediate future.

Such pessimism should be confined, however, to the specific type of aid which has been the focus of this study, general grants for elementary and secondary education. Specific grants for special purposes can be devised which avoid the problems that block the approval of federal aid. The past experience has been that pressures for federal aid have most frequently found expression in the passage of just such specialized programs. The agitation of the 1870's and 1880's was capped by the enactment of a vocational education law. The struggles of 1948 and 1949 brought educational legislation for impacted areas. And the 1956-57 House battles culminated not in a construction bill, but in the NDEA.

At the present time the same trend seems apparent but in this case the deflection of purpose has been toward higher education. Indeed it might be argued that if federal aid legislation of a general character for elementary and secondary schools is not approved in the next few years, the pressure for action at the federal level may begin to slacken. Since the passage of NDEA particularly, the interest of the Office of Education in the field of higher education has been growing rapidly. At the same time one of the Office's most active programs at the elementary and secondary level has been the Cooperative Research Program which, in practice, largely consists of the awarding of grants for research to personnel at institutions of higher education.

The reasons for this shift in emphasis are not far to seek. A general aid program at the elementary and secondary level steps on many toes and generates much opposition; federal programs at the graduate professional level step on virtually no toes and are readily approved. Undergraduate programs, especially when associated with the natural sciences, encounter little more in the way of opposition. Even general aid programs for college facilities and scholarships appear to find easier going in the political world. The racial issue is largely irrelevant and the problem of aid to religious schools becomes more negotiable when it includes large numbers of non-Catholic religious colleges. It is within the realm of possibility that the Office of Education, if balked for a few more years in expanding into the general aid field within elementary and secondary schools, while scoring breakthroughs in higher education, may drastically redefine its conception of its own role.

Such drastic shifts in the direction of federal involvement in education are only speculative. What does appear clearly from the record is the strength of the forces holding the federal government back from a deeper commitment in elementary and secondary education. In 1937, the Senate Majority Leader, Joseph T. Robinson, described education as "the one last field into which federal activity is to be extended."[20] In 1937, at the high tide of the New Deal, it must have appeared incredible that any major field of government action could be maintained aloof from federal participation. Twenty-five years later, education remains the one last major governmental function assigned primarily to state and local government.

XI. Issues in Federal Aid

The traditional case for general federal aid to education rests on what is essentially a value judgment—a judgment that there are national interests in elementary and secondary education, and not wholly state and local interests. This judgment is supported by a fiscal fact—that children and money are not always found in the same place; the ability of the states to support education varies widely. Finally, the case for federal aid rests on considerations affecting the goals of American education. Federal aid can be used as an instrument in the accomplishment of specific educational improvements, to bring larger numbers of schools toward specified standards. These latter purposes can also be accomplished by categorical aid programs, as well as by general aid. Experience with the most important and recent categorical aid programs is examined in Chapters XII and XIII.

The General Case

Perhaps the most obvious evidence of the character of the national interest in education lies in the interrelatedness of the regions of the national economy. The educational system of Puerto Rico is of critical significance to people in New York City, Chicago, or Cleveland. What Indiana or Arkansas do to educate their young people is of importance to California, Michigan, and Florida. The educational ideals and the accomplishments of communities in the Middle West and mountain states have a bearing on the prosperity and civic progress of cities all over the nation. Such interrelation is not alone due to the fact that Americans tend to migrate freely, although the fact of migration is perhaps the most obvious indication of the unity of the United States. In both theory and practice, the political, social, and general economic well-being of the nation is a unity in its diversity. We are a nation and our parts are functionally interrelated. Aspects of these interrelationships are economic, political, and social.

But beyond the facts of economic and educational interdependence are more fundamental ideological considerations. A great part of the American dream is that the basic guarantees of political and legal equality imply equality of opportunity. The major means of securing

This chapter is based on materials prepared by Sidney C. Sufrin.

equality of opportunity is education. Thus the ideal of educational opportunity—the availability of substantial free education regardless of the social status of the prospective student—is a vital part of American ideology. Mental and social capacities, acquired from parents and family, are the givens of a person's life. Society, through law and institutions, attempts to enhance and develop the natural character of people, restraining only when social harm would otherwise be inflicted. The American dream realistically insists that the success of individuals is related both to natural endowment and to education.

The natural endowment of people, scientific and popular belief hold, generally tends to be greater than their accomplishment. Chance, opportunity, and education are the keys to success in most instances, for sufficient resource of natural potential for personal success is locked up in most of us. The potential needs only to be set free to make us more vital and effective.

This is a good and comforting public philosophy for a democratic society which sets high store by social change and progress. But how are the keys of opportunity, chance, and education supplied?

Chance may be subject to a degree of social control by limitations on privilege, special rights, and on the exercise of monopoly power, but in many of its aspects, chance will, as its gambling connotation suggests, remain a matter of luck or probability. Opportunity, however, is subject to a much higher degree of social control.

Opportunity may be defined as the freedom to enter or leave an activity, usually an economic activity. Yet the freedom to enter a trade, profession, or business with hope of success requires not only financing, but knowledge, skill, and experience. Education is the very foundation of technical awareness, and the freer the educational opportunity, the freer the economic opportunity. Thus, the ideal of a society which sets high store by social mobility, individual choice, and private and social growth requires that education be freely available.

These considerations would not, of course, make a strong case for general federal aid to education if it were not for the fact that some states and some communities tend to rank education low in the scale of public and private values. For reasons that are frequently obscure, alternative public and private needs simply appear to be more pressing at any one moment. Other states and communities suffer from low levels of economic development and are unable to break the circular intercausality of low income, low skills, and low productivity. If it were possible to be confident that the economic development of states and regions were coming into common patterns, and that all disparities between rich states and regions and poor states and regions were being eliminated rapidly, it might be concluded that a uniform national pattern for the support of education would emerge. Such, however, is not the case.

Regional Economic Structures

Recent studies of regional economic development in the United States support the general conclusion that income discrepancies among states are narrowing slowly. Many poor states persist in their poverty and many rich states persist in their relatively favorable position.[1] Moreover, rates of growth are far from uniform among states in terms of their "richness" or "poorness." A simple comparison of per capita income between 1950 and 1960, state by state, demonstrates this. The average per capita increase in income in current dollars for the New England states was 51 per cent in these years, but in Maine it was 59 per cent and in Rhode Island only 35 per cent.[2] In the plains states, per capita income increase amounted to only 37 per cent for the poorest state—North Dakota—between 1950 and 1960. Missouri, with the highest per capita income in this region in 1960, had a 52 per cent increase during the decade.

In the southeast the equalizing tendencies were more evident. Both Arkansas and Mississippi, lowest in 1950 per capita income, had above average growth rates for the region during the decade. But heterogenous patterns are evident in the growth experience of the southwest, the mountain states, and the far west.

General tendencies toward equalization of income among states are indeed present, but with many exceptions. Relatively high per capita income states (for example, those of the northeast) tend to persist as high per capita income states while other states, such as in the southeast, tend to persist as low per capita income states. The relative pattern of per capita income distribution tends to be fairly rigid. Similar conclusions emerge when the data are adjusted for price level differences among states and regions.[3] In general, the rate of increase in the per capita income of low income states tends to be greater over the years than the rate of increase in the per capita income of high income states, but the absolute increases in high income states are greater than those of low income states.[4]

The lack of uniformity in patterns of per capita income increases is matched by a lack of uniformity in the extent to which states translate these income increases into expenditures for public elementary and secondary education. Comparisons of this relationship, which may be defined as the elasticity of current expenditure for public education, require the computation of increases in current expenditure per pupil (ADA) in relation to increases in per capita personal income, in this case for the years 1949 to 1959.[5]

Some of the poorer states did extremely well in translating income increases into expenditures for education, notably Mississippi and Maine. Some of the poorer states, however, did very badly—Alabama and Tennessee, for example. Correspondingly, some rich states had a high elasticity of expenditure for education—Ohio, California, and New York. But some wealthier states, such as Connecticut, were well below the national average.

The computations for the states suggest that improvement in elementary and secondary school programs, by way of increased expenditures per pupil, is not wholly related to income changes viewed on a state by state basis. Increases in income do not automatically channel into additional school expenditures. The preferences of the citizenry for education as against other public and private goods and the ability of the tax system and political leadership to translate income into tax revenue will, in a general way, account for these differences.[6]

When the performance of the states is viewed in terms of the quality of teachers and the quality of school facilities, it is again evident that the attainment of educational standards is not wholly a matter of income level. The proportion of teachers with substandard credentials is relatively great in all sections of the country. For example, the District of Columbia, Delaware, Maryland, New Jersey, and Vermont (all in the North Atlantic area) suffer from appreciable shortages of qualified teachers in their school systems.[7] Yet these deficiencies are relatively no more significant than those to be found in states in the Great Lakes region (Michigan and Ohio), or in the southeast (Alabama, Louisiana, and Mississippi), or in the west and southwest (California, Oregon, Utah, and Washington).

A similar varied pattern exists for school facilities, although admittedly the concept of "classroom shortage" is difficult to define. According to Office of Education data, the states of the southeast stand out in terms of measurable classroom shortage.[8] In Alabama there was approximately a 50 per cent shortage of classrooms in 1958; in Florida, 25 per cent; in Mississippi, 30 per cent. Again, however, the shortages are not limited to low income states. New York, New Jersey, Massachusetts, Arizona, and California, all with high personal income, also show relatively large shortages. Again, income is not the only factor that has a bearing on the shortage of classrooms.

It might be hoped that population emigration from the relatively poor states to the relatively wealthy states would tend to equalize educational burdens. However, regional population projections by the Bureau of the Census suggest that this will be a modest equalizing factor at best.[9] The Pacific and mountain states, areas of relatively high income, are, of course, expected to enjoy rapid population growth in the remainder of this decade. Other areas of high income, however, such as the Middle Atlantic and New England states, are expected to fall below the national average of population increase. Some of the poorer states, such as Arkansas and Alabama, have lost population since 1950, and these trends are expected to continue. But the low income South Atlantic states are also expected to increase in population more than the national average.

Objectives of Grants in Aid

Assistance to education in the states implies some notion of standards, else federal aid becomes merely an exercise in the redistribution of income among states. But aid for education would be a very poor mechanism for redirecting the flow of income in the economy, at least in the short run, and to use education for this purpose would abuse the whole educational enterprise. It must be assumed, rather, that the federal government has some standards in mind which it hopes to realize by a program of assistance to elementary and secondary education.

The tendency of federal government officials to avoid discussions of and direct concern with educational standards is perhaps understandable because of popular fears about federal controls and because of the confusion which surrounds the distinction between controls and standards. However, if education is a national problem, as the proponents of aid to education must argue, explicitly or implicitly (else their activity in the field is unwarranted and probably unconstitutional), the federal government cannot long avoid active concern with standards.

There are at least two techniques by which federal standards can be wedded to state standards of education. The first is by frequent meetings of the federal government and the state governments to discuss the question of standards. Such meetings, to be effective, should be supported by a great deal of experimental data, as well as by thoughtful exchange of opinions and ideas. Then gradually a body of doctrine regarding the nature and content of the educational process may evolve. The idea that the states are laboratories for educational experimentation, or that each state requires its own individual system of education unrelated to the nation is excessive parochialism. Neither every man nor every state can become his or its own educational authority any more than every man can be his own judge or psychiatrist. Granting that individual states or localities have special problems, nevertheless, principles, objectives, goals, techniques, and means are, in many instances, national in scope and conception and rarely, if ever, unique in a locality. There is unity as well as diversity in the nation.

A second way in which the federal government can implant its goals in the states is to secure the cooperation of the states through subsidies, grants-in-aid, or other tangible benefits which are given to the states, conditional on the attainment of certain standards. Opponents of this approach will call it bribery. Proponents will assert it assures that the government gets its money's worth.

The subsidy approach may be a tough, hard-boiled way to reach a goal, and the first method, that of discussion, may be too slow and inefficient. A combination of these methods may, however, be reasonable, for conversation ceases to be empty when someone is willing to pay for the implementation of a program, particularly if the payment is a supplemental one.

The federal government, by supplementing the educational budgets of the states, would become a partner of the states in education. The partner suggests the terms and conditions of his limited partnership. Since none of the states is likely to be entirely or even largely dependent on federal funds, the power of the federal government to impose educational standards would not be very great. On the other hand, the recognition on the part of some states that their standards are low might make them willing to improve their standards, if assisted in doing so by federal grants. When a state voluntarily accepts federal funds, it is exercising a choice. To be sure, the attractiveness of the federal money may be hard to resist, but it is also likely that the federal funds are for purposes which have widespread approval.

Educational funds, whether secured from state or local governmental units or from the federal government, do structure the allocation of resources in some other fashion than would have been the case were such educational funds not secured. When the federal government determines to subsidize state educational activity, there is the clear implication that, in the opinion of the Congress and the administration, although not necessarily in the opinions of lesser jurisdictions, greater social, economic, and political returns are to be secured from additional expenditures on schooling than from expenditures on some other public or private activity. Once this decision is made, no subsidy should then be permitted to reduce state school expenditure or to divert actual or potential funds from schools to some other purpose. The essential point is that the federal government has in its wisdom made the decision that additional expenditures for education at the state and local level will result in greater social returns, when measured by criteria that the government thinks relevant, than would be secured if similar expenditures (or no expenditures) were made in fields other than state and local education. In brief, Congress, and the administration, has the authority to decide that public policy requires the expenditure.

Therefore, the federal government is justified in insisting on certain standards as a condition of joint action. To require the state to follow certain patterns of behavior toward its subjurisdictions, when the federal government is offering assistance to the state for the benefit of these subjurisdictions, is not unreasonable and has precedent. For example, the federal housing, highway, and area redevelopment programs require the states to follow certain general rules laid down by the federal government as donor and administrator.

No attempt will be made here to outline the nature of desirable rules which the federal government might require of states with respect to the apportionment of funds within a state. However, the general principles which the federal government may follow in grant patterns to states will be examined.

There are three types of aids or grants which may be utilized. These are (1) flat grants, (2) equalizing grants, and (3) incentive grants.[10]

Flat Grants

Flat grants are based upon some absolute criterion. For example, grants might be awarded to states in terms of their population size, or the number of students in average daily attendance (ADA), or the number of students of school age. Such grants will affect states differentially with respect to funds spent for schooling. Flat grants do not specifically adjust for need or tax burden differentials.

Using any of these bases a state with a large population would receive more total money than a state with a smaller population. Since the money spent on schooling need not be, and in fact is not, proportional to the population of any two states, the prime effect of the flat grant in this respect would be to change relative educational expenditures of the states. The changes in relative expenditure cannot be determined *a priori.* If ADA is used as the basis for determining the flat grant, the states which spend more money on each student in education would benefit relatively less than the states which spend less money, and again the effects among the states would be different. In this case, the flat grant would act as an equalizing factor since the educational outlays of the low expenditure states would increase, and the position of the states which spend more per capita on education would improve relatively less.[11]

The important consideration, however, is not the change in the relative expenditures of states. It would seem that of far greater importance is the effect of the subsidy or grant on education level. If a state whose expenditures per pupil are low receives relatively greater aid than a high-expenditure state, the purpose of education would be served. This assertion assumes that the level of education is a direct function of expenditure, an assumption which probably has general validity for present purposes.

One of the great weaknesses of flat grants is that the payment of federal funds for aid to education might conceivably be used to replace a fraction of state and local funds which previously had been used for educational purposes, or would have been used for educational purposes, were no grant made. This criticism, however, is not necessarily limited to flat grants, as will be argued below. In such cases, the grant is of no help to education, although it might be of value in reducing the tax burden of the state, or in providing funds for other than educational purposes at no cost to the state.

The most obvious measure to use as a basis for flat grant subsidies is the number of school-age children, or the number of children in average daily attendance.[12] These measures of aid presuppose that differences in educational expenditures, economic status of the states, value of production and rate of productivity, patterns of ownership (in-state *vs.* out-of-state), incidence of state and local taxes—these and many other significant variables are of minimal consequence among the states. However, flat grants have a historical sanction in the United States, associated with various indexes, e.g., population (roads), payrolls (unemployment compensation), and uniform state grant (agricultural experimentation).

Equalizing Grants

Equalizing grants are the result of a conscious policy on the part of the federal government to close the gaps between and among states, insofar as some public service is concerned. Closing the gap is accomplished by giving relatively larger sums to those states which spend relatively less on the service in question, e.g., education.

One of the great differences between the flat grant approach and the equalizing approach is that whereas the former produces what might be called unplanned changes in relative expenditures, the latter is designed to produce explicitly desired changes in relative expenditures; specifically, it raises the relative position of the less favored states vis-à-vis the more favored states. The policy of requiring states to match federal funds tends to equalize expenditures by making each local dollar worth more via the additional of federal dollars. This "extra value" will be more significant for a poor state than a rich state.

There are many alternative possible equalizing criteria in educational aid. Per capita income, disposable income, that is, the per capita income of the state corrected for federal taxes, or possibly for federal, state, and local taxes, may serve. School expenditures per student or per capita income per student may also be used. If specific items, such as teachers' salaries, amounts spent on buildings, or the size of the annual building program are to be equalized, these items may be used as the relevant basis for determining the amount of equalization due any state. As in the case of flat grants, the federal government—the donor—would have no assurance that all or even a fraction of the federal funds are, in fact, used to supplement state or local funds which would have been made available in the absence of equalizing funds. It would be possible but difficult in a program of equalization to require that, to retain eligibility, states and school districts not reduce the size of school budgets, or to require that budgets be increased at some historical average rate of expenditure per student. This would amount to a fixed, or slowly rising, expenditure floor as a condition of federal aid. Some such condition could be required regardless of the criteria used in determining the equalization.

Equalizing formulas give a little more scope to ingenuity in their preparation than do flat rate formulas. The basic question which underlies the choice of an equalizing formula is, "What is to be equalized?" One may attempt to equalize, in elementary and secondary education, such diverse expenditures as teachers' salaries, school construction, vocational education, etc. One may attempt to equalize the entire educational effort. Or one may try to equalize personal income or tax burdens.

Incentive Grants

Incentive grants are designed to induce the states to undertake some particular action, in this case to improve their elementary and secondary school systems.

The most clearly needed and readily secured incentive is for the federal government to pay all or a proportion of a specific study or of a continuing study of any state school system as a basis for improvement programs. Clearly the state in question must desire the study and be willing to change its educational system. Unless these conditions are met, the exercise is meaningless. Universities and colleges of education, through their educational research bureaus, are readily available to assist a federal-state investigation. Standards devised to measure school accomplishment would be a joint product of state, federal, and professional interests, and so would avoid the charge of being dictated by the federal government. Such standards, incidentally, could easily satisfy "national goals" as well as state and local goals or needs.

Any incentive, to be effective, must have a goal. To argue that states and school districts need federal assistance without defining the purpose of the assistance does not seem to be good policy. The concept of education is broad and not well defined. What is needed, if one is to justify federal expenditures, is an explicit, distinct purpose. This implies standards—not necessarily federal standards but standards which are acceptable to the federal government.

The question of financing any changes in school curricula and methods suggested by the federally supported study remains unresolved in this approach. It is probable that to some extent the existing plant and financing could support some of the nonphysical, noncostly reforms. Other reforms would, however, need financial support. An early problem in federal aid is to determine a way to subsidize needed reforms by inducing the state in question to extend itself to accomplish the end in view. The education of legislators, public administrators, and the general public are clearly the immediate steps.

The next step is to devise a formula which would induce any state to spend more for education, since by so doing it would receive a bigger share of an incentive fund. Equalizing and incentive techniques are not exclusive. Any equalizing expenditure should not be so large as to discourage or make unattractive the incentive fund, if both are to be used. Limiting the life of the equalizing fund to a definite time span, say five years, or, after three years, reducing annually the equalizing fund by a known amount each year for five or ten years might induce the state to plan ahead to better its incentive position. The incentive should be arranged so that it will be easier for the poor states to make a good showing in equalizing their efforts than for the richer states to accomplish this end.

It would seem that wisdom would dictate employing a system of incentive payments plus other types of grants, but using the most simple criteria to determine the basis of distribution. A tolerable incentive system might even be devised by providing for flat or equalizing grants as a basic amount, with incentive payments above the base. Such a technique might induce low school tax effort states to improve their educational positions rather quickly.

Taxable Capacity

The measurement of the taxable capacity of states is an issue in federal aid to education for two reasons. First, if the taxable capacity of the several states could be clearly defined and measured, it would then be possible to point out that some states, at least on a relative basis, are quite capable of further support of public education out of their own resources. In these circumstances the pressure of public opinion might be such as to bring about necessary needed improvement in educational standards.

Second, measures of relative taxable capacity among states could be utilized as the basis for the payment of general federal aid. Such measures are commonly used within states for the distribution of state aid to education among school districts. Measures of taxable capacity are also used in some existing federal grant-in-aid programs, including hospital construction, school lunches and public health programs. Unfortunately, useful as the measurements would be, the concept of taxable capacity is not a simple one; it is a complex of economics, politics, and value judgments.

Viewed in one way, tax payments are a public claim on the community's current economic activity. Taxpayers yield up to government a portion of their claims on goods and services currently produced. The extent of this taxpaying must, therefore, be viewed in relation to levels of current economic activity, that is, to income produced or received. Tax burdens are commonly measured as a proportion of income by states, and indexes of tax effort are devised in these terms. For these purposes, it is customary to use income received by the residents of the state.[13]

Neither aggregate income, however, nor per capita income, is an unambiguous concept for these purposes. Capacity to pay is also affected by changes in the level of income. Similarly, the distribution of income is relevant. A substantial concentration of income in upper brackets may increase capacity to pay out of a given aggregate or per capita level of income.

Apart from the difficulties with the concept of income in the measurement of taxable capacity, there are further differences in state economic structures not wholly measurable in income terms. Southwestern states with oil resources, and western states with mineral resources have taxable capacities that exceed that of other states with equivalent income simply because oil and mineral resources are commonly subject to special levies. States with race tracks that attract the gambling-minded from outside their borders acquire additional taxable capacity not measured by the income of residents. For many years New Jersey had an unusually favorable tax advantage in the location of a heavy concentration of railroad property in the northern part of the state. Such cases could be multiplied indefinitely, as could the converse where states possess no such special taxable resources.

There is the additional matter of citizen preferences for public versus private goods. In one state the citizenry may prefer to keep their expenditures largely in the private sector, for food and clothing and for yachts and motor cars. This citizenry would be unwilling to yield up additional command over resources to the public sector. In another state, however, citizen preferences may be more favorable to the public sector. It may be that the measurable taxable capacity of the two states is identical, but in the latter state the public services, including public education, will flourish; in the former state they will languish. It seems somewhat beside the point to argue that the former state is capable of taxing more heavily when, in fact, citizen preferences do not run in this direction.

Finally, there are those states that might wish to tax more heavily but are hindered in the exercise of their preferences by the impediments of constitutional restrictions. Pennsylvania, for example, might wish to tax more heavily by way of a personal income tax, but it takes four years in that state to amend the constitution.

It would thus appear to be possible to move through a spectrum with respect to the concept of taxable capacity. At one end is personal income as the sole measure of capacity. As one moves along the spectrum, modifications must be introduced—in the concept of income itself, modifications to reflect the economic structure of the state, attitudes of citizens toward taxpaying, and legal restrictions. The other end of the spectrum simply measures current tax collections in any state. The closer one comes to modifying the concept of taxable capacity in accordance with institutional reality, the closer one comes to defining the taxable capacity of states as the revenues that states are now collecting.

Some of the possibilities and problems encountered in defining and measuring a concept of taxable capacity among states are set forth in a recent publication by the Advisory Commission on Intergovernmental Relations.[14] The commission sets forth, for the year 1959 for all states, five different measures of per capita income as possible indexes of fiscal capacity. These are: (1) personal income, (2) the income of families as reported in the 1960 census, (3) the income of families above a minimum amount, (4) income produced, and (5) a composite series made up of personal income minus federal tax payments, income produced, and corporate net income. In addition, the commission developed a measure of fiscal capacity based on a "representative tax system." This system was selected on the basis of the types of taxes now dominant in state tax structures levied at average tax rates.[15]

The commission found that "conclusions about the relative capacity and effort position of a number of States are strongly dependent on which index is used."[16] States in the southeastern region revealed relatively less and states in the far west revealed relatively more fiscal capacity, regardless of the index used. States in other regions, however, exhibited strikingly different indices of tax effort, depending on the choice of index.

The commission concluded that there is no very strong reason for preferring one measure of fiscal capacity over another. Interestingly enough, the indexes could be used to demonstrate that every state could exert additional fiscal effort where effort is measured as the relationship between actual tax collections and one or more of the indexes; that is, no one state stands at the top in all of the measures.

The fact that the concept of taxable capacity, and hence of tax effort, is both elusive and arbitrary does not mean that all measures of these concepts are without significance. The states *do* differ in their capacity to pay taxes. On the other hand, measurements of tax effort should not be employed as a basis for concluding that taxes have reached their limit in a particular state and that federal aid is therefore necessary if the public sector is to be strengthened. But if it is determined that general federal aid to education is desirable, more or less arbitrary measures of fiscal capacity could appropriately be used as a basis for the distribution of such aid.

Federal Control

No one sensitive to the American tradition and familiar with the American temper seriously argues that the curricula, textbooks, school buildings, faculty requirements, and all the other factors which make up a school should be controlled by the federal government. Nor does anyone seriously argue that any of these should be controlled by the federal government unless the federal government is buying a specific service. Nevertheless, the fear of federal control has been widely expressed and is an important source of continued objection to federal aid to education.

The traditional ideal of local or institutional autonomy and free play is related to individualism, and is deep-seated. It is a great social strength in the American system. But its virtues and requirements are not known only to the public. Administrators, including the federal government's, are also familiar with what is expected of them and with what is acceptable. The federal government is administered by persons very similar to those who run state governments, businesses, or schools. In a democratic society government officials simply do not and cannot operate by laying down hard and fast rules and forcing citizens and nonfederal institutions to adjust to these dictates. The area of education which affects literally millions of people is a particularly sensitive one. No administrator can long or successfully dictate in education-at-large. Persuasion, discussion, and mutual adjustment with a strong admixture of compromise are the techniques of government in all spheres, and particularly in education.

Much of the argument against government control is designed to knock down a straw man. It is sometimes implied that the Congress or the discretionary administrative body would prepare formulas and rules to determine the conduct of state and local school authorities. This kind of control has never been proposed and is not worthy of consideration.

First of all, the sanctions available against any departure from standards, however arrived at, are too slight in recently proposed legislation to have the ability to coerce any state or locality. The payment of three-quarters of a billion dollars a year by the federal government, as proposed in the administration bill in 1961, to elementary and secondary school budgets that exceed $16 billion a year, and will increase vastly in the immediate future, does not provide a handy control to federal administrators, regardless of how subtle and devious they might be.

Furthermore, the very concept of the application of formulas or rules to education is not realistic. Some matters of public concern can be, and indeed should be, governed by hard and fast rules. Building codes dealing with health and safety should properly have minimum fixed requirements. Tax laws should not be fashioned to meet the needs of each individual taxpayer but should be generally set and generally conformed to. Physicians and lawyers properly have to meet minimum requirements of education, skill, and moral integrity. But these areas of public concern are not comparable to educational policy and procedure. Differences, based on regional needs and values, on economic and technical considerations, and on custom and esthetics, emerge of necessity from the variations in the American culture. To deny such differences is to invite disaster for the administrator.

Strict uniformity in education is neither a reasonable ideal nor a practical goal. Discretion, variance, and tailor-made plans and programs for particular areas and types of people are required. The role of the local school board and of the state school administration, as a practical as well as a philosophical and political matter, should not and cannot realistically be neglected in any reasonable school program. Local and state interests and knowledge are of inestimable weight in decision-making.

The question of discretion at the various levels of operation, or variability in educational planning and programming is not at issue. It is accepted. It is clear, then, that a system which relies upon rigid administrative control will not serve the purposes of American education whose unity embraces great diversity.

An alternative to rigid control is one which may be called a system of administrative discretion. Let it be assumed, for the sake of argument, although contrary to fact, that the federal government supplies a major share of the funds for elementary and secondary education. Clearly the Congress could not write into law all the administrative provisions necessary to run a national school system. Congress would, from the very nature of things, delegate authority to an executive agency or to an agency created for the purpose. The agency which received the delegation of power would then be in a position, theoretically at least, to prepare rules, policies, and guides to the school system of the entire United States.

But this in itself is not sensible, since in the American scene education is historically, by tradition and by operating custom, a local and state matter. In all states, the authority to control and regulate the school system lies in the department of education. Yet local interest and concern has been so great that a large fraction of the administration is turned over to local school boards which, as time runs its course, consider themselves the ultimate source of authority, sharing it when it is necessary, and when they are induced to do so, with the state department of education. The theory that educational concern is centered in state government is largely legalistic. The social process, the basis on which people behave, is one which reacts as if the local agency had primary responsibility, although the responsibility is shared with the state agency. It is unthinkable in the American scene to have some central federal agency, such as the Office of Education, assume unilateral control.

From the viewpoint of control over the purse strings, as well as the fact and morality of operations, the federal government at best can share with state and local authorities. The concept of administrative discretion determining policy unilaterally, as applied to a federal agency, makes no sense in the educational picture.

The Need for Cooperative Action

Local school boards, state school agencies, and the federal government all have an interest in elementary and secondary education, and all are participating in the financing of such education. The interdependence of the various parts of the United States requires certain general standards of excellence and accomplishment in the final product; and this excellence can be achieved by sharing technical knowledge, discussing values which should be the goals of a school system, and bringing to the knowledge of all concerned the interrelations of communities which for better or worse are mutually dependent on each other. Here, clearly, is an area which requires cooperative action.

The Office of Education can become a more effective office which assists state and local bodies to solve or reduce problems peculiar to them. In their turn, state and local bodies must be willing to look to the Office of Education for assistance. Local, state, and federal officials should utilize increasingly the advisory and technical services of professional persons trained in the art and technique of education; these include the faculties of schools of education and other faculties, as well as knowledgeable laymen. The horizons of local boards and of state departments of education would undoubtedly be widened by frequent contacts with persons from outside the school system. Similarly, the Office of Education personnel would learn much, and would transmit that learning throughout the United States, by increasing their contacts with local and state boards of education. Professional educators from colleges and universities would find their own knowledge and experience made richer by more contacts with school officials.

Total federal expenditure for such a program would not necessarily be extremely large. Arrangements which have the sanction of time in a given school, community, or state may have neither the sanction of good sense nor efficiency. Changes in program and method would occur more easily if the experience of other communities were available to all. The most fruitful discussions are likely to be those which deal with very specific matters—for example, curriculum, vocational training, or administration. Where the federal government and local and state officials find that a particular program is worthy of being instituted, or at least experimented with, the federal government would be in a position to assist the experiment or the new approach with funds. Here the incentive technique of matching funds in some fashion would make a federal dollar very effective in mobilizing non-federal dollars. Guidance, mutuality, and the spread of ideas are as significant as securing funds for programs.

Administrative and structural changes would undoubtedly have to take place in all the states and in the Office of Education if the program suggested here is to be made effective. The major change would probably be in the Office of Education which would cease to be an agency administering federal funds and holding occasional meetings with state departments of education. The Office of Education would become an integral part of the educational system of America, motivated by ideas and sharing responsibility for programs and their implementation. It would be necessary for the Office to build on the kinds of foundations represented in the Cooperative Research Program, which, since 1956, has provided important financial support for educational research in colleges and universities. The challenge is to develop new leadership patterns and to utilize citizen and expert advisory groups in the settled tradition of American government.

Educational values now unthought of in many communities would become vital guides to public behavior were an institution—the suggested tripartite arrangement—developed to concern itself with the educational process. Values do not spring from the minds of isolated people; values come from the social process and are adopted by people. The major purpose of federal aid to education is not to equalize or improve educational opportunity in any of the several states. The major purpose is to improve the effectiveness of the total educational structure of the United States. To equalize educational opportunity the policy of bringing poorer and less fortunate states up to the standards of the richer states would seem sufficient. Yet in any real sense this is insufficient because it neglects the opportunity and challenge of raising the better states to even higher standards of excellence as well as raising the level of less fortunate states. In education the mode, the median, and the mean have no overwhelming significance. The whole structure must be raised, for education does not have a fixed goal. The goal of education, like the goal of an expanding universe, is ever outward.

One of the great fallacies, often advanced by the proponents of federal aid to education, is the assumption that the only significant feature of such a program is the money which the federal government would distribute to the states. This is, indeed, a short-sighted and narrow view. Federal money is undoubtedly significant; but of greater significance are ideas, organizations, and programs.

The consideration of who would lose power in such a new working arrangement—the local school board, state department of education, the professional, academic, or layman adviser—is a meaningless one because a new institutional framework for the educational process would increase the responsibility of all and would make the tasks of all more difficult, but surely more interesting, provocative, and meaningful. As institutions grow in size and complexity the challenge of all concerned increases. To be sure, individuals who are unwilling to accept change or different ways of doing things are bypassed and become disgruntled. But the persons and groups accepting change and challenge usually find that the new situation brings greater responsibility. The state departments of labor became more, not less, significant in social life with the passage of the Social Security Act. State highway departments became more, not less, significant with the development of a federal road system. Collaboration with the FBI does not reduce the task and authority of state and local police officials; it makes them more effective. The County Agent Program virtually created local and state interest in agricultural problems. And so it goes. Centralization, federal control, dictation—these are words without very much meaning in the light of experience.

The greatest challenge is not to state and local school agencies, but is to the United States Office of Education when, as, and if a program of general federal aid to education is enacted. A reorganized Office of Education will have to become a clearing house for imaginative ideas, a practical research agency ready and able to work with local and state bodies, an idea-creating institution developing programs but remaining flexible enough to adjust, throw out ideas, and receive new ones. The goals suggested here for the Office of

Education are difficult to attain, but are indeed worthy of great effort. In fact, with or without a program of general federal aid, the U.S. Office of Education must come to exercise a positive leadership role in American education if the national interest is to be successful in strengthening state and local educational institutions.

XII. Administering the NDEA

The National Defense Education Act is in the tradition of American federal aid to education, a tradition that requires the coordination of local, state, and federal administrations to achieve specific purposes. Federal aid for fairly well-defined, categorical purposes interacts with the equally persistent and more powerful commitment to state and local autonomy. In this approach the educational establishment is held to be the responsibility of the people—voters exercising the franchise for the election of local officials who administer local educational institutions.

There is, of course, a strong element of myth in both of these traditions. Federal aid given for one purpose relieves funds for other purposes, and so is not simply categorical. Local and state authorities, in fact, share responsibility in various fashions, and both are subjected to the forces and pressures of economics, politics, world events, technological changes, and the simple availability of funds.

Governmental responsibility in education is divided, with federal, state, and local authorities all playing changing roles. These roles may alter in relative significance to each other, but as the educational establishment grows, the roles of each of the three governmental participants will become larger.

While categorical aid is in the American tradition, change—purposive change—in administration is also in the tradition. School administration in America is now ripe for change. The increase in the size of the educational enterprise, its economic significance, and public and political concern demand new ways to administer the function. Furthermore, the very nature of education, its content and technical apparatus, requires a revamping of the administrative institution. Federal aid to education, along lines similar to that employed under NDEA, represents important possibilities for purposive change.

The Background of Legislation

The immediate postwar period did not bring major changes in the relative roles of the federal, state, and local governments in financing and administering elementary and secondary education. But one dramatic event—the Soviet launching of the first Sputnik in the fall of 1957—did bring an important restructuring of the role of the federal

This chapter is based on materials prepared by Sidney C. Sufrin.

government. Sputnik was the catalyst that hastened what was probably an inevitable reconsideration of ways and means to support and direct public education in the United States.

This chapter is concerned with the administration of the NDEA insofar as it affects elementary and secondary schools, although the Act itself is directed to many phases and levels of education and of educational administration. The NDEA is now part and parcel of the American educational scene. The introduction of this complex structure produced remarkably little friction or difficulty in the elementary and secondary educational system. Some of the problems that have seemed vexatious in the first years of the Act are probably short-run frictions. The two major issues, (1) the role of the federal government in the determination of educational standards, and (2) categorical *vs.* general aid, have, however, not been resolved by NDEA. On the other hand, the inherent pragmatism of American politics seems to be leading toward a reasonable solution even to these problems.

Some critics have considered the Act a mistake because it put the federal governments into education, which they consider to be a state and local matter. Others consider the Act a mistake because it does not put the federal government sufficiently into the educational process; still others believe the Act to be a mistake because it is too narrow, while yet others think it too broad in coverage and implication. The Act is controversial but, as indicated, it does not represent a great deviation from the traditional way in which the federal government has assisted education in the United States. The novelty, if it is novelty, is in its scope and content.

The national government has been concerned with education since the beginnings of the Republic. The Northwest Ordinance of 1787 and the Morrill Act of 1862 are familiar landmarks of national educational policy. Congress became interested in general federal aid as early as 1870, and although nothing came of this interest at that time, an important categorical aid program eventually was enacted.[1] This was the Smith-Hughes Act for vocational education which was, in a very specific way, the precursor of the National Defense Education Act.

The Smith-Hughes Act of 1917 provided for federal, categorical, vocational aid to schools. Under this Act the national government undertook to assist the several states in financing instruction in trade and industrial occupations, agriculture, home economics, and distributive trades. Both part-time and full-time programs were within the scope of the Act.

The Smith-Hughes Act was followed by other federal legislation in 1929, 1935, 1937, and finally the George-Barden Act of 1946. Each of these pieces of legislation strengthened the vocational training programs of the states, and the George-Barden Act in turn was incorporated into the National Defense Education Act. In recent years the Kennedy administration has proposed, and Congress has enacted, the Area Redevelopment Act of 1961 and the Federal Manpower Development and Training Act of 1962, both of which provide for vocational training for chronically unemployed adults. Most recently, the administration and the Congress have been concerned with the extension of vocational training to cope with the unemployment of Negro youth.

Federal support for vocational training has never encountered the intense opposition that has characterized general federal aid to elementary and secondary education. Neither has this type of categorical assistance been as controversial as the issue of categorical *vs.* general aid in legislation at the state level. Moreover, the programs have grown tremendously with substantial and generalized public acceptance. More than half of the persons enrolled in vocational courses throughout the nation are adults, and the numbers have increased from 165,000 in 1918 to 3,850,000 in 1961.[2]

Apart from national government support of vocational education, a further precedent for the NDEA approach to education is to be found in the programs of the National Science Foundation. Since 1950 this agency has been concerned with the improvement of scientific education at all levels. Both summer and in-service institutes have been made available for high school teachers of science and mathematics.[3] Other NSF programs have been directed toward the training of additional research and teaching personnel at the postgraduate level.

The Act—a Categorical Instrument

The NDEA is a monumental legislative reaction to the great national concern with education. It follows tradition insofar as elementary and secondary education is concerned. Funds are provided for specific educational programs with a set of fairly general instructions as to how the money shall be spent and for what purposes. The administration of the funds and the programs is essentially a concern for the states. The funds are not given to the states without strings, however. There is at least the auditing requirement to assure that the purposes of the grant are being accomplished. NDEA monies are given to the states for special purposes, e.g., education in mathematics, science, and language, or construction of scientific laboratories in secondary schools. Since the money is given for well-defined purposes, the program takes on some of the character of the vocational education programs.

The controversial issues here are, first, whether the federal government has chosen the proper areas for assistance and, second, whether federal assistance for specific purposes tends to frustrate state educational policy.

These are difficult questions. If, in the opinion of the federal government, i.e., the Congress and administration, young people should be trained in the sciences and mathematics, the federal government presumably has the responsibility to do something about it. But if a particular state finds that its own overwhelming need is not to train young people in the sciences and mathematics but to train them in spelling and shop work, the availability of federal funds might very well thwart the accomplishment of state policy. Federal funds on a matching basis become difficult for a state to refuse, even at a cost to other unsubsidized programs. This is the issue of categorical aid which has become so controversial in educational-administrative circles.

The immediate stimulus to the passage of the National Defense Education Act of 1958 was the belief that the Soviet educational system had surpassed that of the United States. Yet it would be improper to argue that the NDEA was hastily put together and devised solely to "catch up" with the Soviet Union. No experienced legislator or public administrator could believe that the new programs undertaken in 1958 would have any great immediate effect in the technological competition with the Soviet Union. Educational programs and policies are of long-run, not short-run, impact.

Popular interest in science has been extremely strong throughout the whole of the 20th century, particularly stimulated by the role science played in World War II; it is not strange, then, that science and its handmaiden, mathematics, received prominent roles in NDEA. Certain aspects of the legislation, those related to guidance, counseling, improvement of administration, and even assistance to students studying in colleges and universities, had long been discussed in educational and governmental circles. NDEA may have been enacted under the pressures which the Congress felt from the Russian success in space, but the contents of NDEA represent both traditional activities of the federal government with respect to the educational programs of states, and substantive considerations which professional educators and public officials had been considering for some time.

The provisions of the Act may be divided into three major categories. The first is the assistance to students at the university and collegiate level. Such assistance is given through loans and fellowships (Title II, Loans to Students in Institutions of Higher Learning; Title IV, National Defense Fellowships). Second are the programs for assisting state education at the elementary and secondary levels. These programs include funds for strengthening science, mathematics, and foreign language instruction; funds to strengthen the guidance, counselling and testing programs of schools; and finally area vocational programs (Title III, Financial Assistance for Strengthening Mathematics and Modern Foreign Language Instruction; Title V, Guidance, Counselling, Testing: Identification and Encouragement of Able Students; Title VIII, Area Vocational Programs). The state programs are administratively aided by federal government funds to strengthen the statistical services of state departments of education (Title X, Improvement of Statistical Services of State Departments of Education). The third area of concern of the Act is to assist interested research scholars in finding better ways to teach. This is contained in Title VII (Research and Experimentation in the Effect of the Utilization of Television, Radio, Motion Pictures and Related Media for Educational Purposes).

Thus it can be seen that the Act has as its purpose to assist some students at the university and collegiate level, to assist states in their own educational programs, and to assist higher educational institutions generally to train people who will in their turn become teachers at the elementary, secondary, or higher levels of education. Viewed in this way, the purposes of the NDEA are not unlike the vocational program structures of the past, although the present conception of assistance is somewhat broader. It now includes the training of teachers, which is in itself a vocational task, to train young people in well defined categorical areas of education. This approach shares with vocational study the characteristics of being instrumental and more sharply defined than are "general" education or "cultural" education. It is in this area that NDEA does represent a novel broadening of traditional federal aid.

There are many educators and state administrators who favor federal aid provided it is given as general assistance to the educational programs of the states. Such proponents believe that federal funds should be used to assist the states to accomplish the broad complex of programs which each state has devised. Intervention by the federal government with respect to curriculum, standards, textbooks, or teaching technique is therefore considered anathema.

At the other extreme are those who argue that the only way to assure that the federal government will not control, direct, and ultimately monopolize the educational system of the United States is to keep the federal government out of education entirely. This view does not usually argue that present programs of vocational education or impacted areas assistance should be abandoned; rather it asserts that no additional activities should be undertaken by the federal government.

Between these extremes are those who argue for categorical aid, insisting that if the federal government is to support education it has a right, in a sense, to choose what it buys. Federal funds, when, as, and if used, must be employed for specific, defined purposes. This specific requirement is not because the federal government distrusts the states. The essential reason for it is that the federal government should not use public funds except for well defined purposes.

Five years after its enactment the NDEA would appear to be firmly established as national government policy. It is likely to continue to win congressional approval for the foreseeable future. Categorical aid has attracted a substantial political coalition.

Provisions and Operation

The purpose of the National Defense Education Act is to improve the educational system of the United States. If this were not the case, the Act would not have been needed, would have been a waste of money, and would represent an unconscionable interference by the federal government in the affairs of states and localities. That the NDEA presupposes a cooperative partnership between the government on the one hand, and state and local school administrations on the other, is clear; but the Act also defines, in its several titles, the limits and directions of the partnership action.

The Act is a complex instrument—in its coverage, in its administration, and in its patterns of intergovernmental relations. Most of the provisions of the Act are administered by the U.S. Office of Education, but the National Science Foundation has responsibility for fellowship programs for higher education and for the establishment of a Science Information Service. The bulk of NDEA funds are directed, in one way or another, to elementary and secondary education, but loans to college students are the largest single program. The Titles of the Act, authorizations and appropriations for fiscal 1962, and the basis on which grants are made, are outlined in Table 5.

TABLE 5—NDEA FUNDS, BY TITLES, FISCAL 1962

Title	Purpose	Authorized, Fiscal 1962	Appropriated, Fiscal 1962	Basis
I	Statement of Policy			
II	Loans to students	$90,000,000 plus annual share of $25,000,000 for 4-year loans to colleges and universities	$73,845,000 contributions to loan funds; $1,300,000 loans to institutions; $60,000 cancellations of student loans	Shared by states in proportion to full-time college students
III	Assistance to science, math, and modern language instruction in secondary schools	$70,000,000 of which $5,000,000 is for state administration, $8,400,000 for loans to private schools	$47,520,000; $3,750,000 for state administration; $6,480,000 loans to private schools	50-50 state matching*
IV	National Defense Fellowships	$22,262,000	$22,262,000	Direct grants
V	Guidance, counseling, and testing	(a) $15,000,000 state program (b) $7,250,000 counseling institutes	(a) $15,000,000 state program (b) $7,100,000	(a) 50-50 state matching* (b) direct grants
VI	Language development	(a) $8,000,000 (centers, research, and fellowships) (b) $7,250,000 (institutes)	(a) $8,000,000 (b) $7,250,000	(a) by contract to 50% of cost (b) contractual (cost)
VII	Research experiments in communication media	(a) $5,000,000 experimental (b) by contract	(a) $4,770,000 experimental (b) by contract	(a) direct grants (b) by contract
VIII	Area vocational programs	$15,000,000	$12,800,000	50-50 state matching†
IX	Science Information Service	in National Science Foundation budget		
X	State statistical services	$2,750,000	$1,490,000	Grants to state up to 1/2 cost, not to exceed $50,000 per state

* State school-age population × state allotment ratio = each share

$$\text{Allotment ratio} = 100 - 50 \times \frac{\text{state income per child school age}}{\text{U.S. income per child school age}}$$ (minimum value 33-1/3%, maximum 66-2/3%)

† See next page.

Title III, for the support of science, mathematics, and modern foreign languages, has the greatest direct significance for elementary and secondary education. Grants are available for equipment and for remodeling of laboratories and other space, and for the expansion or improvement of supervisory and related services in the schools and in state departments of education.

The method of allocating the major share of federal funds to the states under Title III varies directly with school-age population and inversely with income per child of school age. A strong equalization element, therefore, exists in the allocation formula. The 50-50 matching provisions require that the states be more than passive if they are to benefit.

---

† Within the NDEA, titles III, V, VIII, and X require the matching of federal funds on the part of the states. Using Title III as the basic example, this allotment procedure may be briefly reviewed. Of the total amount appropriated, the Commissioner of Education must hold in reserve a maximum of 2 per cent for allocation to territories and possessions and 12 per cent for loans to non-public schools.

The remaining 86 per cent is allotted to each state in the same ratio as the product of the school-age population of the state and the state's allotment ratio. (One-half of the fraction of the income per child of school age for the state over the income per child of school age for the continental United States subtracted from 100 per cent.) "Child of school age" is defined as any member of the population between the ages of 5 and 17 years inclusive; and "income per child of school age" in this context is taken to mean the total personal income for the state and the continental United States divided by the number of children of school age in the state or United States. The exception to this allotment ratio is that in no case shall it be less than one-third nor more than two-thirds of the average income per child of school age as determined by data available to the Department of Commerce for the last three consecutive years.

A state's allotment for equipment and minor remodeling is available for payment until the end of the fiscal year immediately following the year for which the allocation was made.

Under Title III, the Commissioner allots to states an amount for expansion or improvement of state supervisory services in public elementary or secondary schools in science, mathematics, and modern foreign languages in the same ratio as the school-age population of the state to the total U.S. school-age population. A minimum amount, $20,000, is set up per fiscal year for any state. On the other hand, no state may receive payments for any period in excess of its allotments for such a period whether it be for remodeling, equipment, or supervisory services.

Title V is allocated according to the same ratios and standards as Title III. However, Title VIII allotments are based upon the ratios set up under Title I of the George-Barden Act (Vocational Education Act) as of March 18, 1950, and Section 9 of the Act of August 1, 1956, to the total amounts assigned to all states per year. The amount apportioned to a state for a given fiscal year which is not used may be reallocated, at a time determined by the Commissioner, to other states in proportion to their original allocations.

An examination of state-by-state experience for the fiscal year 1962 suggests that the states overmatched for Title III projects.[4] The federal government contributed $45.4 million in that year, but the gross budgeted amount was more than double this—$99.7 million. For any one state in a single year there may be substantial departures from the 50-50 ratio since funds for equipment and remodeling under this Title may be carried over for two fiscal years.

Federal-state government agreement on projects under Title III has been generally close. More than 90 per cent of the states in fiscal 1961, for example, had 90 per cent or more of their requested projects, measured in dollar terms, approved. No state had less than 70 per cent of its requested projects authorized by the U.S. Office. This would suggest that there has been a high degree of accommodation between the federal administration of NDEA and administrators in the states. It is reasonable to expect that administrative relationships between the U.S. Office and state personnel will be increasingly harmonious as the states employ additional supervisors and consultants to assist school districts in the preparation of Title III projects. Between fiscal 1959 and fiscal 1962, 35 states who had not previously employed such personnel had retained them. Since Title III provides matching federal funds to the states for personnel to administer the Act, it can be expected that the remaining states will soon employ the necessary staff.

The distribution of projects under Title III by subject matter for fiscal 1962 is shown in Table 6. As might be expected, both in terms of numbers of projects and cost, outlays for science education have

TABLE 6

Distribution of Approved Projects under Title III, by subject matter, fiscal 1962

	Per cent of Projects*	Per cent of Cost†
Science only	55.9	72.3
Mathematics	21.5	9.0
Languages	13.4	18.7
Science and mathematics	3.7	
Science and languages	1.0	
Mathematics and languages	.0	
Science, mathematics and languages	4.5	
Total	100.0	100.0

* Total number of projects: 51,752

† Total cost: $99,746,047

Source: U.S. Office of Education, *Report on the National Defense Education Act: Fiscal Years 1961 and 1962* (Washington, 1963), 72.

predominated. Mathematics projects have exceeded language projects in numbers but not in terms of cost.

In general, responses among the states to the availability of NDEA funds and programs have been far from uniform. An examination of enrollment by states in summer institutes for guidance and counseling shows wide variation in the ratio of attendance to teachers or attendance to student enrollment. These disparities would suggest that some states have been far more effective than others in disseminating information and securing the participation of teachers in the strengthening of guidance and counseling. Similar sharp differences among states are noticeable in the administration of Title X (the improvement of state statistical services). Some state departments of education have been aggressive in the pursuit of federal funds to strengthen their own research and data gathering; others have not.

State experience under Title VIII for vocational training allotments is also varied. In fiscal 1962 over one-third of the enrollees were from one state, California. The remaining two-thirds were thinly spread over the entire United States. Such states as Michigan, Pennsylvania, and Indiana, which have had substantial numbers of chronically unemployed, have had modest enrollments under these federal programs.

Reactions to NDEA

From the wholly pragmatic viewpoint, NDEA has much to recommend it, since federal funds and interests are not devoted to a vaguely defined, unstructured concept of "education," but to educational specifics. It is at this point, however, that criticism begins, for the federal conception of educational policy may not be congruent with any particular state or personal conception. The existence of (or fear of) such noncongruence is reflected in state and local views. The philosophy of NDEA is that the national interest and public policy are intimately connected with specific programs and activities in the general area of education. This conception is not widely shared by state and local school administrators.

While education, or indeed any other social institution and endeavor, must ultimately be viewed in its broad general aspect, changes and improvements in such broad endeavors are best accomplished by rather well defined means. These may include specific activities and interventions which are either meaningful in themselves or in their interaction with other parts of the social endeavor. The result of these detailed and specific changes may very well affect the whole institutional purpose of education.

The views of the U.S. Office of Education on the general philosophy of NDEA are well revealed in the early annual reports on its administration. The first commissioner of education to report on the Act, Dr. Lawrence G. Derthick, stated that the essential purpose of NDEA was to assure "that every young person from the day he first enters school should have an opportunity to develop his gifts to the fullest."[5] Commissioner Derthick viewed the Act as offering "a challenging opportunity for shared responsibility and creative cooperation among public and private agencies, individuals, and institutions."[6]

In the fiscal 1960 report, Dr. Sterling M. McMurrin, Commissioner of Education, stressed that NDEA was a partnership "in which the Federal Government assists State educational agencies and institutions of higher education with programs—pioneering new ones as well as strengthening existing ones." The role of the Office of Education is "to operate in the spirit of leadership without domination, and assistance without interference."[7]

Leadership without domination and assistance without interference are obviously difficult administrative goals. The extent to which these have been achieved is, of course, impossible to appraise with precision. Fortunately, some materials are at hand which permit at least a partial evaluation. The late Senator James E. Murray requested the Legislative Reference Service of the Library of Congress to prepare a report in 1961 on the operations of NDEA.[8] This report brought together information concerning the experiences of state agencies and professional associations directly and indirectly concerned with NDEA operations. Reactions were solicited from associations of teachers at all levels of instruction, and representatives of various subject matter areas, from scientific organizations, school administrators—public and private, religious institutions, and organizations of business, labor, and agriculture. The survey solicited the opinions of parent-teacher associations and the various departments of the National Education Association.

As might be expected, so disparate a collection of populations with different interests, goals, and experiences, typically offered varying and sometimes conflicting views. By and large, among associations of professional educators the survey found a strong current of feeling running in support of general federal aid rather than the categorical type represented by NDEA. However, many professionals concerned with particular disciplines urged special categorical consideration for their area. For example, teachers of English or other studies outside the scope of the Act suggested that funds might be made available to assist their programs.

Administrators found red tape, that is, administrative ineptness, to be serious in many instances. On the whole, it was felt that some financial and administrative relief tended to flow from the Act. That federal funds might be or had been a threat to the existing balance of programs was frequently expressed by administrators, although documentary support of such contention was not presented.

As a rough approximation, replies to the questionnaires suggest that in the neighborhood of two-thirds of those directly concerned with administration had more favorable than neutral feelings toward NDEA. No one believed that the Act had solved the major financial and educational problems of schools or that it was likely to. A very small fraction of administrators, on the other hand, felt that the Act was harmful or useless. In the main, the educational world in 1960 was not wildly enthusiastic about NDEA, but it was far from disapproving. The body of educators was ready to take a second look, but it did have some important reservations.

A search of the educational literature, other than that reported by the Legislative Reference Service, indicates that the contributors to educational journals, by and large, share the views of their colleagues as summarized in the Legislative Reference Service report. Almost all of the writings of professional educators stress the complexity of NDEA administration and complain about the red tape of bureaucracy. The feeling that general aid is to be preferred to categorical aid is reflected in frequent comments that NDEA should cover the social sciences, English, the humanities, and the arts. NDEA funds are financially helpful but not basic to most of the programs they support. Categorical aid tends to unbalance the curriculum. Among professional educators the programs directed toward teacher training and the strengthening of counseling and guidance are deemed to be most important. Among educational administrators there is frequent complaint about financial and auditing procedures under the Act and, as in any federal aid program, there is always concern that the federal government will or can by its sheer power and size overwhelm state and local government units. Many state and local educational administrators fear that state and local educational autonomy might be or has been reduced in some measure by federal aid to education.

Views of Administrators

As a part of the research underlying this report, an effort was made to secure additional insight into the operations of NDEA by interviewing state and local school administrators with experience under the Act. Those interviewed had the same general attitudes toward

NDEA as did the representatives of educational organizations surveyed by the Legislative Reference Service.

Among those interviewed there was emphatic feeling that federal aid was desirable but that it should be general, not categorical. Aid for particularly defined objectives such as mathematics or language tends to support aspects of education which the Congress or some national administrative agency in Washington believes to be significant. What appears to be significant on the national level, however, need not be significant on the local or state level.

For example, in some sections of the country, state officials believe that additional funds spent on improving foreign language instruction pay less in social dividends than equal funds spent for other purposes, such as technical and vocational training or improvement in English. Personal and social needs, from the viewpoint of training and education, are so different in various parts of the country that categorical aid is an ineffective device to solve the range of problems. Yet when categorical aid is offered, local and state officials feel reluctant to pass up a chance for "cheap" money, even though it involves matching. Matching, it is sometimes feared, is a means of federal control.

What frequently occurs is that the categorical aid grant is accepted and then the funds are used, in part at least, for other purposes, This, in the language of one state administrator, "makes crooks out of local boards and local principals." In a less dramatic form, the argument is that categorical aid tends to create imbalances in the curriculum offerings because of the attractiveness of cheap money, and also tends to induce local school administrators to seek and find questionable accounting techniques and rationalizations for the use of equipment for purposes other than those contemplated by the categorical program.

Yet the improper use of categorical aid is not the major concern which gives rise to criticism. Of great immediate importance is the feeling that the NDEA program involves paper work, both at the local and state levels, far beyond that for funds of similar size secured from state sources. The growth in the size of the Office of Education is often seen as a prelude to more pressure by the expanded bureau.

There is a general feeling that the whole administrative NDEA process is bathed in the threatening shadow of the General Accounting Office. Federal funds, it is believed, require accounting and auditing care and justification far beyond reasonable requirements. State school administrators who have contact with the Washington federal officials are perhaps more conscious of the GAO spectre than local boards and local school officials. Local officials are less sensitive to "Washington" as a direct threat, since it is a kind of threat by state reference and they are often unimpressed. Consequently state officials constantly fret over the handling of funds by the local boards and local schools, and require more information and records than local boards and schools are willing or perhaps able to provide. The result is a frustration of the state officials, a frustration which they feel to be unnecessary and which might be relieved by appropriate action from Washington.

Similarly, state officials feel their position threatened by the Office of Education. Evidence was not cited to show where the Office of Education had intervened in any markedly untoward sense; nevertheless, state officials are jealous of their own control over curriculum and administration. They fear that federal funds, even though slight, are a vehicle by which the Office of Education can ride into what has up to now been a state domain—the supervision of elementary and secondary education.

Yet the fear of the Office of Education and, to a certain degree, the fear of federal auditing are paradoxical because state officials understand and support the view that where federal funds are involved the federal government has an obligation to concern itself with how and for what the funds are spent. No one can object to auditing; the only objection can be to unnecessary auditing and record-keeping. The resolution of this paradox—fear of Washington, but a recognition of Washington's responsibility—is not at all clear.

There was general agreement that the accounting, auditing, and purchase order procedures are burdensome and probably irrelevant in that they do not reflect the needs for accountability. Part of this unhappy situation, according to the respondents, is attributable to the administration of NDEA from Washington, and part is due to the uncertainty and insecurity which state officials feel, both with respect to Washington and to their local administrations. A third part is due to the unwillingness (or inability) of the local school agencies to perform properly the functions expected of them.

Examples were adduced to show that local administrators sometimes do not understand that the Act provides for the purchase of new equipment and programs and, having a fondness and respect for established programs, local officials try hard to use the federal funds to pay for such programs and their extension. For example, many believe that tape recorders may be secured under the foreign language provisions of the NDEA. The reader can understand, without approving, the subsequent action of the local school principal, who is always short of funds.

It would appear that very large school districts—those with complex accounting and administrative controls and a well organized purchasing system—find the NDEA requirements not especially excessive. Some large districts, however, have educational programs which are above the average in effectiveness in relation to need, even without NDEA's help.

To such districts and to larger cities generally NDEA has probably been more of a boon than to some of the smaller communities. This view was frequently expressed both by state and local officials. Richer (and often larger) communities, it is averred by some school superintendents, have taken more advantage of the NDEA than poorer communities. The NDEA funds, in a sense, were incorporated into the plans that the local schools already had for the extension of their mathematics, language, and science programs. Furthermore, the equipment and remodeling, in many instances, would have occurred perhaps a year or two later without NDEA help. This led one of the state officials to suggest that NDEA aid should be allocated in accordance with ability to pay. Thus a poor state might only match federal funds with 20 per cent of its own funds while a richer state might match federal funds with 70 per cent of its own funds. This keenness of feeling with respect to ability to pay and equalization was apparent in the discussions with the school officials, and there was a strong feeling that these principles of equity were not being met by NDEA.

Categorical versus general aid is the one problem to which the discussions with the school administrators always returned. No school administrator interviewed was opposed to the principle of federal aid. No administrator interviewed supported categorical aid as a wise and inclusive policy; all supported general aid. However, some administrators argued that the federal government might properly provide funds for bettering teachers' salaries, building schools, or strengthening the training in given fields such as mathematics. While this view, in a sense, supports categorical aid, those school officials who supported this also went on to argue that the expenditure of the funds and the standards required of the local schools should be entirely a matter of state control rather than of federal control.

The views of school administrators with respect to categorical versus general aid are based on an almost universal philosophical principle that the curriculum and personnel control of education is and should be state-oriented. This view is held as a belief or even an assumption, rather than as a rational conclusion, although many arguments of a rational sort are adduced to defend the position of state autonomy.

There was but little attempt on the part of the respondents to consider the wisdom and propriety either of federal standards for education or for more strict local control of education. Insofar as the local school superintendents and state school administrators are concerned, the issue of the location of the central power to control elementary and secondary schools has been determined, and the locus of authority, in the American tradition, is the state. The implication that local administrators lack breadth of vision and that federal administrators are domineering is clear. Thus, by exclusion, state administration remains. On this issue there seems to be little tendency to engage in debate.

All the administrators interviewed, without exception, believe that federal aid is necessary, yet they fear federal control. They even fear the sheer technical control over funds by a federal agency because, they argue, technical control over funds can ultimately lead to control of substance. That state and local governments pay, and for the foreseeable future will continue to pay the major share of the costs of public education is not considered a conclusive argument. The inherent fear of the power of the federal government is not defined merely by its share of any money payments.

Providing funds in greater quantity for the sciences, it is feared, can lead to over-emphasis on the science curriculum. Ultimately, allocating varying sums of money to the several disciplines, it is argued, might control the planning of curricula by local schools. This is but one step from determining the specifics of what is taught.

It was also argued that if NDEA continues for a relatively few years then it (or something like it) must be continued forever because the programs which the schools undertake with NDEA funds are built into the total curriculum and budget. Withdrawal of federal funds would then be disastrous, and Congress, under the pressure from "back home," could not countenance it. In this view the appropriate role for the federal government in curriculum building should be stimulative rather than shaping.

There was a unanimous belief among those interviewed that the Office of Education should not initiate any advice to the state or local school authorities, and state officials felt the Office of Education should not deal with the local school authorities except through state school authorities. On the other hand, all believed that the advice, technical studies, and technical assistance of the Office of Education would be most desirable—but only when requested. Both state and local officials obviously desire to be administratively independent of Washington, which in this case means the Office of Education.

The Educators' Model

In the view of a great many educators the whole of the United States is broken into fifty compartments. Each compartment contains a cluster of functioning local school boards, the central agency of the state school administration, and a little opening in the compartment through which can flow federal power. The federal power is small compared to that generated within the compartment. Somewhere in the middle of the model, but not part of any compartment, is the Office of Education. At the moment its power (NDEA funds) flows through very small apertures into each one of the state compartments. The feeling is, however, that should the flow of funds, which is the carrier of power, increase, the apertures will prove too small and will be widened, and in widening will break down the compartment walls, thus attaching the educational structure directly to the federal mechanism by the flowing funds. The result will be a diminution in the importance and role of state and local school bodies.

It is thought that as and if the Congress votes more funds, the Office of Education will increase in size and the flow of funds carrying power will press further upon the local and state school boards. To carry the model further, the ultimate effect would be that the flow of federal funds and power would regiment the state and local bodies in such a fashion that state differences would tend to disappear, with a resulting homogeneous mass whose structure and form is directed from Washington.

This, in part, is the argument made frequently which claims that federal aid to schools of necessity implies some kind of federal control. The model and its presumed operation may or may not be appropriate in analyzing the situation in the United States. Indeed, one would be inclined to argue that it is a static picture in which the boundaries of the universe of discourse are fixed, and the boundaries surrounding the state institutions are made of such flimsy material that a modest increase in federal funds would cause the apertures through which these funds flow to widen and destroy the walls which make up the boundaries of the state administrations.

A more dynamic model would suggest that as federal funds are distributed to the states, the universe of discourse, the whole area of education, would expand and part of the federal funds would be devoted to widening, deepening, and strengthening the educational enterprise so that the pressures of federal funds would not grow intolerable in compressing state and local activity. If the universe of discourse expands, and if the state compartments expand, what might well happen is that the functions and responsibilities undertaken by local boards, the state school administration, and the central government will all increase. The relative positions of state, local, and federal influence might change, probably giving a greater role to the federal government, but the absolute position of all might increase. More decisions will have to be made at all levels and, if the whole model expands, more important ones, too. The greater role of the federal government would not necessarily be at the expense of other authorities. Increasing federal funds in such a fashion as to call forth more local and state funds might actually increase the responsibilities, activities, and effectiveness of state and local school administrations, and at the same time serve the national interest and the interest of cities and states which presently suffer because of inadequate programs of other states and communities. Certainly large cities and industrial states would benefit if the educational standards of rural areas and states of population emigration were improved.

The conventional and static model seems to assume that federal, state, and local administrations are without imagination or will, that they act merely mechanically. But surely the educational process in the United States must be carried on differently, with different goals, techniques, and aspirations in different parts of the country. With this view so frequently expressed by administrators one can be thoroughly sympathetic. Regional differences need not be destroyed by the expenditure of more money, whatever the source of the money, provided that state and local administrations have a coordinate voice in determining how the money is to be spent. One can easily imagine a situation in which the programing and expenditure of federal funds in either local school districts or through state agencies receives the thorough approval of local and state administrators. Many intergovernmental activities bear witness to this.

Where the pressures are great the federal government, jointly with the states, does act and react rapidly, and often with remarkable cooperation and good will. Such cooperation and good will in the educational field, as in any other field, can only be achieved when the parties at interest are mutually informed as to each other's needs, desires, and purposes. Schoolmen generally believe that federal aid to education is inevitable and necessary. When inevitability and necessity join, administrative machinery can and will somehow be devised.

THE VIEWS OF THE U.S. OFFICE OF EDUCATION

The unofficial reactions of various staff members of the Office of Education to the complaints and concerns of state and local administrators fall into two categories. First, there is the denial that many of the complaints and fears of state and local officials have any basis in fact and practice. The second reaction is that the appropriation of federal funds necessarily requires an accounting to assure that adequate care and responsibility are exercised in the expenditure of these funds.

The Department of Health, Education, and Welfare (as is true of all federal agencies) does not employ the General Accounting Office as an auditing agency. GAO is a creature and an arm of Congress and not of the administration. Auditing and accounting are done by the department concerned, in this case the officials of the Department of Health, Education, and Welfare assigned for these purposes to the Office of Education. Departmental audits and state and/or local audits are initially the relevant ones. GAO audits are not very likely to be on a continuing basis.

But, the officials of the Office of Education insist, their policy goes even further. The Office of Education and its parent department, HEW, are desirous of building up state responsibility with respect to administrative and substantive matters. Therefore, whenever possible, existing state procedures rather than federal rules are followed in the accounting and auditing of funds. The states are responsible for the auditing of local projects and no specific rules are laid down for state accounts other than they "shall be adequate to permit an accurate and expeditious audit of the program."

The Office of Education is thus willing to accept state accounting and auditing forms and methods provided they permit an accurate audit. State officials must first of all have an acceptable audit system. Still, disagreements between federal and state officials may occur as to what is acceptable and accurate. This is presumably what state officials fear, for their control over local school districts is sometimes less than complete.

The Office of Education has given a responsibility to the states which they are reluctant to accept. A gift can be very expensive at times. The issue between the state and federal officials may well be one more of communication than of substance.

As is so often the case in controversies regarding administrative procedure, the issues are not clearly drawn. The Office of Education is formally correct in its contention that administrative auditing is in the hands of its own staff. However, this is not the concern of the school administrators. The General Accounting Office is in truth a legislative arm, but it has the authority to conduct investigations and audits of federal grants-in-aid. The General Accounting Office, upon learning of the possibility of fraud or chicanery, would doubtless investigate the matter to see whether federal funds were actually being misused. It is this that the school administrators are wary of.

To be sure, no one would knowingly defend the misappropriation of funds. School administrators, however, fear, according to their comment, that what the federal government would consider misappropriation of funds is not what school administration at the local level might so consider and, furthermore, that state officials cannot control or easily oversee the actions of local bodies.

On the whole, however, it would appear that the concern with the GAO is in a sense a bogeyman. Time and experience alone will fashion a local-state-federal relationship within which each can operate effectively. Audits are an aid to good administration, not a drawback.

In this the position of the Office of Education is not a happy one. If it insists upon certain auditing practices and procedures, it is accused of financial dictation. If it agrees to use a state system with the caveat that the system be adequate, the personal judgments of the federal officials become an easy complaint by state officials that whim and caprice rather than rule and regulation are the mainstays of the Office of Education administration. Yet one cannot reasonably argue that state auditing systems should not be accurate and understandable.

As pointed out above, the major criticism by state and local educators is that categorical aid tends to imbalance local and state programs. A corollary of this criticism is that the larger school districts, with a greater number of programs than the smaller school districts, are not so restrained by the categorical aid approach since there is a greater probability that with many programs some can be expanded profitably with the help of federal money. On the latter point, the respondent officials of the Office of Education are in agreement. Their view is that the larger school districts, generally the big city school districts, are likely to have not only many projects to choose from as justifying improvement which would secure federal funds, but also greater administrative and financial sophistication and will therefore make better use of NDEA.

While granting this, however, the officials of the Office of Education are not ready to grant the first part of the criticism—namely that the categorical aid program leads to widespread or serious imbalancing of local projects. There is the obvious argument that the state or local government has the right simply to refuse to allocate any of its funds to a program which does not make sense to it. This, to be sure, would deny the use of federal funds but, on the other hand, would conserve state funds. Yet the total of federal funds would not be reduced by a state or local district's not following one particular categorical line. So long as there are other categories which can be profitably expanded, federal aid would be forthcoming. The limitation is, of course, that other categories must be judged worthy of expansion, and fit under the rubric of the Act. In general, the feeling on the part of Office of Education respondents was that the categories which receive aid under the Act are generally accepted as so necessary that the imbalance feature is likely to be very small indeed.

Of perhaps greater importance than the imbalance concern is the fiscal problem—that dealing with ability to pay as it affects local districts. Some state and local administrators argue that school districts which need assistance least because of their greater wealth, income, and better tax basis, are likely to be in a preferred position in securing federal help because of their size and administrative sophistication. Therefore, the argument is that the 50-50 matching fund arrangement improves the position of these well situated school districts as compared to the poorer school districts.

The Office of Education respondents point out, however, that the matching fund provision is on a state basis—that each state, in its turn, can use other than a 50-50 provision at the local level. Only the total contribution of the state must equal the federal grant. Indeed, some states have changed the conditions of local matching. Thus a poor district might receive $7 for every $3 spent on a new, approved project, while a rich district might enjoy the inverse of this ratio, $3 of federal funds for every $7 of local funds spent. The program is entirely a matter of state administration and discretion within the total state matching limitation. The states have not generally provided for variable matching because of internal administrative difficulties or because of other policy considerations. However, the option is open to them.

The essential argument made by the Office of Education respondents is that the purposes of their administrative concern are program and educational excellence rather than money. They realize that federal funds are not great compared to the total expenditure of the states on education, but the persistent Office of Education effort is to assist in improvement of the states' educational enterprises.

To gain the ends of its policy, the Office of Education has held frequent meetings to explain to state officials its policy and program and to stress that the accounting and auditing procedures, which officials in the Office of Education expected to be troublesome, were to be determined by the states, with the proviso that they be sufficient to permit an accurate and expeditious audit of the program. That the Office of Education has not been entirely successful in this communication problem seems to be illustrated by the attitudes expressed in an earlier part of the chapter.

In relations between the Office of Education and state and local school bodies, officials of the Office of Education are emphatic in saying that they do not desire to dictate school curriculum or educational (or any other) policy to state and local school bodies. There is almost a reflex response to any question which even vaguely touches on state or local autonomy. In specific, the Office of Education respondents insist that they come into states only on the request of the states, and even then usually make it a point never to deal with local officials unless state officials are present.

What Can Be Done?

It would sometimes appear that local school boards are relatively impervious to direct influence from the U.S. Office of Education. The local school boards' major contacts with the educational world tend to be with state educational authorities. Therefore, state bodies are the ones with which the Office must work to improve educational standards. The great national concern with educational excellence cannot, in all likelihood, be secured by federal mandatory action. Persuasion, advice, and cooperative action are the keys to improvement. Even the expenditure of more funds offers no assurance that teaching methods will be improved or that the subject matter taught will be any better. The way to educational excellence is to improve teaching personnel.

The great needs of the educational system are research which provides a fund of knowledge and ideas, people to administer the school system and do the teaching, and facilities and tools to accomplish the educational program. Pilot projects are of extreme value. Showing school officials at the local school level that improvement can occur because it is occurring in the pilot operation is an irrefutable argument. State contact with the universities and research agencies on the one hand, and with the Office of Education on the other, are also promising paths to excellence.

Although progress may be slow, the states can be helped by federal aid of money and advice. The local boards become the major problem since their awareness, knowledge, and even interest in the educational enterprise are often less than are required. Yet the local boards cannot be skirted and thus isolated from the educational process. Most local boards now sustain a very adequate interest in the business management aspects of the enterprise. Steps should be taken to encourage a comparable interest in the educational process itself. This can be done primarily by assisting the states to work with the local boards.

The differing points of view of state officials and of federal officials with respect to NDEA and other educational policies are not easily reconcilable. It is clear from this investigation that there is a strong tendency on the part of state and local school administrators to look askance at the potential or actual inroads of the Office of Education into the state and local educational enterprise. On the other hand, from the viewpoint of the Office of Education, there seems to be the feeling that contacts between the Office of Education and the states should be strengthened, and this in turn would strengthen the relations between the states and the local school boards.

A jointly financed state-federal agency, housed in the state departments of education and operating under state-federal rules, would do much to smooth the relations between the Office of Education and the state and local authorities. Such a staff would have easy access to the localities, and would operate in accordance with the policies agreed on by the states and the Office of Education. An important outcome of such an arrangement might be to strengthen the position of the Office of Education in the hierarchy of federal agencies.

The disparity between the self-image of the Office of Education and the image which the state and local authorities have of the Office is very much at issue in the future of intergovernmental relations in public education. One can suggest that improved communications, contacts, meetings, and joint ventures would develop a more reasonable and common image both at the state and local level and at the Washington level. Furthermore, the cost of federal aid involves, insofar as state and local authorities are concerned, contacts with federal officials who have an obligation to their own agencies. Mutual adjustments must be made, since it is inconceivable that each participant will have his own way all the time.

Reasonable administration requires that the administered be willing to see good in the administrator and his actions. Whether the criticisms of the state and local school officials by the Office of Education are justified is not the point. The point is that doubt and insecurity exist in a situation where doubt and insecurity are anathema. This is a more important issue than any detail of administrative regulation.

The Office of Education has an enormous challenge to better its relations with the states, to make its contacts more regular and more welcome, so that the Office can become the major clearing house of ideas and experiences between and among all the states and local educational agencies of the United States. Ideas need desperately to be transferred, transmitted, evaluated, and ultimately used. The Office of Education similarly has an obvious role cut out for it to extend and expand the function of acting as a contact between professional groups, universities, and other persons of expertise on the one hand, and the state and local bodies on the other.

The most significant and vital function which the Office of Education might accomplish would be to assist the states, and through the states the local agencies, to develop and define categories of educational activity which are meaningful and fruitful to the whole society and to the individuals involved. The nation as an ongoing society must be considered in the state and local educational process, but general national policy considerations in no way deny the role and significance of state and local policy considerations.

The Educational Public

The school system appeals to no particular public which is utterly and single-mindedly devoted to its purposes. The Parent-Teachers Association is concerned with elementary and secondary education, but the Parent-Teachers Association members as ordinary citizens are also concerned with taxes, school athletics, and a host of other school and nonschool matters.

There are a great many groups in addition to PTA's that have an interest in elementary and secondary education. These include associations of professional educators, chambers of commerce and other civic organizations, and the interests that support adult education, vocational education, or driver education. But these groups are often divisive in their impact, with an inability to view the educational process in its entirety.

All professional educators should in the future, as they have not done in the past, spread their interests to elementary and secondary education if those levels are to be improved substantially. This spread of interest on the part of the educators at the university and college level should not be limited to those in the college of education faculty as it has been in the past, but should include all other faculties. How this is to be done is not at all clear, but unless it is done, a most valuable resource will be lacking in the accomplishment of educational excellence.

The Behavioral Science Subpanel of the President's Science Advisory Committee asserts:

> Outstanding men in the behavioral sciences should follow the lead of their colleagues in physics, mathematics and biology by devoting special efforts to preparing superior instructional materials for use at the secondary school and introductory undergraduate level.[9]

This view, which is the same as that expressed here, argues for the joint effort of all educators in strengthening the substance of elementary and secondary education.

The National Defense Education Act was not merely a reaction to the Russian scientific advance as exemplified by Sputnik. The National Defense Education Act can best be viewed as a major attempt at federal aid to education at the elementary and secondary levels. Although the program is categorical, the categories are so wide and diffuse and so academically oriented as to make them unlike the previous vocational training programs supported by the federal government.

Federal aid to elementary and secondary education makes sense only if the expenditure of funds strengthens educational standards and accomplishments at the state and local levels. Similarly, general aid by the federal government to the states would make sense only if the states and local school boards would adopt standards which are high and desirable. Categorical or general aid both end up as categorical aid because expenditures are for specifics. The nature of the specifics—the standards, the programs, the quality—these are the relevant considerations.

Federal assistance via the NDEA or some other categorical program is likely to continue and to expand modestly in the immediate future. However, the great potential contribution of the federal government will not be money. The great challenge, and hence potential contribution, is to develop the necessary patterns for orientation, guidance, and leadership of American educational systems. Federal funds as such are likely to be a marginal contribution to this development. Ideas and organizations to disseminate these ideas are necessary to meet the challenges that now face the educational system.

XIII. Science Education: Two Programs

In 1956 the Physical Science Study Committee was organized to undertake a massive improvement in the teaching of high school physics. Two years later, in 1958, Congress enacted and the President signed the National Defense Education Act. Title III of that Act was likewise directed toward an improvement in the teaching of science in American high schools. Both of these programs were undertaken as major attacks on what was felt to be a national weakness—science education in the high schools. The two were in some ways parallel, in many ways diverse, and their comparative experience illuminates both the possibilities and the differences in the organization of programs for the improvement of learning in the public schools. The two programs also illustrate the utilization of very different techniques in the use of federal funds for the support of public education.

In the academic year 1956-57 there were over 9,540,000 children of high school age, and somewhat more than 4,000,000 of these were enrolled in science courses, usually general science or biology. Of this group about 310,000 were studying physics, and this was about one-quarter of all high school seniors, the group to whom the course is most commonly offered. Fewer than 5 per cent of all high school students attended institutions that did not offer physics or chemistry.

In its first four years of operation after 1956 the PSSC caused the spending of about $8 million in federal funds and $500,000 locally. By that time it had reached over 2,200 science teachers and perhaps 1,000 classrooms. In its first three years of operation Title III Science spent about $8 million on its own administration and caused state and local expenditures of about $116 million to match its own disbursement of the same amount for federal assistance to some 15,000 science projects. The PSSC was and is essentially a privately organized venture supported by both private and government funds. NDEA Title III Science is wholly governmental in character but with funds available for private schools.

The Physical Science Study Committee

The roots of the PSSC date back to World War II, and the role of such prominent scientists as Vannevar Bush who began at that

This chapter is based on materials prepared by Paul E. Marsh and Ross A. Gortner.

time to think in terms of an organized national science program for the postwar period. By 1950 the Congress became convinced of the need for strengthened federal support for science, and the result was the National Science Foundation, established as an independent agency in the Executive Office of the President. By charter the Foundation was expected to develop "a national policy for the promotion of basic research and education in the sciences." In its first years NSF emphasized the promotion of research but not science education. By 1953, however, NSF was supporting four summer institutes for 250 science teachers from small colleges with some additional support for high school science affairs and clubs. This program continued to expand and by 1956 NSF came to be increasingly concerned about the quality of science education in the high schools. In this year NSF initiated a massive nationwide program to bring up-to-date science to high school students by means of summer institutes. Twenty-five were scheduled for 1956 and 95 for 1957.

In the meantime, Jerrold R. Zacharias, Professor of Physics at the Massachusetts Institute of Technology, had begun to address himself to the problem of teaching materials available for the high school physics course. His proposal was to prepare a number of short films of about twenty minutes each, with some 90 films in all, based on new content for the course. These materials would form the basis for a year-long course with weekly laboratory work.

Professor Zacharias' plan survived the scrutiny of his colleagues at MIT and was submitted to the National Science Foundation for their consideration. It was hoped that the program would eventually reach all high school students enrolled in physics—roughly the upper quarter of all juniors and seniors in secondary schools with more than 300 pupils. Confident of ultimate support for the project, Professor Zacharias organized, in the fall of 1956, a group designated as the Physical Science Study Committee. The group was a distinguished one and included Professor I. I. Rabi of Columbia, James R. Killian of MIT, Edwin Land of the Polaroid Corporation, and Professors Nathaniel H. Frank, Martin Deutsch, and Francis L. Friedman from MIT. In its initial statement of purpose it was agreed that "This committee will revalue the content of courses in physical science, hoping to find a way to make more understandable to all students the world in which we live, and to prepare better those who will do advanced work. It is probable that such a presentation would also attract more students to careers in science."[1]

The group organized a steering committee and added to it a college and a high school chemist, and an expert on secondary schools.

It created a curriculum committee charged with basic responsibility for the course itself: ". . . to outline a two year course in physical science and list the topics to be covered; outline texts, questions and answers, and teachers manual; supervise the evaluation of the pilot work with the Educational Testing Service and consider the type of examination suitable for the course; approve script outlines for films; choose demonstrations that should be included in films and approve materials to be used."[2] The steering committee planned, as its first venture, for a group of six physics teachers to prepare material for a twenty-minute film on Newton's Law.

A second meeting was held six days later and within a month the committee was augmented by the additional membership that it sought. Some of the original ideas were almost immediately modified; the program for a filmed course began to decline as the major preoccupation of the committee, and increased attention came to be paid to textbooks and course content.

An initial grant from NSF in the amount of $300,000 was almost immediately forthcoming. The first meeting of PSSC had been organized in September and by December of 1956 physicists from other universities had joined the group. Major emphasis now came to be placed on the preparation of a course of study. By December the PSSC came into general agreement that this course should aim for teaching concepts rather than facts, and for selecting a few fundamentals to be studied in depth rather than skimming over a large number of concepts. The new course was to be publicized in the 1957 institutes sponsored by the National Science Foundation. The National Education Association agreed to cooperate in recommending that high school science teachers work on the project; new grant proposals were submitted and approved by NSF.

It took just two years to prepare the new course; it was ready for introduction in the fall of 1958. The crucial conference on the nature and composition of the course came in December of 1956 at MIT. Forty-eight participants attended—physicists from the universities and from industry, representatives of the National Education Association, teachers of science education in teacher training institutions, and one classroom teacher. At the end of a three-day conference the basic course outline was established.

At the same time that the course was planned it was necessary to give attention to a program for dissemination. The PSSC steering committee felt that NSF science institutes for high school teachers provided exactly the right vehicle for telling large numbers of physics teachers about the new course and for training them to teach it.

The National Science Foundation, however, did not as a matter of policy seek out colleges to give institutes. Initiative lay wholly with the colleges themselves. It followed that the PSSC must arrange for the introduction of its course in the NSF institutes.

Responsibility for ultimate publication also had to be decided early. It was concluded that:

> The committee felt that the federal government should not be put in the position of supporting competition with private enterprise in the education field, nor subsidize the writing of textbooks which would be distributed by the government. . . . When the work is ready for distribution it should be made a part of the public domain.[3]

Meetings with staff of the National Science Foundation sought to clarify the role of that organization. It was determined that federal funds could support the national meetings of scientists to discuss the need for new science courses in the schools and to explore what these courses might be. Federal funds would support the invention and development of the whole range of new educational materials the courses might require. Federal funds might be used to train numbers of teachers to use the new materials but only if the training institution itself wanted to do so. Federal funds might not be used to compete with private enterprise in the production and distribution of teaching materials. NSF was prepared to budget an additional $242,000 beyond the initial grant of $300,000.

With these funds in hand at the beginning of 1957, Professor Zacharias proceeded to recruit scientists as consultants. Faculty from some 30 colleges and universities were soon drawn into the PSSC effort, occasionally as full-time employees for a year or more. A surprising number of industrial physicists were likewise enlisted for short or long periods of time. To recruit science teachers in the high schools was more difficult simply because few of the PSSC physicists knew any science teachers professionally. Therefore letters were sent to all 48 chief state school officers describing the work of the PSSC and asking each to recommend the best high school physics teacher in his state to join the committee in the summer of 1957. A dozen top teachers were secured by this approach and later two dozen more.

To this core group of scientists and science teachers were added, from time to time, other specialists—a professional artist, two photographers, an editor, engineers, and technicians to prepare laboratory apparatus. Encyclopaedia Britannica Films were retained for the preparation of filmed materials. The Educational Testing Service in

Princeton prepared a new college entrance examination based on the PSSC course.

What with writing and rewriting, the preparation of films and art work, and the testing and retesting of techniques of presentation, the PSSC agenda was a full one. Nevertheless, by the spring of 1958 the course had taken shape. The outcome was a comprehensive package of carefully interlocking learning material. The text was organized around the development of a single basic but specific theme in physical science. The laboratory was treated as the logical indispensable extension of the text. The films explored both aspects of the theme which neither words nor high school laboratories could cope with efficiently. The coherence was definite and exact, and typically and purely scientific.

The NSF institutes turned out to be a ready-made instrument for the dissemination of the PSSC course; the arrangements were relatively simple. A college or university science department would propose to hold a summer institute if the NSF would pay for it. The host institution would supply administration, instruction, and facilities, and the Foundation would contribute the funds, including a percentage for overhead. Decisions about curriculum and the selection of teachers to attend the institutes were the responsibility of the college. The high school teachers who attended paid no tuition and often received academic credit.

In addition to the summer institutes NSF initiated in 1956 a series of in-service training programs. High school teachers would meet regularly for some thirty weeks at the host institution, usually for an evening or on a Saturday morning. They paid no tuition or fees but usually received a travel allowance. PSSC moved to embrace this program as well. Its first sponsored in-service training program took place at Bowdoin College in 1957-58, during the time that the course was still in preparation.

In the summer of 1958 five institute directors—at Reed College, the University of Minnesota, Oak Ridge, the University of Connecticut, and Bowdoin—agreed to offer the PSSC course. These enrolled 276 participants, and MIT conducted a summer institute with 60 participants. Additional colleges and universities offered both summer institutes and in-service institutes in the next few years. By the end of the summer of 1960 sixty-seven PSSC institutes had been held at 42 different host institutions.

During this time there were innovations in the sponsorship pattern. In 1959-60 two in-service programs in Greater Boston were supported by local funds, not by NSF. In suburban Denver a county science supervisor almost singlehandedly financed, recruited, and administered a PSSC in-service institute for science teachers in the area. Moreover, the PSSC course had a momentum of its own, apart from the institutes. In 1958 there were ony eleven teachers who taught the course without institute preparation, but by the next year 36 did, and in 1960, 130 more introduced the course.

In 1958 there were about 250 classrooms that used the PSSC course; in 1959 this had increased to 625. In that year the materials were distributed by a commercial publishing firm at a cost per pupil of approximately $5. Since that time between 850 and 1,100 schools have used PSSC materials with a continued expansion in the number of teachers and students—about 1,800 teachers with perhaps 75,000 students in 1961-62.

The progress of the PSSC through the nation's school system seems to have depended very little on government action apart from the decisions of school boards and administrators to budget for it. In only two instances has action at the state level been a decisive factor—in New York and in Florida. In the former state the Department of Education determined on a three-year testing program and moved to restrict the use of the course during that time. In consequence, although the state had more PSSC institute participants than any other, only about a third of these actually taught the course in their classroom. In Florida the State Education Department moved in the other direction, and under its stimulus by 1959-60 some 80 per cent of all high school students in the state were in schools where the PSSC course was offered.

By 1960 all 50 states had had institute participants, and all but four—Alaska, the Dakotas, and Mississippi—had at least one teacher. Nevertheless there was a heavy concentration in the metropolitan areas on the Pacific Coast and in the northeastern quarter of the nation bounded by Washington, D.C., St. Louis, and Minneapolis. An examination of the geographic spread of schools using PSSC shows clearly the impact of the institutes, both summer and in-service. There are, of course, lone outpost offerings but, in general, the heavy concentration of PSSC courses has been in areas around the colleges and universities offering the institutes.

In matters of financial support, as in other characteristics of the PSSC venture, there has been a mixture of public and private activity. As mentioned, the National Science Foundation provided the initial financing and NSF continued as the major source of funds. All told, its grants to the Committee amounted to $4.1 million. The Committee, at first sponsored by MIT, was eventually transferred to a private corporation called Educational Services, Inc. The Committee also secured support from the Ford Foundation in an amount of $500,000, and from the Alfred P. Sloan Foundation for about half that total.

The PSSC conference program was expensive, but the largest part of its expenditures went for the preparation of the text material and other materials for teachers—in an amount approximating $1.8 million. Expenditures for film making came to about the same total.

To these amounts should be added the NSF support for summer and in-service institutes. Generally these amounted to outlays of somewhat less than $1,000,000 a year in the first years of operation. The average summer institute appears to have cost about $68,000, and the average in-service training course about $31,000. The summer programs, however, handled about twice as many participants as the in-service programs. The average cost per participant amounted to about $1,200 during the school year, and only about $300 more than this during the summer. In the first years it may be estimated that the cost of preparing a teacher to teach the course—since not all institute participants actually taught the course—amounted to about $3,300 per teacher. By 1962 it would appear these costs were in the neighborhood of about $2,000 per PSSC teacher. To this should be added the costs of the materials themselves, which have amounted to about $600 per teacher or $25 to $30 per pupil for a class of 24 students. Thus the PSSC was an expensive course to offer, but the burden on local school budgets has been substantially eased since 1958-59 by the availability of funds under Title III of the National Defense Education Act. Grants available here permitted the assumption of from 21 to 42 per cent of the costs of instructional materials for the course.

During the winter of 1959-60, after considerable discussion with representatives of publishing firms, the PSSC handed over to its choice all its printed materials. Similarly, a scientific apparatus manufacturer assumed responsibility for PSSC equipment, and an educational film distributor the printing and renting of PSSC films. The Physical Science Study Committee had established a program for massive improvement in science education. Henceforth the responsibilities for dissemination were in the hands of private firms.

The National Defense Education Act—Title III Science

In January, 1958, President Eisenhower sent to Congress a special message on education. Eight months later Congress enacted the National Defense Education Act, and on December 2, 1958, President Eisenhower signed it.

The legislative process had been time-consuming. The House Committee on Education and Labor and the Senate Committee on Labor and Public Welfare devoted countless hours to hearings. Under the leadership of Representative Carl Elliott, of Alabama, the House Subcommittee on Special Education held 35 hearings with 2,000 pages of testimony. The Senate committee under the leadership of Lister Hill, of Alabama, was only slightly less burdened. It held 22 hearings with 1,600 pages of testimony. Moreover, these two committees between them considered more than 30 bills directed toward federal assistance to one or more aspects of public education.

The political problems were formidable. All forms of federal aid have encountered long-standing opposition.[4] Long-time advocates of federal aid saw this as an occasion for the enactment of general support legislation for public education and proponents were often divided between those who wanted categorical aid and those who wanted general aid.

It soon became evident that substantial consensus could be reached on federal aid for science, mathematics, and foreign languages. Scientists who testified before the committees generally applauded the NSF support of the PSSC. Science education could be further strengthened by the use of federal funds for equipment, and federal aid to state departments of education to hire specialists in science education. High school science laboratories were expensive, ranging in cost from $6,000 to $12,000. Many schools were unable to purchase the necessary equipment; financial stimulus was necessary.

Out of this came Title III of the National Defense Education Act to provide funds for consultants in science education at the state level and to provide funds to local schools on a matching basis for the purchase of science equipment. In fact, this Title had a rather easier legislative course than other aspects of NDEA. Insofar as Title III embodied a philosophy, it was simply that the nation's scientific establishment could be strengthened by the disbursement of federal funds for science education. The Congress could lighten the financial burden of science improvement by state and local educational agencies. The federal government, however, would not play a direct role in the improvement process apart from the stimulus by way of federal aid.

The National Defense Education Act carried with it an appropriation of $57,350,000 for the support of science, mathematics, and foreign language education.[5] Of this first appropriation, $1,350,000 was earmarked for matching by state departments to increase supervisory services and for the administration of their share of NDEA. The bulk of the remainder was for local schools, with each state's maximum share predetermined by formula.

The language of Title III Science was simple enough. Funds were to be provided for

> . . . acquisition of laboratory and other special equipment, including audio-visual materials and equipment and printed materials (other than textbooks), suitable for use in providing education in science, . . . minor remodelling of laboratory or other space used for such materials or equipment; . . .[6]

Each state was required to submit a plan to the U.S. Commissioner of Education and secure his approval before funds could be released. To expedite this the Council of Chief State School Officers collaborated with the U.S. Office of Education in preparing forms for the plans. Some of the states had completed their proposals by the end of 1958, all of them had plans approved by July of 1959.

Instructions issued to the states for the preparation of their plans were quite simple. Three short sections in the instructions defined who in the state could administer the plan and what the state's fiscal arrangements and procedures must be. Beyond this, each state was required to describe present state services in science education and anticipated improvements. Additional information was required about local laboratory equipment and remodeling projects. The state was required to list its priorities for reimbursing local projects and to describe the kinds of projects and standards for equipment it would help to pay for.

To overcome any possible friction with state departments of education the U.S. Office worked closely with state officials in the preparation of the state plans. Administrative regulations were submitted in advance for comment by state officials before their adoption by the U.S. Office. A series of national conferences and regional meetings was held to explain and consider the Act. To ease the administrative problem of the U.S. Office, the Commissioner of Education created a new branch within the Office's Division of State and Local School systems to advise and consult with state departments on specific projects as they were proposed.

Very little professional attention was devoted to defining the specifics of scientific materials for which Title III funds could be spent. Instead a private schoolbook publishing house recognized a burgeoning new market and compiled a catalog of scientific, mathematical, and linguistic equipment and reference books that would appear to qualify for state reimbursement. This publication was reviewed by the Council of Chief State School Officers and became a nonofficial guide to both state departments and local school districts.

Although the Act was signed after schools opened in the fall of 1958, by June of 1959 thousands of districts were already enjoying new science equipment. The limitations on disbursement were minimal. Federal aid was generally unencumbered by federal control other than financial and auditing, but it was also innocent of scientific guidance and advice. The PSSC could offer to teachers a scientific discipline, Title III Science could not.

Under the provisions of the statute itself and the procedures worked out by U.S. Office and state departments of education, initiative under the law rests with the states. Federal personnel are on tap to give advice and information, but the states do the work. By and large they have. Every year since the Title went into effect more federal funds have left Washington to reimburse states for their efforts to improve education in science, language, and mathematics. Year after year science ends up with about 75 per cent of the funds. In part this is attributable to the somewhat broader coverage of the science grant program. Elementary schools participate here to a greater extent than in mathematics and languages and, of course, science equipment is expensive.

The real question lay in determining what constituted a science project to begin with. The U.S. Office did not ask, and most state plans hesitated to say. Nevertheless states frequently had precise notions about other characteristics needed to support a project. Maine favored projects in high schools in the consolidated country districts it was anxious to create. New York and Vermont wanted projects in districts that were exceeding state program requirements or existing state expenditure averages in order to give lagging districts goals to aspire to. Missouri, on the contrary, decided that only the total expenditure in the state need match the federal allotment so that projects could be supported on a sliding scale from 10 to 100 per cent and thus equalize the local costs of science facilities among school districts.

Getting the plans approved in Washington was relatively easy, but securing funds in the states was not always so simple. In nearly every state, implementation of the plan depended on expanding state department staffs. In some cases state personnel could be reassigned to qualify, but additional positions had to be created and state funds appropriated therefor. But by the end of state legislative sessions in the spring of 1959 only five state legislatures had refused to provide matching funds. By the next year every state except Arizona had approved budget increases for state science supervision. The lawmakers of that state have continued to oppose NDEA.

It was a difficult task to hire additional state-level science supervisors. Nevertheless, by December, 1962, the Office of Education reported impressive gains. In the nation as a whole there were 79 new state science supervisors or consultants, and 17 more for both science and mathematics, six times as many as there had been prior to the Act. Thirty-five states had added supervisors where none had previously been retained.[7]

Almost all states interpreted leadership under Title III as the encouragement of local effort. State personnel, therefore, organized area meetings and workshops for science teachers and administrators to explain the state's plan for Title III. State departments then prepared and distributed newsletters, reports, guidelines, standards, catalogs, applications, bulletins, instructions, regulations, order forms, and summaries for each subject material, and sometimes at each grade level.

The U.S. Office of Education had deliberately kept its scientific guidelines within the broad generalities of the Act; there was to be no hint of federal control. In modern foreign languages the problem of equipment selection was simplified by the existence and widespread acceptance of standard audio linguistic language laboratories, but in science the only new and complete package was the PSSC. It is not surprising that a large proportion of PSSC schools simplified their selection problem by ordering PSSC materials under Title III. Every state, of course, was anxious to have as many projects as possible and from as many districts as possible. No state wished to turn back Title III allocations unspent.

The projects were organized and funds were spent in a remarkably short time. In fiscal 1959, 684 high school science laboratories were remodeled, and there were 2,658 equipment projects. In fiscal 1960 there were 1,915 remodeling jobs and 12,536 equipment projects, and the number of projects has remained at about this level in subsequent years.

Title III developed early in its existence a tendency for large expenditures on a few projects and small expenditures on a very large number of projects. In 1959, for instance, $23.5 million was disbursed among 8,947 Title III projects (5,108 in science alone). About 11 per cent of these accounted for half the total funds. This disparity has continued and indeed has been accentuated in subsequent years.

Part of the explanation for this lies, of course, in the behavior of large city school districts that can sometimes match very large reimbursements without substantial fiscal strain. Nevertheless Title III seems to have developed a tendency to massive smallness and small massiveness.

Loans to private schools have proved to be inconsequential in the total operations of Title III. In the first two years of the Act only 129 such loans were negotiated, and the numbers have declined year by year. Title III loans have not bridged the gap between federal aid and private education.

Title III Science involves outlays of two types—for administration and for grants. A substantial part of the administrative costs are those of the U.S. Office which, as noted, organized a new section for the administration of NDEA. Although it is not possible to disentangle completely specific costs associated with NDEA, it would appear from a comparison of budgets that after the first year of operation of the Act the U.S. Office's administrative costs amounted to about $1.5 million. This is about 16 per cent of total U.S. Office administrative costs. Grants to the states after the first year moved up to $1.8 million, which means that total state budgets for science supervision and administration have increased by about $3.6 million. Most of these expenditures are, of course, for science supervisors and not for administration as such. What might be described as purely administrative costs for Title III as a whole was estimated by the U.S. Office at the end of 1960 as amounting to 0.9 per cent of all Title III outlays. The bulk of the funds, of course, are for laboratory remodeling and science equipment. These have increased from expenditures of $18.0 million in 1959 to $79.3 million in 1960, with a drop to $72.0 million in 1962.

Experience among the states and from year to year has varied widely. In the first year of operation, fiscal 1959, the states that disbursed all they could seem to have done so by spending on large projects. In Maryland, for example, $745,000 was disbursed for 10 projects; Nevada put its whole $47,000 allotment into a single science project. On the other hand, Louisiana reported more than a thousand projects and was the only state to spend its total allotment on projects averaging less than $1,000 each.

In 1960 assistance available for grants practically doubled in the states, but the states, even with a year's experience, often failed to take up all of the funds available. Only 17 states managed to use all of their allocations. However, 16 states doubled the number of projects approved. Georgia alone developed 6,990 projects in that year.

In 1960 the median reimbursement figure was $1,260, but West

Virginia had an average project size of $8,791. Nineteen states had average reimbursements between $1,000 and $2,000 per project. For the nation as a whole, 52 per cent of all projects cost less than $600, and 25 per cent were in excess of $3,000.

Experience under Title III thus far would suggest that there is very little correlation between the wealth of a state and its reimbursements under Title III. A comparison of personal income per school child with reimbursements per child reveals no pattern to suggest either that the rich states have benefited the most from Title III or, conversely, that Title III has been important in equalizing the fiscal burdens of education. Some low income states have had high reimbursements, such as Mississippi, Arkansas, Kentucky, and North Dakota, and some high income states, such as Delaware and California, have had relatively low reimbursements per pupil. But there are 12 high income states in the top half of a ranking of Title III reimbursements, and 12 low income states in the bottom half.

The pattern of Title III expenditures in relation to the income of a state is conditioned by two factors—the statutory allotments which favor poorer states and the ardor with which states pursue the availability of federal funds. The former factor may operate consistently in favor of some modest redistribution, but the latter will vary from year to year in accordance with the proclivities of state departments of education and the school districts that must initiate grant proposals. In some states there has undoubtedly been a failure to take advantage of the grant provisions because of constraints dictated by local economy pressures. The extent to which this has been significant is, unfortunately, impossible to determine.

Contrasts and Comparisons

Although the Physical Science Study Committee and Title III Science of the National Defense Education Act had the same end in view, each provided its own means of accomplishing this. The PSSC proceeded on the basis that the way to improve science education was to create better teaching materials for science courses—textbooks, laboratory apparatus, films—everything necessary for a viable introduction to the content and discipline of modern physical science. Title III, on the other hand, proposed to improve science education by giving money to schools to buy laboratory equipment and to do the minor remodeling of buildings necessary to house it. Each proposition was defensible. Neither was exclusive. Indeed, they might be taken as complementary.

When these programs were conceived there was general concern about whether they would involve federal control of the content of education. The early actions and accomplishments of each must lead to the conclusion that they do not. On the other hand, the reasons differ sharply and have had far-reaching influence on what they did accomplish.

Even though the PSSC's course materials, used as the PSSC prescribes, discipline teaching, federal support does not control the PSSC's new course and never has. Although most of the money for the program came from a federal agency, the National Science Foundation, NSF has concerned itself solely and continually with the feasibility of the undertaking, not with its content. Feasibility was a hard master; it insisted that every major stage in the new course be spelled out, judged by its appropriate peers, and revised on the basis of their judgment. Continuing private evaluation of the course has been made every time a college decides to hold a PSSC institute and every time a high school teacher decides to teach the course.

The course passed its final test when it found private commercial publishing, supply, and distributive houses willing to take over further management of the new materials. While large federal grants made this uniquely thorough schedule of testing possible, no federal employees had taken part in the evaluation. Scientists, classroom teachers, and educational businessmen, acting in their private capacities, had passed judgment on the PSSC before it became generally available. The new course did not control; it disciplined.

Title III Science was different. The money it provided for school use had no intrinsic rigor, nor could Congress make it an instrument of discipline. What the program had was magnitude and flexibility, but there could have been no program if its proponents had insisted on course standards as well. In order to command support in Congress, the Act had to be carefully and explicitly worded to deprive the federal government of means of curriculum control through the funds the Title would disburse.

For this reason, states must report their Title III Science activities to the U.S. Office of Education anonymously—in terms only of dollars and projects. Even their annual narrative reports do not spell out in concrete, usable ways how the dollars and projects have improved science education. The federal role is limited to little more than analyzing and reporting fiscal and jurisdictional characteristics of improvements in science education—and to handing out the money for them.

Nevertheless, Title III Science has introduced a new approach to curriculum development. It has given state departments of education control over sizable funds for science education which were not appropriated by their own state legislatures. This departmental autonomy at the state level, coupled with congressional intent to prevent federal control, has given entirely new powers of discretion of the state administrators of the Title. So far, their reticence in reporting specific improvements in science education brought about by the aid they have disbursed makes it impossible to judge the impact of the Title on curriculum development. In the early years, most of its money went to hard-pressed big city school districts, although most of its projects were relatively small and reflected the distinct administrative and financial styles of various states. Such results suggest the absence of federal control and also a common professional response at the state level to large-scale educational poverty and to idiosyncracies of local financial access characteristics of each state.

There are no impartial criteria by which to judge whether any Title III project may be a scientific or educational improvement. No provision for any such evaluation exists in the Act or in state plans or in terms of local projects. Apparently, negotiating a science project is test enough of its scientific worth. In their anxiety to avoid federal control, the authors of NDEA's Title III Science have gone a long way toward ruling out scientific control as well. As it stands, the sole objective criterion for an improvement in science education under Title III is that it cost money.

A detailed examination of the diffusion of both programs in the northeastern states suggests strongly that a prime factor in the spread of each has been the probable immediate influence of like-minded teachers and administrators in neighboring schools. Concerted small group responses to these nationwide programs for the improvement of science education emerge as key forces in their growth. This is the antithesis of federal control.

The major issue raised by the PSSC and Title III Science is the relative efficiency of private and public action in improving curriculum in American schools. Such improvement is now taken for granted as a matter of national concern. Both the PSSC and Title III Science are responses to the problem from the national level, but quite different ones. Each has demonstrated that national action can be undertaken in this area without specific federal direction. Each is now on the nation's educational scene, probably for good, and there are clear indications where and how each fits into it.

The PSSC represented intrinsically private action in curriculum improvement with large public support. The program was to require financial backing that only a handful of sources could supply. The most readily available resource turned out to be federal appropriations. Furthermore, a good deal of the PSSC's work was done with private support. During the time of major revisions, as much of the course's financial backing came from private foundations as from the NSF. Later, almost 20 per cent of all PSSC institutes in the first three years were sponsored by sources other than the NSF. The NSF's interpretation of national scientific responsibility made it the leading backer of the PSSC, but private sources helped and, if so inclined, could easily have underwritten the whole program. Finally, the PSSC handed its products over to the private economy of American education for continuing distribution. This act capped the consistency of the entire program.

Such privateness was overwhelmingly advantageous to the PSSC—indeed, essential for the work it proposed. In the face of all but unanimous popular opposition, no government agency could have set out to write a course for national school use. The PSSC could, and could also inform it with discipline appropriate to the subject. For this research and development, the PSSC was able to recruit scientists of international stature, and personnel who, on principle, might refuse to do the same work for government. And the PSSC could pay them according to going rates of return, not on the basis of civil service scales. As a private organization, the Committee also had full control of its own personnel policies and so could keep its staff in line with its aims and changing responsibilities. Then, with materials in hand, the PSSC was not arbitrarily restricted in its selection of channels for nationwide diffusion. They had to be scientific, but beyond that they could be public or private, national or state or local, secular or denominational, academic or industrial. This network of scientists was widespread and dense, capable of responding precisely and efficiently to needs of the program. Finally, as a private agent for modern science, the PSSC at the classroom level could ignore public, independent, and parochial tags as impertinences. Altogether, the predominantly private nature of the PSSC was indispensable to the fulfillment of its scientific mandate.

On the other hand, the very existence and drive of the PSSC raised a jurisdictional issue which no public agency could have ignored. In a failure of short-run, practical tactics, the Committee delayed early expansion in the use of its new course by not explaining the program to school administrators. The PSSC treated teachers as representatives of modern science in classrooms, but to the school administrators, teachers stood on the bottom level of the educational hierarchy and should, therefore, take part in curriculum development only with the knowledge and consent of their superiors. Professional control of curriculum was still a recent and jealously held political victory for school administrators and a cornerstone in their professional canon. In the dark about the PSSC, many felt neglected, and some, professionally threatened. What they failed to realize—and the PSSC did not tell them—was that the Committee was as strongly against the actual selection of textbooks by school boards as any school administrator.

Furthermore, efficiency and style combine to suggest that such curriculum work as that of the PSSC could hardly afford not to be essentially private. Here the advantages lie in sensitivity of evaluation. The feasibilities that NSF required the PSSC to demonstrate supersede total, inscrutable evaluation by the educational market place with tests at each step of curriculum development and research. The PSSC had to prove itself acceptable to scientists, teachers, students, foundations, institutes, and schoolbook publishers, with each group looking at it hard from special perspectives. This series of judgments brought out the testable aspects of the new course in an orderly way and in small steps. Scrutiny exposed flaws before they became fossilized in the new course and consequently expensive to alter. The PSSC had to satisfy at each step before it could feel sure of financing for the next. The program set a precedent for prepublication testing by a wide variety of interests with special dispassionate points of view.

The demands of this procedure took at least a third of the PSSC's time and about half its money. No commercial organization could afford such charges for quality control; no governmental agency would expose itself to such fiscal control. Because of its essentially private nature, the PSSC could look for support of all kinds from a wide variety of sources. By exactly the same token, however, every search involved evaluation of its program.

Title III Science avoided such evaluation and was at the same time much less candidly intimate with fundamental aspects of school curriculum. For one thing, the Act of which it was a part and the money which it disbursed were governmental and federal. This program was locked into the public government of the nation's school system. Title III monies went from jurisdiction to jurisdiction—from the U.S. government through state or territorial departments of education to about 30,000 local school districts. While the Title did provide a percentage of each annual appropriation for loans to independent schools, there were few takers. The impulse and character of the Act were public.

Its governmental nature, particularly federal, gave the Title's science some undeniable advantages. Assistance could be massive, as indeed it was, and available to support science education at any grade level from 1 through 12. This permitted access to aid for every local district in the nation. Besides, as a matter of course, the Title was so written as to avoid jurisdictional disputes. Its provisions for science improvements could hardly rub the profession the wrong way, for they did not control and they strengthened the professional hand by increasing its financial resources. Then, too, the U.S. Office fully understood its own administrative role and the order of educational hierarchy. The Office made certain that commissioners, supervisors, and superintendents understood the Title so that they could lead their teachers. The program would not want for districts to help or for professional backing in reaching them.

Still, there is more than this to improving science education. Congress could appropriate money to hire federal administrators of the Title and state science supervisors so that the Title would not wither for lack of enough people to manage it. On the other hand, Congress could neither recruit this manpower nor determine the policies by which states disbursed the aid. Thus, while the federal government could decide the size and scope of Title III, its thrust was determined by state administrators to whom Congress could not give specific directions.

Judging by results, state professionals and their local colleagues made their own use of the competence Title III gave them. Large projects were favored, usually in urban school districts where financial need appeared to be greatest. Even though specific relationships between urban school poverty and science education are not clear, those between such poverty and state school aid politics are. Traditionally and consistently, state aid formulas undersupport big cities and state schoolmen have not been able to prevent such discrimination. Title III gave them the chance to do so. Once this major professional requirement had been met, state departments directed the Title to whatever other such ends they and their local school districts could agree on. These goals were applied in the context of science education, but their relevance to science improvement was equivocal at best. Projects appear to have been undertaken by districts which could afford them and which were encouraged to undertake them by the state and by neighboring districts participating at the same time. This process probably improved science education and stimulated local spending, but it is not clear whether the spending in every case brought the improvement. The federal government has no way of finding out, or of so defining Title III Science as to assure this outcome.

Although the Title's accomplishment cannot be measured directly, public action at the federal level can certainly provide unique and perhaps indispensable assistance to curriculum improvement. No agency but Congress can provide enough funds on a national scale in categories broad enough to let any school district make any curriculum improvement it can buy. The location of Title III's large science projects and the size of its most numerous projects already combine to suggest that the program is moving toward such fiscal independence. Although on a per pupil basis, improvements the Title has made possible are small, and on a scientific basis minimal, each project can be assumed to have filled a classroom need unmet by existing state and local school finance. To the extent that public action at the federal level can enable schools to overcome such poverty, federal aid like Title III Science can be a valuable adjunct to curriculum development.

In the final analysis, the Physical Science Study Committee and Title III Science of the National Defense Education Act are both expressions of a statesmanlike impulse to better the nation's schooling in science. Scientists, led by Professor Zacharias in 1956, and statesmen, marshalled by Representative Elliott and Senator Hill in 1958, analyzed American science education as they saw it, devised improvements for the weaknesses they found, and successfully launched their remedial programs. Remarkably different, each program has enjoyed widespread local school acceptance, wholly free of specific federal curriculum control. By now, each has begun to become a part of the American educational scene.

A close look at what each program has done and how each has worked cannot deny either one a place in the nation's educational system. Nevertheless, the weight of experience indicates that a priority can be suggested. Historically, there was logic in the Congressional view that the PSSC and undertakings like it represented the first order of educational business. Title III Science could then be a useful complement. On scientific, educational, political, and economic grounds, this order of preference continues to be a sensible one.

XIV. Federally Affected Schools

For a dozen years, the federal government has systematically provided special aid for the construction and operation of public schools in communities especially affected by its activities. The present comprehensive programs were initiated under two laws enacted by the 81st Congress and approved September 23 and 30, 1950. They have become widely known by the numbers of the original laws—Public Law 815 for school construction and Public Law 874 for school operation and maintenance (current expenses).

Essentially, these laws provide systems for paying tuition charges (designed, like most tuition charges, to cover only part of the expense) for federally connected pupils in local public schools outside the national capital.

In the twelve years after 1950 the federal government appropriated $2.5 billion under these two laws and their several amendments. For school building construction, the sum of $1,088 million was provided; for the operation and maintenance of schools, $1,426 million. Nine-tenths of this was paid to local school authorities. During the period, at least 11 per cent of all the public schools in the country, with nearly one-third of all the enrollments, received one or more payments. Hundreds drew federal payments in every one of the twelve years.

These broad nationwide programs were initiated on a temporary basis as part of an effort to cushion the varying local impacts of national defense activities associated with the United Nations action in Korea. Nevertheless, the legislation along these lines almost certainly would have been enacted even if there had been no emergency. The proposals had been prepared by the executive branch and initially studied by congressional committees in the interval of postwar readjustment when renewed defense expansion was not generally expected. The original recommendations were advanced as a means of generalizing diverse piecemeal authorizations that had accumulated over the preceding 150 years and of filling gaps between them.

A brief account of the antecedents of this legislation will help to define the special problems of intergovernmental relations toward which P.L. 815 and 874 were directed. Many of these problems emerged early in our federal system; some persist in spite of systematic legislation designed to deal with them.

This chapter is based on materials prepared by I. M. Labovitz.

Uncle Sam's Children: Strangers in the States

Over the last century, it has become an accepted objective of public policy in the United States that every child shall have access to elementary and high school education at public expense. Nevertheless, there have been gaps between the objective and its realization in practice. One of these gaps had its source in the historic doctrine of intergovernmental immunities—specifically, the legal inability of state and local governments to tax federal reservations and activities. In this situation, free access to local public schools was denied in some communities to children of federal government personnel, both military and civilian, residing on government-owned or controlled property, and also to children of other residents of property owned or controlled by the government.

Families in Limbo

An early influential precedent for denial of access for federally connected children in local schools—even where the parents were subject to local taxes—was provided by the justices of the supreme judicial court of Massachusetts in 1841. Their advisory opinion noted that some acts of cession conferred upon residents of federal reservations the privileges and duties of town inhabitants. Nevertheless, said the court, persons who resided on lands purchased by, or ceded to, the United States for Navy yards, forts, and arsenals, where the only jurisdiction reserved to the state was a right to serve civil and criminal process, were not entitled to the benefits of the common schools for their children in the towns in which the lands were situated. Nor did residents of federal reservations acquire the "legal inhabitancy" necessary to qualify them for poor relief in time of need, or for the elective franchise. They were not, however, exempted from state, county, and town taxes.[1]

The Massachusetts ruling has been followed in many other court decisions relating to federally connected children in public schools, although judicial rulings concerning the rights, privileges, and obligations of the residents of federal properties have been characterized by uncertainties, contradictions, and occasional doctrinaire pronouncements. The treatment of the public school problem has been a specific manifestation of general confusion and diversity about the practical implications of federalism. Enveloped in the same fog were birth records, citizenship in a state, marriage, divorce, the custody or adoption of children, suffrage, access to the courts, probate, sanity proceedings, admittance to state colleges and other institutions, eligibility for occupational, driving, hunting, and fishing licenses, and a variety of other civil matters.

Consigned to a sort of legal no man's land—a zone in which the American tradition of free public schooling for every resident child became entangled with the practical necessity that someone stand ready to pay the heavy and mounting expenses of the schools—many federally connected families paid special tuition charges in those public schools that would accept their children. Others were forced to seek private schools—not always available near the workplace to which the parent was assigned.

Denial of local government services provoked strong discontent, especially among those who lived where state and local taxes were collected from them or on federal properties subject to payments in lieu of taxes. To the families assigned to federal property, its jurisdictional status seemed a remote technicality, in no way subject to their control. Even in areas of exclusive or near-exclusive federal jurisdiction, the barring of children from nearby public schools seemed inexplicable, since the families nearly all came from communities where it was taken for granted that every resident child was eligible to enroll, whether or not he was the child of a local taxpayer.

A few states devised statutory accommodations. Others sought to minimize the difficulties through local adjustments that detoured legal niceties. Available statistics suggest that, in fact, a majority of the federally connected children may have been accommodated in this way until the middle of the 1930's. Still, thousands of children were required to pay tuition or fees. Varying state and local solutions might have sufficed and massive nationwide programs might have remained unnecessary if the federally connected children and the affected schools had remained relatively few in number and widely spread. But national and world developments beginning in the 1930's rapidly changed the dimensions of the problem and have continued to alter it from year to year.

By the middle 1930's, with government activities growing in diversity and size so that an increasing number of persons lived or worked on federal properties, the plight of the federally connected children attracted widespread notice. Four staff studies for the President's Advisory Committee on Education in 1937-38 reexamined the problems of special federal jurisdictions, and the committee offered a series of recommendations for each type of jurisdiction.

Reports submitted by government agencies to the committee indicated that children of federal employees lived on government reservations and projects in every state and territory (as well as in the

District of Columbia). In all, nearly 21,000 school age children were reported for 620 reservations and projects in the 48 states. Army posts and naval stations were the homes of 71 per cent of the children; some 15 per cent were at reclamation projects; and nearly 5 per cent were at veterans' facilities. The others were at lighthouse stations; navigation, flood control, and power projects; national parks; prisons, fish hatcheries, and soil conservation projects on public land.

Nearly all these children were enrolled in schools. More than 16,000 attended public schools, and more than 14,000 of these paid no tuition. In every state, in fact, some federally connected children attended public schools without paying tuition charges; and more than 1,000 such pupils were reported for each of the states of Washington, Texas, and California. Another 2,000 paid tuition in the public schools of 28 states. Tuition fees also were paid by some 4,000 children in government agency schools and in private or other schools. The government agency schools were reported only from army posts and naval stations.

A large majority of the children who paid tuition lived on reservations under exclusive federal jurisdiction, but the legal extent of the federal jurisdiction did not appear to be controlling. In some places, children from exclusive reservations paid tuition in the public schools; in others, they did not pay.

Whether children were accepted in the public schools or not, a related matter of widespread concern was the difficulty and cost of transporting them to school. Few local school districts arranged transportation for children on federal properties, and rarer still was the school district that gave them free service. Many employees assigned to isolated stations complained that they had to pay rent, board, and often tuition as well, to maintain their families or individual children near schools far from the fathers' work stations.[2]

Increasingly it was evident that the difficulties associated with the schooling of federally connected children were no longer confined to localized differences over jurisdiction and control, questions of the eligibility of a few individuals for particular public services, and other legal complexities. They could not be resolved by individual arrangements and local negotiations. State action was infrequent and inadequate to relieve local pressures.

The President's Committee urged appropriations adequate to give the affected children the right to an education "free from tuitional costs to the individual and comparable in quality, so far as possible, to the public schools maintained by the states." In the few cases where a federal school or service might be required, the U.S. Office of Education should allocate funds to the responsible federal agencies, which should maintain the schools under its general supervision.[3]

New spurts of federal employment expansion followed the outbreak of war in Europe in 1939, and especially the initiation of major military and lend-lease programs in 1940. Arms contracts and military establishments attracted new residents to many communities. Yet government acquisitions of property for military use, defense production, and other national defense purposes took from many a school district part of its base for local taxation and borrowing while adding to its school-age population.

The new federally connected residents—and especially the military personnel—commonly were regarded as visiting strangers who might return soon to their permanent homes. Few had even nominal title to local real estate, and fewer still became local voters—especially if they lived on federal reservations. In many instances, the local community had exerted political influence and other forms of persuasion to win the location or expansion of a federal government establishment. Nevertheless, even in such places the newcomers brought in to staff the activities could not gain full membership in the local community.

To local school authorities, the inflow of federally connected children appeared chiefly as a further handicap in an already difficult race (too often a losing one) between mounting inescapable expenditure requirements and sluggish revenues. Just as they turned to the state government for help with their basic fiscal problems, so they turned increasingly to the national government for assistance with those special difficulties that appeared to be attributable to federal government activities. At the same time, the continuing failure of perennial proposals for general federal aid for local public schools may have influenced some persons to support special assistance for those places where a degree of direct federal responsibility might be discerned.

Thus, the question of responsibility for providing elementary and secondary education for federally connected children may be said to have mounted to national proportions as a repercussion of the governmental adjustments in the depression and then, more emphatically, the larger changes that preceded United States military engagement in the war.

Arrangements During World War II

Particular difficulties in housing defense workers emerged early in 1940. As more workers and their families were drawn from small towns and rural areas to man production lines, and many families of military personnel also were relocated, it quickly became evident that these people could not be housed in their new locations without special federal assistance. In June, 1940, Congress made provision for such housing, and in the Lanham Act approved in October added a general authorization for the planning and building of community facilities at federal expense.[4]

The enactments of 1940 contained no provision for direct federal support of local government operations beyond a grant of authority for the Federal Works Administrator to pay annual sums in lieu of taxes to any state or political subdivision with respect to real property. However, in the following year, after a survey of educational needs in federally affected areas by the U.S. Office of Education, Congress amended the Lanham Act to authorize the Federal Works Administrator to make loans or grants or both to public and nonprofit private agencies for public works and equipment—with emphasis on schools and certain other facilities essential to community life—and to make contributions for maintenance and operation of the public works. Direct federal government operation of the public works was authorized only if and to the extent that local agencies were unable or unwilling to carry the responsibility. A specific prohibition concerning "supervision or control" over schools was included in the law.[5]

The Lanham Act authorizations affecting schools in war-congested areas were extended and enlarged at intervals during the war. Under the provisions authorizing facilities construction, 1,239 school plants were built, with a federal government investment of $84 million. For 701 of these buildings there was joint federal-local financing, with local sources providing some $18 million. The last of the Lanham Act schools was completed during 1945-1946. Schools financed entirely by the federal government were owned by it and leased to the school districts without charge; those in which local financing was substantial were turned over to the school districts. Disposal of the federally owned schools began immediately after the war. By mid-1948, 171 buildings were transferred to school districts, with a return to the federal government of about one-fourth of their cost.[6]

Under the provisions for assistance in financing current operations, 896 different schools received payments during six school years, 1941-42 through 1946-47. The sums paid rose sharply from less than $3 million in the first year to nearly $13 million in 1944-45. A temporary extension for 1946-47 resulted in payments of about $6 million to 191 schools.[7]

Continuing Need

Wartime newcomers did not move away at the close of the war. Many could find no housing in other areas and the employment outlook was uncertain. Some remained in the expectation that war production plants would be converted to peacetime uses and would provide new jobs. To urgent pleas for a longer period of transition, Congress responded in 1946 with what was expected to be "absolutely" the last action of this kind. It extended the Lanham Act current expense program through the fiscal year 1947, with eligibility limited sharply.[8]

By early 1947, it was evident that some schools in war-affected areas would continue to need financial assistance. The Federal Works Agency held firmly to the position that its obligations would be discharged with the expiration of the Lanham Act extension. The Office of Education, however, encouraged informally by the Bureau of the Budget, arranged a series of interdepartmental meetings. Budget Bureau staff was increasingly concerned about the growing diversity among federal agencies in their arrangements for public school attendance and tuition payments for children of government personnel and residents on government reservations, and the absence of a general continuing plan to follow expiration of the Lanham Act.

War-swollen communities were only one facet of a much larger problem. The continuing peacetime requisite was for measures to meet needs that were already visible before the war and which, in many cases, had not been touched by the Lanham Act—that is, to make public schools accessible to children living on tax-exempt federal properties, often outside any school district. Despite postwar reductions in the armed forces and federal civilian staffs, the number of affected children and school districts was larger than ever. Confronted by rising enrollments, rapid increases in operating and construction costs, and public pressures for program improvements, local school systems were disinclined to accept federally connected children without recovering the expense from either the government or the parents.

School officials met early in 1947 with a large group of members of Congress and persuaded several that the Lanham Act should not be allowed to expire without further federal action. Half a dozen identical bills were introduced proposing to authorize the Office of Education to administer a permanent, enlarged program for children residing on federal property for which no real property taxes or tax equivalents were paid. The House Committee on Education and Labor conducted hearings on this legislation during May and June, 1947, but made no recommendations. As the session drew to a close the Congress enacted a one-year extension of Lanham Act payments. In 1948 and 1949 much the same pattern was repeated, with continued interest in permanent legislation and last-minute action on one-year legislation at the end of each session.

In these years the administration and the Congress gradually moved toward consensus. The Bureau of the Budget continued to be interested in comprehensive legislation if for no other reason than to reduce disparities in the appropriations. The Office of Education and several operating departments gathered data and helped to review various proposals. A well publicized task force report, prepared for the first Hoover Commission by the Brookings Institution, described the wide variety of educational situations for which the federal government was providing an estimated $23.5 million in 1949 and recommended comprehensive legislation to recognize federal responsibility.[9]

Meanwhile, an increasing number of members of Congress had their attention drawn to the continuing financial difficulties of federally affected school districts and the erratic treatment of federally connected children. Finally, after the Lanham Act extension in 1949 the chairman of the House Committee on Education and Labor appointed two subcommittees to report on comprehensive legislation early the next year.

The House subcommittee made extensive investigations including a statistical study of affected school districts. They conducted hearings, beginning with officials of the interested federal agencies and school districts of the Washington metropolitan area. Field investigations took the subcommittees into 23 other communities. Testimony was given by approximately 600 witnesses from 42 states. These included school district officers, representatives of state departments of education and local offices of federal agencies, and spokesmen for other interested organizations. The resulting transcript filled nearly 2,400 closely printed pages.

Statistical reports for 410 school districts were sufficiently complete and accurate to be included in subcommittee tabulations. Fragmentary reports were received from many others. The 410 districts were believed to comprise from two-thirds to three-fourths of the federally affected districts of the nation. They had a total school enrollment of 1,816,000 during 1949-1950, a combined increase of more than 70 per cent, over the "last normal school year" of each district.

The subcommittees' joint 149-page report in early 1950 incorporated the survey data and their recommendations for action. The subcommittees were convinced that federal government activities imposed severe financial burdens on a considerable number of school systems—burdens so severe that, in many cases, children were deprived of minimum educational opportunities; and that contemporary developments would intensify the difficulties in some areas. They proposed that the federal government establish a permanent policy accepting responsibilities for both operating expenses and additional facilities construction in school districts overburdened by federal activities. It should give these districts financial assistance that would enable them to provide adequate educational opportunities. The Commissioner of Education should administer both types of aid, with help from the Federal Works Agency in the construction field.

The recommendations were limited to the federal responsibility in specially affected school districts. The selective programs were not intended to provide assistance that would be available under proposals for general federal aid. Their provisions should encourage state and local units of government to accept responsibilities.

The subcommittees proposed also that the legislation provide for federal operation of schools on reservations where operation by state or local educational authorities was prohibited or where, for other reasons, local school agencies were unable to assume responsibility. They hoped this could be temporary, emphasizing that the objective should be to have all schools for residents of federal property operated by regular public school authorities. Existing provisions for assistance to school districts educating children from Indian reservations should be retained temporarily. Atomic Energy Commission reservations should be excluded from the proposed legislation.[10]

In January, 1950, the president endorsed a Senate-passed bill for construction aid that would serve two objectives: (1) help solve a general national problem of school-building shortages by providing grants to states for surveys of their building needs and their resources available to provide them, and (2) help meet special problems by authorizing grants for facilities construction in those particular areas where federal activities were responsible for increased enrollments. As to current school expenses in such areas, the president urged enactment of comprehensive legislation that would establish a single program for all agencies.[11]

The impetus given by the president and the subcommittee report made it highly probable in early 1950 that the pending comprehensive bills for aid to federally affected school districts would be enacted in some form before Congress adjourned. In late June, hostilities erupted in Korea and the legislation took on new importance. Conceived in peacetime as a long-term adjustment of intergovernmental relations in which the major problems were part of the aftermath of World War II, the proposals now acquired urgency as means for helping the public schools accommodate the quick and massive new population movements that accompanied the rapid expansion of military forces and armaments production. Final action took place on September 15 for the construction bill and September 20 for the current expense bill. President Truman signed S. 2317 on September 23, making it Public Law 815 of the 81st Congress. He signed H.R. 7940 on September 30, making it Public Law 874.

Financing Buildings and Classrooms (P.L. 815)

Under Title I of P.L. 815 the commissioner of education was authorized to make grants to states to assist them to inventory existing schools, survey the need for additional facilities, develop construction programs, and study the adequacy of available state and local resources. A federal appropriation of $3 million was provided for distribution among the states, primarily in proportion to their school-age populations. Equal matching was required. The inventory and survey were not confined to schools or communities affected by federal activities.

Title II provided for a three-year program of federal financial assistance for construction of school facilities in communities where federal activities had been or were being carried on. Payments could be made to local educational agencies where children lived on federal properties, their parents were employed on federal property, or increased attendance resulted from government activities.

"Federal property" was defined as real property owned or leased by the government and not subject to state or local taxation. It included certain real property held for or by Indians.

The Act specified minimum numbers and percentages of pupils in attendance as a basis for determining the eligibility of an applicant school district and the amount of aid it might receive. A school system with fewer than 35,000 children in average daily attendance in 1939 could qualify for school construction aid under the new law subject to the following conditions:

(a) If 15 or more children in average daily attendance lived on federal property with a parent employed on federal property, and these constituted at least 5 per cent of estimated average daily attendance during the current fiscal year, the school district would be entitled to 95 per cent of the cost of constructing complete school facilities for these pupils. The number of children for whom payment was made could not, however, exceed the net increase in average attendance since 1939.

(b) If 15 or more children in average daily attendance either lived on federal property or lived with a parent employed on federal property, and these constituted at least 5 per cent of the estimated average daily attendance in the current year, the school district would be entitled to 70 per cent of the cost of constructing complete school facilities for these pupils. As for group (a), the number in group (b) counted for payment could not exceed the increase over 1939.

(c) The school district might be entitled to 45 per cent of the cost of constructing complete facilities for pupils who were in the area because of federal activity carried on either directly or through a contractor. However, the group had to include 20 or more children, constituting at least 10 per cent of the estimated average attendance during the current year. The district had to show that construction of additional school facilities for this group of children had imposed or would impose an undue financial burden on its taxing and borrowing authority. In determining eligibility and maximum payments for this category, the commissioner could take into account only government activities carried on after June 30, 1939, and he was required to ignore activities connected with certain real property excluded by definition. In this group, the first 10 per cent of increase in average daily attendance over that in the fiscal year 1939 was not to be counted.

Where a pupil might fit into two or more of these categories, the school district was permitted to make a choice among them. For a school district which had more than 35,000 children in 1939, eligibility tests for construction were substantially tighter and proportionately more local financing was required.

Construction outlays for which reimbursements might be allowed were determined by the number of eligible children in average daily attendance multiplied by the average cost per pupil for constructing complete school facilities in the state where the district was located. The concept of "school facilities" was defined as including classrooms and related facilities and initial equipment, machinery, and necessary utilities, but not athletic stadia or facilities intended primarily for athletic exhibitions or other events for which admission fees would be charged to the general public. Land and off-site improvements also were excluded. School facilities would be deemed adequate for a given number of pupils if, under applicable state standards, they were adequate for full-time education of this number.

The act also provided for special cases. Where the federal impact would be temporary, assistance was limited to the provision of or payment for temporary facilities. Where no school district was able to provide for children living on federal property, facilities could be built by the commissioner of education. Where the federal government after 1939 had provided or paid for school facilities in a district, their value was to be deducted from the amount for which the district was eligible. Where schools built under the Lanham Act during World War II were still in federal ownership, they were to be donated immediately to the school districts. Where a school district had used its own resources to construct adequate facilities for children for whom it might otherwise be eligible for payments under the act, it could apply for and presumably receive the federal payment as a reimbursement.

Procedural provisions of the act included a requirement that the commissioner of education ascertain, after consulting the state and local educational agencies, that each project was not inconsistent with over-all state plans for school construction.

A provision forbidding federal direction of local school systems was included, in the form common to many bills relating to federal aid for education:

> In the administration of this Act, no department, agency, officer, or employee of the United States shall exercise any direction, supervision, or control over the personnel, curriculum, or program of instruction of any school or school system of any local or state educational agency.

Financing School Operations (P.L. 874)

Assistance to local educational agencies under P.L. 874, to help cover their current expense, is guided by a formal declaration of policy that has stood without amendment since it was enacted. The Act begins with this statement:

> In recognition of the responsibility of the United States for the impact which certain federal activities have on the local educational agencies in the areas in which such activities are carried on, the Congress hereby declares it to be the policy of the United States to provide financial assistance . . . for those local educational agencies upon which the United States has placed financial burdens.

The particular educational agencies eligible for assistance are those on which financial burdens have been placed by reason for any of these facts:

1. Revenues available to such agencies from local sources have been reduced as the result of federal acquisition of real property.
2. Such agencies provide education for children residing on federal property.
3. Such agencies provide education for children whose parents are employed on federal property.
4. A sudden and substantial increase in school attendance has resulted from federal activities.

Public Law 874 included a prohibition on federal direction of local school systems, identical with that in P.L. 815.

Reduction in the Tax Base

Instances of the first type, involving reduction of the local tax base through acquisition of real property, are covered by section 2 of the Act. Originally applicable for the fiscal years 1951 to 1954, the provision stated that where the commissioner of education reached certain conclusions about the effect of federal acquisition upon a local educational agency, that agency would be entitled to receive an amount "equal to the continuing federal responsibility for the additional financial burden." The entitlement could not exceed the amount which, in the commissioner's judgment, the school district would have derived from the acquired property and had available for current expenditures in the particular year, minus amounts available from other federal payments.

To establish an entitlement, the commissioner was required to determine, upon consultation with the local and state educational agencies, that the United States owned federal property in the school district acquired after 1938, with an assessed value at the time of acquisition aggregating 10 per cent or more of the assessed value of all real property in the district at that time; that the acquisition had placed a substantial and continuing financial burden on the local educational agency; and that the revenue loss was not being substantially offset by other federal payments or by increased local revenues accruing from the federal activities with respect to the property.

Children of Residents and Employees

The second and third types of cases defined in the policy declaration—those where the school district provides education for children living on federal property or with a parent working on federal property—are governed by section 3 of the statute. Subsection (a) relates to children who live on federal property with a parent who works on federal property. Subsection (b) relates to children who do not meet both tests but either live on federal property or live with a parent who works on such property. Several additional subsections control the computations of amounts to be paid in any given case. Section 3 has been amended often.

Subsection (a), as originally enacted, declared that for each of the four fiscal years 1951 to 1954 each local educational agency which provided free public education during the year for children who resided on federal property with a parent employed on federal property would be entitled to an amount equal to the number of these pupils in average daily attendance multiplied by the "local contribution rate" determined under another subsection.

Subsection (b) in its original form was a close parallel of (a), but with entitlement for each pupil set at one-half of the local contribution rate. A child would be counted in this group if the federal property on which his parent was employed lay at least partly within the same state as the school district.

To receive any payment under either subsection (a) or (b), a school district had to show that its average daily attendance for the year included at least ten children to whom the subsection applied and that they were 3 per cent or more of the total number for whom the agency was providing free public education. The commissioner could waive the percentage requirement in exceptional circumstances. For large districts with enrollments of 35,000 or more in 1939, the eligibility test was 6 per cent and it could not be waived; also, the payment would cover only the excess over 3 per cent of average attendance.

Every pupil in group (a) would qualify also in group (b), and the local educational agency could choose which subsection should apply. An applicant ordinarily would not elect to shift (a) pupils to the other group, but in certain circumstances this choice might yield a larger federal payment—for example, if the number of (a) pupils in a district was less than ten or 3 per cent of average attendance.

In determining the local contribution rate, the commissioner was required to consider expenditures of those local school districts in the state which, in his judgment, were most nearly comparable to the applicant district. The procedure for making the computations included a requirement of prior consultation with both the state and the local educational agencies. If expenditures in the applicant district were affected by unusual geographic factors, the commissioner could compensate for this by increasing its local contribution rate.

Sudden and Substantial Increases

Section 4 of P.L. 874 made provision for sudden and substantial increases in school attendance—those that had occurred prior to its enactment and also any that might follow. In the case of increases already experienced, the relief was transitional, to be tapered off over the four fiscal years 1951 to 1954. Eligibility and payments were limited by a series of specific requirements.

As to attendance increases occurring after September 1950, during any of the four fiscal years 1951 to 1954, the law provided entitlements that would extend over a three-year period. Payments could be made where the commissioner determined that federally induced increases equaled at least 10 per cent of the average attendance in the preceding three years; government activities had placed "a substantial and continuing financial burden" on the local educational agency; and the local agency was unable to meet the increased costs despite "a reasonable tax effort" and "due diligence" in availing itself of other financial assistance. For the larger districts, the eligibility test was 15 per cent instead of 10 per cent, and payment would be based on only the excess over 10 per cent of the average daily attendance in the year for which the payment was to be made. The amount of the entitlement was to equal the required current expenditures, not otherwise financed, for the increase in average attendance resulting from government activities.

Direct Federal Operation and Contractual Arrangements

In enacting P.L. 874, Congress sought to have the schooling of federally connected children provided, wherever possible, by local educational agencies under state supervision. It recognized that in some places, however, the local school district might not be able to accommodate federally connected children even if special federal assistance were available—for example, where state law prohibited giving free public education to children living on a reservation where federal legislative jurisdiction was exclusive. Accordingly, section 6 provided that the commissioner should make the necessary arrangements to provide free public education for children residing on federal property in any cases in which (1) no tax revenues of the state or any political subdivision may be expended for free public education for such children, or (2) it was the commissioner's judgment, after consulting with the appropriate state educational authorities, that no local educational agency was able to provide suitable free public education for them. The arrangements could be made by the Office of Education directly or on its behalf by officials of other federal departments or agencies. To the maximum extent practicable, education under this provision was to be comparable to free public education provided in similar communities in the state.

Amendments and Extensions

Public Laws 815 and 874 as enacted in 1950 were statutes of considerable complexity, designed to deal with an intricate problem in intergovernmental fiscal relations. Moreover, they have become more complex through successive amendments that have generally eased the terms of eligibility and liberalized the amount and duration of payments. The legislative process for these amendments has itself been tortuous. Modifications and extensions of P.L. 815 and 874 sometimes have been caught up in the same issues as general federal aid to education. In some years congressional consideration of the fate of legislation for federally affected public schools has been dictated by the strategies of those who would advance or retard the course of general federal aid in the Congress.[12]

Important changes in both statutes were enacted in 1953, 1956, and 1958.[13] In 1953, for example, the definitions of federal property were broadened to include real property owned by the United States and leased to another user, even though the lessee's interest was subject to state or local taxation. The current expense program was liberalized to increase payments to school districts where expenditures were particularly low. This was accomplished by providing that in no event would the local contribution rate be less than one-half the average current expense per pupil in all public schools in the state.

Amendments in 1956 included further liberalization of the rules for setting the local contribution rate. This rate now became the highest of three factors: (1) the average local contribution rate (that is, locally financed current expense) of districts in the same state which were most nearly comparable to the one for which the computation was being made; (2) one-half of the average current expense per pupil in the state; or (3) the national average per pupil local contribution rate. A ceiling also was established: where the national average gave the most favorable rate, the local contribution rate could not in any event exceed the average expenditure per pupil in the state.

In 1958, however, Congress tightened somewhat the provisions for the determination of local contribution rates, at the same time that other liberalizing amendments were enacted. Transition payments, for example, were provided for districts that lost their eligibility—about 200 a year were in this group. Qualifying conditions were eased somewhat for districts with sudden and substantial increases. Large school districts (enrollment of more than 35,000) were no longer required to absorb without payment an average increase in enrollment. The 1958 amendments made both P.L. 815 and 874 permanent for pupils in category (a), those who live on federal property with a parent who works on federal property or is on active military duty.

In 1961 President Kennedy proposed a substantial reduction in the scope of P.L. 815 and 874, with general federal aid to education to serve as a better method of equalizing educational opportunities. However, with the defeat of general federal aid, the Congress reenacted the special programs without important changes.

Any future enactment of general federal aid would very likely bring some narrowing of the coverage of P.L. 815 and 874. But unless this occurs, there is every prospect that the statutes will continue to be liberalized.

Financial Dimensions[14]

Construction Aid

In the twelve-year period from fiscal 1951 through fiscal 1962 P.L. 815 grants were extended to 5,271 projects. About two-thirds were elementary school facilities; one-fourth were secondary schools; and the remainder, multipurpose rooms, kitchens, and other facilities which do not directly increase the number of pupils accommodated. Approved projects included 1,494 new elementary schools and 464 new high schools and a greater number of additions of existing structures.

More than 94 per cent of all approved projects were those of local educational agencies. These claimed $947 million in federal funds reserved for 4,961 projects to accommodate 1,547,000 children. Direct federal construction took $123 million in funds reserved to cover the whole cost of 310 projects to house more than 98,000 pupils at about 100 installations. The P.L. 815 payments to local school system projects covered only a part of their costs.

School districts in all states shared in the program. In 22 states, funds reserved for local educational agencies averaged $1 million or more a year over the period 1951-52. The cumulative 12-year total exceeded $1 million in 46 states. The largest aggregate for any state was in California, with $172 million provided for 710 projects in several hundred school districts and 33 projects on 13 federal installations. Second highest was Virginia, with $74 million for 145 local projects and 17 others on 5 federal installations.

For the country as a whole, one in every twenty public school systems made at least one successful application for P.L. 815 assistance from 1951 through 1962. Participation varied considerably, running highest in some western and southern states. Through 1961, one-fourth or more of all public school systems in Hawaii, Nevada, New Mexico, Alaska, Utah, Oklahoma, Alabama, and Maryland received construction aid. Other states in which a substantial proportion of school systems qualified for assistance were Washington, California, Arizona, Tennessee, Florida, Georgia, South Carolina, Virginia, Connecticut, and Rhode Island. In the midwest and Great Lakes states, with their large numbers of separate school systems, participation was much less frequent.

P.L. 815 payments appear to have financed from 3 to 6 per cent of all capital outlays of local public schools during each of the fiscal years 1952-56, and about 2½ per cent during 1957-61. The highest proportions, 5 to 6 per cent, were provided during 1953-55. This suggests that on a national scale the federal payments were hardly an important element in financing school construction over the decade as a whole.

The allotments were, of course, relatively much more important in several states and must have been a crucial factor in many individual school systems. An Office of Education report indicates that federal payments under P.L. 815 financed 10 per cent or more of all the capital outlays for local public schools in nine states and two territories during 1951-57. Federal financing equaled more than 10 per cent of the cost of all school facilities constructed in 7 states in the fiscal year 1952, 18 states in 1953, 14 states in 1954 and again in 1955, 10 in 1956, and 4 in 1957.[15] In the later years, federal financing was substantial in only a few states.

Current Expense Aid

Despite a rapid reduction in the number of separate public school systems in the United States, there was a marked increase during 1951-62 in the number of eligible applicants for current expense financing under P.L. 874. At the same time, the average entitlement of successful applicants more than doubled in amount.

In the first fiscal year of the law, 1,172 school districts were eligible, and in the second year, 1,763. These were only 2 or 3 per cent of all United States public school systems in those years. By 1962, the number of eligible districts was 4,065—11 per cent of all school districts.

Eligible districts accounted for substantially more than a proportionate part of the school attendance and expenditures of all United

States public schools, even though special statutory barriers excluded most large school systems. In fact, total current expense of federally affected districts was 10 to 15 per cent of the nationwide aggregate in 1951 and 1952 and rose to 30 per cent in 1961.

The rise in the number of eligible districts meant, of course, an increase in the proportion of all public school pupils for whom federal payments were made. In 1951, one of every 48 pupils enrolled in public school grades 1-12 was federally connected under section 3 or 4 of P.L. 874; in 1956, one in every 33; and in 1962, one in every 21.

Aggregate attendance in eligible districts in 1962 was four times the total in 1951. The rate of increase in number of federally connected pupils was a trifle slower. In 1951, these school systems reported 2.9 million pupils in average daily attendance, of whom 17 per cent were federally connected. By 1962, total attendance in eligible districts was 11.7 million, including 15 per cent federally connected. Net entitlements for P.L. 874 payments multiplied almost by eight, from $29.6 million to $223 million.

Average entitlement for each federally connected pupil in eligible districts rose from $58 to $133. This is somewhat more proportionately than the increase in average over-all current expense of these districts for all their pupils. P.L. 874 payments averaged 5.7 per cent of all current expense in eligible districts in the first year of the program, and dropped to 4.9 per cent during 1955-61. In 1962, payments rose to 5.2 per cent.

Despite the decline of local district entitlements from 5.7 to 5.2 per cent of the aggregate current expense of eligible districts, the increased number of these districts meant that the federal payments gradually grew in relative importance as a source of public school revenue for the country as a whole. In 1951 they covered six-tenths, and in 1952, eight-tenths of 1 per cent of all current expenses of all public school systems in the United States. In 1956, the federal payments financed 1 per cent, and in 1961, 1.5 per cent, of all public school current expense.

Almost from the beginning, school districts in every state shared in the current expense payments in every year. The number of states in which assistance was less than $100,000 a year dropped steadily, from 9 in 1951 to 3 in 1956 and 1 (Vermont) in 1961 and 1962. At the same time, the number of states with entitlements above $1 million a year rose rapidly, from 8 in the first year to 21 in 1956 and 41 in 1962. In 3 states, the total net entitlements of local school systems in 1962 exceeded $10 million: Texas, $14.0 million; Virginia, $15.6 million; and

California, $42.0 million. Entitlements in these three states were close to one-third of the nationwide total.

A compilation by the Office of Education for a Senate committee indicated that among the 437 members of the House of Representatives, only 122 had no participating school systems in their constituencies in the fiscal year 1960. (In 2 of the 122 congressional districts, assistance was being given for 6 construction projects under P.L. 815.) In 100 congressional districts in 37 states, P.L. 874 entitlements exceeded $500,000. In 53 of these districts in 28 states, they were above $1 million.

Federal Connection and Fiscal Equalization

Statistical records for the special assistance programs, though voluminous and informative, are inadequate for a full objective evaluation of accomplishments and costs in relation to the declared purpose—the opening of local public schools to federally connected children without the imposition of unwarranted and inequitable fiscal burdens on local taxpayers in particular communities. That kind of appraisal calls for field investigations and research that have not been possible here. Even an incomplete review, however, establishes certain trends and raises key questions.

With each passing year, the tag of federal connection has been attached to more and more children. An increasing number of communities has shared in the payments. How closely are these trends tied to the changing circumstances that might equitably define federal responsibility? There is no hard evidence on this point. Indeed, there can be no conclusive array of facts. The central uncertainty, as has been suggested, is the policy issue involved in setting limits to the federal obligation.

For some communities, the federal payments have been a crucial factor in local school finance. But in most eligible school systems, and consequently in most states, the federal payments remain decidedly a minor source of school revenue. Minute as is the participation of many school districts, it is so widespread and so assiduously sought that the programs may reasonably be viewed as a substitute for general federal aid insofar as the affected communities are concerned.

Yet the test of eligibility that is used in these selective programs is irrelevant to a broad objective of financial equalization. A low level of local contribution does not establish that the combined amount of local and state financial support for the public schools of a district is below standard. It does not demonstrate the existence of financial inability to support schools. School district claims are based on the presence of a specified number of federally connected pupils. Financial need alone, without the special federal connection, bestows no eligibility and wins no federal payment. Undoubtedly hundreds, perhaps thousands, of ineligible school districts could demonstrate greater financial need than many of the districts where the floor provisions yield federal payments at rates above unadjusted local contribution rates.

Individual payments may be small, but they are part of a national total that has mounted to a third of a billion dollars a year. Experience in the states has shown that even a small fund can promote some degree of fiscal equalization. The more general equalization of school district needs and resources remains, of course, a state responsibility, to be discharged by state aid legislation.

The Question of Federal Control

Explicit prohibitions incorporated in both laws are evidence of concern lest the special aids inadvertently carry with them an element of national direction over personnel, curricula, or programs of instruction. Nevertheless, federal control as an issue is surrounded by a kind of mysticism, an ethereal remoteness, unrelated to the administrative procedures by which local, state, and federal school officials operate under these two laws.

Because these are not formula programs, there are no allocations of federal money to any state or to local school districts other than in response to specific, detailed applications filed by school officials or for contractual current expense payments. Consequently, there are no sanctions for compelling observance of prescribed standards or conditions—such sanctions, for example, as the withholding of an allocated amount which sometimes occurs, in, say, a highway aid or public assistance program. School district officials presumably file no application if they consider any requirements of P.L. 815 or 874 onerous. This means there is no way to determine whether any qualified school systems have deliberately refrained from applying; eligibility can be ascertained only with an application officially reviewed.

Inquiries about federal controls within these programs usually have taken the form of questions addressed to successful applicants. Invariably the responses have been close to unanimous, to the effect that there has been no federal control. Many replies have included laudatory comments about the laws and the administrative staff in the Office of Education.

Most extensive among such studies was a dissertation completed by Robert I. Sperber in 1957, analyzing "potential control factors" in P.L. 874.[16] Questionnaires sent to one-fourth of all school officials who received P.L. 874 payments in the fiscal year 1955 brought replies from 500, or 70 per cent, with at least one response from every state. It was the view of 99 per cent of the respondents that federal control did not accompany federal payments.

Among four respondents who said they had experienced "control," one mentioned only that he had to make reports and maintain records and added that the curriculum was not affected; another felt "control" because of uncertainty about the amount to be received, and two did not explain. Among 416 school officials who had experience with discretionary powers of the commissioner of education none reported any federal control.

A summary question asking whether the subsection prohibiting federal control was complied with by the commissioner of education, his representatives, and other federal departments drew 489 replies. Of these, 484 said "completely," and three "most of the time." One reported that the section was "often disregarded," explaining that delays in filing field reports held up aid to his district and this caused cancellations of courses of study or orders for necessary supplies.[17]

Similar evidence has emerged from congressional testimony. In 1958 a spokesman for the Massachusetts State Department of Education stated that there were strong forebodings that federal assistance of any type would bring with it federal control of the local school systems, but these fears had been dissolved by experience. Federal government officials in Boston "succeeded in making clear the distinction between assistance and advice on the one hand and authoritativeness and outright direction on the other. A very harmonious relationship exists in our state between federal and state officials."[18]

Senator Vance Hartke reported in 1961 that Indiana school officials responded with "a consistent and emphatic 'no'" when he asked whether acceptance of P.L. 815 and 874 grants had resulted in "any federal regulation, specific or implied, with regard to school curriculum, personnel, or administration." He added: "Not a single instance of federal control or regulation was reported." In the 1961 debates on general aid, Senator Lee Metcalf and others remarked that congressional committees had made repeated efforts to discover instances of federal controls (other than labor-standard requirements) under P.L. 815 and 874, but had found none.[19]

It may be concluded that there is nearly universal agreement that operations under P.L. 815 and 874 have conformed to the statutory requirements of no "direction, supervision, or control" over "personnel, curriculum, or program of instruction" of any school or school system.

Segregation As an Issue

Federal policy with respect to segregated schools arose very early in the history of P.L. 815 and 874. In 1951 the Congress adopted several amendments to the year-old statutes, one of which would have required that schools operated either directly by the federal government or under contract by local districts provide education "on the same terms, in accordance with the laws of the state," as it was provided for other children in the state. President Truman refused to approve this requirement. He declared that under this amendment schools on federal property, some of them operating successfully on an integrated basis, would have to be segregated if they were located in any of 17 states. The federal government, said the president, had not desegregated all its schools and would not do so without considering "pertinent local factors," but this amendment "would constitute a backward step in the efforts of the federal government to extend equal rights and opportunities to all our people."[20] The Congress did not attempt to override the president's veto, nor did it heed his invitation to reenact the other amendments.

During the decade following the veto, Congress took relatively little explicit action on the question of racial segregation in schools under P.L. 815 and 874, but the executive branch took selective action to curtail the practice.

Just before President Truman left office, the Department of Defense let it be known that it regarded racially segregated schools on military bases as contrary to its policy and that of the president. The Office of Education was asked to "clarify" its position on the use of P.L. 815 and 874 appropriations to finance the operation of segregated schools on government property by local educational agencies. The still unsettled question was reopened at a press conference early in 1953. President Eisenhower said flatly that he did not see how any American could justify legally, logically, or morally any discrimination in an activity that involved the use of federal funds. A few days later the White House announced that segregation would be stopped in schools then operated by the Army and that the Army was negotiating with local officials to end the practice in locally operated schools at its posts. Only the Army-operated schools at Fort Benning, Georgia, would be affected immediately; similar schools at five other bases already were desegregated.

The Department of Defense declared in August 1953, that it had fixed September 1, 1955, as a "target date" for eliminating segregation in locally operated schools on all military bases. Where a district failed to conform, the federal government would operate the schools. A formal order issued by the secretary of defense on January 12, 1954, forbade the military services to open any new segregated schools and required that by the 1955 deadline they end the practice on installations where local educational agencies still were operating schools with federal financing. The ruling was expected to affect 21 posts in Alabama, Arkansas, Florida, Maryland, Oklahoma, South Carolina, Texas, and Virginia, although officers at some installations reported that segregation was already abolished.

The two-year interval was allowed in recognition of "complicating factors," such as the rigidity of school segregation laws in several states and unexpired leases under which school districts used government buildings on military bases. The federal agencies also faced complex problems in the event they had to take over the operation of additional schools. These included the possible loss of teachers and school accreditation, as well as the need to construct or to remodel facilities. When the deadline arrived in 1955, the Defense Department reported that all but two installations had complied with the desegregation policy, several of them in 1954 or earlier.[21]

The Congress did not inquire into segregation under P.L. 815 and 874 until 1962. In that year a special subcommittee of the House Committee on Education and Labor heard testimony on a bill, H.R. 10056, to deny payments to any federally affected school district that did not operate its school on "a racially nondiscriminatory basis." At the opening hearing on February 27, the Secretary of Health, Education, and Welfare, Abraham A. Ribicoff, said he was disposed to favor the legislative proposal. The Commissioner of Education, Sterling McMurrin, also favored the bill.

The secretary indicated that under existing laws the federal government could build and operate schools on federal installations but, in the case of nonfederal public schools not on federal property, the commissioner could not refuse payments because of a failure to desegregate if the district were otherwise eligible. The commissioner later commented that it would be the practice of the Office of Education to withhold funds from any school district that was in defiance of a court order to integrate—though there has been no instance of such withholding. Of course, most segregated school districts were not under court orders, as the secretary had pointed out.

In a second appearance on March 30, the secretary made a policy announcement which he characterized as a "significant step forward in the continuing effort to end racial discrimination." It would affect children residing on federal property.

The secretary reminded the congressmen that the statutes impose upon the commissioner the responsibility for determining whether a local school district can make available to these children "suitable free public education." If he determines that suitable free public education is not available, the commissioner is directed by law to make other arrangements and is given authority to build and finance the operation of schools on federal property. The secretary continued:

> It is our belief, and I can announce to you today that we shall so rule, that under the terms of section 10 of P.L. 815 and section 6 of P.L. 874, local public education which is segregated by race is not suitable. . . .
>
> If, in the course of its 1963 review, the Congress should see fit not to act on the matter of suitability, we will feel obligated to implement the decision we have made and resolve as best we can the resulting administrative problems. Beginning in September, 1963, we will, exercising sound discretion, take appropriate steps as set forth in the law with respect to those children still attending segregated schools who by law are entitled to a suitable education.[22]

The secretary noted that in some forty-five instances in fifteen states it had been determined that suitable free education was not available, primarily because of restrictions in state laws. About two hundred federal installations were served by school districts with segregated schools. The 1954 Supreme Court decision raised a question as to whether segregated public schools could be deemed "suitable," and, ". . . if they are not suitable, where the duty of the Commissioner of Education lies."

The assistant attorney general in charge of civil rights, testifying in mid-April, also emphasized the "particular duty" of the government to the children affected—many of them the children of soldiers, sailors, and airmen who reside in areas of racial segregation under military orders and may have come from places where schools were desegregated. He pointed out that the military services themselves had long been desegregated, that personnel who lived on the base occupied housing made available without regard to race, and that the children lived and played together freely. He contended that the government had an obligation to provide desegregated schools for these children, particularly since the schools they attended were constructed and operated with federal financial support.

The delay until autumn of 1963 in applying the new test would provide time for setting up schools. Also, as the secretary emphasized, it would give Congress an opportunity "to adjust the statutes if necessary, and in general to work its will on this important question."

As to the larger number of federally connected children who do not live on federal property, the secretary and the assistant attorney general emphasized that there was no clear statutory directive for executive action. The apparent congressional purpose, they noted, was to provide federal funds even though educational facilities were racially segregated. This was being done. A clarification of purpose would be desirable and the proposed legislation to withhold federal payments was "best suited to that end" if no more effective remedy were available. But administration support of the bill was much more reserved in April than in February. The threat of withholding, said the officials, would be "preferable to doing nothing" but was "essentially negative and punitive in character." The Department of Justice was studying the feasibility of a lawsuit to compel desegregation in school districts receiving federal funds under P.L. 815 and 874. Successful litigation, it was suggested, would accomplish the desired result more rapidly and more effectively than H.R. 10056, and without the undesirable consequences. Accordingly, action on the bill might be deferred until the alternative had been fully explored.

Instead, the subcommittee recommended favorable action on H.R. 10056, and a majority of the full committee voted on May 23 to make a favorable report to the House. The committee report, submitted by Chairman Adam Clayton Powell, declared that federal payments were being used "to enhance the practice of segregation," despite the Supreme Court decision of 1954. Among 3,961 eligible school districts receiving payments under P.L. 874, approximately 1,280 were in 17 southern and border states. Among 1,890 districts reported as having construction projects under P.L. 815, about 540 were in these states. In three states, segregation continued in all school districts.

The bill would have prohibited P.L. 874 payments, beginning with the fiscal year 1964, to a school district if the commissioner of education determined it was not operating its schools "on a racially nondiscriminatory basis" or was not "making progress toward that end with all deliberate speed." It would have required, as a condition of

P.L. 815 payments, an assurance from the school district that its schools would not be segregated. The House bill died in the Committee on Rules.

Shortly thereafter Justice Department officials planned to bring a test suit in Key West, Florida. The school district chose to desegregate rather than face litigation. In September, 1962, a suit was filed to compel desegregation of the public schools of Prince George County, Virginia, on the ground that many children of Army personnel at Fort Lee attended these schools and the government provided financial support under P.L. 815 and 874. This was the first public school desegregation suit in which the federal government was the plaintiff. The attorney general, in announcing the action, emphasized that the suit did not threaten to end financial assistance to the school district but sought "an end to unconstitutional school segregation in an area where such segregation directly affects the armed forces." At about the same time, the Department of Defense instructed all military installations to assist the Office of Education in a survey of the availability of desegregated schools for pupils of service families. In January, 1963, the Department of Justice filed several law suits against school systems in Alabama, Louisiana, and Mississippi.[23]

Congress could, of course, require desegregation as a condition for the receipt of monies under P.L. 815 and 874. In the absence of such a statutory condition, the administration may pursue the present selective policy of litigation and negotiation to bring desegregation in schools attended by federally connected children from military reservations. Alternatively, the administration may, within the scope of existing law, build and maintain desegregated schools on federal installations.

Military operation of post schools is by no means an innovation; these have been sanctioned by the Congress since at least 1821. However, P.L. 815 and 874 were designed to reduce the need for such schools—to open local school doors to federally affected children. In fact, post schools were almost eliminated by 1953, although their number has increased again recently in support of desegregation policies in the armed forces. Unless other measures are successful, there may be a further proliferation of schools operated directly by the military services.

If this occurs, differences in the patterns of community life off-base and on-base will be emphasized, for the federally operated schools on military posts will be desegregated schools adjacent to communities where the local schools continue to operate on a segregated basis.

The proximity of the two systems might accelerate or it might slow down the general trend toward desegregation in public schools; such effects are speculative. But a clear result of this arrangement is that groups of children will be treated as were earlier generations of federally connected children: as strangers in the states, foreigners to be sequestered in special schools.

PERSPECTIVES

During a dozen years of intensive use and frequent amendment, P.L. 815 and 874 have revealed limitations and imperfections. Still, by any relevant standard, this pair of laws must be adjudged a successful social invention. These programs have cushioned the federal impact, and they have done this not only broadly, or on the average, but with a considerable degree of selective adjustment to local diversities. Policy issues which remain open relate generally to the possibilities for adapting payments still more closely to local circumstances or for measuring on a finer scale the relative federal, state, and local responsibilities. The question of local delays in racial desegregation carries broader implications, far beyond the mechanics of intergovernmental adjustment.

Federal administration has been fully sympathetic and responsive to the views and sensibilities of local school officials and sensitive to the interests of state departments of education. A result is that the programs have served their special objectives well without significant side effects. They have entailed no discernible shifts between levels of government in the exercise of leadership or authority for the provision of public school service.

Experience with P.L. 815 and 874 establishes that federal control of personnel, curricula, or programs of instruction cannot stand as a substantive argument in debates over federal aid to education. In these special programs, even though state governments have exercised no substantial policy role, the record of federal restraint is overwhelming. This restraint is universally acknowledged. Both Congress and the Office of Education have been constantly attentive to the interests of the affected school districts. These programs have demonstrated conclusively that control is no necessary concomitant of federal aid.

Another indication, perhaps less decisively affirmed, is that once an aid program is on the books, it acquires a kind of momentum that overrides efforts to impose limits and modifications. Restrictive amendments proposed by President Eisenhower and President Kennedy attracted little support in Congress; liberalizing amendments and extensions have generally won adoption.

A third point, closely related, is that congressional popularity of the program is a function of the geographic distribution of benefits. This observation from the legislative history of P.L. 815 and 874 is consistent with the converse assertion that has appeared frequently in debates over general federal aid to education: "that it is politically impossible to secure a majority for a bill that leaves some states out of its benefits altogether."[24]

In the evolution of formal intergovernmental financial arrangements in the United States, the enactment of P.L. 815 and 874 was a major event. The action was neither unprecedented nor isolated, since earlier federal laws already had achieved important adjustments in the pattern of intergovernmental fiscal relations. Nevertheless, the 1950 legislation may fairly be described as the first comprehensive and systematic national program for handling on a continuing basis the peculiarly intergovernmental problems of local public school systems.

Perhaps the most obvious conclusion from this experience in federal-state-local accommodations is that liberal monetary allowances are tremendously persuasive. It does not necessarily follow, however, that a somewhat more selective rationing of payments would have opened fewer local school doors. The clear lesson is that decisive and specific congressional action is required for significant progress in solving intergovernmental problems of national concern and that such action need not be coercive. P.L. 815 and 874 demonstrate that permissive techniques can be devised and can be effective.

By assuring free access to local schools for Uncle Sam's children, the programs established under these laws have brought nearer to realization the historic American ideal that all children shall have equitable opportunity to obtain a suitable education in the public schools at public expense.

XV. Patterns for Resource Mobilization

It is the theme of this volume that the resources for a more adequate support of public education are available; the task is to mobilize these resources and to utilize them effectively. In the public finance traditions of this country, both the mobilization of resources and the concern for their effective use is intergovernmental; it is shared by the national government, the states, and local school districts. The responsibility for public education and its financing is different at each of these levels, but in a general way the task of those who wish to strengthen public education is very much the same: to change the preference patterns of citizens, to organize political leadership, and to encourage the kind of administrative and organizational changes within public education that can produce more effective educational results.

The research findings that underlie this volume suggest that a more effective mobilization of resources is possible. In the study of the determinants of school district expenditures and in the study of the community determinants of school support there is an important common finding. The data of the real world, whether explored by an economic model or a sociological model, reveal that community willingness to pay taxes for schools is not a simple function of income, occupation, social status, or any other tightly structured set of relationships. Situational factors appear to be highly influential in tax willingness, and existing attitudes toward school support are not translated into community tax decisions through any simple and straightforward political mechanism.

This finding may be interpreted to mean simply that the ability of economists and sociologists to analyze complex phenomena continues to be limited, and that interactions among variables are sufficiently complex as to elude the grasp of social scientists using presently available techniques. Indeed it would be difficult to deny this interpretation. But the fact that neither economic nor social determinants appear to rigidly structure and control the resources directed toward the support of public education may also demonstrate that society is more open than might have been thought. There is leeway for the allocation of additional resources to public education; there is scope for exercise of leadership; community attitudes toward the support of public education can and do respond to new influences.

In short, there is adequate opportunity for all manner of social invention with respect to organization for the mobilization and more effective use of resources for public education.

Unfortunately, social invention is not easy. It emerges most readily when there is crisis, but there have been all manner of crises in public education since the end of World War II and the organizational response rate has not always been reassuring. Perhaps this is attributable to an overabundance of crises in the contemporary world. Those who have lived through a major depression, one major war and several minor ones, and the tensions of armament and space races may well become inured to the crises that lie closest at hand. Therefore the prescriptions for assuring an adequate public attention to public education and its support are not always clear, not by any means as clear as recognizable needs.

These educational needs and their organizational implications have been explored in the previous chapters. Rapid technological changes in the techniques for the transmission of knowledge offer very great promise for increasing productivity in elementary and secondary education. New educational technologies will facilitate the specialization of teaching skills—and skill specialization is the motivating force for increases in productivity in any organization. But technological change requires organizational change, and unless systematic attention is directed to the internal organization of public education, the promise of the new technology in education will never be realized.

The examination of the politics of state aid points to similar conclusions. Those states in the northeast that now enjoy the most effective state aid programs came to this enviable position because educational statesmen saw that organization was necessary—an organization of the academics to do the necessary research, an organization to build local support for state aid measures, an organization to enlist the support of governors and legislators, and some coordination among the three. And in the relations between suburban schools and other local governments there is an evident need for working out new patterns for organizational cooperation if there is to be appropriate attention to the range of planning, fiscal and program problems that schools have in common with other governmental units at the metropolitan level.

The same kinds of lessons emerge from the study of grant-in-aid programs. Both the record of past successes and the best hopes for the future of strengthened financial support of education come with new organizational forms and patterns. General federal aid, the traditional proposal for federal support, has foundered on the most deeply rooted social and political cleavages of our time, but important progress has been made in federal support where there has been willingness to experiment with new techniques for categorical aid or a willingness to wrestle continuously with the impact of federal activities on the needs of local districts. And one of the most successful of recent curriculum innovations—the Physical Science Study Committee's high school course in physics—required organizational invention of a high order, with wholly new patterns of communication among professional physicists and high school teachers.

There are other areas of school finance where there has been recent progress but where that progress has not been marked by a high degree of organizational innovation. The sources and techniques of finance for state and local support of public education have remained very largely unchanged in the last fifteen years. In a very few states—Wisconsin, Rhode Island, and New York—there has been significant experimentation with incentive-type grants-in-aid. But for the aggregate of states such experimentation has not been significant, nor have the states moved importantly and dramatically in the past decade to increase their relative fiscal support of public education.

At the local level there has been even less experimentation. Ten years ago local nonproperty taxes seemed to offer some hope for new and important revenue sources but these have not become a panacea for local public finance ills. Instead the traditional instrument of local finance—the property tax—has responded surprisingly well to serve the needs not only of public education but of other local governmental functions as well. And this has been accomplished with very little organizational improvement in any aspect of property tax administration. If, somehow, some very ordinary and well known kinds of modest reforms could be injected into its administration there would appear to be no reason why the property tax should not serve public education as well in the next fifteen years as it has in the past fifteen.

If organizational and structural changes inside and outside education are the key to more adequate support for public education, how is this to be accomplished? Surely there is an abundance of commissions of inquiry of all types and kinds working in and on public education. A simple multiplication of this kind of activity, important as it may be in some situations, local, state, or national, is not necessarily the answer. But it is reasonable to expect that the pace of organizational change in public education can be greatly increased simply by a substantial increase in the volume of research and development expenditures in all aspects of education. The U.S. Commissioner of Education recently estimated that research and development expenditures now amount to no more than one-tenth of one per cent of the nation's total educational outlay, a proportion very much below almost every other area of organized endeavor, public or private.

It is evident that vastly enlarged research efforts in education will be necessary in the decades ahead, if only for the examination and testing of new techniques for the transmission of knowledge, for study of the cost-benefit aspects of innovation, and for exploration of the organizational implications of such techniques within elementary and secondary education.

Again there are great possibilities for organizational inventiveness. Some of the most fruitful of these are well within the present scope of responsibilities of state departments of education. These are the agencies that now have clearly defined legal responsibilities for establishing patterns of relationship with school districts, with graduate schools of education, and with other professional groups for the improvement of educational techniques. State departments of education, if adequately staffed, are in a position to establish centers for research activity and demonstration projects, and to assist school administrators in identifying the research-minded among their own teachers and assistant administrators.

Research in educational methods must somehow be made more honorific. At the local level school boards need to become convinced of its value and thus willing to accord it financial support. It is most anomalous that school board members who participate day by day in the research and development efforts of their business firms are so reluctant to promote community support of research activities sponsored and supported by the schools.

In this field, as in other specialized programs in elementary and secondary education, there are abundant opportunities for interschool cooperation, and for the development of new patterns of relationship with the faculties of graduate schools of education and other faculties. Research and development in elementary and secondary education means not only the production of new techniques for teaching and learning but also their testing and adaptation in classroom situations. The great promise of team teaching, for example, is likely to be unrealized unless there is careful and immediate attention to the organizational changes that must accompany its introduction and use.

Another kind of organizational innovation is required to set in motion the processes of participative planning for education and educational finance. Here the needs are quite different at the different levels of government. For the national government it is certainly not now appropriate to contemplate the establishment of broad national educational goals, supported by detailed plans and programs for the achievement of those goals. This is not within our tradition of decentralized public education, and neither, as a practical matter, is there immediate prospect that federal funds and federal organization will be available for such purposes. What can be contemplated in the immediate years ahead is that the national government, starting with the U.S. Office of Education, and joined by a dozen or more federal agencies that are already involved in the support of educational programs, will establish goals in some limited areas of existing responsibility and develop some new organizational patterns for attaining such limited objectives.

For the national government this does not mean, necessarily, the establishment of a Department of Education at the cabinet level, but it should mean the strengthening of the U.S. Office of Education within the Department of Health, Education, and Welfare. When federal agencies are engaged in competing and duplicating programs with resulting waste and inefficiency, as in the space programs a few years ago, there is a compelling need for increased centralization of administrative authority and new agencies for such centralization must be established. But this is hardly the case with existing federal programs for elementary and secondary education. Here the need is not for the elimination of competition and duplication but for the more vigorous promotion of existing responsibilities and the development of some closely related new responsibilities in specific program areas. What are the next steps in federal support of education in science, mathematics, and foreign languages now that equipment is provided under the National Defense Education Act? What should the federal government do to assist the states in restructuring their vocational education programs? Now that the federal government supports vocational guidance under NDEA, what can be done to improve the quality of guidance counseling for students who will not seek higher education? These are the kinds of specifics which should press for attention on the national agenda of public elementary and secondary education. Developments along such lines will require the closest kind of collaboration among federal agencies now involved in the support of public education, and a high degree of coordination with state and local educational agencies. Such developments will give substance to the concept of participative planning.

It may be that there is also need for a kind of loosely structured National Advisory Council on Education, such as was proposed in the 1963 session of the Congress.[1] But the pressing need at the national level is for stimulation, not for coordination. At some time in the future, when the national government is far more committed to the support of public elementary and secondary education than is now the case, some higher degree of administrative coordination may be required.

At the state level organizational prescriptions are somewhat easier. Every competent chief state school officer is well aware of the needs of his state education department. Unfortunately, he is very often much less aware of how to function within state political processes in order to strengthen his department and to strengthen state aid programs for the districts within his state. Very often his frustrations are manifest in perverse demands for independence from politics when, in fact, immersion in the political process of public resource allocation decisions is required.

Chief state school officers and state departments of education are in a very much better position to impart precision and substance to processes of participative planning than are national government agencies. Reasonable accuracy can attach to short-range projections of educational needs and educational resources. Specific goals for a state's vocational education program, for example, can be outlined and these can be related to manpower requirements and needs for identifiable skills for several years ahead.[2] The state education department is in a pivotal position in the development of organizational patterns for metropolitan area programs for the gifted and the handicapped and for the stimulation of all manner of specialized educational programs that require the cooperation of a number of school districts.

At the school district level the most pressing needs for organizational innovation are for citizen participation in the work of the schools in the community. The study of community attitudes toward school support reported in this volume found that citizen participation was far more important in shaping attitudes toward schools than any underlying variable such as income, occupation, or educational attainment. If additional fiscal support is to be forthcoming from the community the conclusion is inescapable—citizen involvement in school affairs cannot be restricted to attendance at the annual parents' night sponsored by the PTA.

Citizen involvement at the district level can extend as well to fiscal analysis. Every school board in a growing suburban community is by now well aware that it must engage continuously in planning for new school facilities. Land must be acquired in advance of need;

space requirements must be projected; bond issues must be prepared. A few districts also engage in a limited kind of educational planning for the immediate future, with projections of teacher, classroom, equipment, and program requirements. What is needed, and is so very often lacking, is a planning package—for physical facilities, for programs, and for financial requirements—in short, a comprehensive program budget projection.

There is nothing mysterious about the techniques for such projections. All that is required is an extension of existing and well known procedures now used for the preparation of next year's school budget. School board members and administrative staff may or may not possess the requisite skills for longer-range program budgeting, but these skills can either be found in the community or co-opted from schools of education or from state departments of education. Moreover, the techniques for such projections are far less important than the development of the participative planning which should characterize the process. The projection of educational needs and resources is the occasion for measuring the preferences of citizens, and the occasion for an interchange of viewpoints on program and finance among teachers, administrators, school board members, taxpayers who are parents, and taxpayers who are not parents.

Beyond doubt the most pressing need of all for organizational innovation in public education is in the large cities of the nation. There are serious educational deficiencies in the rural south, but at least the number of persons affected by such deficiencies is diminishing with the processes of urbanization. Unfortunately, the tasks now facing elementary and secondary education in large cities, north and south alike, are overwhelming and increasing, as James B. Conant has so well dramatized in his *Slums and Suburbs*.[3]

The root difficulty, of course, is that the educational problem in the depressed areas of large cities is the derivative of a complex of social and economic ills that constitute our most serious domestic problem. The outlines of this problem have become distressingly clear. Increased productivity in agriculture forces families out of rural areas and into urban areas. Those who emigrate are unskilled, with inadequate education and training and without previous exposure to the routines of urban existence. The cities who receive the migrants practice discrimination—specific ethnic discrimination and general discrimination against low income families. The migrants come predominantly into the central cities, where housing is already deteriorated, and where public services now suffer an imbalance between needs and resources. To compound all else, automation continually reduces the job opportunities for the unskilled. Levels of aggregate demand are inadequate, and the American economy moves along sluggishly with a growing volume of unemployed and unemployables. The Negro Revolution captures public attention and public support, but the problems that the revolution reflects run far deeper than discrimination in housing, in jobs, and in public accommodations.

The poverty of the urban Negro will not be eradicated without the most strenuous attention to education. As Joseph P. Lyford has said,

> There is no question that racial tensions are going to make life impossible for all of us unless we develop an educational program that enables the Negro to enter our society and the white man to place a high value on his entry. It should be fairly obvious that education is the only method by which we can overcome our institutionalized system of cheating Negroes, halt the growth of a public welfare community, and slow down the emergence of a new group of aliens, the teen-age school dropouts. We are either going to broaden the boundaries of America to include the exiles, or most of us are going to be joining them.[4]

There are now some outstanding programs in some large cities for the strengthening of education in slum areas. The Higher Horizons program in New York City is best known, but St. Louis, Cleveland, Detroit, and other cities all have programs, usually with support by the Ford Foundation. These programs are very much in need of expansion within the cities where they now operate, and in need of extension to other cities. And, as with all experiments in education, there is a pressing need for evaluation of comparative experiences and for additional understanding of the possibility of transferring successful educational techniques for underprivileged children from one environment to another. Only small beginnings have been made here.[5]

If there is recognition that education is at the center of the urban poverty problem, there must also be recognition that education is not sufficient in and of itself. In 1940 young white males averaged four more years of schooling than nonwhites in the same age group. By 1960 this gap had been narrowed to one-and-a-half years, but the earnings differential between whites and nonwhites did not change in the 20-year period. The average wage and salary income for nonwhites continued at about three-fifths of that of whites at the same age level.[6] This may simply mean that years of educational attainment is not a meaningful measure of education and that the quality of education for nonwhites is considerably inferior to that for whites. It may very well mean that nonwhite earnings are also held down by job discrimination. Unless segregation barriers to employment opportunities are eliminated, an improvement in Negro education will make little contribution to narrowing income differentials between whites and nonwhites.

The poverty of the urban Negro is an important part but not the whole of the problem of urban poverty. A concerted attack on general poverty requires a simultaneous advance on two fronts: growth rates for the economy must be improved by increases in aggregate demand; a broad program for the development of human resources must be put underway. Educational programs in schools for underprivileged children may very well be the most important place to start, but in-school programs cannot be both the starting point and the stopping point. The development of human resources requires attention to educational influences within the home, to housing, to health, to recreation, in short, to social welfare broadly conceived.

Organizational prescriptions for such programs are far more difficult than prescriptions for the traditional tasks of mobilizing resources for education at national, state and local levels. Indeed, given the present state of our knowledge about the development of human resources, it is evident that a high order of experimentation is needed, and that much of this experimentation will be characterized by a considerable degree of groping.

The public services of large cities are not now organized and staffed to cope with the responsibilities they face. Large city slums and slum dwellers occupy the administrative attention of almost all local government agencies, affecting at least some aspects of the programs of the police department, the fire department, and the highway department, to say nothing of the health department, the recreation department, the welfare department, and the board of education. The social cost of poverty is very high. To estimate this cost for urban areas would be difficult; the resulting figures would be sobering.

Perhaps the most that can be said with assurance is that the development of the human resources of the urban area must proceed in terms of coordinated programming of education, health, welfare, and recreation. It may be that a modest start toward a broadened approach could be made by creating councils for human resources in metropolitan areas with planning responsibilities comparable to those that municipal governments now direct to physical capital facilities. Such councils must be representative of the whole of the metropolitan area, suburbs as well as central cities, to underline that urban poverty is not the sole responsibility of the municipal jurisdiction that happens to contain that poverty.

It may also be possible to establish, in colleges and universities in metropolitan areas, institutes for research in human resources to serve as counterparts to governmentally established programming agencies. Research programs here would be policy oriented, emphasizing analysis of the characteristics of poverty, and techniques for the evaluation of programs directed to the lowest income groups.

It would be comforting to feel that the education-health-welfare-recreation needs of large cities will somehow be met in the immediate years ahead, or even to feel that organizational structures exist for constructive work on the problem. Such, obviously, is not the case. Perhaps one solace can be derived from the present state of affairs—there is at least in existence an evident public concern—which was not the case even a few years ago. Moreover, whatever is accomplished will redound to the good of the economy. Public and private programs for education-health-welfare-recreation for low income urban areas are growth-inducing outlays, which will contribute to the skills and productivity of the economy as a whole and hence to generally improved standards of material welfare.

Notes to Chapters

I. The Economics of School Finance

1. It is, of course, a rediscovery, as one excellent survey makes clear. See John Vaizey, *The Economics of Education* (London: Faber and Faber, 1962), 15-25.

2. Burton A. Weisbrod, "Does Better Health Pay?" 75 *Public Health Reports* (June 1960), 557-60; Selma J. Mushkin, "Health as an Investment," LXX *The Journal of Political Economy* (October 1962), Part 2, 129-57.

3. See Fritz Machlup, *The Production and Distribution of Knowledge in the United States* (Princeton: Princeton University Press, 1962).

4. See Alice M. Rivlin, "Research in the Economics of Higher Education," in Selma J. Mushkin, ed., *Economics of Higher Education* (Washington: U.S. Office of Education, 1962), 357-83; Harold M. Groves, *Education and Economic Growth* (Washington: National Education Association, 1961); William G. Bowen, *Assessing the Economic Contribution of Education: An Appraisal of Alternative Approaches,* paper prepared for the Organization for Economic Cooperation and Development, Paris, 1962. This last includes a review of studies of manpower projections and educational planning which have been important aspects of the research on the economics of education.

5. See Robert M. Solow, "Technical Change and the Aggregate Production Function," XXXIX *Review of Economics and Statistics* (August 1957), 312-23; Solomon Fabricant, *Basic Facts on Productivity Change* (New York: National Bureau of Economic Research, 1959).

6. Mary Jean Bowman, "Human Capital: Concepts and Measurements," in *Economics of Higher Education, op. cit.,* 72.

7. "Capital Formation by Education," LXVIII *The Journal of Political Economy* (December 1960), 571-83.

8. "Reflections on Investment in Man," LXX *The Journal of Political Economy* (October 1962), Part 2, 1-8.

9. Edward F. Denison, *The Sources of Economic Growth in the United States and the Alternatives before Us* (New York: Committee for Economic Development, 1962), 67-79. For a criticism of Denison's procedure for estimating the contribution of education to growth see Moses Abramovitz, "Economic Growth in the United States," LII *American Economic Review* (September 1962), esp. 769-71.

10. Gary S. Becker, "Underinvestment in College Education?" L *American Economic Review* (May 1960), 346-54.

11. "Education and Economic Growth," in Nelson B. Henry, ed., *Social Forces Influencing American Education* (Chicago: University of Chicago Press, 1961), 46-88.

12. Rudolph C. Blitz, "The Nation's Educational Outlay," in *Economics of Higher Education, op. cit.,* 147-69.

13. Vaizey, *op. cit.,* 40-46.

14. For similar comments on the relationship of education to the determinants of economic growth see Bowman, *op. cit.,* 91-92.

15. Werner Z. Hirsch, *Analysis of the Rising Costs of Public Education* (Washington: Joint Economic Committee, 1959).

16. Approximated from data in Machlup, *op cit.*, 72-79.

17. *Ibid.*, 51-107.

18. Burton A. Weisbrod, "Education and Investment in Human Capital," LXX *The Journal of Political Economy* (October 1962), Part 2, 106-23. See also Vaizey, *op. cit.*, 46-49.

19. *Op. cit.*, 69-70.

20. This section is based on materials prepared by Jerry Miner.

21. For a discussion of public-private provision of education see Jerry Miner, *Social and Economic Factors in Spending for Public Education* (Syracuse: Syracuse University Press, 1963), 24-26; for an examination of taxation patterns see Chapter VIII, this volume.

22. See *The Theory of Public Finance* (New York: McGraw-Hill Book Co., Inc., 1959), esp. 3-57.

II. Administration of the Public Schools

1. Concepts used in this chapter are based upon the general theory of administration contained in the author's *The Governing of Organizations: the Administrative Struggle,* (in press), (New York: The Free Press of Glencoe, 1964).

2. The author hereby expresses his gratitude for the detailed assistance and advice received from Richard C. Lonsdale, Robert C. Stewart and Dean Virgil Rogers of Syracuse University's School of Education. Appreciation must also be expressed for the helpful comments of many others: E. Gil Boyer, Deputy Commissioner of Education, Rhode Island: William W. Brickman, School of Education, University of Pennsylvania; Jack Culbertson, Executive Director, University Council for Educational Administration; Finis Engleman, past Secretary, American Association of School Administrators; Eric F. Gardner, Chairman, Psychology Department, Syracuse University; Daniel E. Griffiths, Dean, School of Education, New York University; Clayton D. Hutchins, School Finance Section, U.S. Office of Education; Thomas James, School of Education, Stanford University; Harold F. Clark, Teachers College, Columbia University; Sam M. Lambert, Director, Research Division, National Education Association; William P. McLure, Director, Bureau of Educational Research, University of Illinois; Sidney G. Tickton, The Ford Foundation; Lorne Woollatt, Associate Commissioner, New York State Education Department; and J. Wayne Wrightstone, Acting-Deputy Superintendent of Schools, New York City Board of Education.

3. Jerome S. Bruner, *The Process of Education* (Cambridge: Harvard University Press, 1961), 4.

4. The Report of the President's Commission on National Goals, *Goals for Americans* (Englewood Cliffs, New Jersey: Prentice-Hall, 1960).

5. For a further discussion of these possibilities see Chapters XII and XV.

III. The Determinants of School Expenditures

1. For a review of other historical and analytical studies of government expenditures see Jerry Miner, *Social and Economic Factors in Spending for Public Education* (Syracuse: Syracuse University Press, 1963), 39-65.

2. Several indexes of taxpaying capacity of local governments have been developed. For example, see Advisory Commission on Intergovernmental Relations, *Measures of State and Local Fiscal Capacity and Tax Effort* (Washington, 1962).

3. See Harvey E. Brazer, *City Expenditures in the United States* (New York: National Bureau of Economic Research, 1959).

4. For additional discussion of the sampling technique, the data, and methods of analysis, see Miner, *op. cit.*, 87-92.

5. Debt service is excluded because data were not obtained for all states. Equalized property valuations are available for only six of the states included in the study.

6. The results of the simple correlation analysis are reported in Miner, *op. cit.*, 96-100.

7. For the state-by-state analysis see *ibid.*, 107-31.

IV. Cost and Quality

1. See Chapter I.

2. For an alternative set of estimates see Fritz Machlup, *The Production and Distribution of Knowledge in the United States* (Princeton: Princeton University Press, 1962), 104-05.

3. See Chapter II.

4. For a critical evaluation of existing salary practices in public education and a proposal for differentials in accordance with scarce teaching skills see Joseph A. Kershaw and Roland N. McKean, *Teacher Shortages and Salary Schedules* (New York: McGraw-Hill, 1962).

5. For an eloquent condemnation of contemporary emphasis on narrow "business-like" administration of the schools see Raymond E. Callahan, *Education and the Cult of Efficiency* (Chicago: University of Chicago Press, 1962).

6. For a brilliant analysis of the relationship between the value patterns and academic performance of high school students see James S. Coleman, *The Adolescent Society* (New York: The Free Press of Glencoe, 1961).

7. *Procedures in School Quality Evaluation, A Second Report of the Quality Measurement Project* (Albany: The University of the State of New York, 1961).

8. See, for example, *The Encyclopedia of Educational Research, The Review of Educational Research*, and *The Journal of Educational Research.*

9. Elton Mayo, *The Human Problems of an Industrial Civilization* (New York: The Macmillan Company, 1933); F. J. Roethlisberger and William J. Dickson, *Management and the Worker* (Cambridge: Harvard University Press, 1939).

V. The Politics of State Aid

1. Jean Gottman, *Megalopolis* (New York: Twentieth Century Fund, 1961).

2. *Statistical Abstract of the United States.*

3. Theodore Powell, *The School Bus Law* (Middletown: Wesleyan University Press, 1960), 6.

4. Quoted in Daniel P. Moynihan, "How Catholics Feel About Federal School Aid," 24 *The Reporter* (May 25, 1961), 36.

5. Everson vs. Board of Education (330 U.S. 1, 1947).

6. H. H. Horner, ed., *Education in New York State, 1784-1954* (Albany:

The University of the State of New York, The State Education Department, 1954), 1-2.

7. George D. Strayer and R. M. Haig, *The Financing of Education in the State of New York* (New York: Macmillan, 1923).

8. Paul R. Mort, *State Support for Public Schools* (New York: Teachers College, Columbia University, 1926).

9. In an interview with Dr. Paul Mandry, Executive Secretary, New Hampshire Association of School Boards, August 22, 1961.

VI. Governments, Schools, and Suburbs

1. See National Citizens Commission for the Public Schools, *How Have Our Schools Developed?* (New York: The Commission, 1955); and Edgar W. Knight, "The Evolving and Expanding Common School," in *Critical Issues and Trends in American Education*, 265 *The Annals* (September 1949), 92-100.

2. United States Census of Population, 1960, *United States Summary: General Population Characteristics* (Washington, 1961), Tables 44, 46, 49, 50.

3. Summarized from United States Census of Governments: 1962, Vol. I, No. 2, *Local Government in Standard Metropolitan Areas* (Washington, 1963).

4. LI *National Civic Review* (March 1962), 113.

5. John R. Seeley, R. Alexander Sim, Elizabeth W. Loosley, *Crestwood Heights: A Study of the Culture of Suburban Life* (New York: Basic Books, 1956), 224.

6. U.S. Office of Education, Biennial Survey of Education in the United States, 1954-56, *Statistics of Local School Systems: 1955-56* (Washington, 1960).

7. Alpheus L. White, *Local School Boards: Organization and Practices* (Washington: U.S. Office of Education, 1962).

8. National Commission for the Defense of Democracy Through Education, *Indianapolis, Indiana: A Study of the Sudden Forced Resignation of a Superintendent* (Washington: National Education Association, 1960).

9. William Ellis Gould, "A Study of School Board Elections in Santa Clara County" (Stanford: Stanford University, unpublished doctoral dissertation, 1953), especially Chapter X. The sentence quoted occurs on p. 210.

10. The gruesome vendetta which has beset the public schools of one new suburb would seem enough to cast at least some small doubt on the system of election. See Joseph F. Maloney, *"The Lonesome Train" in Levittown* (University of Alabama: University of Alabama Press, ICP Case Series, 1958). But see also a news story published in *The New York Times* of January 11, 1962, in which, under the headline "Schools Analysis Chides Levittown," a commission of the National Education Association identifies the problem with the absence of skilled lay leadership.

11. Vincent A. Ostrom, "School Board Politics: An Analysis of Non-Partisanship in the Los Angeles City Board of Education" (Los Angeles: University of California, unpublished master's thesis, 1945).

12. For a description of this questionnaire survey, see Roscoe C. Martin, *Government and Suburban School* (Syracuse: Syracuse University Press, 1962), 108-12.

13. A recent study pleads for an end to nonpartisanship in municipal elections, citing the importance of party organization in developing vigorous leadership, arousing popular interest, rallying the people in support of (or in opposition

to) a program, bringing criticism effectively to bear, and providing a vehicle for the exercise of public accountability. See Marvin A. Harder, *Nonpartisan Election: A Political Illusion?* (New York: Henry Holt and Company for the Eagleton Foundation, 1958).

14. Martin, *op. cit.*, 49.

15. Richard F. Carter, *Voters and Their Schools* (Stanford University: School of Education, Institute for Communication Research, 1960), 7, 16.

16. It should be noted that of the eleven "All American" cities selected "for their citizens' exemplary conduct in the game of civic progress" by the National Municipal League and *Look* magazine in 1961, four were central cities and four were suburban. LI *National Civic Review* (March 1962), 113.

17. For the view that teachers and teachers' organizations, not administrators, must have primary responsibility for all aspects of public education see Myron Lieberman, *The Future of Public Education* (Chicago: University of Chicago Press, 1960).

18. In a significant study of both internal, school-centered issues and public or political issues, Alan Rosenthal found the influence of the superintendent to be truly overwhelming. "Community Leadership and Public School Politics: Two Case Studies" (Princeton: Princeton University, unpublished doctoral dissertation, 1960).

19. Nelson B. Henry and Jerome G. Kerwin, *Schools and City Government* (Chicago: The University of Chicago Press, 1938).

20. Thomas H. Eliot, "Toward an Understanding of Public School Politics," LIII *The American Political Science Review* (December 1959), 1032-51.

21. Julius Margolis, "Metropolitan Finance Problems: Territories, Functions, and Growth," National Bureau of Economic Research, *Public Finances: Needs, Sources, and Utilization* (Princeton: Princeton University Press, 1961), 261-66.

22. Theodore L. Reller, "The Preparation of Administrators: New Perspective" (a mimeographed paper delivered at a national conference sponsored by the University Council for Educational Administration, Chicago, October 16-18, 1961), 2-3

23. Richard C. Lonsdale, *The School's Role in Metropolitan Development* (Syracuse: Syracuse University Press, 1960), 51-60.

VII. Suburban Values, Decisions, and Taxes

1. For further detail on the characteristics of the suburbs see Warner Bloomberg, Jr. and Morris Sunshine, *Suburban Power Structures and Public Education* (Syracuse: Syracuse University Press, 1963), 26-42.

2. The procedures used here were first developed and tested in the Metropolitan Leadership Research Project. See Linton Freeman, *et al.*, *Local Community Leadership* (Syracuse: University College of Syracuse University, 1960).

3. For a further description of this technique see Bloomberg and Sunshine, *op. cit.*, pp. 88-93.

VIII. State and Local Tax Support

1. For further discussion of state differences see I. M. Labovitz, "The Property Tax: Quicksand or Bedrock?" *Proceedings of the Annual Conference on Taxation, 1960* (Harrisburg: National Tax Association, 1961), 58-70.

2. Eugene Peter McLoone, "Effects of Tax Elasticity on the Financial Support of Education" (Urbana: College of Education, University of Illinois, unpublished doctoral dissertation, 1961), 50.

3. Data supplied by the Advisory Commission on Intergovernmental Relations.

4. Richard A. Musgrave, "The Incidence of the Tax Structure and Its Effects on Consumption," *Federal Tax Policy for Economic Growth and Stability* (Washington: Joint Economic Committee, 1955), 97-98.

5. See Jesse Burkhead, *State and Local Taxes for Public Education* (Syracuse: Syracuse University Press, 1963), 31-38.

6. Dick Netzer, "Financial Needs and Resources over the Next Decade: State and Local Governments," National Bureau of Economic Research, *Public Finances: Needs, Sources, and Utilization* (Princeton: Princeton University Press, 1961), 23-65; Robert J. Lampman, "How Much Government Spending in the 1960's," 1 *Quarterly Review of Economics and Business* (February 1961), 7-17; McLoone, *op. cit.*, 75.

7. For a description of techniques and procedures see Burkhead, *op. cit.*, 53-65.

8. For a description of techniques and additional details of findings, see *ibid.*, 57-65.

9. Findings for other states were less conclusive, due in part to imperfections in available data. See *ibid.*, 65-70.

10. Charles S. Benson, *The Economics of Public Education* (Boston: Houghton Mifflin Company, 1961), 171.

11. See the study by Frederick L. Bird, *The Role of the States in Strengthening the Property Tax,* Vol. I, (Washington: Advisory Commission on Intergovernmental Relations, 1963).

12. Selma J. Mushkin, "Population and Public Finances," *Financing Education for our Changing Population* (Washington: National Education Association, 1961), 25-34.

13. Selma J. Mushkin, "Intergovernmental Aspects of Expenditure Decisions in Localities," Conference on Public Decisions in the Urban Community (Washington: Resources for the Future, Inc., 1962).

14. Data for the analysis of state revenue systems were derived from U.S. *Income and Output* (Washington: U.S. Department of Commerce, 1958); issues of the *Survey of Current Business;* U.S. Bureau of the Census, *Historical Statistics of the U.S.* (Washington, 1960); U.S. Bureau of the Census, *Compendium of State Government Finances in 1960* (Washington, 1961).

15. This includes the states of New Hampshire and Tennessee, where the tax is on income from interest and dividends only.

16. For example, Netzer, *op. cit.*, 23-65.

17. "State and Local Tax Prospects for the 1960's," paper prepared for the 1960 Conference of the Government Research Association (St. Louis, 1960).

18. Carl S. Shoup, "Suggested Changes in the State and Local Tax System of Michigan," Paul W. McCracken, ed. *Taxes and Economic Growth in Michigan* (Kalamazoo: The W. E. Upjohn Institute, 1960), 149-67.

19. The history of these levies and detailed statistics on their rate, base and yield is contained in Advisory Commission on Intergovernmental Relations, *Local Nonproperty Taxes and the Coordinating Role of the State* (Washington, 1961). See also National Education Association, *New Local Sources of Tax Revenues* (Washington, 1959).

20. See Robert A. Sigafoos, *The Municipal Income Tax: Its History and Problems* (Chicago: Public Administration Service, 1955), esp. 105-51.

21. Milton C. Taylor, "Local Income Taxes after Twenty-One Years," XV *National Tax Journal* (June 1962), 114.

IX. State Aid Patterns

1. Albert R. Munse and Eugene P. McLoone, *Public School Finance Programs of the United States, 1957-58* (Washington: U.S. Office of Education, 1960), 34. Less complete descriptions of aid programs are available for 1959-60; totals by major categories of grants show that there were then 413 separate programs for 50 states. See Albert R. Munse, *Revenue Programs for the Public Schools in the United States, 1959-60* (Washington: U.S. Office of Education, 1961), 9.

2. Munse and McLoone, *op. cit.*, 35. Where the school department is itself an adjunct of some other unit of local government, the problem exists of seeing that school grants are actually used for school purposes. This simply points up the fact that all educational grants are special purpose in the sense that they are designated for one of the functions of local government.

3. Even this is subject to dispute, however, if one takes account of the possible harmful effects of grants on the allocation of human resources. A. D. Scott, "A Note on Grants in Federal Countries," 17 *Economica*, New Series (November 1960), 416-22.

4. Some equalizing grants would be expected to have stronger results in meeting the equity objective than others, as will be discussed below. Here it should be noted (a) that a nonequalizing grant may have some equity effects in the "right" directions, i.e., aid poor districts more than rich, and (b) that it is possible for a grant which is ostensibly in equalizing form to have anti-equalizing effects.

5. See, for example, Paul R. Mort, Walter C. Reusser, and John W. Polley, *Public School Finance* (New York: McGraw-Hill Book Company, Inc., 1960) Chap. 15; Roe L. Johns and Edgar L. Morphet, *Financing the Public Schools* (Englewood Cliffs, N.J.: Prentice-Hall, Inc., 1960) Chap. 12. For a broader view of the issue of general vs. specific grants, see Selma J. Mushkin, "Barriers to a System of Federal Grants-in-Aid," XIII *National Tax Journal* (September 1960), 198-207.

6. If A_i represents the state subsidy in the ith district, then the formula for fixed-unit equalizing type of aid can be written as $A_i = N_i u - rY_i$. Note that both u and r are constant for all districts.

7. The net grant is given by the following formula:

$$V_i = [N_i u - rY_i] - \Sigma A_i / \Sigma Y_i \cdot Y_i$$

8. Educational Finance Inquiry Commission, American Council on Education, *The Financing of Education in the State of New York* (New York: The Macmillan Company, 1923), 173-76.

9. Ellwood P. Cubberley made the case in 1906 for distribution of aid on the basis of number of teachers employed. (*School Funds and Their Apportionment*, New York, Columbia University.) Ideally, he said, teacher grants would be supplemented by a distribution on the basis of pupil attendance and he would have paid an extra sum to very poor districts. His main concern was to drain money from the cities to the towns and rural areas. Now, we have come full

circle and find that the cities are viewed as standing in an unfavored position relative to the suburbs—the richer ones at least.

10. The variable-unit equalizing formula is thus $A_i = N_i u_i - rY_i$, where $u_a \leqslant u_i \leqslant u_b$. Here, only the term r is necessarily the same for all districts.

11. The basic formula, hence, is $A_i = (1 - x \cdot y_i / y) E_i$, where E_i represents total educational expenditures in the ith district.

12. The first proposal of this kind for educational grants in the United States appears to have been advanced by Harlan Updegraff and Leroy A. King in their *Survey of the Fiscal Policies of the State of Pennsylvania in the Field of Education* (December, 1922), Chap. II.

13. However, Utah in 1957-58 used a device to withdraw excess local resources. This could be done because localities had a choice of only a discrete number of expenditure levels. Another device to accomplish the same purpose is to use a system of state taxation which is discriminating among the districts with respect to income.

14. Conversely, if rich districts are the ones to move ahead, the state share will fall. This is so even when income in the rich districts increases in proportion to the rise in school expenditures.

15. It is not, as under Strayer-Haig, intended to be a statement of what an adequate educational program costs. The difference is subtle but important.

16. For a further discussion of "necessary" costs, see D. S. Lees, *et al.*, *Local Expenditures and Exchequer Grants* (London: Institute of Municipal Treasurers and Accountants, Inc., 1956), 3 ff.

17. For example, Professors Johns and Morphet state that while "the more alert districts will employ a higher proportion of well qualified teachers and consequently receive a somewhat larger share of the funds than the others . . . the evidence seems to indicate that reasonable differentials have stimulated improvement in the preparation of teachers in many areas where standards previously had been quite unsatisfactory." *Op. cit.*, 285-86. One way to reduce the anti-equalizing effect is to vary r_i directly with that u_i chosen by a district. This device was employed by Utah in 1957-58. The result is to move the variable grant toward the percentage equalizing form.

18. There are a number of ways that greater stimulation could be provided; for example, the state could offer a "bonus" for high rates of advance in school spending. For those who object to the percentage equalizing form as offering too high an inducement to spend it should be noted that the stimulation effect of most present grants appear to be extremely low. See Edward F. Renshaw, "A Note on the Expenditure Effect of State Aid to Education," LXVIII *Journal of Political Economy* (April 1960), 170-74.

19. The committee proposed the formula $A_i = (1 - .51 \frac{y_i}{y}) E_i$. The recommendation was similar to the plan for New York that was developed by Paul R. Mort. See *A New Approach to School Finance* (Albany: New York State Educational Conference Board, 1961).

20. Because of the existence of the flat grants, the guaranteed valuation figure of $33,000 (which is above the state average) does not represent the point at which districts come under equalization aid. It is closer to $28,500.

21. Since the plan functions on a reimbursement basis, high growth districts, however, may face a slightly higher tax rate than low growth ones. Two articles

by William C. Kahl, one in 89 *Wisconsin Journal of Education* (March 1957) and one in *Problems and Opportunities in Financing Education* (Committee on Tax Education and School Finance, National Educational Association, 1959) give a good description of the plan.

22. There are other incentives to establish integrated districts: the debt limit is higher but the tax limitation for current operation is lower, this latter figure being the point at which the state assumes full financing of the program. There is a further general incentive in Wisconsin, namely, that when the ratio of pupils to teachers rises above 25 to 1, the district receives a reduction in state aid.

23. When expenditures rise above the tax limit or when the state meets 50 per cent or more of current school expenditures, the budgets of the districts are subject to approval by the State Department of Public Instruction.

24. Eugene P. McLoone, "Are School Revenue Sources Adequate for the 1960's?" 44 *School Life* (September 1961), 11.

25. The plan is described in E. Gil Boyer, *Financing Tomorrow's Schools Today* (Providence: State Department of Education, 1961) and in "How to Get Aid to Education," 4 *School Management* (July 1960).

26. Gerald T. Kowitz and William C. Sayres, *Size, Cost, and Educational Opportunity in Secondary Schools* (Albany: New York State Department of Education, 1959).

27. William P. McLure, "Fiscal Policies of the Great Cities in the United States" (A study for the Great Cities School Improvement Studies Group, Urbana: Bureau of Educational Research, mimeo., 1961).

28. Boston Municipal Research Bureau, III *Bureau Blotter* (November 15, 1961), 1.

29. William D. Firman, *et al., Education for the Sixties—How Much Will It Cost?*" (Albany: New York State Department of Education, 1961), 70.

X. National Politics and Federal Aid

1. 80:2 *Congressional Record* (1948), 3290.

2. Gordon Canfield Lee, *The Struggle for Federal Aid—First Phase: A History of the Attempts to Obtain Federal Aid for the Common Schools, 1870-1890* (New York: Teachers College, Columbia University, 1949).

3. U.S. National Advisory Committee on Education, *Federal Relations to Education* (Washington, 1931).

4. 76:1 *Congressional Record* (1939), 516

5. See Chapter XIV.

6. House Committee on Education and Labor, *Federal Aid to School Construction,* 81st Congress, 2nd Session (1950), 146.

7. House Committee on Education and Labor, *Federal Grants to States for Education,* 85th Congress, 2nd Session (1958), 252.

8. See Chapter XII.

9. The identical sequence of events occurred in 1890 when two decades of efforts to secure federal aid to common schooling terminated in the second Morrill Act for higher education.

10. 78:1 *Congressional Record* (1943), 8399.

11. Hugh Douglas Price, "Race, Religion, and the Rules Committee: The Kennedy Aid-to-Education Bills," in Alan F. Westin, ed., *The Uses of Power* (New York: Harcourt, Brace, and World, Inc., 1962), 2-71.

12. Roger A. Freeman, *School Needs in the Decade Ahead* (Washington: Institute for Social Science Research, 1958); Roger A. Freeman, *Taxes for the Schools* (Washington: Institute for Social Science Research, 1960).

13. House Committee on Education and Labor, *Federal Aid to States for School Construction,* 84th Congress, 1st Session (1955), Vol. II, 437.

14. Senate Committee on Education and Labor, *Federal Aid for Education,* 79th Congress, 1st Session (1945), 749.

15. House Committee on Education and Labor, *School Support Act of 1959,* 86th Congress, 1st Session (1959), 105.

16. 80:2 *Congressional Record* (1948), 1460.

17. Anne Gibson Buis, "*An Historical Study of the Role of the Federal Government in the Financial Support of Education, with Special Reference to Legislative Proposals and Action*" (Columbus: Ohio State University, unpublished doctoral dissertation, 1953), 659-60.

18. Richard F. Carter, "Voters and Their Schools," 42 *Phi Delta Kappan* (March 1961), 244-49, at 244.

19. Price, *op. cit.*

20. 75:1 *Congressional Record* (1937), 3368.

XI. Issues in Federal Aid

1. Harvey S. Perloff, Edgar F. Dunn, Jr., Eric E. Lampard, Richard F. Muth, *Regions, Resources, and Economic Growth* (Baltimore: The Johns Hopkins Press, 1960), esp. 489-519.

2. Data from *Survey of Current Business,* August issues.

3. Abner Hurwitz and Carlisle P. Stallings, "Interregional Differentials in Per Capita Real Income Change," *Regional Incomes, Studies in Income and Wealth,* XXI National Bureau of Economic Research (Princeton: Princeton University Press, 1957), 195 ff.

4. Frank A. Hanna, *State Income Differentials, 1919-1954* (Durham: Duke University Press, 1959), Chap. I.

5. The computations reported here are based on data from the *Survey of Current Business,* August issues, and *Rankings of the States* (Washington: National Education Association, 1961), Tables 43, 50.

6. Measurements of the elasticity of educational expenditure must be viewed with caution. Current expenditures per pupil can increase as the number of pupils declines with a consequent lag in the adjustment of school budgets. An increase in the population in economically productive age groups may be associated with an increase in per capita income, but this may not necessarily be associated with an increase in the number of children of school age. Educational budgets may be dominated by capital expenditures that are partially financed out of current revenue and thus tend to hold down the measure of current expenditures per pupil.

7. Samuel Schloss and Carol Joy Hobson, *Enrollment, Teachers, and School Housing* (Washington: Office of Education, 1958), 12.

8. *Ibid.,* 13.

9. Regional projections are contained in U.S. Bureau of the Census, *Current Population Reports,* Series P-25, No. 160 (Washington, 1957).

10. For a detailed discussion of types of grants at the state level see Chapter IX.

11. For a careful examination of the equalizing effects of grant arrangements see Ray O. Werner, "Federal Aid to Education: Some Economic Aspects of Major Legislative Proposals for Support of Primary and Secondary Schools in the United States, 1946-1958" (Lincoln: University of Nebraska, unpublished doctoral dissertation, 1959).

12. The choice between these measures will affect the distribution of aid among states in accordance with their nonpublic school enrollment.

13. See, for example, the annual compilations of the National Education Association in *Rankings of the States;* also, James A. Maxwell, *Intergovernmental Tax Credits* (Washington: The Brookings Institution, 1962).

14. *Measures of State and Local Fiscal Capacity and Tax Effort* (Washington: The Advisory Commission on Intergovernmental Relations, 1962).

15. *Ibid.,* 31-51.

16. *Ibid.,* 89.

XII. Administering the NDEA

1. See Chapter X.

2. H. M. Hamlin, "National Aid to Agricultural and Vocational Education," 45 *High School Journal* (January 1962), 170; see also U.S. Office of Education, *Trends,* in the 1962 *Annual* (Washington, 1962), 139.

3. See Chapter XIII.

4. Data are from U.S. Office of Education, *Report on the National Defense Education Act, 1959; 1960; 1961-62.*

5. Office of Education, *Report on the National Defense Education Act: Fiscal Year ending June 30, 1959* (Washington: Office of Education, 1960), 1.

6. *Ibid.,* 3.

7. Office of Education, *Report on the National Defense Education Act: Fiscal Year ending June 30, 1960* (Washington: Office of Education, 1961), 1.

8. Subcommittee on Education, U.S. Senate Committee on Labor and Public Welfare, *Operation of the National Defense Education Act and Proposals for Its Extension,* 87th Congress, 1st Session (1961).

9. President's Science Advisory Committee, "Strengthening the Behavioral Sciences," 136 *Science* (April 20, 1962), 233.

XIII. Science Education: Two Programs

1. Physical Science Study Committee minutes (unpublished, M.I.T., Cambridge, September 8, 1956), 1.

2. *Ibid.,* 2.

3. PSSC, "Memo for the Record" (unpublished, Cambridge, December 21, 1956), 1-2.

4. See Frank J. Munger and Richard F. Fenno, Jr., *National Politics and Federal Aid to Education* (Syracuse: Syracuse University Press, 1962), especially 1-18.

5. P.L. 85-864.

6. *Ibid.,* Section 303 (a) (1).

7. Data for this section are from U.S. Office of Education, *Report on the National Defense Education Act, 1959; 1960; 1961-62.*

XIV. Federally Affected Schools

1. Advisory opinion in 42 Mass. (1 Metc.) 580 (1841). See also Newcomb vs. Inhabitants of Rockport, 183 Mass. 74 (1903); Davis vs. Inhabitants of Chilmark, 199 Mass. 115 (1908).

2. The Advisory Committee on Education, Staff Study No. 17, *Education of Children on Federal Reservations,* by Lloyd E. Blauch and William L. Iversen (Washington, 1939), 18, 27-80.

3. The Advisory Committee on Education, *Report of the Committee* (Washington, 1938), 171-73, 217-18.

4. 54 Stat. 681-83, Chap. 440, P.L. 76-671; and 54 Stat. 1125, Chap. 862, P.L. 76-849, esp. sec. 9.

5. 55 Stat. 361-3, Chap. 260, P.L. 77-137, adding Title II and Title III to the Lanham Act.

6. Hollis P. Allen, *The Federal Government and Education: The Original and Complete Study of Education for the Hoover Commission Task Force on Public Welfare* (New York: McGraw-Hill, 1950), 105-06; FWA, *Annual Report, 1948,* 34; and *1946,* 149.

7. House Committee on Education and Labor, *Emergency Educational Aid for Government Reservations: Hearings on H.R. 2650 . . . ,* Vol. 2, 80th Congress, 1st Session (1948), 235; FWA, *Supplement to Final Report of the War Public Service Programs* (Washington, 1947, mimeo.), tables at 11, 19.

8. 60 Stat. 314, Chap. 498, P.L. 79-452.

9. *Functions and Activities of the National Government in the Field of Welfare, A Report with Recommendations,* prepared by the Brookings Institution for the Commission on Organization of the Government (Washington, 1949).

10. House Committee on Education and Labor, Special Investigating Subcommittees, *Federal Assistance for Educating Children in Localities Affected by Federal Activities: Hearings . . . on H.R. 4115,* 81st Congress, 2nd Session (1950), 2 parts; and *ibid., Report of Special Investigating Subcommittees . . . on H.R. 4115* (Committee Print, Washington, 1950).

11. *Budget of the U.S. Government for the Fiscal Year 1951* (Washington, 1950), M56-57; 271.

12. See Frank J. Munger and Richard F. Fenno, Jr., *National Politics and Federal Aid to Education* (Syracuse: Syracuse University Press, 1962), 167-69.

13. For further detail see I. M. Labovitz, *Aid for Federally Affected Public Schools* (Syracuse: Syracuse University Press, 1963), 50-95.

14. Most of the data reported here are derived from publications and records of the U.S. Office of Education. For further detail on sources see Labovitz, *op. cit.,* 96-137.

15. Clayton D. Hutchins and Elmer C. Deering, *Financing Public School Facilities* (Washington: U.S. Office of Education, 1959).

16. Robert I. Sperber, "An Analysis of the Potential Control Factors in Public Law 874" (New York: Teachers College, Columbia University, unpublished doctoral dissertation, 1957).

17. *Ibid.,* Chapters 6-7.

18. House Committee on Education and Labor, *Hearings,* 85th Congress, 2nd Session (1958), 414.

19. 87:1 *Congressional Record* (1961), Part 7, Senate, 8504; 8772; 8954; and Part 14, 18962.

20. White House press release, November 2, 1951.

21. *New York Times,* January 15, March 20, 26, 27, June 11, August 24, November 16 and 24; February 1 and 2, 1954; August 21, 1955.

22. House Committee on Education and Labor, Subcommittee on Integration in Federally Assisted Education Programs, *Hearings,* 87th Congress, 2nd Session (1962), 69.

23. *New York Times,* September 8, 18, and 23, 1962; *Washington Star,* January 18, 1963; See also *ibid.,* A-1, A-3 January 30, 1963; *Washington Post,* February 28, 1963.

24. Munger and Fenno, *op. cit.,* 37.

XV. Patterns for Resource Mobilization

1. H.R. 6595, 88th Congress, 1st Session, introduced by Congressman John V. Lindsay.

2. For an excellent example of this kind of projection see Bureau of Educational Research, *Vocational and Technical Education in Illinois* (Urbana: College of Education, University of Illinois), 1960.

3. New York: McGraw Hill Book Company, Inc., 1961.

4. Joseph P. Lyford, "Proposal for a Revolution: Part I," *Saturday Review* (October 19, 1963), 22.

5. A. Harry Passow, ed., *Education in Depressed Areas* (New York: Teachers College, Columbia University, 1963).

6. Herman P. Miller, "Is the Income Gap Closed? No!" *New York Times Magazine* (November 11, 1962), 50.

Index